Never has a book in employment studies had such a fine pedigree and been so eagerly awaited. This is *the* definitive diagnosis of the state of employment relations in Britain in 2004 and charts changes over the period of the Labour government since 1997. The breadth is huge (literally something for everyone), the depth enviable, the conclusions often disturbing.

**John Purcell,** *Professor of Human Resource Management,*
*University of Bath, UK*

For nearly a quarter of a century the Workplace Employment Relations Survey has been the gold standard survey of personnel and labor relations. *Inside the Workplace* uses data gathered from firms, worker representatives and workers in 2004 to provide a comprehensive picture of the state of labor practices in the UK in the 21st Century. If only the US was smart enough to imitate this masterful survey and study!

**Richard Freeman,** *Professor of Economics,*
*Harvard University, USA*

The UK continues to lag behind our major competitors in the productivity and management stakes. Moving to more evidence-based management practice is an important component for closing this gap and there is no better, more comprehensive and authoritative source of evidence than WERS. The fifth survey covers not just the traditional areas of employee relations but also contains valuable information on a wide range of communication and HR practices, making it essential reading for all those who are responsible for and interested in these fields.

**Duncan Brown,** *Research Director,*
*Chartered Institute of Personnel and Development*

This book is a prime reference point for every serious student or analyst of UK employment relations. It provides the highest quality of information in three senses: by being representative and large-scale, by providing authoritative information on longitudinal change and by combining information at the workplace from the employer, worker representatives and individual employees. Such richness of information is a rare commodity indeed.

**Jill Rubery,** Professor of Comparative Employment Systems,
*Manchester Business School, University of Manchester, UK*

# Inside the Workplace

*Inside the Workplace* presents a detailed analysis of the 2004 Workplace Employment Relations Survey (WERS 2004). WERS 2004 is the fifth survey in the series of surveys that have generally been considered to be one of the most authoritative sources of information on employment relations in Great Britain. Interviews were conducted with managers and employee representatives in over 3,000 workplaces. Over 20,000 employees completed and returned a self-completion questionnaire. The survey links the views from these three parties, providing a truly integrated picture of employment relations.

Providing an up-to-date portrait of the state of employment relations and working life in Britain, this text also examines what has changed inside British workplaces since the 1998 survey was conducted. Current debates in employment relations are examined, including an assessment of the impact of the Labour Government's programme of employment relations reform.

*Inside the Workplace* is a unique contribution to the field of employment relations and an invaluable resource for students, academics and practitioners in the fields of employee relations, human resource management, organizational behaviour and sociology.

**Barbara Kersley** (Head of the WERS Research Team) and **Carmen Alpin** are both Principal Research Officers at the Department of Trade and Industry. **John Forth** is a Research Fellow at the National Institute for Economic and Social Research. **Alex Bryson** is a Principal Research Fellow and **Helen Bewley** is a Research Fellow, both at the Policy Studies Institute. **Gill Dix** is a Principal Research Officer at the Advisory, Conciliation and Arbitration Service (Acas). **Sarah Oxenbridge** also made her contribution while working as a Senior Research Officer at Acas.

# Inside the Workplace

Findings from the 2004 Workplace
Employment Relations Survey

Barbara Kersley, Carmen Alpin,
John Forth, Alex Bryson, Helen Bewley,
Gill Dix and Sarah Oxenbridge

Routledge
Taylor & Francis Group

LONDON AND NEW YORK

First published 2006
by Routledge
2 Park Square, Milton Park, Abingdon, Oxon OX14 4RN

Simultaneously published in the USA and Canada
by Routledge
270 Madison Ave, New York, NY 10016

*Routledge is an imprint of the Taylor & Francis Group, an informa business*

Department of Trade and Industry. http://www.dti.gov.uk/

Typeset in Garamond by Taylor & Francis Books
Printed and bound in Great Britain by TJ International Ltd, Padstow, Cornwall

*British Library Cataloguing in Publication Data*
A catalogue record for this book is available from the British Library

*Library of Congress Cataloging in Publication Data*
Inside the workplace : findings from the 2004 workplace employment relations survey / Barbara
Kersley... [et al.].
          p. cm.
"Published by Routledge on behalf of the Department of Trade and Industry with
permission of the Controller of HMSO."
Includes bibliographical references and index.
1. Industrial relations–Great Britain. 2. Industrial relations–Government policy–Great Britain.
I. Kersley, Barbara. II. Title.
  HD8391.I76 2006
  331.0941–dc22
                          2005036069

ISBN10: 0-415-37812-5 (hbk)
ISBN10: 0-415-37813-3 (pbk)

ISBN13: 978-0-415-37812-3 (hbk)
ISBN13: 978-0-415-37813-0 (pbk)

# Contents

# Figures

# Tables

# Acknowledgements

The 2004 Workplace Employment Relations Survey (WERS 2004) is a truly collaborative venture. The study is jointly sponsored by the Department of Trade and Industry (DTI), the Advisory, Conciliation and Arbitration Service (Acas), the Economic and Social Research Council (ESRC) and the Policy Studies Institute (PSI). The Steering Committee is drawn from representatives of the sponsoring bodies. Mark Beatson of the DTI initially chaired the Committee in his former role as Director of the Employment Market Analysis and Research (EMAR) Branch. He was succeeded by Grant Fitzner in April 2003. Another change in membership of the Steering Committee was the departure of David Guy of the ESRC, succeeded by Paul Rouse, in turn succeeded by Fiona Armstrong. Long-serving members have been Andrew Wareing (Acas), Professor Keith Whitfield (ESRC), and Bernard Carter (DTI). A grant from the Nuffield Foundation, together with the Wertheim Fellowship from Harvard Law School and the National Bureau of Economic Research (NBER), has facilitated PSI's involvement in the study. Jim Skea, the former Director of PSI, was an original member of the Committee and has been succeeded by Malcolm Rigg. John McQueeney, Head of Research in EMAR, DTI, has also attended a number of Steering Committee meetings and has provided valuable support to the DTI Research Team throughout the course of the study. Funding from the Small Business Service (SBS) has permitted the extension of the survey sample to include smaller workplaces, and the involvement of David Purdy and Stella Mascarenhas-Keyes has been appreciated.

The WERS Research Team is drawn from three of the four sponsoring bodies. The team comprises Barbara Kersley (Head of the WERS Research Team, DTI), Carmen Alpin (DTI), John Forth (National Institute of Economic and Social Research and on contract to DTI), Alex Bryson (PSI), Helen Bewley (PSI), Gill Dix (Acas) and Sarah Oxenbridge (Acas). It is noteworthy that Carmen Alpin provided maternity leave cover for Ms Kersley during a critical design phase of the survey.

The Sponsors are indebted to the teams of academic researchers who assisted in the development of specific question areas. This exercise was successfully led by Professor Keith Whitfield. The sponsors would like to thank: Professor Robert Blackburn, Kingston University; Professor William A. Brown, University of Cambridge; Dr Andy Charlwood, University of Leeds; Professor Simon Deakin, University of Cambridge; Professor Paul Edwards, University of Warwick; Professor Francis Green, University of Kent; Professor David Guest, King's College London; Professor Richard Harris, University of Glasgow; Professor Stephen Machin, University College London; Professor Paul Marginson, University of Warwick; Professor Robert McNabb, Cardiff University; Dr Sarah Oxenbridge (Acas), formerly University of Cambridge; Professor Riccardo Peccei, King's College London; Professor Andrew Pendleton, Manchester Metropolitan University; Professor Michael Rose, University of Bath; Professor David Storey, University of Warwick; Professor Mike Terry, University of Warwick; and, Professor Stephen Wood, University of Sheffield. Other academic researchers, lawyers and government officials also made valuable contributions to other areas of the survey.

Fieldwork for the survey was conducted by the National Centre for Social Research (NatCen). Sponsors offer particular thanks to Stephen Woodland who led the team at NatCen from June 2003 until August 2004. His knowledge and experience of working on the 1998 WERS proved invaluable to the exercise. Joanna Chaplin ably took up the reins after Stephen left NatCen and was assisted by a strong team of researchers: Jane Mangla, Susan Purdon, Rachel Breman and Colin Airey. They were backed up by a first-rate team of interviewers, fieldwork managers and data processors, under the overall supervision of Sandra Laver. The Sponsors would like to thank the NatCen team for their commitment to the execution of the survey.

Finally, and most importantly, the Sponsors and the Research Team would like to thank the managers, employees and employee representatives who gave freely of their time to participate in this study. Without their cooperation, the study, and a publication of this kind, would not be possible.

The authors write in a personal capacity and their views do not necessarily reflect those of the sponsoring bodies.

# Abbreviations

| | |
|---|---|
| ABI | Annual Business Inquiry |
| Acas | Advisory, Conciliation and Arbitration Service |
| CABx | Citizens Advice Bureaux |
| CAPI | Computer Aided Personal Interviewing |
| CIPD | Chartered Institute of Personnel and Development |
| CSOP | Company Share Option Plans |
| DDA | Disability Discrimination Act |
| DTI | Department of Trade and Industry |
| EMAR | Employment Market Analysis and Research |
| EMI | Enterprise Management Incentive |
| EPQ | Employee Profile Questionnaire |
| ESOS | Employee share ownership scheme |
| ESRC | Economic and Social Research Council |
| EWC | European Works Council |
| FPQ | Financial Performance Questionnaire |
| HIM | High involvement management |
| HRM | Human resource management |
| ICE | Information and Consultation of Employees |
| ICTs | Information communication technologies |
| IDBR | Inter-Departmental Business Register |
| IiP | Investors in People |
| ILM | Internal labour market |
| IPM | Institute of Personnel Management |
| JCC | Joint consultative committees |
| LFS | Labour Force Survey |
| NatCen | National Centre for Social Research |
| NBER | National Bureau of Economic Research |
| ONS | Office for National Statistics |
| PBR | Payment by results |
| PRP | Profit-related payments |
| PSI | Policy Studies Institute |
| SAYE | Save As You Earn |
| SEQ | Survey of Employees Questionnaire |

| | |
|---|---|
| SIC | Standard Industrial Classification |
| SIP | Share incentive plan |
| TUC | Trades Union Congress |
| ULR | Union Learning Representatives |
| WERS | Workplace Employment Relations Survey |
| WLB2 | Second Work–Life Balance Survey |

# Reporting conventions

Unless otherwise stated, the results presented in this publication exclude cases where the respondent did not provide an answer (i.e. they refused to provide one or were unable to express a view). The level of missing cases never exceeds 10 per cent, unless otherwise stated. Where differences or associations are highlighted, these have all been tested and are statistically significant at the 5 per cent level.

## Symbols within tables

0    Represents less than 0.5 per cent, including none.

( )   The unweighted base is 20–49 observations and should be treated with caution.

\*    Unweighted base is less than 20 observations and so is considered too low to produce a reliable estimate.

–    Not applicable/No estimate available

# 1 Introduction

This book provides an up-to-date and nationally representative portrait of the state of employment relations and working life inside British workplaces. It is based on an in-depth exploration of the findings from the 2004 Workplace Employment Relations Survey (WERS 2004). It also examines what has changed inside British workplaces since the 1998 WERS. The book will be of key interest to anyone concerned with the relationship between managers and employees, employment relations issues more generally, and how the world of work has changed in recent years.

There is perennial interest in the changing nature of work. This is evident not least from the extensive research conducted in recent years to identify patterns of change and interpret what these might mean for the future (for example, the Economic and Social Research Council's 'Future of Work' programme and the Leverhulme Trust-funded programme of work into the 'Future of Unions').[1] Today's global economy means that many employers are faced with an increasingly competitive market, and it is of growing interest how employers have responded to such an environment (White *et al.*, 2004: 5–6). There have also been significant changes within the labour market, with an increased focus on the position of women, the nature of employer and employee flexibility and the impact of technical change (Kingsmill, 2001; Machin, 2001; HM Treasury, 2003). Change within the political arena has also had an impact on the employment relations landscape. With the election of the Labour Government in 1997, legislation has been introduced or reformed in a number of policy areas, including: working hours; rates of pay; union recognition; work and family life; workplace conflict; equal opportunities; and, most recently, information and consultation. There has been a growing interest in the impact of these legislative and policy changes on employers (see, for example, Dickens *et al.*, 2005). The nature of research into the practice of employment relations has also altered in some respects, with an increasing focus on efficiency and the diffusion of what have been termed 'high involvement' or 'high performance' management practices. This 'new paradigm' stands in contrast to the traditional focus on institutions – principally trade unions – although a consensus has emerged which emphasizes the value of a holistic approach (Edwards, 1995, 2003; Godard and Delaney, 2000, 2002; Kochan, 2000; Budd, 2004).

It is the intention of the WERS Sponsors that this latest survey should continue in the footsteps of its predecessors by making a valuable contribution to on-going debate on these and other employment relations issues. The survey provides up-to-date empirical evidence on the changing nature of work as well as providing a unique opportunity to examine the potential determinants of change. It also provides an important source of data for those wishing to understand more about the detailed practice of employment relations and how it affects (or is affected by) each of the actors that take part. The dissemination of results began with the publication of the initial findings from the survey, shortly after the end of fieldwork (Kersley *et al.*, 2005). This volume represents a second, more substantial, contribution in that vein.

## About the survey

WERS 2004 is the fifth survey in the series of surveys conducted by the Department of Trade and Industry (DTI), the Economic and Social Research Council (ESRC), the Advisory, Conciliation and Arbitration Service (Acas), and the Policy Studies Institute (PSI). Previous surveys were conducted in 1980, 1984, 1990 and 1998. The Workplace Employment Relations Survey (WERS) series has mapped the contours of employment relations and informed the development of policy and practice in this area over the past quarter of a century.

Some of the survey questions have been asked consistently over the period, producing comparable data across the period 1980–2004. However, the series has also responded to changing interests in the employment relations arena by adding new areas of enquiry and reducing other areas in scope. In particular, the 1998 survey underwent substantial redesign, including a move away from detailed questioning on union organization and collective bargaining, a greater focus on employment relations practices and the adoption of the Survey of Employees. These changes were reflected in the change in the title of the survey: from 'industrial relations' to 'employee relations'. While the Sponsors considered that major revisions to both the structure and content of the 2004 survey were not necessary, changes were made in a number of key areas and these are reflected in the final survey design and survey instruments. Three key innovations to the 2004 design were: (1) the extension of the Cross-Section sample to include workplaces with between five and nine employees; (2) the sampling of greater numbers of non-union employee representatives; and (3) the adoption of a Financial Performance Questionnaire. The title of the survey was changed again, from 'employee relations' to 'employment relations', in order to reflect the most commonly used title for this broad field of study (see Edwards, 1995, for example). The development and the design of the 2004 survey are considered in some detail in the next section.

## Survey development

In order to inform the Sponsors' thinking about the overall design and scope of the fifth WERS, in the summer of 2002, the potential user community was consulted and views were sought on all aspects of WERS, including its broad design, the sampling population, the survey content and the survey outputs. The consultation exercise had two distinct elements: (1) a consultation with the academic community, led by the ESRC; and (2) a consultation with practitioners, think-tanks, and policy-makers and analysts across government, conducted by the DTI. The results of the ESRC-led and DTI-led exercises and other commissioned papers culminated in a paper setting out the Sponsors' decisions on how the fifth WERS would proceed (DTI/Acas/ESRC/PSI, 2003).[2] Sponsors considered that continuity in the design of the survey was very important, particularly given the strong interest in assessing the nature and extent of change since the previous survey. Nonetheless, the consultation exercise with user groups suggested the need for change in a number of key areas and these changes are considered in the section on 'questionnaire design'.

## Survey design and sample coverage

For the purposes of the survey, a workplace was defined as comprising 'the activities of a single employer at a single set of premises'. A branch of a high street bank, a head office or a factory were all considered to be workplaces in their own right. The terms 'workplace' and 'organization' were thus not interchangeable, except in the situation where an organization was located at a single site. The sample of workplaces was randomly drawn from the Inter-Departmental Business Register (IDBR) maintained by the Office for National Statistics (ONS). The Register is continuously updated from PAYE and VAT records and is considered to be the highest quality sampling frame of workplaces available in the United Kingdom. The sampling unit is the IDBR's 'local unit' which conforms to the definition of workplace used in the survey in most circumstances.[3]

Data were collected from three different perspectives: from workplace managers, employee representatives and employees. Managers and employee representatives were asked to act as informants of their workplace, and so the majority of the data collected in those interviews relates to the features of the workplace rather than to the particular characteristics of the individual respondent. The broad structure of the survey follows the design adopted in previous surveys, with both a Cross-Section and a Panel element (see Figure 1.1), albeit with some additional innovations and these are discussed below.

### *The 2004 Cross-Section*

An important innovation in WERS 2004 was the greater coverage of small workplaces. Funding from the Small Business Service enabled workplaces that employed between five and nine employees to be included in the Cross-Section Survey for the first time. Their inclusion expanded the scope of the survey so that the population from which it was drawn covered 700,000 workplaces (33 per cent of all workplaces in Britain) and 22.5 million employees (89 per cent

*Figure 1.1* Structure of the survey

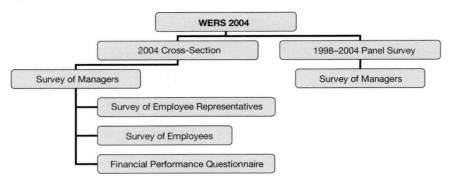

of all employees in employment).[4] The 1998 survey extended its scope to a lower workplace employment threshold of 10 or more employees, from 25 or more previously. Consultation with a team of academics specializing in research into small firms and subsequent piloting of the survey confirmed that a further extension would be possible. However, while the 2004 survey covered work-places with five or more employees, the findings reported in this book focus on the subset of workplaces with 10 or more employees. The main reason for this approach was so that straightforward comparisons could be made with the 1998 survey. A separate publication examines employment relations in small work-places and organizations (Forth *et al.*, 2006). All figures reported in the book are weighted and are representative of this subset of the population, which accounts for 18 per cent of all workplaces and 80 per cent of all employees in Britain.

The sample for the Cross-Section was stratified by workplace size and indus-try. Workplaces were randomly selected from within a particular size band and industry. Larger workplaces were given a greater probability of being selected across the sample so that statistically reliable comparisons could be made with smaller workplaces. Certain industries (e.g. Utilities) were also given a higher probability of being selected so that comparisons could be made between industrial sectors. Weights were applied to ensure that the final achieved sample was representative of the survey population from which it was drawn (the IDBR) and to take account of any non-response bias by workplace size and by industrial sector.[5] Further information about the design of the sample and the weighting strategy adopted for the Cross-Section is provided in the Technical Appendix to this book. A fuller account is provided in the Technical Report of the survey (Chaplin *et al.*, 2005).[6]

The intention was to conduct interviews in 2,500 workplaces as part of the Cross-Section Survey, comprising approximately 250 workplaces with between five and nine employees and the remainder drawn from workplaces with at least 10 employees. The main element of this survey was an interview with the senior manager responsible for employment relations on a day-to-day basis at the workplace (the 'Cross-Section Survey of Managers'). There were three further elements to the Cross-Section Survey, each being attempted in those workplaces that participated in the Survey of Managers. First, a short self-completion questionnaire was distributed to a random selection of (up to) 25 employees (the 'Survey of Employees'). Second, interviews were conducted with both a union and a non-union representative at the workplace, where present (the 'Survey of Employee Representatives').[7] This meant that, in some workplaces, two interviews were conducted with employee representatives. This constituted a departure from previous surveys where a single interview took place with an employee representative, and where preference was given to interviewing union representatives in workplaces where both types of representative were present. The main purpose of the revised selection rule was to increase the number of interviews with non-union representatives. This was considered to be desirable, given the decline in union representation and the increasing interest in non-union representation, and to establish an effective baseline against which to monitor the impact of the forthcoming Information and Consultation of Employees (2004) regulations. Third, a new self-completion questionnaire was designed to collect quantitative data about the financial performance of the workplace (the 'Financial Performance Questionnaire'). The questionnaire was completed either by the workplace manager or the financial manager. The questionnaire was adopted to supplement the existing subjective measures of performance collected in the management questionnaire and to provide additional information in areas not hitherto covered by WERS, such as data on research and development expenditure.

All of the elements of the Cross-Section are linked, thus providing an opportunity to examine the nature of employment relations from three different perspectives. This can assist in providing a balanced and rounded picture of the state of employment relations at the workplace. This book compares parties' reports in some areas. For example, Chapter 8 assesses employee representatives' and managers' accounts of collective conflict. Chapter 10 uses the link between the management questionnaire and the Financial Performance Questionnaire (FPQ) to compare subjective measures of productivity with 'accounting' measures derived from the FPQ.

### *The 1998–2004 Panel Survey*

As Figure 1.1 illustrates, the other element to the survey was the 1998–2004 Panel Survey. This was conducted in a random sub-sample of workplaces that had participated in the 1998 survey, had continued to be in operation throughout the six-year period, and employed at least 10 employees at the time of the 2004 interview (hereafter referred to as 'continuing workplaces'). A sample of 1,479 workplaces was taken with the aim of achieving approximately 900 interviews. In these workplaces, a single interview was conducted with the senior manager responsible for employment relations on a day-to-day basis. The remaining WERS 1998 establishments that were not selected to participate in the Panel were screened by telephone to establish whether they were still in existence and, where possible, to establish the current level of employment at that workplace. Like the Cross-Section Survey of Managers, weights were applied to ensure that the final achieved sample was representative of the population of continuing workplaces. Further information can be found in the Technical Appendix to this book and the full Technical Report of the survey (Chaplin *et al.*, 2005).

The Panel element of WERS is integral to understanding change. Combining data from the 1998 and 2004 Cross-Section Surveys of Managers together with data from the Panel Survey allows an assessment of how much change is due to alterations in the composition of the population of workplaces – for example, the move away from manufacturing towards service-sector workplaces – and how much is due to changes in the behaviour of continuing workplaces.

## Questionnaire design

Turning to the development of the survey instruments, the WERS Sponsors consulted with a number of academic researchers, who formed specialist teams to advise on the following discrete areas: Governance; Partnership; Skills, Job Satisfaction and Stress; Performance and Technology; Small Workplaces; and Worker Representation. These teams, together with other academic researchers, lawyers and government officials, made valuable contributions to the development of the survey. This work informed the development work undertaken by the WERS Research Team who were responsible for designing the final instruments.

Piloting of the draft questionnaires prepared by the Research Team took place between August and November 2003. The process began with the cognitive testing of the new questions which had been added to the Survey of Managers and the Survey of Employees. This was followed by a two-stage pilot, with the first stage focusing on the content, comprehension and length of the questionnaires and the second stage, 'the dress rehearsal', used to finesse the instruments and contact procedures.[8] Computer Aided Personal Interviewing (CAPI) was used for each of the interview based instruments in the pilot. Following the outcome of the pilots, in December 2003 the Research Team finalized the research instruments to be used in the main fieldwork.

A number of new topics were included in the Cross-Section Survey of Managers, such as trust, business strategy and computer use. Question sets were also expanded in the areas of consultation, dispute resolution, work–life balance and equal opportunities, and questions on organizational status, employee representation and payment systems were refined. The Survey of Employee Representatives was completely revised, seeing a reduction in the number of questions that duplicated those asked of managers and an expansion in questions considered particularly relevant to non-union representatives. Questions were also added to better identify the personal characteristics of employee representatives; to better understand the activities of joint consultative committees; and to investigate the extent of union recruitment activity. In the Survey of Employees, new questions on well-being, trust and computer use were included, and questions on job satisfaction, work–life balance and consultation were revised. The revisions and additions to the Survey of Employees increased its length by about one-fifth in comparison to the 1998 Survey of Employees. The Panel Survey questionnaire was based on that used in the 1998 Cross-Section Survey of Managers. However, it was shorter in length and collected less detail about particular practices, extending to only one-third of the length of the full 1998 Cross-Section Survey of Managers.

An initial analysis of many of the new items was presented in the booklet of first findings (Kersley *et al.*, 2005). Further analyses are presented at various points throughout this volume. It is hoped that the development of these data items will demonstrate the value of collaboration between those from different disciplines and methodological backgrounds, in particular, adding weight to the view expressed by Godard (2001a) that a healthy interaction between quantitative and qualitative methods of enquiry can achieve more than if one method were to be favoured to the exclusion of the other.

## Conduct of the survey

Fieldwork for the survey was conducted between February 2004 and April 2005 by the National Centre for Social Research, who were also responsible for conducting the fieldwork for the previous surveys in the series.

The fieldwork outcomes are provided in Table 1.1.[9] In the Cross-Section Survey of Managers, 2,295 workplaces with five or more employees took part, and the response rate was 64 per cent. The response rate for workplaces with 10 or more employees equated to 65 per cent, which was lower than the 80 per cent rate achieved in 1998. This might partly be explained by the longer interview length in 2004, the additional interviews with employee representatives conducted in some workplaces and the additional Financial Performance

*Table 1.1* Fieldwork outcomes

|  | *Total responses* (*no.*) | *Response rate* (*%*) | *Average duration* (*mins*) |
|---|---|---|---|
| *2004 Cross-Section* |  |  |  |
| Survey of Managers | 2,295 | 64 | 118 |
| Survey of Employee Representatives | 984 | 77 | 52 (union) |
|  |  |  | 43 (non-union) |
| Survey of Employees | 22,451 | 61 | – |
| Financial Performance Questionnaire | 1,070 | 51 | – |
| *1998–2004 Panel Survey* |  |  |  |
| Survey of Managers | 938 | 75 | 42 |

Questionnaire. However, a number of environmental factors may also have been at work, including: the overall research burden on large employers, who given their low incidence in the survey population, are asked to participate in employer surveys on a regular basis; an increase in the extent to which organizations survey their own employees on a regular basis; difficulty in getting to speak directly to the respondent due to the increased use of voicemail; and a general decline in response rates across all types of survey research.

The total number of interviews achieved with managers was below the intended target of 2,500.[10] Reserve samples were issued for workplaces with between five and nine employees, and single independent establishments with 10–49 employees, because of the lower than expected yields in these groups. The response rate achieved among the smallest workplaces (with between five and nine employees) was the lowest at 58 per cent.

In addition, 984 employee representatives were interviewed, representing a response rate of 77 per cent. Employee questionnaires were distributed in 86 per cent of workplaces; 22,451 of these questionnaires were completed and returned, representing a response rate of 61 per cent.[11] The Financial Performance Questionnaire was placed in 2,076 workplaces and 1,070 questionnaires were returned. When expressed as a proportion of those placed, this represents a response rate of 51 per cent.

In the Panel Survey, 938 workplaces participated out of the 1,479 selected. Sixteen per cent of the initial sample was found to be ineligible, with 10 per cent of workplaces having closed down and 3 per cent were continuing to operate but had less than 10 employees. Calculated as a proportion of eligible cases, the response rate for the Panel Survey equates to 75 per cent.

To sum up, good response rates were achieved for each of the different instruments. While they were lower than those achieved for the 1998 WERS, they still constitute some of the best response rates for a survey of this scale. They also provide a sound basis for analysis.

## The political, economic and labour market context since the 1998 survey

Before turning to the contents of the book and the nature of the analyses undertaken, it is worth considering the changes in the political, economic and labour market context which have taken place since the previous WERS in 1997/8, all of which have a bearing on interpretation of the findings reported in this book.

### *The political context*

As previously mentioned, the election of the Labour Government in 1997 is notable when considering the findings on the conduct of workplace employment relations in Britain. Since the previous survey was conducted, the UK Government has introduced a programme of legislative reforms with the intention of setting minimum standards in work.[12] In 1998, the Working Time Regulations came into force, restricting the circumstances in which employees could be required to work more than 48 hours a week and introducing an entitlement to four weeks' annual leave. In 1999, the National Minimum Wage was introduced. Under the Employment Relations Act 1999, new rights to parental leave and time off for dependants were introduced, including enhanced maternity leave. The same Act also introduced a right to statutory trade union recognition and the right to be accompanied in grievance and disciplinary hearings. The Employment Act 2002 introduced paternity leave, further enhancements to maternity leave and pay and a duty on employers to consider seriously requests for flexible working by parents of children under the age of 6 or disabled children aged under 18. Legislation introduced in 2003 outlawed discrimination on the grounds of sexual orientation and religion or belief. In October 2004, the law required all employers to have minimum statutory procedures in place for dealing with dismissal, disciplinary action and grievances in the workplace, known as the 'three-step' statutory dispute resolution procedure. In April 2005, the Information and Consultation of Employees Regulations 2004 came into force. This gave employees in organizations with 150 or more employees the right to be informed and consulted about important managerial decisions affecting the business they work for.[13] Legislation outlawing age discrimination is due to be in force by the end of 2006.

The 1998 WERS was conducted before most of these legislative changes came into effect. The 1998 survey therefore provides a baseline against which the impact of many of these changes in employment legislation can be assessed. However, it should be noted that this book only attempts to provide a broad assessment of the impact of the legislation. This is largely done by highlighting any changes which have occurred in relevant areas of policy or practice within workplaces. A broad assessment of the impact of legislation is considered in Chapter 11.

## The economic and labour market context

Turning to the economic context, at the time when the survey was conducted, the economy was experiencing a period of economic stability. The UK economy was enjoying the longest period of sustained low inflation since the 1960s (standing at 1.3 per cent in 2004) and the longest period of economic growth on record (3.2 per cent in 2004). Interest rates were historically low (4.75 per cent in 2004) and so too was unemployment (4.7 per cent in 2004). The number of people in work had increased by over 2.1 million from Spring 1997 and close to 28.5 million people were in work.

Also of relevance were a number of significant changes in the labour market between 1997 and 2004, including an increase in the employment rate of women with young children (from 49.1 per cent to 52.8 per cent). This period also witnessed an increase in the employment rate of older workers (aged 50 years and over but below retirement age), up from 64.7 per cent to 70.0 per cent. Conversely the same period saw a decline in the employment rate of younger workers (aged between 16 and 17 years), falling from 48.6 per cent to 41.3 per cent in 2004, driven in large part by higher staying-on rates at school. There have also been a number of changes in respect of 'non-standard' forms of employment. Between 1997 and 2004 there has been a fall in the proportion of employees in temporary jobs (from 7.7 per cent to 6.0 per cent), while the proportion of employees in part-time work has remained stable at around one quarter since the late 1990s. The composition of the workforce is examined in Chapter 2. The increase in the employment rate of women with young children in recent years has also led to an interest in the availability of flexible working arrangements for employees with caring responsibilities. There is also some existing evidence which suggests that employer provision and employee take-up of a number of flexible working arrangements have increased since 2000 (Woodland *et al.*, 2003; Stevens *et al.*, 2004). The incidence of flexible working arrangements is examined in Chapter 9.

While the WERS series charted the decline in trade union membership and density up to 1998, in recent years, membership levels appear to have stabilized. In 2004, 6.3 million employees were union members in Great Britain and density stood at 28.5 per cent. Overt workplace conflict was seen to be low with 34 working days lost per 1,000 employees to labour disputes in 2004 (Monger, 2005).

## Structure of the book

The broad style adopted in this book is similar to its immediate predecessors (Cully *et al.*, 1999; Millward *et al.*, 2000), with the aim being to locate the results in a broader context and to engage with wider debates within the policy-making communities. However, the current volume differs, in that it seeks to integrate the analysis of the most recent Cross-Section with an analysis of change in a single volume. It adopts a thematic approach in which the findings from each of the different Cross-Section Survey instruments are discussed together rather than in separate chapters. An outline of the contents of the book is provided below.

Chapter 2 begins by providing a profile of the population of workplaces and employees in Great Britain in 2004. These characteristics will be used to help better understand the practice of employment relations considered in the chapters that follow.

Chapter 3 considers the changing roles and responsibilities of employment relations managers and the involvement of line managers in people management. It also provides an analysis of managers' attitudes towards the employment relations function, and reflects upon the links between managing employment relations and the achievement of wider business goals.

Chapter 4 assesses the recruitment, training and appraisal of employees as well as work organization. The change in the incidence of employer practices in these areas is also explored. Employees' experiences of work are also considered through investigations of issues such as job influence, work intensity and employee well-being.

Chapter 5 looks at the incidence and operation of a number of arrangements for employee representation, consultation and communication, along with changes since 1998. It also investigates the effectiveness of different arrangements, as seen from the perspective of employees.

Chapter 6 provides a portrait of the senior employee representatives who 'staff' the structures of representation and consultation as discussed in Chapter 5. It includes an analysis of their profile, describes their roles and activities, the nature of their constituencies, and considers the nature of management–representative relations.

Chapter 7 considers the way in which pay and non-pay terms and conditions are determined. It also examines the effects of pay determination methods on the pay distribution, fringe benefits provision and pay satisfaction. Consultation on collective redundancies and health and safety is also considered.

Chapter 8 provides an overview of the nature and extent of workplace conflict in 2004, and examines the degree of change and consistency since 1998. It also looks closely at organizational procedures for addressing and resolving disagreements between managers and trade unions, and managers and employees.

Chapter 9 examines employers' equal opportunities policies and practices, including arrangements aimed at assisting employees to achieve a work–life balance and assesses whether their incidence has changed since the late 1990s. It also examines attitudes towards 'work–life' balance from both managers' and employees' perspectives.

Chapter 10 investigates the factors that influence outcomes associated with the climate of employment relations and workplace performance.

Finally, Chapter 11 provides a summary of the main findings and examines a number of debates of interest, including the impact of the government's programme of employment relations reform. It concludes by considering the design issues for a possible sixth WERS.

## Nature of the analyses

The analyses presented in this book are, in the main, cross-tabular in nature. However, multivariate analyses have been conducted on occasion where the aim has been to isolate the impact of a particular variable of interest on another variable, holding other variables constant. The bulk of the analysis presented in Chapter 10, for example, draws on multivariate techniques. Where such techniques have been used, the results are presented in a simple form and the full results are available from the website accompanying this book.[14] The same website also provides a set of tables containing a number of key variables cross-tabulated against a range of workplace characteristics.

While the primary focus of the book is to provide a mapping of the 2004 results, the intention has also been to provide an analysis of change since 1998, where consistent questioning permits. In order that straightforward comparisons can be made with the results from the previous survey, the findings presented in this book focus on the subset of workplaces with 10 or more employees, as noted earlier. Most of the analyses reported in the book relate to the population of workplaces, but there are some analyses that relate to the population of employees. The latter provide an indication of the nature of the employment relationship for employees, a high percentage of whom work in larger workplaces.

The reporting conventions used are discussed on p. xviii, and it is important now to comment on the accuracy of the results. The high response rates achieved in WERS 2004 (both for the survey as a whole and for individual questions) help minimize response biases, but non-response weights have also been computed to ensure, as far as is practicable, that one can extrapolate from the survey to the population from which it was drawn. Like other sample surveys, however, WERS 2004 is subject to sampling errors whereby the results computed from the sample provide only an estimate of the true figure within the population as a whole. It is possible to quantify the degree of error through the calculation of standard errors and confidence intervals. For ease of reading, these are not reported within the text, which reports estimates as if they were exact. However, the Technical Appendix to this book includes tables which allow the reader to approximate standard errors for various percentages, based on average design effects, for both the 2004 Cross-Section Survey and the 1998–2004 Panel Survey.

# 2 A profile of workplaces and employees

## Introduction

This first substantive chapter presents a profile of workplaces with 10 or more employees. In doing so, it considers a number of basic establishment characteristics, such as workforce size, industrial activity and patterns of ownership, as well as discussing the nature of the product markets in which different workplaces operate. It also presents some of the key characteristics of the employees who staff these workplaces, illustrating the diversity and homogeneity that often are present at establishment level.

Such characteristics are of interest because they represent the accumulated choices of employers in organizing their available resources to produce goods and deliver services, all of which impact upon the deployment of labour and the practice of employment relations. They are also commonly associated with many of the attitudes, behaviours and practices that are discussed in the chapters which follow. For example, many of the institutional features of employment relations, such as trade union representation, are found to be less common among smaller workplaces, establishments under private ownership and those employing high proportions of young workers. With these points in mind, the chapter introduces most of the key characteristics that are used in later chapters to illustrate how employment relations vary across the population. The chapter also provides some of the context that is necessary to understand why the practice and character of employment relations may have changed in certain respects since the previous WERS in 1998.

## Workplace and organization characteristics

### Employment size

The number of employees at a workplace can be expected to have a fundamental impact on the practice of employment relations. The task of managing a large number of employees is necessarily complex, bringing with it questions of efficiency and consistency that are likely to arise less often when all the employees report directly to a single owner or manager. For instance, in larger workplaces the senior manager responsible for employment relations is likely to devote a greater amount of time to employment relations issues, to delegate more aspects of the managerial function to departmental managers or supervisors, and to place a greater reliance on employee representatives to communicate the wishes and concerns of the workforce.

The surveys in the WERS series take the employees of a workplace to be those who have a contract of employment with the employer at the sampled establishment and who either work at, or principally report to, that address. This includes any sales persons and other employees who may spend much of their time off-site, but who nonetheless report to the sampled establishment. It excludes any outworkers and casual staff who do not have a contract of employment, as well as freelance workers working under contracts for services and temporary staff working under agency contracts.[1]

The population of workplaces with 10 or more employees is dominated by small workplaces (Figure 2.1). These might include workshops, small retail outlets, restaurants or surgeries. At the time of the survey, around two-fifths (57 per cent) of workplaces employed 10–24 employees, while a further fifth (23 per cent) employed 25–49 employees. The proportion of larger workplaces was correspondingly small, but such workplaces employed a disproportionately large share of all employees. Workplaces with 500 or more employees, which might include some hospitals, manufacturing plants or local government offices, made up only 1 per cent of all establishments, but accounted for one-fifth (22 per cent) of total employment.

*Figure 2.1* Distribution of workplaces and employment by workplace size

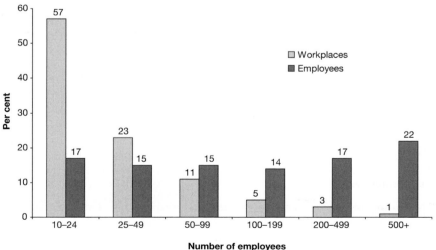

Base: All workplaces with 10 or more employees.
Figures are weighted and based on responses from 2,062 managers.

One important consequence of these figures is that the overall incidence of employment relations practices is heavily influenced by the practices of small workplaces. However, the character of the employment relationship for most employees is determined by practice in larger workplaces. With these points in mind, findings on the percentages of workplaces with particular features of employment relations are interspersed with employee-based findings throughout the remainder of this volume.

Some have pointed to a reduction in the size of the average workplace in recent years, citing this as a key factor in explaining many of the changes that are taking place in the overall incidence of certain employment relations practices (Sisson and Marginson, 2003: 178). However, there is no support for this proposition within the population of workplaces covered by WERS. The profile of workplaces by size in 2004 was no different to that observed in 1998, nor were there any differences across the earlier surveys in the WERS series among the subset of workplaces with 25 or more employees (Millward *et al.*, 2000: 25).

The numbers of employees employed by individual workplaces do, of course, change over time. Some grow from having less than 10 employees to employing 10 or more, or they shrink in the opposite direction, moving into and out of the subset of workplaces with 10 or more employees that is the focus of this book. In some extreme cases, workplaces will close down. The degree of movement in and out of the survey population is extensive and, since those workplaces that join the population also tend to conduct employment relations in a rather different way to those who leave it, these compositional changes commonly have an effect on the overall incidence of employment relations practices that is often at least as great as that caused by changes in behaviour among workplaces that continue in operation (see the discussions of trade union recognition in Chapter 5 and performance-related pay in Chapter 7, for example).

Establishments participating in the 1998 Cross-Section Survey were traced in 2004 in order to ascertain whether each establishment had survived over the intervening six years. Figure 2.2 shows that, overall, one-sixth (16 per cent) of workplaces with 10 or more employees in 1998 had closed down. Whether particular features of employment relations, such as the recognition of trade unions, affect the likelihood of establishment survival has been the subject of some debate (see, for example, Bryson, 2004; Metcalf, 2005); this and other often-cited associations are explored in subsequent chapters. A further tenth of workplaces with 10 or more employees in 1998 had fallen out of scope (having fewer than 10 employees in 2004). The remaining 74 per cent continued in operation with 10 or more employees in 2004; these are referred to hereafter as 'continuing workplaces'.[2] A random sample of these continuing workplaces were interviewed as part of the WERS 1998–2004 Panel Survey in order to identify how their employment relations practices had changed over the six-year period, as discussed in Chapter 1.

Turning to the origins of workplaces with 10 or more employees in 2004 – mapped in the current Cross-Section Survey of Managers – one-sixth (16 per cent) were new workplaces that were not in existence in 1998. The degree of

*Figure 2.2* The changing composition of the population of workplaces, 1998–2004

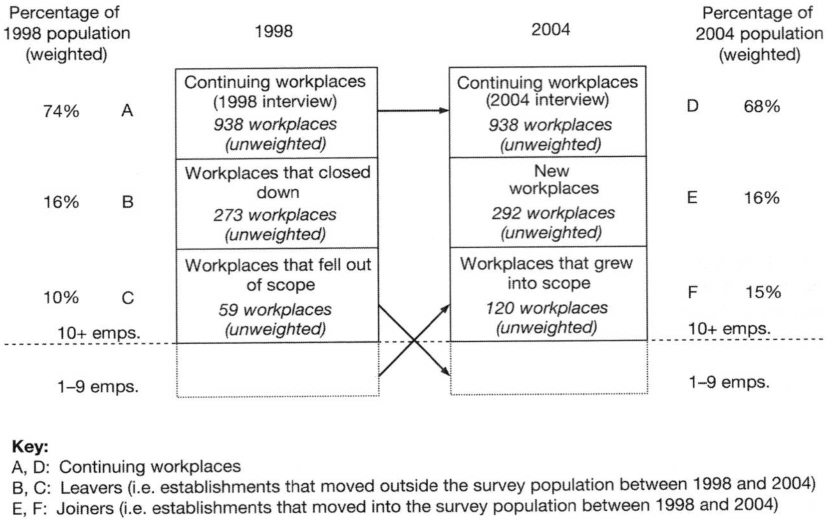

| Percentage of 1998 population (weighted) | | 1998 | 2004 | | Percentage of 2004 population (weighted) |
|---|---|---|---|---|---|
| 74% | A | Continuing workplaces (1998 interview) *938 workplaces (unweighted)* | Continuing workplaces (2004 interview) *938 workplaces (unweighted)* | D | 68% |
| 16% | B | Workplaces that closed down *273 workplaces (unweighted)* | New workplaces *292 workplaces (unweighted)* | E | 16% |
| 10% | C | Workplaces that fell out of scope *59 workplaces (unweighted)* | Workplaces that grew into scope *120 workplaces (unweighted)* | F | 15% |
| 10+ emps. | | | | | 10+ emps. |
| 1–9 emps. | | | | | 1–9 emps. |

**Key:**
A, D:  Continuing workplaces
B, C:  Leavers (i.e. establishments that moved outside the survey population between 1998 and 2004)
E, F:  Joiners (i.e. establishments that moved into the survey population between 1998 and 2004)

innovation and sophistication in employment relations practice in these new workplaces is of particular interest. A further 15 per cent had grown from having fewer than 10 employees in 1998 to having 10 or more in 2004, and the remaining 68 per cent were 'continuing workplaces'. Consequently, just over two-thirds of the population of workplaces with 10 or more employees was consistent in 1998 and 2004; the remainder in 1998 had left the population by 2004, to be replaced by workplaces that had joined it over the same period. The turnover of establishments between 1998 and 2004 was particularly high among smaller workplaces. Just three-fifths of workplaces with between 10 and 24 employees in 2004 had also been part of the survey population in 1998, compared with 76 per cent of workplaces with between 24 and 49 employees and 85 per cent of those with 50 or more employees.

Even among those workplaces that remain in operation, there will almost inevitably be some turnover among the staff employed from year to year. Respondents to the 2004 Cross-Section Survey of Managers were asked how many employees were employed at the workplace 12 months prior to the survey interview, and what proportion of those employees had left the workplace over the intervening period, providing us with an indicator of the degree of labour turnover at the workplace. In aggregate, some 20 per cent of those employed one year prior to the survey interview had left employment at their workplaces during the subsequent 12 months (Table 2.1). This proportion was particularly high in Hotels and restaurants (39 per cent) and in Wholesale and retail (27 per cent). It was particularly low in Electricity, gas and water supply (10 per cent), Public administration (10 per cent) and Education (11 per cent). Almost one-third of all workplaces (30 per cent) had seen at least one quarter of those employed 12 months prior to the survey interview depart over the year. In

*Table 2.1* Labour turnover 2003–2004, by industry

|  | All employees (%) | Workplaces with turnover of 25% or more (%) |
|---|---|---|
| Manufacturing | 17 | 19 |
| Electricity, gas and water supply | (10) | (12) |
| Construction | 21 | 35 |
| Wholesale and retail | 27 | 40 |
| Hotels and restaurants | 39 | 64 |
| Transport and communication | 17 | 20 |
| Financial services | 21 | 22 |
| Other business services | 20 | 24 |
| Public administration | 10 | 6 |
| Education | 11 | 6 |
| Health and social work | 17 | 30 |
| Other community services | 20 | 38 |
| All workplaces | 20 | 30 |

Base (column 1): All employees in workplaces with 10 or more, if employed 12 months prior to the survey interview.
Base (column 2): All workplaces with 10 or more employees.
Figures are weighted and based on responses from 1,973 managers.

Hotels and restaurants, the proportion was almost two-thirds (64 per cent). Public sector establishments were much less likely than private sector establishments to have seen at least one quarter of their staff depart over the previous year (9 per cent, compared with 35 per cent). The distinction between the public and private sectors remained after accounting for differences in workplace size and activity.

## Industry and ownership

Although the nature of employment relations is closely associated with the size of a workplace, it is also related to the type of product that is being manufactured or the service that is being delivered. Broad industrial classifications can mask a great deal of variety but, as Arrowsmith and Sisson (1999) show, workplaces in a given sector also tend to share similar constraints and pressures that may bring about some commonality of practice.

Table 2.2 shows the distribution of workplaces by industry, with each workplace in the survey having been classified to one of 12 Sections of the *Standard Industrial Classification (2003)*.[3] Table 2.2 shows that Manufacturing accounted for just over one-tenth of establishments and 15 per cent of employment. The Wholesale and retail sector accounted for almost twice as many workplaces (21 per cent), but the establishments in this sector were generally smaller, having an average of 39 employees each, compared with an average of 64 employees among establishments in Manufacturing. As a consequence, the two sectors accounted for similar shares of all employment. Other business services and Health and social work were the two other sectors that accounted for more than one-tenth of both establishments and employment.

*Table 2.2* Industry and ownership

| | All workplaces (column %) | All employees (column %) | Private sector workplaces (cell %) | Private sector only | |
| --- | --- | --- | --- | --- | --- |
| | | | | Foreign-owned (cell %) | Family-owned (cell %) |
| Manufacturing | 12 | 15 | 98 | 19 | 62 |
| Electricity, gas and water supply | 0 | 0 | (89) | (17) | (0) |
| Construction | 4 | 4 | 96 | 5 | 69 |
| Wholesale and retail | 21 | 16 | 100 | 18 | 47 |
| Hotels and restaurants | 9 | 5 | 100 | 12 | 35 |
| Transport and communication | 6 | 7 | 74 | 10 | 59 |
| Financial services | 4 | 6 | 100 | 9 | 3 |
| Other business services | 14 | 13 | 95 | 9 | 33 |
| Public administration | 3 | 6 | 1 | * | * |
| Education | 8 | 9 | 14 | 0 | 31 |
| Health and social work | 14 | 15 | 65 | 0 | 16 |
| Other community services | 5 | 4 | 80 | 4 | 26 |
| All workplaces | 100 | 100 | 82 | 12 | 40 |

Base (columns 1 and 3): All workplaces with 10 or more employees.
Base (column 2): All employees in workplaces with 10 or more employees.
Base (columns 4 and 5): All private sector workplaces with 10 or more employees.
Figures are weighted and based on responses from 2,062 managers (1,477 in the private sector).

Industrial activity is closely linked to sector of ownership, with the majority of workplaces in each industry being located in either the private or public sector, but few industries having a mixture of privately and publicly-owned establishments (Table 2.2, column 3). Analysing industry and ownership together, some 12 per cent of establishments operated in private sector Manufacturing, 70 per cent operated in private sector services and 18 per cent were part of the public sector. The equivalent figures in 1998 were 14 per cent, 66 per cent and 21 per cent, respectively. The over-representation of private Manufacturing establishments among workplaces that closed down between 1998 and 2004 (32 per cent of closures were in this sector), and their under-representation among new workplaces (8 per cent), go some way towards explaining the overall changes in composition.

Sector of ownership is an important characteristic when investigating employment relations practice, not least because public sector employers in Britain have historically offered a greater level of support for union representation and placed a greater emphasis on industry-wide terms and conditions than employers in the private sector. While these features are changing to varying degrees (Bach and Winchester, 2003), the public sector remains distinct from the private sector in many areas, as is evident throughout the remaining chapters.

Within the private sector, workplaces can be disaggregated into those that are domestically-owned and those that are foreign-owned. Britain is a major recipient of foreign direct investment and the activities of foreign multi-nationals are seen by many policy-makers as a potentially important source of innovation in a range of areas, not least employment relations (Ferner, 2003). Among private sector workplaces with 10 or more employees, one-fifth (19 per cent) had some degree of foreign-ownership or control, while one-tenth (12 per cent) were predominantly foreign-owned or controlled. The equivalent figures in 1998 were 15 per cent and 8 per cent, respectively, indicating an increase in foreign-ownership since the last survey.

Foreign-owned workplaces were typically larger than domestically-owned establishments. Focusing on workplaces that were predominantly foreign-owned, the majority were located in either Wholesale and retail (40 per cent) or Manufacturing (24 per cent). Along with the small Electricity, gas and water supply sector, these were the industries with above-average proportions of foreign-owned workplaces (Table 2.2). The head offices of foreign-owned workplaces were most commonly located in the United States (37 per cent). In a further 23 per cent of cases, the head office was located in another member state of the European Union and in 16 per cent it was located elsewhere outside the European Union, usually in Japan. The remaining 24 per cent of foreign-owned workplaces belonged to organizations which, although not domestically-owned, located their head office in the United Kingdom.

An alternative route through which employment relations practices may be imported is via the foreign subsidiaries of domestically-owned multinational enterprises. Among the 81 per cent of private sector establishments that were wholly UK-owned, almost one-third (31 per cent) belonged to organizations that owned or controlled subsidiary companies or establishments outside the UK. This figure was particularly high among workplaces in the Financial services industry (83 per cent), but was also above-average in the Transport and communication industry (53 per cent).

A further characteristic of interest among private sector workplaces is the degree of family-ownership and involvement. Research has indicated that family-owned workplaces exhibit a less consultative style of management than is found in other types of establishment (Harris *et al.*, 2004). The results from WERS 2004 also indicate that small, family-owned workplaces feature prominently among the minority that actively discourage union membership (Chapter 5). Family-owned workplaces are here defined as those where a single individual or family owned at least 50 per cent of the organization to which the workplace belonged. Two-fifths of private sector workplaces with 10 or more employees were family-owned under this definition (Table 2.2). However, family-owned workplaces tended to be small – two-thirds (66 per cent) had fewer than 25 employees – and they employed less than one-third (31 per cent) of all private sector employees. It was usual for the controlling owners of family-owned workplaces to be actively involved in day-to-day management on a full-time basis; this was the case in 61 per cent of family-owned establishments. The incidence of family-owned workplaces was notably higher in 2004 than in 1998, when the figure stood at 32 per cent.

## The wider organization

One-third (32 per cent) of workplaces were single independent establishments: in other words, they did not belong to any larger organization (Table 2.3). This proportion was unchanged since 1998. Smaller workplaces were more likely than larger workplaces to be single independent establishments. Equally, private sector establishments were much more likely to be independent than those under public ownership.

Workplaces that belong to a larger organization may have limited autonomy in the way that they manage employment relations, unless the workplace is itself the head office and takes responsibility for the development of policies and procedures on behalf of all sites. This particular issue is explored in Chapter 3. Among the two-thirds of workplaces that were part of a larger organization, one in seven (15 per cent) were the head office of that organization and the remainder were branch sites. In total, 10 per cent of all workplaces were head offices and 58 per cent were branch sites. Many branch sites had a large number of sister establishments in the UK. A small proportion (3 per cent) represented the sole UK establishment of a foreign organization, and a further fifth (20 per cent) had less than 10 sister establishments, but one quarter had between 10 and 99 sister establishments and a further two-fifths (38 per cent) had 100 or more. The remaining 14 per cent of branch sites did not know how many other sites in the UK belonged to their organization, a likely indication that the number was reasonably large.

The number of sites in the wider organization was, not surprisingly, closely associated with the total number of employees in the organization. Accordingly, most workplaces that were part of a wider organization accounted for only a fraction of total organization-wide employment. Although most (76 per cent) of

*Table 2.3* Location within the wider organization (row %)

|  | Single, independent establishment | Head office of multi-site organization | Branch of multi-site organization |
|---|---|---|---|
| *Workplace size* | | | |
| 10–24 employees | 39 | 9 | 52 |
| 25–49 employees | 27 | 12 | 62 |
| 50–99 employees | 19 | 12 | 70 |
| 100–199 employees | 15 | 13 | 72 |
| 200–499 employees | 14 | 13 | 73 |
| 500 or more employees | 15 | 22 | 63 |
| | | | |
| *Sector of ownership* | | | |
| Private sector | 38 | 11 | 51 |
| Public sector | 4 | 8 | 88 |
| All workplaces | 32 | 10 | 58 |

Base: All workplaces with 10 or more employees.
Figures are weighted and based on responses from 2,060 managers.

those workplaces that belonged to a wider organization had fewer than 50 employees, a majority (53 per cent) belonged to organizations with at least 1,000 employees across all sites.

There is a particular interest in employment relations within small firms (see, for example, Ram and Edwards, 2003; Scase, 2003). Definitions vary, but private sector organizations with 10–49 employees are here categorized as small firms, those with 50–249 employees as medium-sized firms and those with 250 or more employees as large firms.[4] Taking the number of employees to represent the size of the organization for single independent workplaces, since the two are equivalent in such cases, 36 per cent of all workplaces were part of small firms. These workplaces employed 13 per cent of all employees. A further 11 per cent of all workplaces were part of medium-sized firms; they accounted for 12 per cent of all employees. Some findings from WERS 2004 that indicate the importance of firm size are presented in this book. However, the nature of employment relations in small and medium-sized firms is investigated in detail in a companion report (Forth *et al.*, 2006).

## *The competitive environment*

Retaining the focus on private sector workplaces, the discussion now moves on to consider the competitive environment in which workplaces operate. Almost all private sector workplaces (97 per cent), including most head offices, traded with consumers or other organizations. The remainder either supplied goods or services solely to sister establishments, or served only as an administrative office for other parts of the organization. Of those that did trade externally, 54 per cent traded only with the general public, 33 per cent traded only with other organizations and 13 per cent traded with both. Two-fifths (42 per cent) relied on a single product or service, while the remaining three-fifths (58 per cent) had different products or services.[5] Small workplaces were more likely than larger workplaces to trade solely with the general public, and were more likely to offer only a single product or service. The provision of a range of products or services does afford an establishment greater protection against market fluctuations, all other things being equal, but it may also necessitate greater complexity in the organization of work, irrespective of workplace size (see Chapter 4).

Turning to the geographical proximity of the market, almost half (45 per cent) of all private sector establishments primarily served a local market, defined as being within one hour's drive. A further 43 per cent operated primarily at regional or national level, with the remaining 12 per cent reporting that their market was primarily international. The proximity of the market was strongly associated with workplace size: only 14 per cent of workplaces with 500 or more employees served primarily local markets and 39 per cent served primarily international markets. Trans-national trade brings the opportunity of a broader customer base, but also brings competitive threats if the flow of exports is accompanied by a corresponding flow of imports.[6] One quarter of workplaces (24 per cent) faced competition from overseas-based suppliers. Foreign competition was particularly common in Manufacturing (58 per cent of workplaces) and Financial services (43 per cent). Perhaps unsurprisingly, it was much less common in Hotels and restaurants (7 per cent), Other community services (4 per cent) and Health and social work (2 per cent).

Managers were asked to rate the degree of competition in the market for their main product or service on a five-point scale: 'Very high'; 'High'; 'Neither high nor low'; 'Low'; and 'Very low'. Around two-fifths (38 per cent) said that the degree of competition was 'very high'. Establishments in Financial services and Wholesale and retail were most likely to say that competition was 'very high' (61 per cent and 47 per cent respectively), while those in Health and social work and Education – two areas where services have principally been provided by the public sector – were least likely to do so (16 per cent and 9 per cent). Establishments facing foreign competition were more likely to say that the degree of competition was 'very high' (53 per cent, compared with 34 per cent among workplaces that did not face foreign competition). The findings from WERS 2004 show that, among other things, the degree of competition was positively associated with employees' ratings of work intensity (Chapter 4).

The final area to be considered in this section is business strategy. Managers were asked to rate the extent to which demand for their main product or service depended on offering lower prices than or superior quality to their competitors, in either case using a five-point scale ranging from 'Heavily' to 'Not at all'. One-fifth (19 per cent) of private sector trading establishments reported that demand depended heavily on offering lower prices, while a similar proportion (15 per cent) said that it did not depend at all on price. Price-dependence varied little by size of workplace but was particularly high in Wholesale and retail (33 per cent) and Construction (32 per cent). There was less variation in the extent to which establishments reported that demand depended on offering superior quality: 43 per cent reported that it was heavily dependent on quality and only 5 per cent said that quality was unrelated to demand. Establishments in Education and Other community services were the most likely to report a heavy dependence on quality (73 per cent and 59 per cent, respectively).

Both price- and quality-dependence were positively associated with the presence of a high degree of competition in the establishment's principal market. However, price and quality were not always seen as alternatives. Overall, 31 per cent of establishments reported that demand was highly dependent on both lower prices and superior quality; 46 per cent reported that it was highly dependent on quality but not price; 12 per cent reported that it was highly dependent on price but not quality; and 10 per cent reported that it was not highly dependent on either factor. When asked to name the two additional factors that were most important to competitive success, establishments were more likely to mention a high level of customer service (65 per cent) and customizing their product or service to meet individual needs (45 per cent) than they were to mention product or service complexity (22 per cent), uniqueness (22 per cent), availability or delivery times (18 per cent) or innovation (12 per cent).

Questions on business strategy were not present in the 1998 WERS, and they provide an interesting insight into the determinants of employment relations practice. The results from WERS 2004 indicated that the emphasis placed on price, quality and other factors was closely associated with a number of features of employment relations, including the provision of training (see Chapter 4).

## Workforce composition

Together, workplaces with 10 or more employees employ 80 per cent of the employee workforce (excluding the self-employed), representing approximately 20.3 million employees. The second half of this chapter draws both on the Survey of Employees Questionnaire and the Employee Profile Questionnaire to describe the characteristics of these employees and the types of workplaces in which they are employed.

A small number of basic characteristics are explored, namely occupation, gender, ethnicity, disability, age, and the incidence of caring responsibilities. The Survey of Employees Questionnaire (SEQ) collected information on such characteristics and the broad proportions are presented here. However, as this information is similar to that available from other surveys of employees, such as the Labour Force Survey (LFS), it is considered only briefly.[7] Instead, the primary focus in this section is on the data provided by managers on the composition of the workforce through the Employee Profile Questionnaire (EPQ). These data give WERS a unique advantage over employee surveys such as the LFS, as they enable analysis of the extent to which employees with particular characteristics are concentrated in different types of workplaces. This information can be useful in understanding the incidence of management practices, such as those designed to promote equal opportunities (see Chapter 9), as well as the character of management–employment relations and levels of labour productivity (see Chapter 10).

### *Occupation*

Managers were asked to detail the number of employees at the workplace within nine distinct occupational groups (as defined in the *Standard Occupational Classification 2000*). On average, each workplace contained employees from four of the nine occupational groups. Table 2.4 shows that 11 per cent of all employees covered by the survey were Managers and senior officials, but nine out of every 10 workplaces (90 per cent) contained at least some managerial employees. The absence of managerial employees from some workplaces is, in part, explained by the presence of owner-managers, who would not be classed as employees. Ninety-five per cent of workplaces with 25 or more employees employed at least one manager. After Managers and senior officials, Administrative and secretarial workers were the occupational group most commonly found in workplaces. More than two-thirds (67 per cent) of workplaces had some administrative staff. By contrast, less than one in five workplaces (18 per

*Table 2.4* Incidence and gender composition of occupational groups

| | All employees | Some employees in the occupation | Largest occupational group | Gender composition of occupation |
|---|---|---|---|---|
| | % employees | % workplaces | % workplaces | % employees female |
| *Occupational group* | | | | |
| Managers and senior officials | 11 | 90 | – | 36 |
| Professional | 12 | 35 | 10 | 48 |
| Associate professional and technical | 15 | 32 | 9 | 56 |
| Administrative and secretarial | 18 | 67 | 12 | 77 |
| Skilled trades | 7 | 29 | 9 | 10 |
| Caring, leisure and other personal service | 8 | 18 | 12 | 82 |
| Sales and customer service | 8 | 38 | 20 | 75 |
| Process, plant and machine operatives and drivers | 9 | 23 | 12 | 18 |
| Elementary occupations | 13 | 43 | 16 | 45 |

Base (columns 1 and 4): All employees in workplaces with 10 or more.
Base (columns 2 and 3): All workplaces with 10 or more employees.
Figures are weighted and based on responses from 21,418 employees (column 1); 2,043 managers (columns 2 and 3); and 21,338 employees (column 4).

cent) contained some employees from Caring, leisure and other personal service occupations.

Regardless of their occupation, employees were asked whether they supervised other staff. Thirty-four per cent of employees reported that they did so. Unsurprisingly, Managers were the group most likely to have some supervisory responsibilities (82 per cent did so), although a sizeable proportion of employees in the Professional and Associate professional and technical occupations also supervised some staff (46 per cent and 40 per cent, respectively). Less than one-third of employees from the other occupational groups had supervisory responsibilities, with those in Elementary occupations being the least likely to oversee the work of others (17 per cent did so).

There were clear differences in the employment of particular occupations between industrial sectors. While Professionals were most likely to be found in establishments in the Education sector (97 per cent), they were only employed in 11 per cent of workplaces in Wholesale and retail or Hotels and restaurants. Less than one quarter (22 per cent) of workplaces in the Hotels and restaurants sector had any Administrative and secretarial staff, but at least half of all establishments in the other industrial sectors had some employees from these occupations. Workplaces in the Hotels and restaurants sector were most likely to employ some staff in Elementary occupations (87 per cent), while establishments in the Financial services sector were least likely to have some employees in this occupational group (15 per cent did so).

Table 2.4 also shows the proportion of workplaces where each occupation constituted the largest non-managerial group of employees in the workplace (column 3). The largest non-managerial occupational group at the workplace was referred to at various points throughout the WERS 2004 Management Questionnaire as a means of focusing on what might be termed the 'core group' of employees at the surveyed establishment. Questions generally focused on these 'core employees' when it was desirable to obtain greater detail on the operation of a particular employment practice, but the constraints of interview length did not permit the survey to repeat the questions for each occupational group in turn. Sales and customer service staff were most commonly the core group of employees, with this being the case in 20 per cent of establishments. However, the identity of the core group varied across industries, with Process, plant and machine operatives and drivers most commonly forming the core group in Manufacturing (44 per cent of establishments), Professionals most commonly forming the core group in Education (56 per cent) and those in Elementary occupations typically forming the core group in Hotels and restaurants (82 per cent). On average, the core group accounted for 69 per cent of non-managerial employees, and 62 per cent of all employees, at an establishment. The ways in which various practices relate to 'core employees' was explored in a number of instances throughout this volume.

### Gender

The WERS 2004 Survey of Employees showed that, across all workplaces with 10 or more employees, 52 per cent of employees were female. Managers reported a similar proportion of female employees (49 per cent).[8] However, the approximate equality in the gender composition of the workforce that exists at the aggregate level often is not replicated at the level of individual jobs or establishments.

Gender segregation has both horizontal and vertical dimensions. Horizontal gender segregation is indicated by a high concentration of women within a particular work group, establishment or sector (as shown in the first column of Table 2.5), and is not necessarily associated with gender inequality, although the two often occur alongside each other (Blackburn *et al.*, 2001). Vertical gender segregation is apparent when women are concentrated in lower-level occupations, or in lower-paying work, and is indicative of gender inequality. WERS 2004 provides measures of both horizontal and vertical gender segregation although, due to space constraints, the measurement of vertical segregation here is limited to an analysis of management status.

Table 2.4 shows the breakdown of occupations by gender, based on employee reports (column 3). Women dominated the Administrative, Caring and Sales occupations, while a fairly similar proportion of men and women were employed as Professionals, in Associate professional and technical occupations, and in

*Table 2.5* Gender composition of the workplace

| | | Proportion female | | |
|---|---|---|---|---|
| | *Female share of employment* | *Mostly women (over half) at workplace* | *25% or less* | *26–74%* | *75% or more* |
| | *% of employees* | *% of workplaces* | | | |
| All workplaces | 52 | 53 | 27 | 42 | 32 |
| *Workplace size* | | | | | |
| 10–24 employees | 61 | 53 | 26 | 38 | 37 |
| 25–49 employees | 55 | 55 | 27 | 42 | 31 |
| 50–99 employees | 53 | 51 | 29 | 47 | 24 |
| 100–199 employees | 50 | 46 | 31 | 57 | 12 |
| 200–499 employees | 44 | 45 | 29 | 63 | 8 |
| 500 or more employees | 52 | 50 | 26 | 60 | 14 |
| All workplaces with 25 or more  employees | 51 | 52 | 28 | 47 | 25 |
| *Organization status* | | | | | |
| Stand-alone workplace | 51 | 45 | 32 | 40 | 28 |
| Part of a larger organization | 53 | 56 | 24 | 42 | 34 |
| *Organization size* | | | | | |
| 10–99 employees | 51 | 46 | 33 | 39 | 28 |
| 100–999 employees | 44 | 39 | 36 | 47 | 17 |
| 1,000–9,999 employees | 54 | 56 | 20 | 47 | 33 |
| 10,000 employees or more | 57 | 70 | 15 | 39 | 47 |
| *Sector of ownership* | | | | | |
| Private | 47 | 47 | 30 | 44 | 26 |
| Public | 66 | 79 | 11 | 31 | 58 |
| *Industry* | | | | | |
| Manufacturing | 26 | 12 | 57 | 40 | 3 |
| Electricity, gas and water | 36 | 7 | 77 | 21 | 2 |
| Construction | 19 | 2 | 87 | 13 | 0 |
| Wholesale and retail | 55 | 45 | 29 | 45 | 26 |
| Hotels and restaurants | 62 | 62 | 5 | 71 | 25 |
| Transport and communication | 29 | 12 | 64 | 27 | 9 |
| Financial services | 57 | 69 | 5 | 56 | 39 |
| Other business services | 49 | 50 | 29 | 53 | 18 |
| Public administration | 54 | 65 | 22 | 42 | 36 |
| Education | 75 | 94 | 0 | 26 | 74 |
| Health and social work | 81 | 94 | 1 | 19 | 79 |
| Other community services | 52 | 60 | 14 | 59 | 27 |
| *Trade union recognition* | | | | | |
| No union recognized | 51 | 46 | 30 | 43 | 27 |
| At least one recognized union | 54 | 68 | 19 | 38 | 43 |

Base (column 1): All employees in workplaces with 10 or more.
Base (columns 2 to 5): All workplaces with 10 or more employees.
Figures are weighted and based on responses from 20,884 employees (column 1) and 1,983 managers (columns 2 to 5).

Elementary occupations. Around one-third of the workforce was female in Managerial occupations. Less than one-fifth of Process, plant and machine operatives were female, while one in ten employees were women in the Skilled trades.

The first column of Table 2.5 shows that the female share of employment was generally higher in smaller workplaces, but also in the public sector. Within the private sector, a greater proportion of the workforce was female in workplaces where unions were not recognized. Women made up more than half the workforce in Health and social work, Education, Hotels and restaurants, Financial services, Wholesale and retail, Public administration and Other community services. In the Health and social work sector in particular, four out of every five employees were female.

The second column of Table 2.5, which is based on management reports, shows that more than half the workforce was female in 79 per cent of public sector workplaces, compared with only 47 per cent of those in the private sector. Women were in the majority in 94 per cent of workplaces in the Health and social work and Education sectors compared to just 2 per cent of workplaces in the Construction industry. They were also more likely to compose more than half the workforce in establishments with at least one recognized union than where no unions were recognized, and this finding held true when public sector workplaces were excluded from the analysis.

The Survey of Employees asked respondents whether the type of work they did was mainly carried out by men or women at their establishment. This provides a measure of horizontal gender segregation at the level of the work group. Across all establishments with 10 or more employees, 6 per cent of employees said that they were the only person doing that particular type of work. Ten per cent of employees did work that was carried out only by men, while 18 per cent said that the work that they did was mainly done by men. Thirty-eight per cent of employees were in jobs which were done equally by men and women. Twenty-three per cent of employees reported that their job was mainly done by women, while 5 per cent had jobs which were done only by women. There was a great deal of variation between sectors in the gender composition of jobs as reported by employees. Thirty-nine per cent of employees in the Construction industry reported that their job was done only by men. Also, one quarter of employees in the Manufacturing sector, and just under one-fifth (19 per cent) of employees in the Electricity, gas and water sector reported that their job was done only by men. By contrast, employees reported that their job was done only by women in less than one in seven workplaces (12 per cent) in any given sector. Employees were most likely to report that their job was done equally by men and women in Hotels and restaurants and the Financial services sector (both 54 per cent). The proportion of employees who said that their job was done equally by men and women went up from 30 per cent in 1998 to 38 per cent in 2004.

Turning to vertical gender segregation, the Survey of Employees indicated that 36 per cent of Managers and senior officials were female; a similar proportion to the management estimate of the gender composition of the occupation, which stood at 34 per cent. According to workplace managers, a greater proportion of

Managers and senior officials were female in public sector establishments than in the private sector (46 per cent and 30 per cent respectively). However, the extent of female under-representation in management grades is better understood by examining the gender composition of these occupations relative to the gender composition of the whole workforce within each workplace. Women were under-represented in management relative to the gender composition of the workforce in 69 per cent of workplaces where there were some managers. By contrast, men were under-represented in management in 30 per cent of workplaces. Women's under-representation in management grades was apparent across all types of workplace. There was little change in the proportion of workplaces where women were under-represented in management between 1998 and 2004 (71 per cent in 1998, and 69 per cent in 2004). Likewise, there was no significant difference in the proportion of establishments where men were under-represented in management in 1998 and 2004 (28 per cent in 1998 and 30 per cent in 2004).

## *Ethnicity*

Aside from the fact that employment levels are lower than average for some ethnic minority groups (Office for National Statistics, 2003: 599), there is also evidence to suggest that employees from ethnic minority groups experience lower pay in work (Blackaby *et al.*, 2002). As WERS contains information on the ethnic composition of the workforce, it provides a valuable source of information in understanding the interaction between employment practices and the ethnicity of employees.

Ninety-four per cent of respondents to the Survey of Employees classified themselves as belonging to a white ethnic group; 89 per cent of employees described themselves as White British, while 1 per cent said that they were Irish, and 3 per cent had another White background.[9] Three per cent of employees classified themselves as Asian or Asian British, while 1 per cent were Black or Black British. A further 1 per cent of employees were of mixed background, and 1 per cent of employees described themselves as either Chinese, or from another ethnic group.[10]

The Employee Profile Questionnaire can be used to distinguish between workplaces in terms of their employment of ethnic minority employees. The proportion of employees thought by managers to be from a non-white ethnic group in 1998 was 5 per cent, compared with 9 per cent in 2004. Although this was three percentage points higher than that suggested by the Survey of Employees (6 per cent), as Chapter 9 indicates, a relatively small proportion of workplaces monitored or reviewed recruitment and selection, promotions, or relative pay rates, by ethnicity. This suggests that management reports were likely to be estimates, rather than based on workplace records, and may explain the divergence between the figures supplied by managers and employees. However, management estimates are useful in that they indicate the types of workplaces in which employees from minority ethnic groups tend to be concentrated.

According to managers, on average only 3 per cent of employees in work-places in the Construction sector were from a non-white ethnic group, but this figure reached 13 per cent in the Hotels and restaurants sector. Table 2.6 shows that 56 per cent of workplaces did not have any ethnic minority employees. Smaller workplaces and organizations were also less likely to have some ethnic minority employees than larger establishments and organizations. Also, single independent establishments were less likely to have some non-white ethnic minority employees than workplaces which were part of a larger organization (35 per cent and 49 per cent respectively) and workplaces with a recognized union were more likely to have some ethnic minority employees than those without union recognition (49 per cent compared to 41 per cent). One-tenth or more of the workforce was from an ethnic minority in 27 per cent of workplaces in the Hotels and restaurants sector, compared to only one in twenty estab-lishments in the Construction sector.

*Disability*

The LFS shows that people with a disability are significantly less likely to be in employment than those without a disability (49 per cent, compared to 81 per cent) (Office for National Statistics, 2003: 598). There is also evidence to sug-gest that disabled employees experience disadvantage in the workplace, for example, being more likely to experience involuntary job separation (Baldwin and Schumacher, 2002). WERS 2004 can be used to identify the types of workplace in which disabled employees are concentrated, and thus provides a useful source of data to enhance understanding in this area.

Twelve per cent of employees responding to the SEQ reported that they had a long-term illness, health problem or disability. However, only 5 per cent of employees said that this affected the amount or type of work that they were able to do. By contrast, managers believed that only 1 per cent of employees had a long-term disability which affected the amount or type of work that they were able to do. The lower proportion reported by managers may be explained by the fact that the disability may not always be apparent to the employer.

Managers reported that disabled employees were present in 19 per cent of workplaces, but while 24 per cent of public sector workplaces had some dis-abled staff, this was true of only 17 per cent of workplaces in the private sector. Larger workplaces were more likely to have some disabled employees than smaller establishments: for example, only 10 per cent of workplaces with 10 to 24 employees had some disabled staff, compared to 79 per cent of workplaces with 500 or more employees. Workplaces with a recognized union were more likely to have some disabled employees than workplaces in which unions were not recognized (28 per cent compared to 15 per cent). This is probably explained in part by the fact that unions were more likely to be recognized in larger workplaces (see Chapter 5) which were in turn more likely to have some disabled employees, although unions may also encourage the employer to recruit and retain disabled staff. Table 2.6 shows that just 11 per cent of Hotels

Table 2.6 Ethnicity, disability and age composition of workplaces

| | All work places | Manufacturing | Electricity, gas and water | Construction | Wholesale and retail | Hotels and restaurants | Transport and communications | Financial services | Other business services | Public administration | Education | Health and social work | Other community services |
|---|---|---|---|---|---|---|---|---|---|---|---|---|---|
| Ethnic minority employees | | | | | | | | | | | | | |
| None | 56 | 65 | 60 | 70 | 61 | 57 | 47 | 41 | 41 | 47 | 60 | 47 | 77 |
| 10% or more | 18 | 12 | 7 | 5 | 16 | 27 | 23 | 26 | 25 | 16 | 16 | 23 | 7 |
| Disabled employees | | | | | | | | | | | | | |
| None | 81 | 80 | 70 | 77 | 86 | 89 | 81 | 82 | 79 | 66 | 82 | 78 | 81 |
| 5% or more | 7 | 7 | 10 | 7 | 5 | 6 | 3 | 7 | 6 | 8 | 5 | 13 | 6 |
| Employees aged 16 to 21 | | | | | | | | | | | | | |
| None | 37 | 37 | 18 | 26 | 20 | 16 | 44 | 22 | 47 | 54 | 71 | 53 | 29 |
| 25% or more | 15 | 3 | 2 | 9 | 35 | 47 | 10 | 0 | 5 | 0 | 2 | 5 | 22 |
| Employees aged 16 to 17 | | | | | | | | | | | | | |
| None | 76 | 83 | 74 | 72 | 54 | 51 | 90 | 90 | 91 | 91 | 96 | 87 | 68 |
| 5% or more | 17 | 8 | 0 | 22 | 37 | 44 | 0 | 4 | 3 | 1 | 1 | 6 | 28 |
| Employees aged 50 or more | | | | | | | | | | | | | |
| None | 14 | 6 | 0 | 9 | 22 | 40 | 12 | 16 | 14 | 2 | 5 | 4 | 20 |
| 25% or more | 32 | 41 | 35 | 34 | 24 | 13 | 36 | 12 | 23 | 42 | 45 | 58 | 26 |

Base: All workplaces with 10 or more employees.
Figures are based on responses from a minimum of 1,899 managers.

and restaurants had disabled employees, compared to around one-third of work-places in Public administration (34 per cent). Overall, 5 per cent or more of the workforce were disabled in 7 per cent of workplaces (13 per cent in the Health and social work sector, but only 3 per cent in Transport and communications).

## Age

WERS 2004 also provides data on the age composition of the workforce within establishments. This is of interest given evidence that employees at the extremes of the working age range may experience discrimination in terms of access to employment, and terms and conditions. Finding employment can be difficult for older workers and problems may be encountered once in work, in gaining access to training and promotion (Department for Work and Pensions, 2001a: 111; Taylor and Urwin, 2001). Also, Saks and Waldman (1998) found that older workers received lower performance appraisals than their younger collea-gues. At the other end of the age spectrum, younger workers have reported difficulties in recruitment and attaining training and promotions due to their age, as well as being paid less than other staff employed in similar work, and not eligible for occupational pensions (Department for Work and Pensions 2001b). In addition, as shown in Chapter 5, young employees are less likely to be union members, thus compounding the likelihood that they are relatively disadvantaged in employment compared to older employees, given that union membership provides some protection from arbitrary employer behaviour and is associated with reduced wage inequality (see Chapter 7). The age composition of the workforce is also of interest given the forthcoming legislation on age discrimination, which is due to be in force by the end of 2006. The 2004 Survey thus establishes a baseline against which to assess the impact of the forthcoming regulations.

Seven per cent of employees across all establishments with 10 or more employees were aged between 16 and 21 according to the Survey of Employ-ees.[11] This is similar to the account provided by managers, who indicated that 9 per cent of employees were aged between 16 and 21. More than twice the proportion of employees in private sector workplaces were in this age range compared to public sector workplaces (11 per cent compared to 4 per cent). Likewise, less than half the proportion of employees were aged between 16 and 21 in workplaces where a union was recognized compared to workplaces with-out union recognition (6 per cent and 13 per cent respectively) and a greater proportion of the workforce was in this age range in establishments which did not recognize unions, even when public sector workplaces were excluded. Also, almost one-third (32 per cent) of the workforce in the Hotels and restaurants sector were aged between 16 and 21. One quarter or more of the workforce was aged between 16 and 21 in 15 per cent of workplaces. Private sector establish-ments were more likely than public sector workplaces to have at least a quarter of their employees in the 16 to 21 age range (18 per cent compared to 2 per cent), as were workplaces which were part of a larger organization, rather than single independent establishments (17 per cent compared to 11 per cent), and establishments which did not recognize a union, compared to those that did (20 per cent compared to 6 per cent). The proportion of workplaces in which at least a quarter of the workforce were aged between 16 and 21 was particularly high in Hotels and restaurants (47 per cent) and Wholesale and retail (35 per cent).

From 1 October 2004, employers were obliged to pay employees aged 16 and 17 the National Minimum Wage. WERS 2004 indicates the types of workplaces most likely to have been affected by the legislation. Overall, 1 per cent of the workforce were aged 16 or 17 according to the Survey of Employees, and 2 per cent were in this age range according to the Employee Profile Questionnaire.[12] Although the 16 to 17 age group comprised a small proportion of the workforce across establishments, in 17 per cent of workplaces this age group made up at least 5 per cent of the workforce. Again, these younger workers were concentrated in the private, rather than the public, sector. In 20 per cent of private sector workplaces, at least 5 per cent of the workforce was aged 16 or 17, compared to just 2 per cent of public sector establishments. Workplaces in the Hotels and restaurants and Wholesale and retail sectors were also particularly likely to draw at least 5 per cent of their workforce from the 16 to 17 age group (44 and 37 per cent respectively), followed by Other community services (28 per cent) and Construction (22 per cent). Establishments without recognized unions were more likely to have at least 5 per cent of their workforce in the age range 16 to 17 than workplaces that did recognise unions (21 per cent and 8 per cent respectively).

Employees aged 50 or over formed 27 per cent of the workforce according to the Survey of Employees.[13] This differed somewhat from management estimates, which suggested that 20 per cent of employees were in this age range. Despite this, management estimates are used here because they provide an indication of the types of workplace in which older employees were concentrated. Only 14 per cent of workplaces had no employees aged 50 or more. Smaller workplaces, and those in the private, rather than the public, sector were those least likely to employ anyone aged 50 or over. Table 2.6 shows that two-fifths of workplaces in the Hotels and restaurants sector had no employees aged 50 or more.

Employees aged 50 or over made up at least one quarter of the workforce in 32 per cent of establishments, and 36 per cent of all employees were aged 50 or more in this subset of workplaces. In contrast to younger workers, high concentrations of older workers were found in single independent establishments and the public sector. At least one quarter of the workforce was aged 50 or more in 40 per cent of single independent establishments, compared to 29 per cent of workplaces that were part of a larger organization. Nearly one half (48 per cent) of public sector establishments drew at least one quarter of their workforce from employees aged 50 or more, compared to less than one-third (29 per cent) of private sector workplaces. Comparing across industry sectors, workplaces in the Health and social work sector were most likely to have a high concentration of older workers (58 per cent), whereas the opposite was true in Hotels and restaurants (13 per cent) and Financial services (12 per cent).

## Caring responsibilities

Employees who take primary responsibility for caring for other adults or dependent children can be disadvantaged in workplaces where arrangements are inflexible and pose barriers to them meeting their obligations outside work (Lane, 1998: 189), or where employees are required to work long hours in order to demonstrate commitment (Lewis, 1997: 16). The Survey of Employees provides information on the personal circumstances of employees, including their caring commitments. Thirty-eight per cent of employees had dependent children, that is, children under the age of 18 whom they considered dependent.[14] Five per cent of employees reported that they had children both of school age and younger, while 7 per cent had pre-school children only, and 26 per cent had only school-age children.

Around three-fifths of employees aged between 30 and 39, and 40 and 49, had dependent children (59 per cent and 62 per cent respectively), while employees aged between 20 and 29, and 30 and 39, were most likely to have pre-school children (14 per cent and 29 per cent). Female employees were less likely than men to have pre-school age children (6 per cent compared to 8 per cent) or pre-school and school-aged children (4 per cent compared to 7 per cent). This reflects the fact that women are more likely to take responsibility for childcare than men, and therefore are less likely to work before children reach school age (Office for National Statistics, 2004). Forty-three per cent of employees in public sector workplaces had dependent children, compared to 37 per cent of employees in private sector establishments. Also, the proportion of employees with dependent children was greater in workplaces which recognized at least one union than in workplaces where no unions were recognized (42 per cent compared to 35 per cent).

Employees were most likely to have dependent children where they were Managers or senior officials (44 per cent) or worked in Associate professional and technical occupations (41 per cent), Skilled trades (42 per cent), Caring, leisure and other personal service occupations (43 per cent), or where they were Process, plant or machine operatives (42 per cent). They were least likely to have dependent children when they worked in Administrative and secretarial (33 per cent) and Sales and customer service roles (32 per cent). Forty-nine per cent of men working in Managerial occupations had dependent children, compared to only 35 per cent of women in these jobs, perhaps because of the difficulties of attaining managerial status while taking responsibility for childcare. It was also the case that, among Professionals and Process, plant and machine operatives, a significantly greater proportion of men than women had dependent children. However, the opposite was the case in the Caring and Sales occupations; that is, the proportion of women with dependent children working in these occupations was greater than the proportion of men with dependent children.

Sixteen per cent of employees looked after or gave help or support to family members or friends with a long-term physical or mental illness or disability, or with problems related to old age. Most commonly (7 per cent of all employees) this was for less than five hours a week, with a further 4 per cent of employees spending between five and nine hours on such caring responsibilities. Two per cent spent between 10 and 19 hours a week on such caring activities, while 1 per cent spent between 20 and 34 hours of their time on this. A further 2 per cent of employees reported that they spent 35 or more hours a week on caring responsibilities other than caring for dependent children.

More than half of all employees (52 per cent) did not have dependent children or any other caring responsibilities, while about one-third (32 per cent) had dependent children only. Ten per cent of employees had some caring responsibilities but did not have dependent children, while 6 per cent of employees had other caring responsibilities in addition to having dependent children. The provisions available to assist employees to balance their work and caring responsibilities are considered in Chapter 9.

## Conclusion

This chapter has covered a wide variety of workplace and employee characteristics in an attempt to provide a profile of the population of workplaces and employees covered by WERS 2004. Without much direct reference to their associations with employment relations practices, or with employees' experiences of work, the discussion of these characteristics can appear somewhat anodyne. While a number of interesting relationships have been highlighted, the full value of these characteristics in understanding the practice of employment relations emerges over the course of the chapters that follow. However, some interesting stylized facts have emerged from the analysis presented thus far.

First, small workplaces may be plentiful but sizeable proportions of employees work in large workplaces, which are scarce in comparison. The majority of workplaces (58 per cent) are small, privately-owned establishments with less than 50 employees, concerned with the provision of services rather than the manufacture of goods. Nevertheless, such workplaces employ only one quarter (23 per cent) of all employees. A similar proportion of employees (20 per cent) work in larger, public-sector establishments, although these comprise only 5 per cent of all workplaces. This distinction between workplace-centred and employee-centred findings is a recurrent feature of the analysis in subsequent chapters.

Second, the organizational structures in which workplaces are located exhibit a great deal of diversity. Foreign investment clearly plays an important role in the ownership structure of British workplaces, particularly in industries such as Wholesale and retail. And this role has increased since 1998, as has the importance of family-ownership.

Third, the workforce as a whole is highly diverse in respect of basic characteristics such as gender and ethnicity, and many workplaces exhibit at least some of this diversity. So, although only 6 per cent of all employees are from an ethnic minority, almost half of all workplaces (44 per cent) employ at least one ethnic minority employee. Similarly, one in five workplaces (19 per cent) employ someone with a long-term disability that affects the type or amount of work they can do, although this characteristic is shared by only 5 per cent of all employees. However, the proportion of workplaces that are truly diverse appears to be rather smaller. For example, it is striking that, in over half (58 per cent) of all workplaces, three-quarters of the workforce are of the same gender.

Finally, there is a considerable degree of turnover in the population of workplaces, which can have just as much bearing on the practice of employment relations as changes in management practice within continuing workplaces. Around one quarter of all workplaces with ten or more employees in 1998 left the population of workplaces over the following six years, to be replaced by new workplaces and those that grew into scope. As the overall changes in employment relations are investigated at aggregate level between 1998 and 2004 ('net' change), it is important to look at the impact of turnover in the population of workplaces, as well as changes in behaviour among continuing workplaces.

This chapter has provided a short introduction to some of the key characteristics of the populations of workplaces and employees. Just how important each of these characteristics is in helping us to understand the practice of employment relations is illustrated throughout the remainder of the book.

# 3 The management of employment relations

## Introduction

During the 1950s and the 1960s there was a clear separation between industrial relations and administrative management, especially in large organizations and public administration. The two decades spanning the 1960s and the 1970s were characterized by the increasing ascendancy and dominance of the industrial relations function. During this period, a debate originated about the state of British management and the implications for competitiveness of poor management practice. It was considered that British management needed to be professionalized. The professionalization encompassed all management areas, including industrial relations (collective relations and the management of conflict) as well as other aspects of the employment relationship (personnel and administration). This issue was addressed by the Wilson Government, most notably through the establishment of the elite management business schools and a network of regional management centres, and coincided with an expansion of the activities of the Institute of Personnel Management (IPM), later to become the Chartered Institute of Personnel and Development (CIPD).

In the 1980s, there was a move towards an increasingly integrated personnel function around industrial relations (later termed employee relations), manpower planning (later termed employee resourcing), and training (later termed employee development). This decade also saw the emergence of the concept of human resource management (HRM), originating in the USA, in British business schools. The growth of business education provided a platform for the dissemination of HRM ideas and the promotion of a strategic view of management (Bach and Sisson, 2000: 13). The significance of HRM can be linked to the broader political and economic context of the period, a context of declining incidence of trade unionism and intensified competition, and the continuing concerns with the state of British management.

In practice, HRM had relatively little impact on the personnel function in the 1980s or the 1990s. According to Sisson (2001: 93), the impact had been partial at best with limited changes in employment practices, and some recognition of the importance of the management of people, the integration with business strategy and the professionalization of the function. Few organizations were pursuing the high-commitment model. In addition, HRM practices were more likely to be found in unionized than in non-unionized workplaces (Cully *et al.*, 1999: 110). The shift then from an operating to a strategic role, from control to commitment, and from collectivism to individualism, advocated by proponents of HRM, did not occur to any great extent.

WERS constitutes one of the few sources of nationally representative data able to shed light on these aspects of the management of employment relations.[1] By the late 1990s, it was possible to map and reflect on some changes, notably: the growth in managers with employment relations-specific job titles, including 'human resource managers'; the 'feminization' of the profession and its movement towards a more formal, qualifications-based footing; the changing roles and responsibilities of employment relations managers; and the contours of the employment relations function at workplace level and above, including the time and staff devoted to managing employment relations (Millward *et al.*, 2000). This chapter returns to these issues to examine how trends have developed since 1998 and considers whether employment relations management has become more strategic. The chapter makes use of several indicators to measure the degree of integration of personnel management into wider business goals, and explores the workplace characteristics associated with a strategic approach to the management of employees.

Much of the analysis in the chapter is based on information provided by managers interviewed on site, thus excluding information on a small minority of workplaces where the management interview took place elsewhere in the organization, generally at a higher level in the organization.[2] The reason for this exclusion is that data relating to individual respondents, such as gender, job tenure and job title, cannot be related to workplace characteristics where the respondent is based elsewhere in the organization. Where these considerations are not relevant, analyses are based on all respondents.

## Who manages employment relations?

Most managers (90 per cent) who took part in the survey said that they were the person 'primarily responsible' for employee relations matters at the workplace. While they might have been the most senior person responsible for these matters at the establishment, employment relations seldom constituted their major job responsibility: only 19 per cent of all managers said that this was their major job responsibility. A much higher proportion (38 per cent) said that they were equally responsible for human resource management and other responsibilities, with the remainder saying that they were more concerned with other matters.

This was reflected in their job titles, as half of respondents described themselves as general managers (Table 3.1, column 6). An additional 22 per cent of respondents were the owners, proprietors or managing directors of the workplace, 6 per cent were finance managers, and the remaining 21 per cent of respondents had job titles that inferred specific responsibility for employment relations

*Table 3.1* Respondent's job title and time spent on employment relations by gender,[a] 1998 and 2004

| | Job title | | | | | | More than 50% of time spent on employment relations | | | | | |
| | 1998 (%) | | | 2004 (%) | | | 1998 (%) | | | 2004 (%) | | |
| | M | F | All | M | F | All | M | F | All | M | F | All |
|---|---|---|---|---|---|---|---|---|---|---|---|---|
| HR manager | 48 | 52 | 3 | 26 | 74 | 12 | 34 | 36 | 70 | 14 | 42 | 57 |
| Personnel manager | 30 | 70 | 8 | 37 | 63 | 9 | 19 | 40 | 59 | 8 | 28 | 36 |
| Employee/ Industrial/ Staff relations manager | (93) | (7) | 0 | (46) | (54) | 0 | (89) | * | (93) | * | * | (100) |
| All | 37 | 63 | 12 | 31 | 69 | 21 | 25 | 38 | 63 | 12 | 36 | 48 |
| Proprietor/ Owner | 86 | 14 | 22 | 78 | 22 | 22 | 1 | (3) | 5 | 1 | (4) | 5 |
| General manager | 71 | 29 | 57 | 58 | 42 | 51 | 6 | 2 | 8 | 5 | 4 | 11 |
| Financial manager/ Company secretary | 65 | 35 | 10 | 66 | 34 | 6 | 0 | (0) | 0 | (0) | (3) | 3 |
| All | 74 | 26 | 88 | 64 | 36 | 79 | 4 | 2 | 6 | 4 | 4 | 8 |

Base: All workplaces with 10 or more employees where the interview is conducted on site.
Figures are weighted and based on responses from 1,945 (columns 1–3), 1,745 (columns 4–6), 1,138 (column 7), 790 (column 8), 1,928 (column 9), 851 (column 10), 889 (column 11) and 1,740 managers (column 12).
Note:
[a] 'M' denotes male managers and 'F' denotes female managers.

matters. However, the proportion of managers with employment relations-specific job titles has doubled since 1998, when only 11 per cent of managers had an employment relations-specific job title. This finding points towards a higher degree of functional specialization in the personnel area and a continuation of the trend emerging in the 1990s of a declining involvement of general managers and a rise of managers with employment relations-specific job titles (Millward *et al.,* 2000: 53).[3]

This increase in managers with employment relations-specific job titles included an increase in the proportion of workplaces with human resource managers (Table 3.1). In 1998, human resource managers were less common than personnel managers. By 2004, however, human resource managers were a little more numerous than personnel managers (12 per cent and 9 per cent, respectively). As in 1998, employee relations and industrial relations managers remained rare. Whether the increase in the proportion of human resource managers signals an expansion of the principles of human resource management

(HRM) or simply a change in nomenclature remains to be seen and is beyond the scope of this book. However, an initial exploration of the profile of HR managers in comparison to other managers with employment relations-specific job titles is provided later in this chapter, in an attempt to address whether HR managers bring something qualitatively different to the management of employees or whether their profile is essentially the same as that of other managers.

Managers spent, on average, 31 per cent of their time on employment relations matters, with 17 per cent of respondents spending more than half of their time on these issues. One-third of managers dedicated less than a tenth of their time to these matters. Greater functional specialization was accompanied by greater management time on employment relations matters. HR managers spent the most time on employment relations, followed by personnel managers. The majority of HR managers spent more than half of their time on this (Table 3.1, column 12). Financial managers spent the least time, with 71 per cent dedicating a tenth or less of their time to these issues. They were followed by proprietors (56 per cent) and general managers (27 per cent).

Although the proportion of managers spending a significant amount of time on employment relations matters increased since 1998, with 17 per cent of managers spending more than half of their time on these issues in 2004 compared with 13 per cent in 1998, this increase was confined to managers with no employment relations-specific job titles (Table 3.1). Both HR managers and personnel managers spent less time on employment relations issues in 2004 than in 1998, continuing the trend since 1984 identified by Millward *et al.* (2000: 58). It seems that in the majority of workplaces that choose not to employ HR or personnel managers, general managers are taking on an increasing employment relations-related workload. In the growing numbers of workplaces that opt for personnel or HR managers, these managers may increasingly be relying on assistants, or may be delegating tasks to line managers, issues which are explored later in the chapter.

## Specialists versus generalists

The responses on the title of the job and the time spent on employment relations were combined in order to identify respondents who could be described as employment relations 'specialists'. Specialists were defined as those whose formal job title was personnel manager, human resource manager, employee relations manager, or industrial relations manager, *or* who spent more than half of their time on employment relations issues. According to this definition, the main management respondent was a specialist in 28 per cent of workplaces, a substantial increase from the 17 per cent of specialists found in 1998. Those whose job title was general manager, financial manager, or proprietor *and* who spent less than half of their time on employment relations issues, were labelled employment relations 'generalists' (found in 72 per cent of workplaces in 2004 and in 83 per cent of workplaces in 1998).

The rise in specialists occurred in workplaces with certain characteristics. The likelihood of having a specialist on site increased in the following workplaces: small establishments with 10 to 49 employees (from 10 per cent in 1998 to 21 per cent in 2004), and workplaces with 100 to 199 employees (from 48 to 66 per cent); multiple establishments (from 21 to 34 per cent); workplaces that belonged to larger organizations of 100 or more employees (from 24 to 38 per cent); both private sector sites (from 17 to 27 per cent) and public sector sites (from 18 to 30 per cent); sites in Construction (from 12 to 31 per cent), Public administration workplaces (from 33 to 56 per cent) and sites in the Health sector (from 19 to 33 per cent); UK-owned sites (from 15 to 25 per cent) and predominantly UK-owned sites (from 17 to 47 per cent); and sites with recognized unions (from 23 to 37 per cent) as well as with no recognized unions (from 15 to 24 per cent).

The discussion so far has focused on the personnel function at workplace level, but in those workplaces that were part of a larger organization, this function was often based elsewhere. The survey allowed for the identification of workplaces with staff dedicated specifically to personnel matters – also defined as specialists – at a higher level in their organization. Putting together these data and those related to the respondent, we found that overall nearly three-fifths of workplaces (58 per cent) had access to employment relations specialists either at the workplace or at a higher level, an increase since 1998, when 53 per cent had access to employment relations specialists.[4] Larger workplaces, establishments belonging to organizations with 1,000 or more employees, and those in the public sector were the most likely to have access to employment relations specialists in their organizations (Table 3.2, column 1). Variations across industries were also substantial. Workplaces in Financial services and Public administration were the most likely to have access to a specialist, either at the workplace or at a higher level. Establishments with recognized unions were also more likely to have access to employment relations specialists in their organizations than workplaces with no union recognition.

The analysis now shifts to workplaces that are part of a larger organization, and reports the incidence of specialists both at the workplace and at a higher level in order to assess the extent to which the personnel function has been decentralized. Overall, 27 per cent of branch establishments had both a specialist at the workplace and a manager at a higher level who spent the major part of his/her time on employment relations matters (Table 3.2).[5] Six per cent of branch sites only had a specialist at the workplace, while half only had an employment relations specialist at a higher level. Close to one-fifth (17 per cent) had no employment relations specialists either at the workplace or at a higher level.

As shown in Table 3.2, the likelihood of having an employment relations specialist at both the workplace and a higher level increased with workplace size. Small workplaces, in contrast, as well as those that belonged to large organizations, were more likely to have an employment relations specialist at a higher level only than larger workplaces and those belonging to smaller organizations.

*Table 3.2* Structure of the personnel function

| | All workplaces | Branch sites | | | |
|---|---|---|---|---|---|
| | Specialist at the workplace or higher (%) | Specialist at workplace and higher (%) | Specialist at the workplace only (%) | Specialist at higher level only (%) | No specialist (%) |
| All workplaces | 58 | 27 | 6 | 50 | 17 |
| *Workplace size* | | | | | |
| 10–24 employees | 47 | 22 | 4 | 53 | 22 |
| 25–49 employees | 64 | 21 | 5 | 56 | 17 |
| 50–99 employees | 76 | 33 | 6 | 51 | 11 |
| 100–199 employees | 86 | 44 | 20 | 31 | 5 |
| 200–499 employees | 91 | 61 | 19 | 16 | 3 |
| 500 or more employees | 99 | 64 | 20 | 17 | 0 |
| All workplaces with 25 or more employees | 73 | 31 | 9 | 48 | 13 |
| *Organization status* | | | | | |
| Stand-alone workplace | 18 | – | – | – | – |
| Part of a larger organization | 77 | 27 | 6 | 50 | 17 |
| *Organization size:* | | | | | |
| 10–99 employees | 17 | * | * | * | * |
| 100–999 employees | 74 | 13 | 14 | 43 | 30 |
| 1,000–9,999 employees | 91 | 31 | 7 | 54 | 9 |
| 10,000 employees or more | 91 | 32 | 3 | 57 | 8 |
| *Sector of ownership* | | | | | |
| Private | 53 | 28 | 7 | 47 | 18 |
| Public | 82 | 24 | 3 | 57 | 16 |
| *Industry* | | | | | |
| Manufacturing | 35 | 25 | 15 | 24 | 36 |
| Electricity, gas and water | (100) | (39) | (7) | (55) | (0) |
| Construction | (44) | (31) | (5) | (21) | (43) |
| Wholesale and retail | 67 | 30 | 3 | 51 | 16 |
| Hotels and restaurants | (50) | (24) | (9) | (52) | (15) |
| Transport and communication | 62 | 34 | 5 | 51 | 10 |
| Financial inter-mediation | 89 | 36 | 7 | 53 | 4 |
| Other business services | 45 | 22 | 17 | 37 | 24 |
| Public administration | 87 | 47 | 3 | 39 | 11 |

*(continued on next page)*

*Table 3.2 (continued)*

|  | All workplaces | Branch sites | | | |
|---|---|---|---|---|---|
|  | Specialist at the workplace or higher (%) | Specialist at workplace and higher (%) | Specialist at the workplace only (%) | Specialist at higher level only (%) | No specialist (%) |
| Education | 71 | 8 | 3 | 68 | 22 |
| Health | 59 | 33 | 8 | 47 | 12 |
| Other community services | (62) | (11) | (6) | (71) | (12) |
| *Trade union recognition* |  |  |  |  |  |
| No union recognized | 46 | 24 | 8 | 43 | 24 |
| At least one union recognized | 85 | 29 | 5 | 56 | 10 |

Base (column 1): All workplaces with 10 or more employees.
Base (columns 2–5): All branch sites with 10 or more employees that are not head offices.
Figures are weighted and based on responses from 1,950 (column 1) and 981 managers (columns 2–5).
Notes:
  Workplace specialists were defined as those respondents whose formal job title was personnel manager, human resource manager, employee relations manager, or industrial relations manager, *or* who spent more than half of their time on employment relations issues. Respondents were asked if there were staff dedicated specifically to personnel matters at a higher level in their organization; these were also defined as specialists.

Organization size was also strongly related to the absence of a specialist at both the workplace and a higher level. Around one-third (30 per cent) of branch sites belonging to smaller organizations of between 100 and 1,000 employees did not have a specialist at all, compared to less than one-tenth (8 per cent) of branch sites belonging to the largest organizations of more than 10,000 employees.

The proportion of branch sites with employment relations specialists at both the workplace and a higher level increased since 1998, when only 15 per cent of workplaces had specialists at both levels.[6] The proportion of workplaces with only a specialist at a higher level, in contrast, decreased by 8 percentage points over the same period. This suggests an increased decentralization of the personnel function and more devolved forms of management structures, which poses the question of whether this has been accompanied by greater delegation of real decision-making power. This issue is investigated later in the chapter.

## The professional profile of employment relations specialists

The Cross-Section Survey of Managers allowed comparisons to be made between on-site specialists and generalists in terms of their experience, job tenure and

*Table 3.3* Professional profile of specialists and generalists, 1998 and 2004

| | 1998 (%) | | | 2004 (%) | | |
|---|---|---|---|---|---|---|
| | *Specialists* | *Generalists* | *All* | *Specialists* | *Generalists* | *All* |
| Holds qualifications in personnel: | 53 | 15 | 26 | 58 | 22 | 35 |
| *Years in job* | | | | | | |
| 11 or more years | 10 | 20 | 17 | 10 | 21 | 17 |
| Between 5 and 10 years | 21 | 25 | 23 | 22 | 25 | 24 |
| Between 2 and 4 years | 35 | 28 | 30 | 37 | 29 | 32 |
| Between 6 months and 1 year | 21 | 17 | 18 | 18 | 13 | 15 |
| 5 months or less | 13 | 10 | 11 | 13 | 11 | 12 |
| *Years in personnel* | | | | | | |
| 10 or more years | 59 | 68 | 65 | 54 | 59 | 57 |
| Between 5 and 10 years | 25 | 24 | 25 | 30 | 25 | 27 |
| Between 2 and 4 years | 12 | 6 | 7 | 12 | 11 | 12 |
| Between 6 months and 1 year | 3 | 1 | 1 | 3 | 3 | 3 |
| 5 months or less | 1 | 1 | 1 | 1 | 2 | 2 |

Base: All workplaces with 10 or more employees where the interview is conducted on site, and where managers' major job responsibility is employment relations or where they are equally responsible for employment relations and other responsibilities.
Figures are weighted and based on responses from 824 (column 1), 479 (column 2), 1,318 (column 3), 855 (column 4), 361 (column 5) and 1,231 managers (column 6).
Note:
  Specialists were defined as those whose formal job title was personnel manager, human resource manager, employee relations manager or industrial relations manager, or who spent more than half of their time on employment relations issues.

qualifications (Table 3.3).[7] Almost three-fifths (58 per cent) of employment relations specialists had formal qualifications in personnel management, a much higher proportion than of generalists (22 per cent).[8] On average, employment relations managers were more likely to be professionally qualified in 2004 than in 1998. However, the proportion of qualified *specialists* was not significantly different in 2004 and 1998.

  Employment relations specialists stayed in their jobs for a shorter period than generalists (one-tenth of specialists had been doing their jobs for more than 10 years, compared to 21 per cent of generalists), but they were not, however, less experienced than generalists (Table 3.3). Specialists had on average 13 years of experience in personnel management, gained either at the sampled establishment or elsewhere, with the majority of them having 10 or more years of experience in personnel, a similar proportion to the generalists. Experience levels of specialists were found to be similar in 1998 and 2004.

  The decline in managers' job tenure observed over the course of the WERS series seems to have been arrested. Managers in 2004 did not move jobs more than they had in 1998. Overall, 17 per cent of all managers had been doing their jobs for more than 10 years in both 1998 and 2004 (Table 3.3), and average job tenure was the same (six years). Job tenure of specialists also remained at the same level: one-tenth had been doing their jobs for more than 10 years in both 1998 and 2004, and average tenure was the same (four years).

Small workplaces, establishments where unions were not recognized, and stand-alone sites were not only less likely to have employment relations specialists (Table 3.2), but when they had specialists, they were less likely to be qualified. The incidence of qualified specialists ranged from 46 per cent in the smallest sites with less than 25 employees to 85 per cent in sites with 500 or more employees. Fifty-five per cent of specialists in non-recognized workplaces and 46 per cent in stand-alone sites had personnel qualifications, compared to 61 per cent in recognized workplaces and 60 per cent in branch sites. Managers in non-recognized workplaces were also less experienced than in recognized workplaces (48 per cent had 10 or more years of experience, compared to 64 per cent in recognized workplaces). However, in single independent establishments, even though managers were less qualified, they tended to have more experience than in establishments belonging to a larger organization (69 per cent had 10 or more years, compared to 50 per cent).

Some have found that public sector personnel managers are less qualified than those in the private sector, and tend to develop their careers within the public sector (Lupton and Shaw, 2001: 34–36). However, the data showed that workplaces in the public sector employed more 'professional' employment relations specialists both in terms of personnel experience and qualifications than private sector workplaces. Three-quarters (74 per cent) of specialists in the public sector had 10 or more years of experience and two-thirds had qualifications in personnel, compared to only 49 and 46 per cent in the private sector respectively. There was little difference in job tenure among specialists in the private and public sectors. Public sector specialists seemed to change jobs as often as private sector specialists, but no data were available about their previous jobs so it is not possible to assess whether they had moved between sectors.

## The feminization of the employment relations function

Women are increasingly taking responsibility for the management of employment relations, a trend already identified by Millward *et al.* (2000: 59–60). Two-fifths (43 per cent) of managers responsible for employment relations matters were women, a substantial increase since 1998, when less than a third (30 per cent) of managers were women. The proportion of women among those managers whose job title inferred specialism in employment relations matters was higher than among other managers, as shown in Table 3.1. Around three-quarters of HR managers and almost two-thirds of personnel managers were women. But whereas the proportion of women among HR managers increased since 1998, the opposite was true among personnel managers; the 'feminization' was, in this respect, confined to managers with 'human resource' in their job title.

The proportion of women among specialists (defined not just on the basis of job title but also on time spent on employment relations issues) was similarly higher (64 per cent) than among generalists (34 per cent) and, again, experienced an increase since 1998, when only 54 per cent of specialists were women. It would appear that women have been breaking the 'glass ceiling' preventing them from attaining managerial positions, at least with respect to employment relations. However, the terminology used to describe personnel management – the so-called 'Cinderella function' – has low status connotations. In addition, women are disproportionately represented in the more junior jobs and categories of CIPD membership (Gooch and Ledwith, 1996: 112). The WERS survey does not have data on the representation of women among board-level employment relations managers or on the gender of managers' assistants, so it cannot be used to test whether this is the case.

The analysis now turns to the types of workplaces where the rise in female specialists has occurred. Women's presence increased in small establishments of between 10 and 24 employees (where 36 per cent of female specialists worked in 2004, compared to 20 per cent in 1998) and in the Construction sector (where 6 per cent of female specialists worked in 2004, compared to 1 per cent in 1998). Their presence decreased, however, in sites belonging to organizations of between 100 and 1,000 employees, where 22 per cent of female specialists worked in 2004, down from 31 per cent in 1998. Similar proportions of female specialists were found in 1998 and 2004 in single and multiple sites, private and public sector establishments, and in sites with and without recognized unions.

So did female specialists differ in any way from their male counterparts? As in 1998, female specialists continued to be less experienced in the personnel function than their male counterparts. Half of them had 10 or more years of personnel experience, compared to 61 per cent of male specialists.[9] Similar proportions of men and women were relatively recent entrants into the profession, i.e. had spent less than five years in the profession. Women were more likely than men to have spent between five and 10 years in personnel, suggesting that the feminization of the profession started some years ago.

Female specialists were more likely to hold personnel qualifications than men: 70 per cent of female specialists were qualified compared to 36 per cent of male specialists.[10] In 1998, in contrast, female and male specialists were equally qualified (51 and 57 per cent, respectively – statistically, not a significant difference). Overall, female specialists were more likely to be qualified in 2004 than in 1998, while male specialists were less likely to be qualified in 2004 than in 1998.

Figure 3.1 shows that the likelihood of a woman specialist being qualified did not differ with the length of personnel experience. Men, in contrast, were more likely to be qualified if they had 10 or more years of experience than if they were relatively new to the profession. The most striking difference

*Figure 3.1* Qualifications and personnel experience of specialists by gender

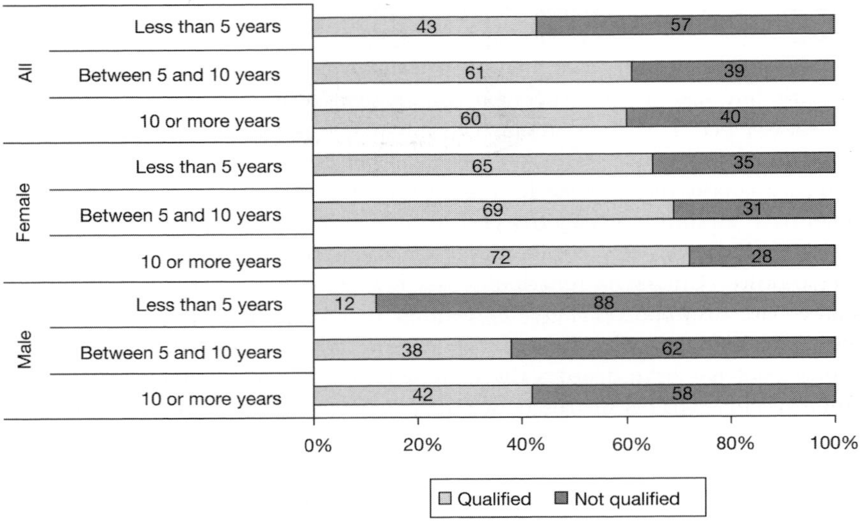

| | | Qualified | Not qualified |
|---|---|---|---|
| **All** | Less than 5 years | 43 | 57 |
| | Between 5 and 10 years | 61 | 39 |
| | 10 or more years | 60 | 40 |
| **Female** | Less than 5 years | 65 | 35 |
| | Between 5 and 10 years | 69 | 31 |
| | 10 or more years | 72 | 28 |
| **Male** | Less than 5 years | 12 | 88 |
| | Between 5 and 10 years | 38 | 62 |
| | 10 or more years | 42 | 58 |

0%    20%    40%    60%    80%    100%

□ Qualified    ■ Not qualified

Base: All workplaces with 10 or more employees where the interview is conducted on site, and where managers' major job responsibility is employment relations or where they are equally responsible for employment relations and other responsibilities.

Figures are weighted and based on responses from 326 male managers and 529 female managers.

Note:

Specialists were defined as those whose formal job title was personnel manager, human resource manager, employee relations manager or industrial relations manager, or who spent more than half of their time on employment relations issues.

between male and female specialists was found among new entrants. A substantially higher proportion of female specialists were entering the profession with personnel qualifications than male specialists: 65 per cent of female specialists entering the profession in the last four years were qualified, compared to only 12 per cent of male specialists.[11] This is clear evidence that a new cohort of women are 'professionalizing' employment relations.

## The changing role of managers responsible for employment relations matters

### Changing responsibilities?

Some commentators have highlighted the substantial changes that HRM has brought about (Storey, 1992); others are more sceptical and conclude that managers did not change their ways in the 1980s but rather continued doing essentially the same tasks, although perhaps in a more sophisticated manner (Armstrong, 2000: 587). An indication of whether the personnel function has changed is provided by the survey data on the job responsibilities that managers had in 1998 and 2004.

Managers who were primarily responsible for employment relations matters were asked about the tasks that formed part of their jobs (or the jobs of their subordinates).[12] They were shown a list of 13 job duties related to the management of employees. Dealing with disciplinary matters or disciplinary procedures, grievances or grievance procedures and recruitment or selection of employees were the most common job responsibilities. Practically all managers said these formed part of their jobs or of someone responsible to them (Table 3.4, column 1). On the other hand, they were less likely to be responsible for working hours, rates of pay, holiday entitlements and, particularly, pensions.

Comparable data were available in 1998 for seven of the 13 job duties: recruitment, training, grievances, staffing plans, equal opportunities, health and safety, and performance appraisals. These work responsibilities of managers remained largely unchanged since 1998, the only change being that equal opportunities were less likely to be part of their job in 2004 than in 1998; 90 per cent of managers were responsible for equal opportunities in 1998, compared to 84 per cent in 2004. It could be that responsibility for this area might have fallen on managers located at a higher level in the organization. The data seemed to point in this direction, as the decline in responsibility for this issue was confined to establishments belonging to a larger organization, suggesting the function had moved elsewhere in the organization. Managers in such establishments had broadly the same work duties as those located in single sites, in both 1998 and 2004. In 2004, the only areas that managers in branch establishments were less likely to be responsible for, when compared with managers in single sites, were rates of pay, working hours, holiday and pension entitlements, reflecting the fact that pay and conditions are often determined at a higher level in the organization (see Chapter 7).

Managers in the public sector were less likely than their private sector counterparts to be responsible for rates of pay, working hours, holiday and pension entitlements, and equally responsible for the remaining tasks. In 1998, public sector managers were less likely to be responsible for pay but more likely to be responsible for equal opportunities and training than private sector managers. The overall decline in responsibility for equal opportunities was confined to public sector managers.

Organization size also played a role in shaping the tasks that managers performed. Managers in workplaces that belonged to large organizations were less likely to be responsible for pay and conditions than those in smaller organizations (Table 3.4). Managers in large organizations were, on the other hand, more likely to be responsible for recruitment, training, appraisals and employee consultation than managers in smaller organizations. Responsibility for equal opportunities did not vary by organization size, and this was also the case in 1998.

There was some variation in the number of tasks performed by specialists and generalists responsible for employment relations matters (Table 3.4). Overall, 27 per cent of managers were responsible for all 13 issues, and generalists were more likely to have responsibility for all issues than specialists. While overall

*Table 3.4* Work responsibilities of employment relations managers

| | All workplaces | Organization size | | | | Trade union recognition | | Type of manager | |
|---|---|---|---|---|---|---|---|---|---|
| | | 10–99 employees | 100–999 employees | 1,000–9,999 employees | 10,000 employees or more | No union recognized | At least one union recognized | Specialist | Generalist |
| | | | | *% workplaces* | | | | | |
| Rates of pay | 68 | 81 | 78 | 52 | 46 | 76 | 48 | 63 | 69 |
| Working hours | 80 | 85 | 80 | 75 | 72 | 85 | 69 | 80 | 80 |
| Holiday entitlements | 62 | 81 | 68 | 46 | 33 | 72 | 38 | 65 | 60 |
| Pension entitlements | 37 | 57 | 38 | 18 | 12 | 46 | 17 | 37 | 37 |
| Recruitment | 94 | 91 | 97 | 97 | 93 | 93 | 94 | 93 | 94 |
| Training | 89 | 84 | 85 | 94 | 96 | 88 | 92 | 86 | 90 |
| Grievances | 95 | 94 | 95 | 97 | 93 | 95 | 93 | 95 | 95 |
| Disciplinary matters | 96 | 94 | 98 | 95 | 97 | 95 | 97 | 95 | 96 |
| Staffing plans | 90 | 88 | 85 | 92 | 92 | 89 | 92 | 82 | 93 |
| Equal opportunities | 84 | 86 | 86 | 84 | 80 | 85 | 84 | 83 | 86 |
| Health and safety | 88 | 87 | 81 | 89 | 91 | 86 | 91 | 76 | 93 |
| Performance appraisals | 88 | 84 | 87 | 92 | 92 | 85 | 94 | 85 | 90 |
| Employee consultation | 90 | 86 | 90 | 93 | 93 | 89 | 92 | 89 | 91 |
| Responsible for all areas | 27 | 45 | 19 | 10 | 10 | 33 | 13 | 22 | 29 |
| Average number of areas of responsibility | 10.6 | 11.1 | 10.6 | 10.3 | 9.9 | 10.9 | 10.0 | 10.4 | 10.8 |

Base: All workplaces with 10 or more employees where the the interview is conducted on site and where the manager is primarily responsible for employment relations matters.

Figures are weighted and based on responses from 1,523 (column 1), 312 (column 2), 293 (column 3), 458 (column 4), 448 (column 5), 730 (column 6), 741 (column 7), 813 (column 8) and 685 managers (column 9).

there was little variation in the type of tasks performed by specialists and generalists, there were two areas that specialists were less likely to be responsible for than generalists: health and safety issues, and staffing plans. It seemed that both specialists and generalists largely covered the same areas. Divergence was greater, however, in 1998, when specialists were more likely than generalists to be responsible for pay or conditions of employment, systems of payment, and grievances while the opposite was true for training, and health and safety. The work responsibilities of specialists were essentially the same as in 1998, the exception being equal opportunities and the handling of grievances, which were less likely to be their responsibility.

Among workplaces in smaller organizations and those where unions were absent, employment relations managers tended to perform more employment relations tasks and were more likely to do all the listed tasks, compared with their counterparts in larger organizations and those in unionized establishments. Task responsibilities were also broader in single independent establishments than in establishments belonging to a larger organization (46 per cent of managers were responsible for all areas in single sites, compared to 17 per cent in branch sites), and in private than in public sector sites (31 compared to 8 per cent).

### Managers' perceptions of the employment relations function

This section explores whether there has been any change in managers' perceptions of their role and their attitudes towards the employment relations function generally. Managers were presented with the 10 statements shown in Table 3.5 and responses were given on a five-point scale from 'strongly agree' to 'strongly disagree'. Responses from managers agreeing or strongly agreeing with each of the statements were combined and these are presented in Table 3.5.

Only one-fifth of workplace managers were in favour of union membership among employees at their workplace (see Chapter 5) but the data showed that managers in 2004 were no more anti-union than in 1998, on the basis of the following statements: 'unions help find ways to improve performance' (item 9), and 'we prefer to consult directly with employees than with unions' (item 10). Nor did they become more pro-union.

The main changes in management attitudes since 1998 were in relation to trust and work–life balance. Managers were less trusting of employees in 2004 than in 1998, being more likely to agree that employees sometimes took unfair advantage of management (item 4). The data also showed that managers were less of the view that employees had the sole responsibility for ensuring their own work–life balance, recognizing the role to be played by other parties such as employers and/or the government (item 3). A more detailed discussion of this particular issue is provided in Chapter 9.

Management attitudes were strongly related to workplace characteristics, as shown in Table 3.5. The management culture differed substantially between small and large workplaces, and between the private and public sectors. Private sector managers were more sceptical of the value of unions (item 9), especially

*Table 3.5* Attitudes of managers towards the personnel function, 1998 and 2004

| Agree with:[a] | 1998 Column % — All | 2004 Column % — All | 2004 Column % — Public sector — All | 2004 Column % — Private sector — All | Private sector — Workplaces with less than 50 employees | Private sector — Workplaces with 50–249 employees | Private sector — Workplaces with 250 or more employees |
|---|---|---|---|---|---|---|---|
| 1. We frequently ask employees to help us in ways not specified in their job description | 54 | 50 | 43 | 51 | 49 | 58 | 52 |
| 2. Employees are led to expect long-term employment in this organization | 79 | 80 | 73 | 81 | 83 | 83 | 79 |
| 3. It is up to individual employees to balance their work and family responsibilities | 84 | 67 | 49 | 71 | 77 | 63 | 67 |
| 4. Employees sometimes try to take unfair advantage of management | 27 | 32 | 20 | 36 | 34 | 34 | 36 |
| 5. Those at the top are best placed to make decisions | 57 | 56 | 44 | 59 | 66 | 67 | 48 |
| 6. We do not introduce changes without first discussing the implications with employees | 70 | 73 | 85 | 70 | 71 | 70 | 70 |
| 7. Most decisions are made without consulting employees | 18 | 17 | 3 | 21 | 22 | 21 | 17 |
| 8. Employees are fully committed to the values of this organization | 72 | 76 | 79 | 74 | 79 | 76 | 70 |
| 9. Unions help find ways to improve workplace performance | 23 | 22 | 51 | 15 | 12 | 16 | 19 |
| 10. We would rather consult directly with employees than with unions | 79 | 79 | 60 | 82 | 88 | 80 | 77 |

Base: All workplaces with 10 or more employees where the interview is conducted on site.
Figures are weighted and based on responses from 1,949 (column 1), 1,751 (column 2), 1,288 (column 3), 474 (column 4), 267 (column 5), 189 (column 6) and 821 managers (column 7).

Note:

[a] Responses to each of the statements were given on a five-point scale from 'strongly agree' to 'strongly disagree'. Figures provided combine responses from managers agreeing and strongly agreeing.

those in the smallest establishments, than their public sector counterparts. They also preferred to a greater extent to consult with employees directly rather than with unions (item 10). Compared to public sector managers, private sector managers exhibited greater levels of distrust towards employees (item 4), and were more of the view that decisions were best taken by senior managers (item 5). Private sector managers, especially in the smallest workplaces, seemed to be less engaged in consultation when introducing changes and when making decisions (items 6 and 7). Managers in the private sector were more likely to consider that employees had the sole responsibility for ensuring their own work life balance (item 3), especially those managers located in small workplaces. Job demarcation seemed to be less strict in the private sector, where a majority of managers asked their employees for help in ways not specified in their job descriptions (item 1). Finally, private sector managers were more likely to think that their employees expected long-term employment (item 2) than their public sector counterparts. There was only one item that both private and public sector managers had a similar opinion about: their employees' commitment to the values of the organization (item 8). Within the private sector, managers in small workplaces perceived greater commitment among their employees than those in large workplaces.

As discussed earlier, employment relations specialists tended to work in different types of workplaces and had a different professional and gender profile than generalists. One could expect these differences to be reflected in some way in their attitudes about the world of work and the role of the personnel function. In comparison to generalists, specialists tended to have a more positive stance towards trade unions (items 9 and 10) and were more sceptical about the level of commitment of their employees (item 8). Most said work–life balance was employees' responsibility (item 3) but to a lesser degree than generalists; they were also more likely to disagree with this statement, suggesting that other parties, such as employers or the government, might also have a role in ensuring employees' work–life balance. With regards to employee consultation and involvement, the picture that emerged was mixed. Specialists had similar attitudes to generalists in relation to employee consultation in decision-making (item 7), but they had a more negative attitude towards consultation before the introduction of changes (item 6). On the remaining issues, the views of specialists did not differ significantly from those of generalists.

## *The size of the employment relations function*

Sisson and Storey (2000b) argue that the size of the personnel function is only partially accounted for by the size of companies and that it is more closely associated to the way in which collective bargaining takes place. They conclude that the largest personnel functions tend to be found in businesses that have multi-establishment pay determination structures, whereas in diversified conglomerates or industrial holding companies with typically decentralized arrangements, the function is smaller or non-existent. The survey data can be used to examine this.

Managers were asked if they had any staff at their workplace to assist them in managing personnel matters. Over two-thirds (68 per cent) of managers did have some assistance. Managers in sites belonging to a larger organization, in the public sector, and where unions were recognized were more likely to have assistants (70, 73 and 72 per cent respectively) than those in single sites, in the private sector, and where unions were not recognized (64, 67 and 65 per cent respectively).

The likelihood of having assistants increased with workplace size, but the relationship with organization size was less clear-cut. Methods of pay determination appeared more relevant than organization size. Managers were most likely to have assistants in workplaces where pay was determined by a pay review body (86 per cent having assistants), or was subject to collective bargaining at the organization level (75 per cent). The positive association between collective bargaining at the organization level and the size of the personnel function held, irrespective of whether the workplace was in the public or the private sector.

On average, managers with assistants had three assistants working on personnel issues, though this varied by broad sector. Managers in the private sector had on average two assistants, while their public sector counterparts had on average four assistants. Specialists relied on more assistants than generalists (three versus two, on average). Again, the method of pay determination was important, irrespective of whether the workplace was in the public or the private sector. In workplaces where collective bargaining for more than one employer took place (e.g. industry-wide agreement), the average number of assistants was highest, with four assistants, followed by workplaces where negotiations took place at the organization or workplace level, with three assistants. In workplaces where pay was determined by a pay review body, or where there was no collective bargaining, managers had on average two assistants. These results seem to support the argument by Sisson and Storey (2000b).

The likelihood of having assistants decreased since 1998, when three-quarters of managers had assistants. However, these managers had fewer assistants on average (two) than in 2004. It appears that in 2004 there were more workplaces with no assistants, but in those workplaces where there were some, the function was larger than in 1998. The fact that there were more workplaces with no assistants in 2004 than in 1998 leaves open the question as to who has taken over responsibility for these issues. It could reflect a move towards centralization of the function, but it could also mean a devolvement of responsibilities to line managers.

While the number of staff that respondents had to assist them in managing personnel matters illustrates whether the personnel function has grown at the workplace, managers' use of outside bodies as sources of advice shows whether the function has expanded beyond the workplace. Seeking expert advice on personnel issues from outside bodies may signal practitioners' attempts to become more professional.

Managers were asked whether they had sought expert advice over the previous year. Overall 57 per cent of management respondents in 2004 said that they had approached at least one of the 10 bodies listed for advice on employment issues.[13] The most common sources of advice were external lawyers (29 per cent) and Acas (26 per cent), followed by external accountants (17 per cent), professional bodies such as the Chartered Institute of Personnel and Development (16 per cent), government departments other than DTI (14 per cent), management consultants (13 per cent), DTI (12 per cent), and Business Links and the Small Business Service (11 per cent).

Recourse to Acas has become increasingly common as illustrated by the growing number of calls answered by their national telephone helpline since 2002 (Acas, 2004: 45; 2005: 3). Managers were more likely to cite Acas and external accountants as sources of advice in 2004 than they were in 1998. In 1998, the proportion of managers relying on these sources was 16 and 13 per cent respectively, compared to 26 and 17 per cent in 2004. No changes were found in the usage of management consultants, external lawyers, external accountants, employer associations and professional bodies such as the CIPD.

The use of Acas as a source of advice increased in the private sector, and although there was also an increase in the public sector, this was not statistically significant. Twenty-eight per cent of managers in the private sector sought advice from Acas in 2004, compared with 17 per cent in 1998.[14] The use of Acas for advice also increased in small establishments of between 10 and 24 employees and in larger establishments of 100 or more employees; in both single and sites belonging to a larger organization; and in sites belonging to large organizations of 1,000 or more employees. The reliance on external accountants for advice increased in the private sector, with 19 per cent of managers reporting having sought advice from accountants, up from 14 per cent in 1998, while in the public sector it stayed at the same level.

The likelihood of managers seeking advice from at least one of the 10 bodies listed was higher than average in workplaces with the following characteristics: large workplaces, stand-alone sites, those belonging to small organizations, private sector establishments, in the Construction, Manufacturing, Other business services and Health sectors, and where unions were not recognized.

One might expect that managers with specialist skills would use outside bodies for advice to a lesser extent than generalists, as they have expert knowledge. However, the results did not support this. Specialists were in fact more likely to seek advice than generalists. Sixty-eight per cent of specialists had sought advice from at least one external source, compared to 54 per cent of generalists.

The size of HR departments can also be altered by either outsourcing or contracting-in HR services such as recruitment, payroll, training, and temporary filling of vacant posts. There have been claims that HR outsourcing is becoming more prevalent and that the restructuring of the personnel function has involved a considerable amount of contracting-out. The picture emerging from the WERS data was, however, rather mixed. One-third of workplaces (34 per cent) outsourced their training function to independent contractors; 28 per cent their payroll activities; 16 per cent their temporary filling of vacant posts; and 12 per cent had outsourced their recruitment. The outsourcing of the payroll function became more prevalent since 1998, when only 19 per cent of workplaces contracted this out; the outsourcing of temporary-vacancy filling became, on the other hand, less common (22 per cent in 1998). Training and recruitment were as likely to be contracted-out in 2004 as in 1998. Contracting-in these services was rare. Only 2 per cent of workplaces had stopped using contractors to carry out payroll activities in the previous five years; 1 per cent had contracted-in their training and recruitment; and less than 1 per cent had contracted-in their temporary vacancy filling.

In summary, the duties performed by employment relations' managers in 2004 were essentially the same as in 1998, but the increased use of outside bodies as sources of advice and the growth in the size of the personnel function in some workplaces may reflect increasing complexity in the employment relations function associated with a more complex legal and regulatory environment. On the other hand, it may reflect an increase in the volume of work of people managers, or even practitioners' desire to do their jobs better; and, in establishments that belong to larger organizations, it is perhaps a reflection of the degree to which the employment relations function has been decentralized. The latter is covered in the next section.

### *The autonomy of workplace managers*

It was reported earlier that the increase in the proportion of branch sites with specialists at both the workplace and a higher level, and the decrease in the proportion of workplaces with only a specialist at a higher level, suggested an increased decentralization of the personnel function. This section explores whether any decentralization has been accompanied by greater levels of autonomy and decision-making power for managers based at the workplace level (also referred to as 'local managers').

Before considering this issue though, several aspects of local managers' autonomy from senior management in their organizations are explored. First, the autonomy of local managers is looked at in terms of their freedom to make decisions and the extent of monitoring from the centre. The degree of autonomy over the employment relations issue being dealt with is then examined, followed by how the local manager's autonomy is related to the structure of the personnel function in their organization. The survey also allowed an exploration of whether the degree of autonomy of local managers differed if the issues being dealt with were employment relations related or not.

Managers in branch sites were asked whether they had to follow policies set by managers elsewhere in the organization on a number of employment relations matters such as rates of pay, training, and trade union recognition. They were also asked whether they had to consult managers elsewhere before making a decision on these matters, and whether they regularly reported to managers elsewhere in the organization on these issues. A distinction can be made between having to follow policies or having to consult others, and reporting one's actions to others. The first two dimensions of autonomy are about the scope for decision-making, whereas the third dimension on reporting refers more to the extent of monitoring systems, rather than about the decision-making process itself.

As shown in Table 3.6, local managers were less likely to have to follow a policy on training, recruitment or performance appraisals than they were on holiday or pension entitlements, health and safety, rates of pay, equal opportunities, grievances or disciplinary matters. This suggests that the latter issues tend to be designed centrally. Local managers in the public sector had to follow policies to a greater extent than their private sector counterparts across most employment relations issues, the only exceptions being training and staffing plans, where no differences between the sectors were found.

*Table* 3.6 Autonomy[a] of local managers, 1998 and 2004

| | % *workplaces* | | | | | |
| | *1998* | | | *2004* | | |
| | *Policy* | *Consult* | *Report* | *Policy* | *Consult* | *Report* |
|---|---|---|---|---|---|---|
| *Job duties* | | | | | | |
| Rates of pay | – | – | – | 74 | 68 | 25 |
| Working hours | – | – | – | 59 | 48 | 27 |
| Holidays | – | – | – | 79 | 75 | 17 |
| Pensions | – | – | – | 79 | 92 | 12 |
| Recruitment | 61 | 29 | 36 | 51 | 34 | 42 |
| Training | 55 | 18 | 41 | 50 | 25 | 39 |
| Grievances | 77 | 36 | 34 | 73 | 55 | 46 |
| Disciplinary matters | – | – | – | 72 | 53 | 49 |
| Staffing plans | 46 | 29 | 49 | 37 | 29 | 33 |
| Equal opportunities | 75 | 46 | 21 | 72 | 64 | 22 |
| Health and safety | 75 | 41 | 51 | 76 | 57 | 50 |
| Performance appraisals | 65 | 27 | 41 | 56 | 36 | 42 |
| Trade union recognition | – | – | – | 54 | 84 | 9 |
| Pay or conditions of employment | 81 | 66 | 31 | – | – | – |
| Systems of payment | 78 | 78 | 20 | – | – | – |

Base: All branch sites with 10 or more employees that are not head offices and where the interview is conducted on site.

Figures are weighted and based on responses from 1,284 (columns 1–3) and 1,031 managers (columns 4–6).

Note:

[a] Three measures of autonomy are included: whether managers had to follow a policy set by managers elsewhere in their organization ('Policy'); whether they had to consult managers elsewhere before making a decision ('Consult'); and whether they regularly reported to managers elsewhere ('Report').

Issues that were more likely to be subject to an external policy were the most likely to require consultation. Managers had to consult on issues such as pension and holiday entitlements, rates of pay, and equal opportunities to a greater extent than when the decision to be made was about training issues, recruitment or appraisals. Some differences were found on this dimension of autonomy between the private and public sector: there was a greater requirement for public sector managers to consult on rates of pay (83 per cent compared to 63 per cent in the private sector), working hours (65 per cent compared to 41 per cent), holiday entitlements (85 per cent compared to 71 per cent), and recruitment (44 per cent compared to 30 per cent), and a lesser requirement for them to consult on pension entitlements (86 per cent compared to 90 per cent).

Local managers may have had greater freedom to make decisions on training, recruitment or performance appraisals relative to other issues, but their decisions were still closely monitored, as indicated by the requirement to report back to management elsewhere. Indeed, the requirement to report back was more widespread than in the case of pension and holiday entitlements, equal opportunities, rates of pay, and hours of work. This finding seemed to indicate that decentralized decision-making can go hand-in-hand with strong central monitoring systems.

Few local managers had a substantial degree of autonomy. Eleven per cent of managers did not have to follow a policy on any of the 13 employment relations issues listed, while 5 per cent could make decisions without consulting on any item. It would appear therefore that central decision-making was widespread. So too was central monitoring, since only one quarter (23 per cent) did not regularly report on any of the specified employment relations issues. The majority of managers had to follow a policy or consult on *most* of the listed issues (at least seven issues), or reported on at least *some* issues (up to six issues). One-tenth of managers enjoyed the least autonomy as they had to follow organization-wide policies and had to consult, as well as regularly report, on most issues.

The analysis now turns to whether there has been a greater delegation of real decision-making power to employment relations managers based at the workplace level since 1998 (Table 3.6). On the first dimension of autonomy, managers' discretion increased on four out of seven issues common to both surveys: branch site managers had to follow policies on recruitment, training, staffing plans and appraisals to a lesser degree in 2004 than in 1998. No change was found with respect to equal opportunities and health and safety, areas subject to long-standing legislation. However, managers' autonomy in relation to consultation decreased on five issues (training, grievances, appraisals, equal opportunities and health and safety) and remained the same on decisions related to staffing plans and recruitment. Levels of autonomy with regard to reporting also remained unchanged on most issues, only increasing with regard to staffing plans, and decreasing in relation to handling grievances and recruitment. Overall, a mixed picture on autonomy levels emerged. Although there seemed to be fewer organization-wide policies that local managers had to follow, personnel departments at the centre increased their control and used their influence in terms of decision-making to a considerable extent.

The structure of the personnel function played a role in determining the levels of autonomy of local managers. Local managers in workplaces that had a specialist at a higher level had the least autonomy across all three dimensions, with nearly all having to follow policies or consult prior to decision-making. These managers were also more likely to have to report back than managers in workplaces without specialists elsewhere in the organization. The presence of a personnel function at a higher level substantially reduced the discretion of local managers, even specialist local managers.

Local managers in foreign-owned workplaces with multiple UK sites had more discretion than managers in UK-owned workplaces across the three dimensions of autonomy. Overall, 11 per cent of local managers in predominantly or wholly foreign-owned establishments did not have to follow a policy or report on any issues, and were able to make decisions on all issues without consulting elsewhere, compared to only 2 per cent of managers in wholly UK-owned sites.

The survey also explored the degree of autonomy of local managers on issues that were not related to employment relations. This allowed us to examine how decentralized the decision-making power on personnel issues was in comparison to other matters such as the quality of the organization's main product or service, or the quantity of output. Local managers had to consult to a lesser degree when making decisions on quantity of output (45 per cent) and product quality (42 per cent) than when deciding on five employment relations issues (rates of pay, holiday and pension entitlements, equal opportunities and union recognition).[15] Only on training and staffing plans did local managers have more autonomy than on non-employment issues, while similar levels were found in relation to recruitment, appraisals, working hours, disciplinary and grievance procedures, and health and safety. Local managers had much less discretion though when dealing with a major physical change in their establishment: 83 per cent of local managers said that they had to consult elsewhere before making a decision. Only on pensions did managers have less autonomy than on decisions about physical changes, with 92 per cent having to consult elsewhere.

Local managers may have had greater discretion when making decisions about the product quality and the quantity of output than about most employment relations matters, but monitoring levels were also much higher. The majority of local managers regularly reported to managers elsewhere in their organization on quantity of output (64 per cent) and product quality (62 per cent), a much higher proportion than on any single employment relations issue. Summing up, local management had greater freedom to make decisions on these non-employment issues, but there was a high level of monitoring of the local unit from the centre. Decision-making on employment relations issues was, in contrast, more centralized but monitoring systems were, in comparison, less apparent.

### *The employment relations functions of supervisors*

All supervisors and line managers have some people management responsibilities. By exploring their role and the level of decision-making power that they have on a number of employment relations issues one can further assess the extent to which the personnel function has been decentralized, a key theme in the HRM literature (Bach and Sisson, 2000; Hoque and Noon, 2001; Storey, 2001).

More than four-fifths (84 per cent) of workplaces had some employees with supervisory responsibilities, a similar proportion to 1998 (82 per cent). In the majority of these workplaces (57 per cent), however, less than one-fifth of employees were supervisors. The proportion of employees with supervisory responsibilities had not changed since 1998, but did supervisors have more decision-making power than in 1998?

Managers were asked whether supervisors could make final decisions on recruiting people to work for them, on pay rises for their staff and on dismissals for poor performance. Supervisors had limited authority over these issues, especially with regard to pay rises and dismissals, with only 6 and 10 per cent respectively being able to make final decisions on these issues. This compared to 21 per cent of supervisors having authority to make decisions on recruitment. This confirms what some commentators (Sisson and Storey, 2000b) have said in relation to recruitment, an area where devolution is most likely to take place, and pay, an area where there is the greatest reluctance to devolve. Of the three areas, pay was, however, slightly more likely to be devolved in 2004 than in 1998, when only 3 per cent of supervisors had the power to make final decisions on this issue. The extent to which decision-making power on recruitment and dismissals had been devolved was similar in 2004 and 1998.

Overall, three-quarters of line managers could not make final decisions on *any* of these issues in both 1998 and in 2004, signalling that the extent of delegation of people management away from personnel departments and employment relations managers continued to be rather limited and restricted to issues such as recruitment.

## From 'personnel management' to 'human resource management'?

As discussed earlier in the chapter, the increase in the number of managers with employment-related job titles was driven by the rise in the number of HR managers. Have these HR managers brought something different to the management of employment relations, and has their role changed since 1998? First, this section investigates whether managers who have the HR label in their job title exhibit a different professional profile to managers with other employment relations-specific job titles (i.e. personnel managers and employee/industrial/staff relations managers). Second, it explores whether the HR label is associated with the degree of discretion that workplace managers have when making decisions about employment relations matters. Third, it looks at the types of workplaces that are most likely to employ HR managers. The analysis follows on from the work by Hoque and Noon (2001), who found, using data from the previous WERS survey, that HR managers were distinct from personnel managers in a number of characteristics and job-related activities.

As shown in Table 3.1, HR managers spent more time on employment relations issues than personnel managers. Also, there were more women among HR managers than among personnel managers, and even more so than among those with no employment relations-specific job titles, i.e. general managers, owners and financial managers.

The increased incidence of HR managers may occur because erstwhile 'personnel managers' have simply been re-labelled. Alternatively, the HR management label may be associated with a new cohort of employment relations managers, something that might be apparent from lower job tenure and employment relations experience than other employment relations managers and − perhaps − better qualifications for the job. HR managers' professional profile differed significantly from that of personnel managers and general managers. Although they had similar levels of experience in employment relations, HR managers were much more likely to have qualifications in personnel management and had been in post for much less time than personnel managers (Table 3.7). These differences suggest that the increase in HR managers is not simply a product of a re-labelling exercise. HR managers' profile in terms of qualifications, job tenure and years of personnel experience was similar in 1998.[16]

Some differences were found in terms of work responsibilities, with HR managers being more likely to be responsible for rates of pay and pension entitlements and less likely to be in charge of health and safety issues than other managers with employment relations-specific job titles. The work responsibilities of HR managers were essentially the same as in 1998, the exceptions being their lesser involvement in equal opportunities (as was the case for all managers and specialists), and staffing plans.

HR managers at branch sites also exhibited a different profile in terms of the discretion that they had when taking decisions on employment relations issues. They had substantially greater levels of autonomy than personnel managers and, to a lesser extent, general managers employed at branch sites. This was especially in relation to one of the three dimensions of autonomy explored by the survey: whether they had to follow a policy set by management elsewhere in their organization. With regard to this dimension, HR managers had greater autonomy on pay, working hours, holiday entitlements and health and safety than personnel managers and general managers. They had similar levels of autonomy to general managers on other issues. Personnel managers had, in contrast, very little autonomy on any issue in comparison to both HR managers and general managers at branch sites. The only exception was in relation to union recognition, with personnel managers having similar autonomy levels to both HR and general managers in branch sites.

HR managers and personnel managers in branch sites had similar discretion levels when it came to the need to consult with others elsewhere in the organization prior to making a decision. This was the case for all employment relations issues but one (rates of pay), with personnel managers having less discretion when taking decisions on this issue than both HR and general managers.

HR managers were as likely as personnel managers to regularly report elsewhere in the organization on most employment relations issues listed in the survey, but they seemed to be subject to less central monitoring than personnel

*Table 3.7* Profile of HR managers and personnel managers

|  | % workplaces | | | |
|---|---|---|---|---|
|  | HR manager | Personnel manager | General manager, Owner, Financial manager | All managers |
| *Professional profile* | | | | |
| Qualifications in personnel | 73 | 52 | 23 | 35 |
| 10 or more years of experience in personnel | 55 | 58 | 58 | 57 |
| 5 or more years in job | 23 | 49 | 45 | 41 |
| *Work duties* | | | | |
| Rates of pay | 72 | 57 | 68 | 68 |
| Working hours | 78 | 77 | 80 | 80 |
| Holiday entitlements | 73 | 64 | 60 | 62 |
| Pension entitlements | 45 | 34 | 37 | 37 |
| Recruitment | 93 | 93 | 94 | 94 |
| Training | 83 | 89 | 90 | 89 |
| Grievances or grievance procedures | 96 | 96 | 94 | 95 |
| Disciplinary matters or disciplinary procedures | 94 | 94 | 96 | 96 |
| Staffing plans | 76 | 83 | 93 | 90 |
| Equal opportunities | 82 | 78 | 86 | 84 |
| Health and safety | 63 | 77 | 93 | 88 |
| Performance appraisals | 79 | 84 | 90 | 88 |
| Employee consultation | 87 | 88 | 91 | 90 |
| Has employees with supervisory responsibilities | 94 | 83 | 82 | 84 |
| *Supervisors can make final decisions on:* | | | | |
| Recruitment | 31 | 25 | 19 | 21 |
| Pay rises | 11 | 3 | 5 | 6 |
| Dismissals | 17 | 11 | 8 | 10 |

Base: All workplaces with 10 or more employees where the interview is conducted on site and, for the professional profile, where managers' major job responsibility is employment relations or where they are equally responsible for employment relations and other responsibilities; for work duties, where managers are primarily responsible for employment relations matters.
Figures are weighted and based on responses from 1,219 managers (professional profile), 1,523 managers (work duties) and 1,551 managers (supervisors).

managers with regard to working hours, holiday and pension entitlements, and training. Both HR and personnel managers were close to the level of autonomy of general managers at branch sites on 10 issues and had less autonomy than general managers on three issues, albeit not on the same issues. HR managers had less autonomy on grievances and disciplinary procedures, and appraisals, while personnel managers had less autonomy on pay and conditions of employment.

The HRM literature advocates the devolution of decision-making to supervisory level. Employees with supervisory responsibilities were more in evidence where HR managers were present than where employment relations were the responsibility of personnel managers. Line managers in workplaces where there was an HR manager also had greater discretion when making decisions on pay rises for people who worked for them than line managers in workplaces with a personnel manager or a general manager. However, supervisors' decision-making power in relation to recruitment and dismissals did not vary between workplaces with an HR manager and workplaces with a personnel manager. Supervisors in workplaces with a general manager had less decision-making power in relation to recruitment and dismissals than HR managers.

HR managers were more likely to be employed in larger workplaces (52 per cent of HR managers but only 36 per cent of personnel managers worked in workplaces with 50 or more employees), branch sites (where 85 per cent of HR managers but only 73 per cent of personnel managers worked), workplaces that belonged to large organizations (85 per cent of HR managers but only 70 per cent of personnel managers worked in organizations of 100 or more employees), and foreign-owned establishments (where 18 per cent of HR managers but only 3 per cent of personnel managers worked). There were no differences in the way HR managers and personnel managers were distributed across sectors and industries, and between workplaces with or without recognized trade unions.

Overall, the different profile and context in which HR and personnel managers work do not support the assertion that 'the name has changed but the game has remained the same' (Armstrong, 2000), although the author recognizes that the way in which the game is being played has altered. An exploration of the reasons why the game may have changed – for example, the different business environment, or the advent of HRM principles – is beyond the scope of the chapter. In addition, whether the presence of an HR manager signalled that the 'textbook principles' of HRM were being applied (i.e. that it was associated with certain employment relations practices) and whether it made a difference, are also beyond the scope of the chapter, but are touched upon in other chapters.

## The integration of employment relations in business strategy

Proponents of HRM as a source of sustained competitive advantage saw the integration of HR issues into business planning as vital to successful people management (Pfeffer, 1995; Storey, 1992; Guest and Peccei, 1994). Since then a consensus has emerged among both practitioners and academics as to the value of strategic HRM in maximizing the value that business derives from the deployment of its workers. Two broad assumptions underpin this approach to the management of employment relations. The first is that management is a 'strategic actor' (Sisson and Marginson, 2003: 160) capable of making choices which can alter the nature of employment relations. The second is that this choice extends to influence over the nature of the business strategy pursued (ibid.). Advocates of the approach therefore emphasize the importance of the HR function in strategic business decisions, and thus the centrality of HR managers in devising and executing business strategy. Others have cautioned against an over-emphasis on this strategic link and have stressed the importance of a more rounded conception of the HR function in effective people management (Buyens and De Vos, 2001). However, the debate on this issue has been characterized by a paucity of empirical evidence regarding the nature and extent of HRM. This section aims to fill this empirical gap by looking at the types of employers who have regard to employment relations in the preparation and coverage of strategic plans, those who have board-level representation of employment relations matters, and those who obtain Investors in People accreditation.

### Who is 'strategic' about employment relations management?

To establish what role, if any, employment relations matters played in business strategy, managers responsible for employment relations matters were first asked whether their workplace was 'covered by a formal strategic plan which sets out objectives and how they will be achieved'. If they had a plan, they were asked which issues were covered by the plan, a showcard prompting them with seven items, including three relating to employment relations: employee development, employee job satisfaction, and employee diversity.[17] Nearly one-third (30 per cent) of workplaces had no strategic plan at all. This rose to half of all workplaces in Construction, Hotels and restaurants, small organizations with fewer than 100 employees, and single independent establishments, but fell as low as 1 per cent in Education and Public administration, and around 5 per cent in workplaces with over 500 employees and 6 per cent across the public sector (Table 3.8).

Sixty-one per cent of workplaces had a strategic plan covering at least one of the three employment relations issues identified in the showcard, with a further 10 per cent of workplaces having a strategic plan that did not cover employment relations matters. Thus, where workplaces had a strategic plan, the vast majority (87 per cent) said it covered employment relations issues. Strategic plans covering employment relations issues were much more common in the public sector than the private sector (85 per cent compared with 58 per cent), particularly in Public administration where they existed in nearly all workplaces. They were least common in smaller organizations, stand-alone establishments and in Manufacturing, where around four in ten workplaces had one.

*Table 3.8 Employment relations and strategic business plans*

| | % workplaces | | | | |
|---|---|---|---|---|---|
| | Strategy covers ER with HR[a] involved in preparation | HR[a] involved in strategic plan preparation but does not cover ER | Strategy covers ER but HR[a] not involved in preparation | Strategy but no HR[a] involved and no ER coverage | No strategic plan |
| All workplaces | 47 | 6 | 14 | 4 | 30 |
| *Workplace size* | | | | | |
| 10–24 employees | 40 | 6 | 12 | 4 | 38 |
| 25–49 employees | 51 | 5 | 15 | 4 | 24 |
| 50–99 employees | 60 | 5 | 20 | 4 | 11 |
| 100–199 employees | 61 | 8 | 17 | 2 | 11 |
| 200–499 employees | 63 | 5 | 18 | 4 | 10 |
| 500 or more employees | 73 | 4 | 13 | 4 | 5 |
| *Organization status* | | | | | |
| Stand-alone workplace | 35 | 7 | 3 | 2 | 53 |
| Part of a larger organization | 52 | 5 | 19 | 5 | 18 |
| *Organization size* | | | | | |
| 10–99 employees | 34 | 6 | 3 | 3 | 53 |
| 100–999 employees | 48 | 8 | 13 | 8 | 23 |
| 1,000–9,999 employees | 52 | 7 | 28 | 4 | 10 |
| 10,000 employees or more | 64 | 2 | 24 | 2 | 7 |
| *Sector of ownership* | | | | | |
| Private | 44 | 5 | 14 | 4 | 33 |
| Public | 64 | 5 | 21 | 3 | 6 |
| *Industry* | | | | | |
| Manufacturing | 34 | 11 | 6 | 4 | 46 |
| Electricity, gas and water | 68 | 1 | 24 | 4 | 5 |
| Construction | 43 | 1 | 4 | 1 | 51 |
| Wholesale and retail | 37 | 5 | 24 | 6 | 28 |
| Hotels and restaurants | 29 | 8 | 12 | 1 | 50 |
| Transport and communication | 41 | 4 | 12 | 0 | 43 |
| Financial intermediation | 59 | 4 | 22 | 8 | 7 |
| Other business services | 46 | 8 | 9 | 6 | 31 |
| Public administration | 67 | 1 | 30 | 1 | 1 |
| Education | 78 | 5 | 13 | 2 | 1 |
| Health | 62 | 3 | 14 | 3 | 18 |
| Other community services | 49 | 7 | 12 | 2 | 30 |
| *Trade union recognition* | | | | | |
| No union recognized | 41 | 5 | 11 | 4 | 39 |
| At least one union recognized | 61 | 7 | 21 | 4 | 7 |

Base: All workplaces with 10 or more employees.
Figures are weighted and based on responses from 2,045 managers.
Note:
  [a] HR refers to all managers responsible for employment relations matters.

Employment relations might have a greater impact on strategic business choices where employment relations managers are involved in the preparation of the strategic plan, especially if that plan explicitly covers employment relations matters. In the economy as a whole, managers responsible for employment relations matters were involved in the preparation of a strategic plan in around half (53 per cent) of all workplaces (Table 3.8). However, management involvement in preparing the plan did not always ensure coverage of employment relations matters in the plan: 47 per cent of workplaces had involved employment relations management in the preparation of a plan that explicitly covered the three specified employment relations issues, while a further 6 per cent had involved employment relations managers in a plan which did *not* cover these issues. Employment relations managers' involvement in a strategic plan that explicitly included these employment relations issues was most common in Education (78 per cent) and least common in Hotels and restaurants (29 per cent).

The issues covered by strategic plans were affected by the involvement of employment relations managers in the preparation of the plan. Although employment relations management involvement made no difference to the inclusion of employee job satisfaction or employee diversity in the plans, employee development was much more likely to be covered where employment relations managers were involved in its preparation than in cases where employment relations managers were not involved in preparing the plan (88 per cent versus 77 per cent). Strategic plans were also more likely to cover 'product or service development' where managers with responsibility for employment relations matters were involved in their preparation (89 per cent versus 80 per cent).

Another indicator of the extent to which an employer may take employment relations into account when devising business strategy is the presence of someone responsible for employment relations on the board of directors or top governing body of an organization. Managers in private sector workplaces with a head office in the UK were asked whether they had such a person on their top governing body; 61 per cent said they did. The likelihood of having a board-level employment relations representative rose with organizational size, union recognition, and among workplaces that were part of larger organizations as opposed to stand-alone enterprises. It also varied by sector, ranging from 86 per cent of those in Financial services to around half in Construction (50 per cent) and Manufacturing (52 per cent).

Board-level employment relations representation was also strongly associated with the inclusion of employment relations in a strategic business plan: 63 per cent of workplaces with board-level employment relations representation had a business strategy covering employment relations issues compared with 40 per cent of those without such representation. Put the other way round, 71 per cent of workplaces with a business plan incorporating employment relations issues also had board-level employment relations representation, compared with 60 per cent of those with a business strategy which did not cover employment relations, and 46 per cent of those with no strategy at all.

Although there is some dispute about the impact of the Investors in People (IiP) award on employment relations practices (Hoque, 2003), employers are accredited with the award by Investors in People UK where they can show that they have a planned approach to setting and communicating business objectives and developing people to meet those objectives. In four-fifths (80 per cent) of IiP-accredited workplaces the manager responsible for employment relations matters said that they had a strategic business plan covering employment relations issues, compared with 48 per cent of workplaces without accreditation, confirming a clear link between accreditation and strategic HRM planning. Across the economy, 38 per cent of workplaces were accredited for IiP. Once again, this indicator of integration between HR and business strategy was more prevalent in the public than the private sector (74 per cent compared with 31 per cent) – though 73 per cent of workplaces in Financial services were IiP accredited. It was also more prevalent in workplaces with recognized unions than in workplaces with no recognized unions (68 per cent and 26 per cent respectively), and it was positively associated with organizational size.

A simple 'strategic' HR index can be constructed by giving workplaces a point for having a strategic plan covering employment relations matters, for involving managers responsible for employment relations matters in its preparation, and for IiP accreditation. If one sums these points to create a scale running from zero to three, just over one quarter (28 per cent) of workplaces scored zero; 16 per cent scored one; one-third (34 per cent) scored two; and one-fifth (22 per cent) scored three. Scoring highly on this scale was strongly associated with larger organizations, unionization and membership of the public sector. The sectors with the highest degree of integration were Education, followed by Financial services whereas Manufacturing had the lowest degree of integration.

## When is strategic HRM used?

There are a number of rationales as to why employers may choose a strategic approach to the management of their employees. One argument, mentioned above, is that employees, as a human resource, can offer the employer a source of sustainable competitive advantage in the production and sale of goods and services. A second proposition is that employers will choose a strategic approach to employment relations when they are engaged in a programme of change which may rely upon employee acquiescence or support. In these circumstances, HR managers may be performing the role of 'change agent' described by Ulrich (1997) and of Storey's (1992) 'changemakers'. A third possibility is that it pays to adopt a strategic approach to employment relations when there are opportunities to cut labour costs, or where labour costs constitute a relatively high proportion of all costs, since a strategic approach to labour deployment may present opportunities to cut labour costs. Each of these propositions is considered below, recognizing that they are not necessarily mutually exclusive.

Thinking first about the role of employee development in business planning, one way to gain insight into the intent behind the inclusion of employee development in strategic business plans is to establish what else strategic business plans contain when they include employee development. The inclusion of 'employee development' in strategic plans was positively and significantly associated with the inclusion of 'employee job satisfaction', 'employee diversity' and with 'forecasts of staffing requirements'. However, it was not associated with the inclusion of 'product or service development', 'improving quality of product or service', nor with 'market strategy/developing new markets'. This suggests that employment development considerations entered strategic business plans when there were concerns about employee well-being or staffing arrangements, but that employee development was treated as somewhat separate from market strategy and product development. Further evidence for this proposition comes from the targets that workplaces say that they are following. Management respondents were asked which of the 11 targets listed on a showcard their workplace followed. Where employment relations were included in the strategic plan, they were much more likely to mention targets for productivity, labour turnover, absenteeism, workforce training, and employee job satisfaction. The inclusion of employment relations in the plan was also positively associated with targets for 'customer/client satisfaction', something that well-trained and motivated staff can have a direct influence over. However, there was no relationship between whether employment relations featured in the strategic plan and targets for profits/returns on investment, total costs, or volume of sales/services provided.

If strategic HRM is linked to product market strategies, one might expect to see this reflected in a link between employment relations managers' involvement in the business plan, or inclusion of employment relations in the business plan, and sensitivity to competition based either on prices, quality or both. In fact, there was no clear link between the importance of price or quality factors in the employer's competitive success and the degree to which managers responsible for employment relations matters were involved in preparing the business plan. Nor was there any link between factors in competitive success and the inclusion of employment relations matters in the business plan.[18]

There is substantial support, however, for the proposition that strategic HR is associated with the amount of change that management has introduced at the workplace. Management respondents were asked, 'Over the past two years has management here introduced any of the changes listed on this card?', the showcard listing eight items.[19] The mean number of changes made across all workplaces was 3.1. The number of changes made rose with strategic integration of HR with business planning: those scoring the maximum of three on the HR integration index (that is, those with a strategic plan incorporating employment relations, with employment relations management involvement in the preparation of the plan, and IiP accreditation) had a mean of 3.7 changes, compared to 3.4 changes among those scoring two, 3.0 changes among those scoring one, and 2.2 changes among those with zero on the HR integration scale. Furthermore, this positive relationship between HR integration and the probability of making changes held across all eight types of change, suggesting a robust relationship between recent change initiated by management and the integration of HR with business planning. It may be that the two are complementary in some way, or that the extent of managerially-initiated change and strategic orientation towards people management are associated with other factors unaccounted for in this simple bivariate relationship.

There is also a clear relationship between HR integration into the business and sensitivity to labour costs. Workplaces whose labour costs exceeded half their sales revenue or operating costs were significantly more likely than those with lower labour costs to have a strategic plan covering employment relations, to involve HR managers in the preparation of that strategy, and to be IiP accredited.[20] This relationship did not hold, however, with regard to board-level employment relations representation. Higher scores on the HR integration index were also associated with a higher incidence of contracted-out services.

## Are workplaces more strategic in their people management?

If practitioners are taking their cue from the vociferous advocates of strategic HRM in the burgeoning literature on the subject, there is little evidence of it judging by the three indicators of HRM integration into business plans presented in Table 3.9. Across the economy as a whole, there has been little change in the percentage of workplaces incorporating employee development in their

*Table 3.9 Strategic people management by broad sector, 1998 and 2004*

| | % workplaces | | | | | | | |
| --- | --- | --- | --- | --- | --- | --- | --- | --- |
| | 1998 | | | | 2004 | | | |
| | *Private manufacturing* | *Private services* | *Public* | *All* | *Private manufacturing* | *Private services* | *Public* | *All* |
| Strategy covering employee development | 43 | 56 | 84 | 60 | 40 | 57 | 84 | 60 |
| Strategy not covering employee development | 17 | 12 | 9 | 12 | 13 | 10 | 11 | 11 |
| No strategy | 40 | 32 | 7 | 28 | 47 | 33 | 6 | 30 |
| HR involvement in preparing strategic plan | 52 | 53 | 76 | 58 | 43 | 50 | 69 | 52 |
| Investor in People | 15 | 32 | 54 | 34 | 13 | 34 | 74 | 38 |

Base: All workplaces with 10 or more employees.
Figures are weighted and based on responses from managerial respondents. In 2004, the strategic plan variables are based on 2,048 respondents and the IiP figures are based on 1,989 respondents. In 1998 the bases were 2,129 and 2,177 respectively.
Note:
   In 1998 the showcard identifying issues covered by strategic business plans did not include employee job satisfaction or employee diversity, so the measure of employment relations coverage in business plans is confined to the inclusion of 'employee development' in this 1998–2004 comparison.

strategic business plans, and some indication of a decline in this practice in private manufacturing. Furthermore, HR managers were less likely to be involved in the preparation of strategic business plans in 2004 than in 1998, a trend discernible in all three broad sectors of the economy. Although IiP accreditation was more prevalent in 2004 than in 1998, the sectoral breakdown reveals that it only rose significantly in the public sector.

## Auditing the employment relations function

So far the chapter has dealt with how the personnel function has been structured. As Sisson and Storey (2000b) say, the debate over how this function should be structured has been accompanied by pressure to establish the effectiveness of the function itself. The pressure is perhaps greater for employment relations specialists, who often have to prove that they are making a significant contribution to the enterprise. They outline three types of indicators that can be used to measure effectiveness: (1) quantitative or hard measures; (2) qualitative or soft measures; and (3) process analysis. The survey collected data on whether managers kept records on a number of quantitative indicators (labour turnover, absenteeism, training, and diversity indicators such as monitoring employment relations practices by gender, age, ethnic background and disability). The survey also had data on one qualitative indicator (employee attitude surveys) and one process indicator (IiP accreditation). All these indicators are covered below, with the exception of the diversity indicators, which are covered in Chapter 9.

Managers were most likely to keep records on absenteeism (81 per cent), followed by labour turnover (63 per cent) and training (53 per cent). Just over half (53 per cent) kept records on all three issues. Specialists were more likely than generalists to monitor what could be seen as the two quantitative employee outcomes: labour turnover (75 per cent compared to 59 per cent) and absenteeism (86 per cent compared to 79 per cent). They were less likely, however, to monitor training (48 per cent compared to 55 per cent). This seems to support the hypothesis of greater pressure faced by specialists than by generalists to prove their contribution; it could also reflect a greater professionalism on their part.

Surveys of employees' views had been conducted during the previous two years in 42 per cent of workplaces and, as mentioned earlier, 38 per cent of workplaces were accredited as Investors in People (IiP). The incidence of surveys and IiP accreditation was also higher in those workplaces where there was an employment relations specialist: over half of specialists (53 per cent) had conducted an employee survey, compared to 36 per cent of generalists. Also half of workplace specialists (49 per cent) worked in IiP-accredited workplaces, compared to a third (34 per cent) of generalists. An even higher proportion of workplaces that had a specialist at the workplace or a higher level were IiP accredited (59 per cent), compared to only 16 per cent of workplaces that had no specialists at any level, illustrating the fact that IiP is sometimes initiated from the centre.

The trend identified by Millward *et al.* (2000) of increasing information collection between 1990 and 1998 did not seem to continue, as similar levels of monitoring were found in 2004 and in 1998 on these indicators, with the exception of employee surveys, for which no comparable data were available for 1998. Given that monitoring is far from universal, this could be an indication that the pressure on practitioners may be easing off. Alternatively, the extent to which these indicators measure the effectiveness of the HR department is questionable, as they can be affected by other factors, such as the state of the labour market and aspects of the job beyond the control of the HR department. Practitioners may find that the benefit they obtain by collecting this data does not justify the expense incurred.

## Conclusion

This chapter has provided evidence on some of the common themes in the HRM literature, including the decentralization of the personnel function, local managers' discretion levels in decision-making, the involvement of line managers in people management, the distinctive role of the HR manager, and the integration of employment relations in the business strategy.

The picture arising is one of increased specialization in the personnel function at the workplace level as reflected by the increased numbers of on-site HR managers and employment relations specialists. The 'feminization' of the personnel profession has continued, with the proportion of women among HR managers being especially high. The data have shown that female specialists have a different profile to that of their male counterparts; they are more likely to hold qualifications in personnel, especially those newly entering the profession, but they still lag behind in terms of personnel experience, and have shorter job tenure.

The rise in the number of specialists has been accompanied by greater management time spent on employment relations matters. However, this has been confined to managers with no employment relations-specific job titles. The amount of time HR and personnel managers dedicate to employment relations matters has decreased since 1998, raising the question as to what other tasks they are devoting their time to. A question that needs to be addressed in the future is whether they are being engaged in more strategic duties.

The increased specialization has not, however, been accompanied by a change in the employment relations-related tasks of managers, apart from a lesser involvement in equal opportunities. Compared to 1998, there has been a convergence in terms of the employment relations duties performed by specialists and generalists. Although the types of duties that managers of employment relations are responsible for have not changed since 1998, the greater use of outside bodies for advice, and the increase in the size of the personnel function in some workplaces possibly reflects an increase in the volume of work and complexity of employment relations tasks and, in establishments that belong to larger organizations, a move towards decentralization.

Decentralization has not necessarily been accompanied by greater levels of autonomy for local managers. Although there seem to be fewer organization-wide policies that workplace managers have to follow, personnel departments at the centre have been increasing their influence in decision-making. The presence of a personnel function at a higher level substantially reduces the discretion of local managers, even when these are specialists themselves. The extent of delegation of people management away from personnel departments to line managers and supervisors has continued to be rather limited and has been restricted to issues such as recruitment. The employment relations function seems to be characterized by centralized decision-making and relatively underdeveloped monitoring systems.

The chapter has also investigated whether managers who have the HR label in their job title are bringing something different to the management of employment relations. HR managers did exhibit a different professional profile to that of personnel managers – they spend more time on employment relations issues, are more qualified, and have been in post for less time – and are more likely to be responsible for pay and pension entitlements than personnel managers. The HR label also makes a difference in terms of the autonomy that local managers have when making decisions about employment relations matters. HR managers seem to have greater autonomy, especially with regard to pay, and line managers in workplaces with an HR manager also seem to have greater discretion on pay issues. These findings suggest that HR managers are a new breed of managers, and that the increase in their numbers is not the product of a re-labelling exercise.

Finally, the chapter has considered the integration of employment relations into the business strategy and whether personnel management has become more strategic since 1998. The data have shown no clear link between strategic HRM and product market strategies; it is, however, associated with the amount of change that management has introduced at the workplace. There is also a clear relationship between HR integration into the business and sensitivity to labour costs. There is little evidence that personnel management has become more strategic since 1998. There has been hardly any change in the proportion of workplaces incorporating employee development in their strategic business plans and HR managers are less likely to be involved in the preparation of strategic business plans in 2004 than in 1998. Although IiP accreditation, another strong indicator of strategic HRM, is more prevalent in 2004 than in 1998, the rise has been confined to the public sector.

# 4 Recruitment, training and work organization

## Introduction

As noted in the previous chapter, the management of employees is now seen by many as a source of competitive advantage. The precise means by which this advantage can be secured are subject to much debate. However, practices that are commonly considered to be important include those which help to recruit and develop skilled and motivated employees, methods of work organization that enhance employees' involvement in job design and problem-solving, and contractual arrangements which provide sufficient flexibility to cope with changing market conditions.

This fairly loose collection of practices has been of great interest to practitioners, policy-makers and researchers alike in recent years.[1] The focus has often been directed towards the impact of such practices on workplace productivity and performance. Such issues are not the focal point here: Chapter 10 provides an introductory analysis in that respect. Instead, this chapter looks primarily at the incidence, or diffusion, of various practices relating to recruitment, training and the organization of work. Employees' experiences also feature through investigations of issues such as job influence, work intensity and employee well-being. The chapter begins by discussing methods of recruitment and selection.

## Recruitment and selection

Employee recruitment and selection are among the most common job responsibilities of employment relations managers (see Chapter 3). A key decision that managers must take when recruiting employees is whether to recruit internally or externally. According to Boxall and Purcell (2003a: 118) 'the ILM [internal labour market] became the defining feature of sophisticated personnel management in the 1960s and 1970s', with the themes of career development and job security being central to the development of the ILM. Recruiting internally offers a number of advantages, tending to be cheaper and also guaranteeing tacit knowledge on the part of recruits, who already have an understanding of the internal workings of the workplace. However, internal labour markets can also be inflexible, potentially unfair and discriminatory, and can act as a barrier to the acquisition of valuable experience from other organizations. These flaws have contributed to what Boxall and Purcell have termed the 'erosion' of ILMs (ibid.: 119–120).

The WERS survey asked managers whether internal applicants were given preference over external applicants when filling vacancies. Although the majority (68 per cent) of respondents said that both internal and external applicants were treated equally, one-fifth (22 per cent) gave preference to internal applicants, while the remaining 10 per cent preferred external applicants. Large workplaces of 100 or more employees were more likely to favour internal applicants than smaller workplaces (32 per cent compared to 21 per cent), the latter being more likely to be constrained in their ability to recruit internally. Private sector workplaces were more likely to favour internal applicants, with a quarter preferring to recruit internally, compared to around one-tenth (12 per cent) of public sector workplaces. This association held after controlling for workplace size. The proportion of all managers preferring to recruit internally was unchanged between 1998 and 2004.[2]

In response to a separate question, four-fifths of managers expressed the view that their employees were led to expect long-term employment in their organization. However, this proportion did not differ between managers who favoured internal or external applicants, and so the data did not corroborate one of the key assumptions of the ILM, namely that managers operating in ILMs are more likely to convey the message of long-term employment to their employees.

It is not surprising that recruitment is found to be a common activity for employment relations managers, given that 84 per cent of workplaces had experienced vacancies among their 'core group of employees' in the 12 months prior to the survey. The 'core group of employees' (or 'core employees') was defined as the largest non-managerial occupational group at the workplace (see Chapter 2). Managers were asked which recruitment channels they had used when trying to fill these vacancies. Newspapers were the most common recruitment channel (used in 65 per cent of workplaces with vacancies), followed by Employment Service offices (57 per cent), internal notices (52 per cent), recommendations by existing employees (45 per cent), and word of mouth (44 per cent). Parts of the job-search literature focus on the most informal methods, such as employee referrals or word of mouth (Holzer, 1988; Simon and Warner, 1992; Pelizzari, 2004); others compare formal and informal channels (Urwin and Shackleton, 1999). For the purposes of the analysis presented here, a distinction was made between employee referrals, direct approaches to potential recruits and word of mouth (categorized as 'informal recruitment channels'), and more formal recruitment channels, with the latter separated into channels involving professional help, such as the Employment Service, and other formal methods. As shown in Table 4.1, 69 per cent of workplaces with one or more vacancies among core staff within the previous year had used at least one formal channel that involved professional help when trying to fill these vacancies. Eighty-eight per cent of workplaces had used at least one formal channel that did not involve professional help, and just under two-thirds (64 per cent) had used at least one informal channel.

*Table 4.1* Recruitment channels, by workplace characteristics

| | % workplaces | | |
|---|---|---|---|
| | Formal channel – professional help[a] | Formal channel – no professional help[b] | Informal channel[c] |
| All workplaces with vacancies in core group of employees in previous year | 69 | 88 | 64 |
| *Occupation of core employees* | | | |
| Professional | 52 | 93 | 42 |
| Associate professional and technical | 61 | 93 | 50 |
| Administrative and secretarial | 64 | 92 | 40 |
| Skilled trades | 73 | 80 | 74 |
| Caring, leisure and other personal service | 66 | 96 | 66 |
| Sales and customer service | 78 | 92 | 70 |
| Process, plant and machine operatives | 68 | 72 | 80 |
| Elementary occupations | 74 | 84 | 74 |
| *Organization status* | | | |
| Stand-alone workplace | 68 | 80 | 72 |
| Part of a larger organization | 69 | 92 | 61 |
| *Organization size:* | | | |
| 10–99 employees | 68 | 80 | 70 |
| 100–999 employees | 72 | 89 | 67 |
| 1,000–9,999 employees | 66 | 96 | 54 |
| 10,000 or more employees | 71 | 95 | 60 |
| *Sector of ownership* | | | |
| Private | 73 | 86 | 71 |
| Public | 51 | 98 | 32 |
| *Industry* | | | |
| Manufacturing | 76 | 78 | 72 |
| Electricity, gas and water | (45) | (100) | (32) |
| Construction | 71 | 83 | 80 |
| Wholesale and retail | 72 | 89 | 72 |
| Hotels and restaurants | 69 | 83 | 77 |
| Transport and communication | 78 | 84 | 60 |
| Financial services | 66 | 93 | 64 |
| Other business services | 82 | 82 | 64 |
| Public administration | 52 | 99 | 28 |
| Education | 38 | 96 | 34 |
| Health and social work | 64 | 97 | 53 |
| Other community services | 60 | 95 | 65 |
| *Trade union recognition* | | | |
| No union recognized | 72 | 85 | 72 |
| At least one union recognized | 61 | 97 | 45 |

Base: Workplaces with 10 or more employees that had one or more vacancies in the core group of employees in the previous year.

Figures are weighted and based on responses from at least 1,291 managers.

Notes:

[a] Job centres, careers service and private employment agencies.

[b] Newspapers, specialist press, notices, replying to speculative applications and internet.

[c] Direct approaches to potential recruits, recommendation or enquiry by existing employees and word of mouth.

The use of informal channels was negatively associated with the use of formal methods of recruitment, although the association was primarily evident in respect of formal channels that did not involve professional help. Comparing across the eight non-managerial Major Groups of the *Standard Occupational Classification (2000)*, formal recruitment methods involving professional help were most commonly deployed in the recruitment of Sales and customer service staff, while formal methods not involving professional help were most commonly used in the recruitment of core employees in Caring, leisure and other personal service occupations. Informal methods were most likely to be used in the recruitment of Process, plant and machine operatives, but were also commonly used to recruit into Elementary occupations and Skilled trades.

Workplaces belonging to smaller organizations and those in the private sector were less likely to rely on formal channels that did not involve professional help compared with workplaces belonging to larger organizations and public sector workplaces. In the public sector, the use of informal channels was particularly low (32 per cent). Within the private sector, informal channels were used most commonly in the Construction and Hotels and restaurants sectors, and there was also greater use of informal channels among workplaces without recognized trade unions: 63 per cent of private sector workplaces with recognized unions had used informal channels, compared with 72 per cent of those where unions were not recognized.

Irrespective of whether the establishment had recently had any vacancies, all managers were given a showcard listing the factors that they might generally consider important when recruiting new employees. Managers were most likely to value experience (86 per cent), skills (83 per cent), motivation (80 per cent) and references (71 per cent). These were followed by qualifications (54 per cent), availability (47 per cent) and personal recommendations (40 per cent). Age was considered to be important by 16 per cent of managers. There were some changes in the prevalence of certain items since 1998. Skills, motivation, qualifications and availability were mentioned slightly less in 2004 than in 1998, when the percentages of managers considering these important were 87 per cent, 85 per cent, 64 per cent and 52 per cent respectively. The slight decline in the prominence of pre-existing skills and qualifications poses the question as to whether employers are opting instead to provide training in order to obtain the skills they require. This is examined in the section dedicated to training.

Forthcoming legislation outlawing age discrimination in recruitment seems to run in tandem with current practice, as age was also cited less frequently in 2004 than in 1998, when the proportion of managers citing age as an important factor was 22 per cent. The 1998–2004 Panel Survey also showed a fall in the proportion of continuing workplaces where age was an important factor in recruitment, from 18 per cent in 1998 to 12 per cent in 2004. The Cross-Section Survey also explored whether union membership was a factor in employee selection and asked managers whether they took any steps to find out whether potential recruits were union members. Four per cent of managers required potential recruits to state whether they were union members. A further 1 per cent of managers used some other method to find out whether potential recruits belonged to a union. The remaining 95 per cent did not take any steps to find out about potential recruits' union status. Further discussions of the use of union membership and age as factors in employee selection are provided in Chapters 5 and 9, respectively.

Current legislation does not allow for 'positive discrimination', requiring candidates to be judged purely on merit, but it does allow for 'positive action', whereby groups that are under-represented in the labour market may be encouraged to apply for vacant posts. This might involve advertising in newspapers targeted at minority ethnic groups, or designing advertisements which explicitly welcome applications from women or people with disabilities. The Cross-Section Survey of Managers explored whether employers were engaging in positive action by asking whether workplaces had special procedures in place to encourage applications from six specific groups. Few employers took positive action of this type: less than one-fifth (18 per cent) of workplaces had special procedures in place. One-tenth of workplaces had special procedures to encourage applications from people with disabilities. A similar proportion had procedures targeting members of minority ethnic groups (9 per cent) and women returning to work after having children (8 per cent). Six per cent had special procedures to encourage applications from women generally, 5 per cent encouraged applications from older workers, and the same proportion encouraged the long-term unemployed. The data suggested a mixture of general and targeted approaches among the minority taking some action: 7 per cent of all workplaces targeted only one of the six groups, while 4 per cent encouraged applications from four or more. Chapter 9 provides a discussion of how the incidence of special procedures varied according to sector of ownership and also examines the change in incidence since 1998.

Having attracted individuals to apply for vacant posts, employers must then choose between the available candidates. Methods such as competency or personality tests have gained importance in the search for greater objectivity in selection. Performance or competency tests are designed to measure recruits' current and potential ability to do the tasks that the job requires, whereas employers use personality tests to see if potential employees will fit in with the organization's culture and will be able to handle the demands of the job in an effective manner. However, the validity and reliability of tests continue to be subjects of controversy, especially with regard to personality tests, which are not always seen as good predictors of performance (Blinkhorn and Johnson, 1990). This may help to explain their lower incidence. Personality or attitude tests were routinely used for at least some types of vacancies in 19 per cent of all workplaces, while performance tests were much more commonly applied, being routinely used in 46 per cent of workplaces.

Other surveys have shown that personality tests are mainly used for managers (IRS, 1997), and the evidence from WERS 2004 partly corroborates this finding. Among the fifth of workplaces that routinely used personality tests, these tests were used when filling managerial vacancies in about two-thirds (67 per cent) of the establishments where managers were employed. They were used when filling Professional vacancies in three-fifths (58 per cent) of establishments employing Professionals, and equivalently in the same percentage of workplaces employing Sales staff. They were used for each of the remaining six broad occupational groups in less than half of workplaces where these six groups were each employed. Around one quarter (23 per cent) of establishments applying personality tests used them for managerial staff only; a figure which had increased from 16 per cent in 1998. Workplaces were more likely to apply personality tests to non-managerial groups if that group was the largest at the establishment (i.e. the core group of employees).

The regular use of personality tests was more common in larger workplaces, workplaces that were part of larger organizations, workplaces in the Electricity, gas and water industry, in Public administration and in Financial services, and workplaces with recognized unions (Table 4.2). In addition, personality tests were more likely to be utilized where a personnel specialist was present at the workplace: 30 per cent of workplaces with an on-site personnel specialist used them, compared to 14 per cent of workplaces without a personnel specialist. However, this association disappeared after controlling for workplace and organization size, industry and the occupation of core employees. The overall incidence of personality tests was similar in the public and the private sectors but, after controlling for each of the factors noted above, personality tests were considerably less common in the public sector.

Among the 46 per cent of all workplaces that routinely used performance tests, these tests were used when filling vacancies for Administrative and secretarial employees in almost three-fifths (56 per cent) of the establishments where this group were employed and in a similar proportion (55 per cent) where Professionals were employed. They were used to a lesser extent when filling vacancies in Elementary occupations. Among workplaces routinely using performance tests, they were used to fill vacancies for Elementary staff in only 28 per cent of the establishments that employed workers in this category. Among workplaces routinely using performance tests, 7 per cent used performance tests for applicants to managerial positions only, with the remaining 93 per cent using them for at least some applicants to non-managerial positions. Performance tests were again more likely to be used when recruiting core employees.

Larger workplaces were more likely to use performance tests, as were workplaces that were part of larger organizations, public sector workplaces, workplaces in Public administration, Electricity, gas and water, Education and Financial services, and workplaces with recognized unions (Table 4.2). Workplaces with a personnel specialist at the workplace were also more likely to make use of these tests: 53 per cent of workplaces with a specialist on site used them, compared to 42 per cent of workplaces without a personnel specialist. However, after controlling for each of these factors simultaneously, the occupation of core employees and workplace size were found to be the key determinants of the use of performance tests.

According to some commentators, the main development in selection testing during the 1990s was an increase in usage, both in terms of the number of

*Table 4.2* Selection tests, 1998 and 2004

| | % workplaces | | | |
| | 1998 | | 2004 | |
| | Personality tests used routinely for some occupations | Performance tests used routinely for some occupations | Personality tests used routinely for some occupations | Performance tests used routinely for some occupations |
|---|---|---|---|---|
| All workplaces | 18 | 44 | 19 | 46 |
| *Workplace size* | | | | |
| 10–24 employees | 16 | 39 | 13 | 39 |
| 25–49 employees | 16 | 45 | 21 | 49 |
| 50–99 employees | 20 | 54 | 27 | 55 |
| 100–199 employees | 26 | 59 | 41 | 62 |
| 200–499 employees | 36 | 61 | 46 | 72 |
| 500 or more employees | 51 | 70 | 56 | 76 |
| *Organization status* | | | | |
| Stand-alone workplace | 14 | 43 | 8 | 40 |
| Part of a larger organization | 20 | 45 | 25 | 48 |
| *Organization size* | | | | |
| 10–99 employees | 12 | 41 | 7 | 38 |
| 100–999 employees | 22 | 49 | 25 | 41 |
| 1,000–9,999 employees | 24 | 47 | 30 | 54 |
| 10,000 or more employees | 22 | 48 | 29 | 58 |
| *Sector of ownership* | | | | |
| Private | 18 | 41 | 20 | 42 |
| Public | 16 | 56 | 18 | 63 |
| *Industry* | | | | |
| Manufacturing | 12 | 44 | 17 | 37 |
| Electricity, gas and water | (69) | (71) | (70) | (73) |
| Construction | 7 | 35 | 10 | 33 |
| Wholesale and retail | 23 | 34 | 23 | 36 |
| Hotels and restaurants | 15 | 23 | 20 | 33 |
| Transport and communication | 23 | 62 | 23 | 54 |
| Financial services | 53 | 69 | 25 | 61 |
| Other business services | 18 | 54 | 22 | 49 |
| Public administration | 16 | 76 | 35 | 74 |
| Education | 10 | 49 | 6 | 61 |
| Health and social work | 17 | 38 | 17 | 50 |
| Other community services | 19 | 49 | 22 | 59 |
| *Trade union recognition* | | | | |
| No union recognized | 16 | 40 | 16 | 39 |
| At least one union recognized | 21 | 53 | 27 | 62 |
| *Employment relations specialist at workplace* | | | | |
| Yes | 30 | 48 | 30 | 53 |
| No | 14 | 43 | 14 | 42 |

Base: All workplaces with 10 or more employees.
Figures are weighted and based on responses from 2,150 managers in 1998 and 2,024 managers in 2004.

organizations using tests and the range of occupations subject to testing (IRS, 1997). However, any such trend did not continue between 1998 and 2004. Overall, the proportions of workplaces using personality and performance tests for selection purposes remained unchanged. This was true across almost all types of workplace. The proportion of workplaces where performance tests were routinely used in two or more occupational groups was also similar in 1998 and 2004 (50 per cent and 48 per cent respectively). With respect to personality tests, the proportion of workplaces where these tests were used in two or more occupational groups decreased since 1998, from 64 per cent to 50 per cent.

## Working patterns

The hours employees are expected to work, and the pattern in which these hours are to be worked, are two of the key elements of an employee's contractual arrangements. Employer will wish to ensure that their employees' working patterns fit with the requirements of the organization, while employees naturally have their own interests and preferences in terms of the amount and scheduling of their contracted hours.

Around one-fifth (22 per cent) of employees reported working less than 30 hours a week on average, thereby meeting the commonly-agreed definition of part-time work.[3] The proportion of part-time employees reported by managers in the Employee Profile Questionnaire was slightly higher (27 per cent), probably reflecting a common discrepancy between contracted hours and actual hours worked.[4] The Cross-Section Survey of Managers showed that part-time workers were more heavily concentrated in the public, rather than the private sector (33 per cent compared to 25 per cent). While part-time employees made up 53 per cent of the workforce in Hotels and restaurants, they constituted less than one in ten employees in Manufacturing (5 per cent), Electricity, gas and water (9 per cent) and Construction (4 per cent).

The proportion of workplaces with no part-time workers fell slightly between 1998 and 2004 (from 21 per cent to 17 per cent) while the proportion in which more than half the workforce was part-time was almost unchanged (29 per cent and 30 per cent respectively). In 2004, private sector workplaces were more than twice as likely to have no part-time workers as public sector workplaces (19 per cent compared to 8 per cent). In contrast, part-time workers comprised more than half the workforce in almost two-fifths of public sector workplaces (39 per cent), compared to just over one quarter of private sector workplaces (27 per cent). However, within almost one-third of workplaces in the Hotels and restaurants sector, more than three-quarters of the workforce worked part-time.

Table 4.3 shows the relationship between the gender composition of the workforce, and the proportion of part-time workers. Eighty-three per cent of part-time employees were female and, generally speaking, a greater proportion of employees worked part-time where women made up a greater proportion of the workforce. Where at least three-quarters of employees were female, part-time

*Table 4.3* Percentage of employees working part-time, by gender composition of the workforce

| | % of employees working part-time | | | | | |
| --- | --- | --- | --- | --- | --- | --- |
| | None | 1–10 | 11–25 | 26–50 | 51–75 | More than 75 |
| | % of workplaces (row %) | | | | | |
| % of employees female | | | | | | |
| 1–25 | 41 | 37 | 14 | 7 | 1 | 1 |
| 26–74 | 12 | 20 | 19 | 21 | 16 | 12 |
| 75 or more | 2 | 6 | 11 | 26 | 33 | 22 |

Base: All workplaces with 10 or more employees.
Figures are weighted and based on responses from 2,052 managers.

staff accounted for more than half of the workforce in 55 per cent of workplaces; in contrast, where three-quarters of employees were male, the figure was just 2 per cent. In more than two-fifths (44 per cent) of all workplaces with at least some part-time workers, none of these part-time workers were male. This figure was almost unchanged from 1998, when 45 per cent of workplaces with part-time employees had no male part-time staff.

Some employers introduce working time practices which allow them to operate around the clock, at weekends, meet surges in demand, or to respond to staffing shortages. A greater proportion of part-time staff were employed in workplaces which were open six or seven days a week, than in those that opened Monday to Friday only.[5] However, workplaces which were open 24 hours a day employed a similar proportion of part-time staff to those which only opened within the hours of 8.00 am–6.30 pm.[6] This is perhaps because workplaces which were open 24 hours a day made use of shift-workers rather than employing part-time staff to cover these hours (84 per cent of workplaces which were open 24 hours a day employed shift-workers). As might be expected, shift-working was relatively uncommon in workplaces where the usual operating hours were between 8.00 am and 6.30 pm (12 per cent of these workplaces had shift-workers), while almost two-fifths (39 per cent) of workplaces which were usually open at some other time, but not 24 hours a day, employed shift-workers. Only 16 per cent of workplaces open from Monday to Friday, and 17 per cent of workplaces open six days a week, employed shift-workers, compared to 56 per cent of workplaces which opened seven days a week.

Overall, 32 per cent of workplaces had some staff working shifts, but large workplaces were more likely to employ shift-workers than smaller workplaces. Use of shifts was far more common in some sectors than in others. Less than one in ten workplaces in Construction (6 per cent), Financial services (8 per cent) and Education (8 per cent) operated a shift system, compared to more than half of all workplaces in Electricity, gas and water (64 per cent), Hotels and restaurants (51 per cent) and Health and social work (59 per cent).

Six per cent of workplaces made use of annual-hours contracts for some employees, while 5 per cent used zero-hours contracts. Annual and zero-hours contracts were generally more common in larger workplaces and establishments that were part of a larger organization, than in small workplaces or single, independent workplaces. A greater proportion of public sector workplaces than private sector establishments made use of annual-hours contracts (14 per cent and 4 per cent respectively). Also, private sector workplaces where unions were recognized were more likely to employ some staff on annual-hours contracts than those which did not recognize unions (13 per cent and 3 per cent respectively), and a difference remained even after controlling for workplace size. Both annual-hours and zero-hours contracts were more common in workplaces that operated shifts than in workplaces without shift-working arrangements.

## Contractual status

The expected length of the contractual engagement is also a fundamental aspect of the employment relationship, not least because the nature of the contract has been shown historically to have a bearing on a number of other conditions, such as access to training and rates of pay (Booth *et al.*, 2000). Employers are now obliged to treat fixed-term workers in the same way as comparable permanent workers, but there remain substantial numbers of employees who are employed under contracts that are not open-ended.

Ninety-two per cent of employees reported that they had a permanent contract, while 5 per cent were employed on a temporary contract with no agreed end date, and 3 per cent had a fixed-term contract.[7] Management respondents also reported that 7 per cent of employees were on temporary or fixed-term contracts (henceforward referred to in combination as fixed-term contracts). The use of fixed-term contracts was most prevalent in Education and Other community services, with 14 per cent of the workforce in these workplaces on these contracts, while their use was least common in Electricity, gas and water (1 per cent) and Financial services (2 per cent).

Thirty per cent of workplaces had at least some staff employed on fixed-term contracts. However, there was considerable variation between different types of workplaces. Larger workplaces were more likely to have some staff on fixed-term contracts than smaller workplaces, and workplaces which were part of a larger organization were more likely to make use of fixed-term contracts than single independent workplaces (34 per cent compared to 21 per cent). More than three-fifths (61 per cent) of workplaces in the public sector had some employees on fixed-term contracts, compared to less than one quarter (23 per cent) of private sector workplaces. Workplaces where at least one union was recognized were also more likely to make use of fixed-term contracts than workplaces where no unions were recognized, but this appeared to be due to the fact that, on average, workplaces where unions were recognized were larger than those without union recognition as this relationship disappeared when workplaces of a similar size were compared. Workplaces in the Education sector were particularly likely to make use of fixed-term contracts (76 per cent did so), while over half of all workplaces in Public administration (54 per cent) employed some staff on fixed-term contracts. Workplaces in the Wholesale and retail and Hotels and restaurants sectors were particularly unlikely to have any fixed-term employees. Just 15 per cent and 11 per cent respectively had any employees on such contracts.

Table 4.4 shows the proportion of workplaces where some employees from a particular occupational group were employed on fixed-term contracts, according to managers. Workplaces were most likely to have Professional and Administrative and secretarial staff on fixed-term contracts (8 per cent of all workplaces had staff from either group on fixed-term contracts). But in workplaces that employed staff in Caring, leisure and other personal service occupations, managers were just as likely to use fixed-term contracts for this group as for Professionals (Table 4.4, column 2). Workplaces were least likely to use fixed-term contracts for Managers and senior officials and for Skilled trades. A comparison of columns 2 and 3 in Table 4.4 indicates that fixed-term contracts were more commonly used when an occupation formed the core group within a workplace. This shows the persistence of the use of fixed-term contracts to augment the core workforce, as observed by Cully *et al.* (1999: 37–38), and is counter to the core–periphery model of labour market segmentation, which suggests that fixed-term contracts are primarily used among the peripheral, rather than the core, workforce.

Managers were asked whether fixed-term contracts had been introduced for employees who in the past would have been employed on open-ended contracts. In almost one-third (30 per cent) of workplaces with some fixed-term workers all of these employees were carrying out work previously done by staff on open-ended contracts. In a further 8 per cent of workplaces, fixed-term contracts were

*Table 4.4* Fixed-term contracts, by occupation

| | % of workplaces | | |
| --- | --- | --- | --- |
| | *All workplaces* | *Workplaces employing some staff in the specified occupation* | *Workplaces where specified occupation is the largest occupational group* |
| All occupations | 30 | – | – |
| Managers and senior officials | 2 | 2 | – |
| Professional | 8 | 23 | 49 |
| Associate professional and technical | 5 | 17 | 30 |
| Administrative and secretarial | 8 | 12 | 26 |
| Skilled trades | 1 | 4 | 8 |
| Caring, leisure and other personal service | 4 | 24 | 28 |
| Sales and customer service | 5 | 12 | 18 |
| Process, plant and machine operative | 2 | 8 | 13 |
| Elementary | 4 | 10 | 16 |

Base: All workplaces with 10 or more employees.

used for some employees who were previously in permanent positions, while in the remaining three-fifths of workplaces this had never been the case. The most common reason for using fixed-term contracts was to respond to a temporary increase in demand. More than one-third (36 per cent) of workplaces with some fixed-term employees made use of them for this reason. Almost one quarter (24 per cent) of workplaces used fixed-term contracts to cover for maternity leave or long-term absence. Fixed-term contracts were used to obtain specialist skills in 17 per cent of workplaces with such contracts, and 16 per cent of workplaces with some fixed-term employees used them to decide whether an employee should be taken on in a permanent job. Less than one in ten workplaces used fixed-term contracts to respond to a freeze on permanent staff numbers, in pursuit of enhanced performance, because of time-limited funding, or due to budget restrictions or financial constraints.

Faced with skills shortages, some argue that employers have engaged in short-term measures such as buying-in, poaching, outsourcing or using temporary workers rather than investing in training (Sisson and Storey, 2000a). The general issue of training is considered next.

## Off-the-job training

The UK has generally been characterized by a 'voluntaristic' approach to training, with employers and employees taking primary responsibility for training matters, while the state performs a facilitator's role.[8] Since 1997, the Labour Government has sought to increase participation in further and higher education, motivated in part by concerns about the UK's performance in comparison with other developed economies. However, it has retained support for a voluntary approach to workplace learning and some argue that, despite the increased focus on the supply of skills, a number of structural factors − such as the erosion of skilled manual employment − continue to limit employers' demand for higher-level skills (Keep and Rainbird, 2003: 415). Nevertheless, the evidence from WERS 2004 and other recent surveys suggests that the provision of workplace training has increased in recent years.

The 2004 Cross-Section Survey of Managers enquired about the extent of training for which core employees were given time off from their normal work duties, whether that training took place at their immediate work position or elsewhere. Over four-fifths of all workplaces (84 per cent) had provided such 'off-the-job' training for some of their experienced core employees over the previous year, while almost half (47 per cent) had provided it for at least three-fifths of core employees (Table 4.5). The available evidence suggests that this represents a marked increase in provision since 1998.

In the 1998 Cross-Section Survey, 73 per cent of employers provided training for some of their experienced core employees and 31 per cent provided it for at least three-fifths of these employees. A change in the wording of this question since 1998 means that direct comparisons with the 2004 Cross-Section are somewhat tentative: the question wording in the 1998 survey was arguably less

*Table 4.5* Off-the-job training and performance appraisals

| | % workplaces | | | |
| --- | --- | --- | --- | --- |
| | *Off-the-job training for …* | | *Regular appraisals for …* | |
| | *Any experienced core employees* | *60% or more experienced core employees* | *Any non-managerial employees* | *60% or more non-managerial employees* |
| All workplaces | 84 | 47 | 71 | 64 |
| *Workplace size* | | | | |
| 10–24 employees | 79 | 41 | 65 | 60 |
| 25–49 employees | 88 | 51 | 77 | 68 |
| 50–99 employees | 94 | 62 | 81 | 72 |
| 100–199 employees | 95 | 51 | 82 | 75 |
| 200–499 employees | 94 | 55 | 89 | 74 |
| 500 or more employees | 98 | 63 | 91 | 81 |
| *Organization status* | | | | |
| Stand-alone workplace | 69 | 36 | 53 | 47 |
| Part of a larger organization | 92 | 52 | 80 | 72 |
| *Organization size* | | | | |
| 10–99 employees | 71 | 35 | 54 | 49 |
| 100–999 employees | 92 | 46 | 73 | 69 |
| 1,000–9,999 employees | 93 | 59 | 83 | 73 |
| 10,000 or more employees | 95 | 59 | 91 | 82 |
| *Sector of ownership* | | | | |
| Private | 81 | 41 | 68 | 62 |
| Public | 98 | 72 | 86 | 77 |
| *Industry* | | | | |
| Manufacturing | 73 | 28 | 51 | 41 |
| Electricity, gas and water | (100) | (82) | (90) | (77) |
| Construction | 78 | 37 | 44 | 38 |
| Wholesale and retail | 87 | 36 | 67 | 61 |
| Hotels and restaurants | 53 | 27 | 54 | 48 |
| Transport and communication | 90 | 55 | 58 | 49 |
| Financial services | 96 | 77 | 96 | 96 |
| Other business services | 87 | 40 | 81 | 74 |
| Public administration | 100 | 72 | 84 | 80 |
| Education | 95 | 73 | 96 | 78 |
| Health and social work | 94 | 69 | 89 | 84 |
| Other community services | 85 | 47 | 62 | 66 |
| *Trade union recognition* | | | | |
| No union recognized | 79 | 39 | 65 | 59 |
| At least one union recognized | 96 | 66 | 86 | 76 |
| *Employment relations specialist at workplace* | | | | |
| Yes | 92 | 53 | 82 | 74 |
| No | 82 | 44 | 66 | 60 |

Base: All workplaces with 10 or more employees.
Figures are weighted and based on responses from 2,025 managers (training) and 2,023 managers (appraisals).

explicit, as it referred directly to 'formal off-the-job training' and offered a definition only by way of an interviewer prompt. However, the 1998–2004 Panel Survey, which did not alter the wording of this question, also shows a notable increase in provision among continuing workplaces: 89 per cent provided some off-the-job training to core employees in 2004, compared with 79 per cent in 1998, and 54 per cent provided it to at least three-fifths of these employees, compared with only 34 per cent in the earlier period. Figures from the Learning and Training at Work surveys also record an increase in employer provision of off-the-job training between 1999 and 2002 (Spilsbury, 2003). And so it seems reasonable to infer that provision has increased, although the precise magnitude of the change among the full Cross-Section population may be difficult to ascertain.

In 2004, provision of off-the-job-training for experienced core employees was most likely in workplaces where core staff worked in Professional occupations (97 per cent) and least likely where core staff worked in Elementary occupations (65 per cent), Skilled trades (75 per cent) or as Plant, process and machine operatives (79 per cent). Comparing across other workplace characteristics, provision was more prevalent in larger workplaces, workplaces belonging to larger organizations, public sector workplaces and workplaces with recognized unions (Table 4.5). Comparing across industrial sectors, provision was most likely in workplaces in the Electricity, gas and water industry and in Public administration, and was lowest among Hotels and restaurants. Provision was also more common, overall, among workplaces with a personnel specialist. After controlling for each of these factors simultaneously, the occupation of core employees and the size of the organization were found to be the key determinants of the provision of off-the-job training.

Provision was higher in workplaces which had a strategic plan that covered employee development: training was provided in the vast majority (93 per cent) of workplaces where the plan covered employee development but only in 80 per cent of workplaces where the strategy did not. The presence of an Investors in People (IiP) award was also related to training provision, with training being provided in the great majority (94 per cent) of IiP-accredited workplaces but only in 79 per cent of workplaces that did not have such an award. Whether workplaces provided training was also related to the basis of demand for the establishment's main product or service. Workplaces for which demand was heavily dependent on price were less likely to provide off-the-job training to at least 60 per cent of their core employees than workplaces facing lower levels of price dependence (31 per cent, compared with 43 per cent). And workplaces for which demand was heavily dependent on quality were more likely to train at least 60 per cent of core staff than those with lower levels of dependence on quality (46 per cent, compared with 37 per cent).

Claims that there has been a shift in the basis of competition from price to product quality and service delivery would imply an increased need to train in customer care and total quality (Sisson and Storey, 2000a). On the other hand, new technology would be expected to lead to training needs on computing skills and the operation of new equipment. Current practice seemed to reflect the salience of all factors. Health and safety was the most common subject of training for core staff, with 70 per cent of workplaces covering this in their training for experienced employees in the core group. But this was followed by the operation of new equipment (50 per cent), computing skills and communication skills (45 per cent each), customer service (41 per cent), and quality control procedures (38 per cent).

In order to further investigate the rationale for providing training, managers were asked whether the training delivered in the previous year had any of five specific objectives, listed on a showcard. Over four-fifths (85 per cent) said that one of the objectives was to improve the skills already used by employees in their current jobs, and a similar proportion (81 per cent) said that the training aimed to extend the range of skills used by employees in these jobs. Around half (49 per cent) said that it aimed to increase employees' commitment to, and understanding of, the organization, and almost two-fifths (38 per cent) said that it provided the skills needed for employees to move to different jobs, perhaps signalling a commitment to multi-skilling. Around one-tenth (13 per cent) of employers said that one of the reasons for providing training was to gain IiP accreditation or some other quality standard, although very few cited this as the only objective. One in twenty (4 per cent) said that none of the five specified objectives applied to their training provision, while most (82 per cent) cited at least two of the five.

A more detailed insight into the types of workers who receive training can be obtained by referring to the Cross-Section Survey of Employees. Employees were asked whether they had received any training during the 12 months prior to the survey, for which they had been 'given time off from [their] normal work duties to undertake the training'. Health and safety training was specifically excluded, but the definition otherwise mirrored that used in the Cross-Section Survey of Managers. Over one-third (36 per cent) of employees had not received any training; almost one half (46 per cent) had received 1–4 days of training and the remaining 18 per cent had received five days or more. The corresponding question in the 1998 survey did not exclude health and safety, but the proportion of employees receiving training rose nonetheless (from 42 per cent in 1998), thereby supporting the picture of increased training provision that emerged from the establishment data.[9] It also corresponded with the trend in employees' responses to a question which asked whether managers at the workplace encouraged people to develop their skills: the proportion of employees either agreeing or strongly agreeing rose from 61 per cent in 1998 to 72 per cent in 2004.

Some argue that the UK is a relatively low-pay economy and that this has led to a 'low-skills equilibrium' with regards to training and development (see Keep and Mayhew, 1999). The data showed that those in the lower skilled occupations were less likely to receive training. Those least likely to receive training were Process, plant and machine operatives (43 per cent), employees in Elementary occupations (44 per cent) and those in Skilled trades (48 per cent);

those most likely to have received training, on the other hand, were Professionals (79 per cent), Associate professionals (77 per cent) and Managers (76 per cent). These employees were also the most likely to have had five or more days of training in the previous year, followed by those working in Caring, leisure and other personal service occupations. Those in Elementary occupations, Process, plant and machine operatives, and those working in Sales and customer service were the least likely to have had five or more days of training. Training provision was positively associated with the level of academic qualifications. Sixty-three per cent of employees whose highest qualification was at CSE, O-level or equivalent grades had received training, compared to 71 per cent of employees whose highest qualification was at A-level standard or equivalent, and 78 per cent of those with a degree or a higher qualification.

The amount of training received by employees appeared to affect their perceptions of the degree to which managers at their workplace encouraged skill development. The majority (57 per cent) of all employees agreed that managers at their workplace encouraged people to develop their skills, but the figure was 77 per cent among those employees that received five or more days of off-the-job training and 61 per cent among employees receiving between one and four days. The fact that 43 per cent of those that did not receive any off-the-job training still agreed with the statement suggests that *on-the-job* training is also important in forming employees' perceptions of the adequacy of their employers' approach to skill development. Employees' responses to a question asking them to rate their degree of satisfaction with the training they received at their workplace also indicate that on-the-job training makes an important contribution. Overall, 51 per cent of employees were either 'satisfied' or 'very satisfied' with the training they received, and this figure rose to 73 per cent among those receiving five days or more. But a substantial proportion (37 per cent) of employees who had received no off-the-job training in the previous year were also satisfied with training provision at their establishment. On-the-job training may have contributed towards their assessment, although it is equally possible that these employees may have been satisfied to have received no training in the year.

Evidence from various sources suggests that many employees are actually 'under-employed' and their qualifications and skills under-used (Alpin *et al.*, 1998; Chevalier, 2003; Green *et al.*, 2002). The WERS data also revealed the existence of a skills 'mismatch'. Employees were asked how well they felt the skills that they had matched the skills they needed to do their job. Twenty-two per cent of employees thought that their skills were much higher than required, while 32 per cent thought that their skills were a bit higher than needed. Forty-two per cent of employees believed that there was a good match between their skills and the skills required in their job. Only 4 per cent of employees thought that their own skills were lower than those needed in their job, with a further 1 per cent believing that their skills were much lower than required. Employees with higher academic or vocational qualifications were more likely to believe that their skills exceeded those needed to do their job than employees with lower levels of qualifications. Fifty-six per cent of employees with the equivalent of NVQ level-four qualifications or higher believed that their skills were higher than needed, compared to 42 per cent of employees with no academic or vocational qualifications. This suggests that, while a large proportion of employees of all qualification levels felt that they did not make full use of their qualifications at work, the most highly-qualified employees felt this most keenly.

Although a similar proportion of employees from each of the nine broad occupational groups felt that their skills were lower than required in their job, there was a difference in the proportion of employees who felt that their skills exceeded those required. Employees in Sales and customer service or Elementary occupations and Process, plant and machine operatives were particularly likely to believe that their skills exceeded those required in their job, while Professionals were the group least likely to take this view, despite having higher levels of qualifications on average. Professionals and employees in Caring, leisure and other personal service occupations were most likely to report a good match between their skills and the skills needed in their job (48 per cent of employees in both occupations did so), while the skills match was lowest for Sales and customer service employees and Process, plant and machine operatives (both 38 per cent).

## Performance appraisals

Appraisals constitute one of the main tools for evaluating and managing employee performance. They may serve various purposes, including the identification of training needs and employee development planning. Some commentators reported an increased use of performance appraisals in Britain in the 1990s, particularly in managerial and professional work (Gallie *et al.*, 1998; IRS, 1999). WERS 2004 shows that this trend seems to have continued: in 2004, 78 per cent of workplaces reported undertaking performance appraisals, compared with 73 per cent in 1998. Performance appraisals were not always conducted on a regular basis or used for all employees. Two-thirds (64 per cent) of all workplaces conducted *regular* appraisals for *most* (60 per cent or more) non-managerial employees. This again represented an increase since 1998, when the equivalent figure was 48 per cent.

Employers are also increasingly exploring different ways of conducting appraisals. This partly reflects their attempts to gain employees' acceptance of the value of the process. Bach (2000) reports on the emergence of a broader approach to performance appraisal, signalled by the shift towards an element of self-appraisal, the use of more diverse criteria, and interest in 360-degree appraisal. Traditionally appraisals have been conducted for managerial staff (ibid.), and this remains common. In almost three-quarters (73 per cent) of workplaces employing managers, they had their performance formally appraised. However, appraisals are rarely restricted to staff in managerial grades; indeed, the proportion of workplaces where *only* managers were appraised decreased from 8 per cent in 1998 to 3 per cent in 2004. Along with managers, workplaces also commonly appraised the performance of Professional staff (82 per cent of workplaces employing Professionals), Caring, leisure and other personal service staff (79 per cent of workplaces employing this group) and Associate professional and technical employees (77 per cent of workplaces with this category of employee).

Almost all workplaces (94 per cent) that appraised the performance of at least some non-managerial staff did so among the core group of employees. Overall, 70 per cent of workplaces appraised the performance of core employees, with the figure being highest where Professionals were the core group (93 per cent) and lowest where core employees were Process, plant and machine operatives (40 per cent). The likelihood that employees in a particular occupation had their performance appraised was generally higher if that group formed the core staff at a workplace, although appraisals were less likely for Process, plant and machine operatives if they formed the core group and there was no difference in respect of employees in Elementary occupations.

The types of workplaces using appraisals were similar to those conducting testing for employee selection purposes. Larger workplaces were more likely to conduct appraisals, as were workplaces that were part of large organizations, those with recognized unions and those with a personnel specialist (Table 4.5). However, the associations with union recognition and the presence of a specialist were no longer significant after controlling for the occupation of core employees, workplace size and organization size. Even though the public sector had little tradition of the use of performance appraisal (Long, 1986), the use of appraisals in the public sector increased in the 1990s partly as a result of governments' attempts to introduce private sector 'best practice' into the public sector (Winchester and Bach, 1995). Indeed, public sector workplaces were more likely than private sector workplaces to conduct performance appraisals in 1998, and this gap remained in 2004. Sixty-nine per cent of public sector workplaces conducted appraisals for non-managerials in 1998, compared to 56 per cent of private sector workplaces; by 2004, the proportions of workplaces conducting appraisals for non-managerials had gone up to 86 per cent in the public sector and 68 per cent in the private sector.

Appraisals were typically conducted annually: 64 per cent of workplaces conducted appraisals for non-managerial staff on an annual basis and a further 16 per cent of workplaces conducted half-yearly appraisals. Ten per cent conducted appraisals on a quarterly basis. The remainder conducted appraisals either bi-annually or to no fixed pattern. Annual appraisals were particularly common in the public sector (76 per cent, compared with 61 per cent in the private sector). In three-quarters of workplaces that conducted appraisals for non-managerial staff these appraisals were conducted by the employee's immediate line manager or supervisor, with appraisals in most other workplaces being conducted by a more senior manager.

Performance appraisals resulted in an evaluation of employees' training needs in the vast majority of workplaces where they were conducted (96 per cent), whereas employees' pay was linked to the outcome in around one-third (36 per cent). The role of individual performance pay and especially the role of training in appraisals seem to have gained in importance. The data showed that appraisals were used for these two purposes to a greater extent in 2004 than in 1998, when 86 per cent of workplaces linked appraisals to a training needs assessment and 31 per cent of workplaces linked them to employees' pay, suggesting a more strategic approach in the use of performance appraisals.[10]

## Work organization

While many have noted the importance of continuous appraisal and development in helping workplaces to secure a competitive advantage, work organization has also been at the forefront of these debates. Much of the recent interest in this area has been focused on arrangements that are intended to encourage a more collaborative and flexible approach to work tasks; the most commonly cited include team-working, functional flexibility and the use of problem-solving groups (see, for example, Ichniowski *et al.*, 1996; Wood and de Menezes, 1998; Wood, 1999; Capelli and Neumark, 2001; Godard, 2001a, 2004).

There has been much discussion about the potential for such practices to enhance employees' sense of involvement in their work, and thus to contribute to improved workplace performance. However, the existing evidence suggests that the take-up of such practices among employers has been far from universal (Cully *et al.*, 1999; Forth and Millward, 2004; White *et al.*, 2004). This has led some to raise questions about the potential costs involved in revising work processes (Godard, 2001a: 28). Others have also questioned the extent to which such arrangements may result merely in effort intensification rather than employee empowerment (Hyman and Mason, 1995).

The sections which follow examine the use of these practices. The degree of job autonomy and influence, and associations with work intensity and employee well-being, are also investigated later in the chapter.

### *Team-working*

Management respondents to the Cross-Section Survey were asked whether any of their core employees worked in 'formally designated teams'. Team-working was present among core employees in almost three-quarters (72 per cent) of all workplaces (Table 4.6). The incidence of team-working varied substantially according to the work being done by core employees, however. Comparing across each of the eight non-managerial Major Groups of the *Standard Occupational Classification (2000)*, team-working was most common where core employees worked in Professional occupations (91 per cent) or Associate professional and technical occupations (90 per cent), and least common where core employees were engaged in Sales and customer service occupations (59 per cent). The likelihood that at least some core employees worked in formally designated

Table 4.6 Team-working arrangements, by occupation of core employees

| | Any team-working | Teams ... | | | | | A–D | A–E |
|---|---|---|---|---|---|---|---|---|
| | | ... are given responsibility for specific products or services (A) | ... depend on each other's work (B) | ... rotate tasks or roles (C) | ... jointly decide how work is to be done (D) | ... can appoint own leaders (E) | | |
| | % workplaces | % workplaces (where team-working) | | | | | | |
| All workplaces | 72 | 83 | 81 | 66 | 61 | 6 | 34 | 4 |
| *Occupation of core employees* | | | | | | | | |
| Professional | 91 | 91 | 74 | 45 | 80 | 9 | 29 | 4 |
| Associate professional and technical | 90 | 89 | 76 | 53 | 69 | 5 | 32 | 2 |
| Administrative and secretarial | 73 | 86 | 79 | 64 | 60 | 6 | 30 | 4 |
| Skilled trades | 68 | 79 | 83 | 57 | 51 | 7 | 18 | 3 |
| Caring, leisure and other personal service | 77 | 80 | 80 | 73 | 69 | 2 | 40 | 2 |
| Sales and customer service | 59 | 92 | 82 | 81 | 48 | 6 | 39 | 5 |
| Process, plant and machine operatives | 65 | 67 | 85 | 70 | 50 | 4 | 37 | 3 |
| Elementary occupations | 67 | 74 | 87 | 79 | 61 | 6 | 42 | 5 |

Base (column 1): All workplaces with 10 or more employees.
Base (columns 2–8): All workplaces with 10 or more employees and formal team-working arrangements.
Figures are weighted and based on responses from 2,050 managers (column 1) and at least 1,745 managers (columns 2–8).

teams increased with establishment size, and was higher in the public sector (88 per cent) than the private sector (68 per cent). Both associations held after controlling for the occupation of the core group of employees. Comparing across industry sectors, team-working was most likely to be found among core employees in Public administration (91 per cent), Construction (89 per cent) and Education (88 per cent); it was least common in Transport and communications (55 per cent) and Wholesale and retail (51 per cent).

Team-working arrangements did not always extend to the full complement of core employees, but 80 per cent of workplaces with team-working among core employees extended these working arrangements to at least two-thirds of core employees and 51 per cent extended them to all core employees. Also, the way in which team-working operated was not always consistent across workplaces. The 2004 survey asked about five specific features of workplaces' team-working arrangements. The survey found that in 83 per cent of instances, teams were given responsibility for specific products or services; in 81 per cent, team members depended on each other's work to be able to do their job; in 66 per cent, tasks were rotated among members of the team; and in 61 per cent, team members jointly decided how work was to be done. But in just 6 per cent were team members able to appoint their own team leaders. The first four characteristics were shared by around one-third (34 per cent) of the instances of team-working, while only 4 per cent shared all five (Table 4.6). These two figures did not vary greatly according to the occupation of those engaged in team-working, but there was some variability across occupations in the prevalence of each of the five individual characteristics. In particular, teams involving Professional workers were among the most likely to have responsibility for specific products and services and to be able to jointly decide how work was to be done, but they were among the least likely to depend upon each other's work and to rotate tasks among team members.

One-third (34 per cent) of workplaces had trained at least some of their experienced core employees in team-working in the year prior to the survey. This figure was 37 per cent in workplaces where core employees worked in formally designated teams and, here, the likelihood of training was positively associated with the proportion of core employees engaged in team-working. The figure was 27 per cent in workplaces without team-working arrangements for core employees, indicating that a minority of workplaces encouraged collaborative working among core employees in the absence of formal teams. Overall, around four-fifths (79 per cent) of all workplaces either had some core employees working in formally designated teams, or had trained at least some core employees in team-working in the year prior to the survey.

The overall incidence and operation of team-working had changed little since 1998, when 74 per cent of all workplaces involved at least some core employees in formally designated teams. But there was less stability among continuing workplaces between 1998 and 2004. Around three-fifths (62 per cent) of workplaces reported formal team-working arrangements among core employees in both years, while 12 per cent had these arrangements only in 1998 and 11 per cent had them only in 2004. The remaining 15 per cent of continuing workplaces did not have formal team-working arrangements in either year.

### *Multi-skilling and functional flexibility*

Multi-skilling, or cross-training, involves training employees to do jobs other than their own. It is intended to increase the degree of functional flexibility within a workplace, and stands in contrast to arrangements designed to enhance numerical flexibility, covered elsewhere in this chapter. Two-thirds (66 per cent) of workplaces formally trained at least some core employees to be functionally flexible (Table 4.7). As in the case of team-working arrangements, the overall incidence of multi-skilling had changed little since 1998, when 69 per cent of all workplaces formally trained at least some core employees to be functionally flexible. However, fewer workplaces in 2004 were training substantial proportions of their core employees in this way: 29 per cent of workplaces in 1998 trained at least three-fifths of their core employees to be able to do other jobs, but this figure was just 19 per cent in 2004.

Comparing core employees from each of the eight non-managerial groups of the *Standard Occupational Classification (2000)*, multi-skilling was most common among Process, plant and machine operatives, with 75 per cent of workplaces in

*Table* 4.7 Multi-skilling and functional flexibility, by occupation of core employees

| | *% workplaces* | | | |
|---|---|---|---|---|
| | *% of core employees trained to do jobs other than their own* | | *% of core employees doing jobs other than their own at least once a week* | |
| | *Any* | *60% or more* | *Any* | *60% or more* |
| All workplaces | 66 | 19 | 65 | 16 |
| *Occupation of core employees* | | | | |
| Professional | 58 | 10 | 47 | 6 |
| Associate professional and technical | 60 | 16 | 60 | 17 |
| Administrative and secretarial | 75 | 19 | 75 | 16 |
| Skilled trades | 63 | 20 | 64 | 13 |
| Caring, leisure and other personal service | 62 | 14 | 57 | 11 |
| Sales and customer service | 66 | 22 | 68 | 22 |
| Process, plant and machine operatives | 75 | 25 | 75 | 19 |
| Elementary occupations | 68 | 19 | 65 | 17 |

Base: All workplaces with 10 or more employees.
Figures are weighted and based on responses from 2,012 managers (columns 1 and 2) and 2,011 managers (columns 3 and 4).

which these were the core group training at least some of them to be functionally flexible, and 25 per cent training at least three-fifths. It was least
common among Professionals, where the equivalent figures were 58 per cent
and 10 per cent respectively. Comparing across industry sectors, multi-skilling
was most common in Manufacturing and Financial services and least common
in Education and Other business services. It was also more common among
workplaces with multiple products or services than among workplaces with a
single product or service, even after controlling for workplace size.

There is an obvious connection between the concepts of multi-skilling and
job rotation, and this association was evident in practice as multi-skilling took
place in three-quarters of workplaces in which core employees worked in teams
with formal job rotation. However, multi-skilling was also common in the
absence of this particular arrangement. It took place in around two-thirds (65
per cent) of workplaces with teams that did not rotate tasks, and in 57 per cent
of workplaces where core employees did not work in formally designated teams.

A new question in the 2004 survey went beyond the issue of training to
establish the extent to which employees were actually being called upon to be
functionally flexible. Overall, 65 per cent of workplaces had at least some core
employees doing jobs other than their own at least once a week, with this
proportion being highest where the core employees were Administrative and
secretarial workers or Process, plant and machine operatives (both 75 per cent)
and lowest where the core employees were Professionals (47 per cent) (Table 4.7).
In only 16 per cent of workplaces did the proportion of employees who were
practising functional flexibility reach three-fifths, with the proportion again
being lowest where the core employees were Professionals (6 per cent) and
being highest where they were Sales workers (22 per cent). These figures indicate that the incidence of functional flexibility was closely associated with the
incidence of multi-skilling. Only 7 per cent of all workplaces trained their core
employees to be able to do jobs other than their own, but did not call upon
these skills on a regular basis, although in many other workplaces the proportion of core employees who had been trained exceeded the proportion regularly
using these skills. There was a small proportion of workplaces (6 per cent) in
which core employees were doing jobs other than their own at least once a week
despite the absence of any formal training in multi-skilling, such that almost
three-quarters (73 per cent) of all workplaces appeared to have at least some
intended capacity for functional flexibility.

## Problem-solving groups

The third arrangement discussed here under the 'work organization' heading
involves meetings between employees to discuss aspects of work performance or
solve task-related problems. These are commonly referred to as 'problem-solving groups' or 'continuous improvement groups' or, in situations where the
prime object is to improve quality, they are often referred to as 'quality circles'. Such
groups comprise one form of direct, upward communication but, in contrast to

the more general forms of upward communication discussed in Chapter 5, the motives here are primarily task-oriented.

Managers in the Cross-Section Survey were asked whether there were any groups of non-managerial employees at their workplace who solved specific problems or discussed aspects of performance or quality. Such groups were present in one-fifth (21 per cent) of all workplaces (Table 4.8). A change in the wording of the question on problem-solving groups between the 1998 and 2004 Cross-Section Surveys, introduced with the intention of excluding groups consisting solely of managers, means that one must be cautious when estimating the degree of change in the incidence of problem-solving groups. However, by comparing the results from the Cross-Section Surveys with estimates from the 1998–2004 Panel Survey, where the question remained unchanged, it is possible to identify a small increase in the incidence of problem-solving groups between 1998 and 2004 under either definition.[11] It is estimated that, in 1998, 16 per cent of workplaces had problem-solving groups under the criteria applied in the 2004 survey. Adopting the less restrictive definition used in the 1998 survey, it is estimated that the incidence has risen from 28 per cent of workplaces to 36 per cent.

In 2004, problem-solving groups were most common in workplaces where core employees were from Professional occupations (44 per cent), Associate professional and technical occupations (30 per cent), and Administrative and secretarial occupations (29 per cent). In workplaces where core employees belonged to any one of the remaining five non-managerial occupational categories, the incidence of problem-solving groups did not exceed 20 per cent. It was therefore not surprising to see that such groups were commonly found in Public administration (42 per cent), Financial services (34 per cent) and Education (32 per cent), each of which have high proportions of white-collar staff. Larger workplaces were also more likely than smaller workplaces to operate problem-solving groups, although few workplaces of any size involved substantial proportions of their staff in such arrangements. Less than one in ten

*Table 4.8*  Problem-solving groups involving non-managerial employees, by size of establishment

|  | *% workplaces* | | | |
|  | *None* | *Temporary* | *Permanent* | *Mixture of both* |
|---|---|---|---|---|
| All workplaces | 79 | 7 | 10 | 4 |
| *Size of establishment* | | | | |
| 10–24 employees | 85 | 4 | 8 | 3 |
| 25–49 employees | 77 | 7 | 11 | 6 |
| 50–99 employees | 66 | 13 | 15 | 6 |
| 100–199 employees | 60 | 16 | 20 | 4 |
| 200–499 employees | 59 | 20 | 13 | 7 |
| 500 or more employees | 49 | 27 | 12 | 12 |

Base: All workplaces with 10 or more employees.
Figures are weighted and based on responses from 2,048 managers.

workplaces (8 per cent) involved at least three-fifths of their employees in problem-solving groups. This figure rose to 22 per cent in workplaces where the core employees were Professionals.

A distinction can be made between groups that come together for a limited period of time, perhaps to discuss a particular project, innovation or problem, and groups who discuss work-related matters on an on-going basis. Half of all workplaces with problem-solving groups (49 per cent) reported that the groups at their workplace were permanent; one-third (32 per cent) reported that they were predominantly in place only for a fixed period of time, and the remaining fifth (19 per cent) reported a mixture of both types of arrangement. Problem-solving groups were more likely to be permanent in smaller workplaces than in larger workplaces. Among workplaces with fewer than 25 employees, 56 per cent of those with problem-solving groups reported permanent arrangements while among workplaces with 500 or more employees, the figure was just 24 per cent.

Questions on the nature of training delivered to core employees over the previous year indicated that training in problem-solving skills was more common than the existence of formal groups; one-third (34 per cent) of all workplaces had trained at least some core employees in problem-solving skills in the year prior to the survey. Less than half (47 per cent) of all workplaces with formal groups had provided such training in the previous year, but it had been provided in almost one-third (31 per cent) of workplaces that did not have problem-solving groups. Consequently, it seemed that there were a substantial number of workplaces which encouraged a problem-solving approach among their employees without necessarily setting up formal groups. This is in keeping with the results in respect of team-working and functional flexibility, discussed above. Overall, 45 per cent of all workplaces either operated formal problem-solving groups among non-managerial employees or had trained at least some core employees in problem-solving skills within the year prior to the survey.

Finally, in this section on problem-solving groups, it is appropriate to include a brief mention of the incidence of suggestion schemes, as these are also intended to elicit comments from employees as to how work processes may be improved. Overall, 30 per cent of workplaces operated suggestion schemes (31 per cent in 1998). They are not discussed in detail here, since such schemes may equally be used as a means for employees to provide comments on broader aspects of the working environment and so they are covered along with other more general forms of direct, upward communication in Chapter 5. But it is notable that suggestion schemes appeared to be complementary to the use of problem-solving groups, rather than acting as substitutes. Two-fifths (41 per cent) of workplaces with problem-solving groups also operated a suggestion scheme, whereas the proportion was around one quarter (27 per cent) in all other workplaces.

## Bundles of 'high-involvement' task practices

Team-working, functional flexibility and problem-solving groups have been much discussed in the extensive literature relating to the prevalence and impact of what is commonly referred to as 'high-performance', 'high-commitment' or 'high-involvement' management. There is little consistency in the way in which this approach is defined or measured, but there is at least a broad consensus that these three practices lie at the core of the approach (see, for example, Geary, 2003: 339–340). As the literature tends to emphasize the co-existence of bundles of practices, this section briefly investigates the extent to which arrangements for team-working, functional flexibility and problem-solving are found together in British workplaces. The precise definition of the practices and how they are bundled may, or may not, have a substantive bearing on any association with performance; an initial exploration of the association between workplace practices and workplace productivity and performance is presented in Chapter 10. But the results which follow show that the definitions used, and the way in which practices are grouped, clearly do have a bearing on estimates of incidence.

One in seven workplaces (14 per cent) engaged at least some core employees in formally designated teams, had at least some who were regularly doing jobs other than their own and engaged at least some non-managerial employees in formal problem-solving groups. Restricting the definition of team-working so as to ensure that team members depended on each other's work and jointly decided how work was to be done – in support of notions of interdependence and team autonomy – reduced this proportion to around one in ten workplaces (9 per cent). It would naturally decline further if one were to require that these arrangements were extended to substantial proportions of employees within each workplace. Moving in the opposite direction, a third, broader definition that encompasses workplaces which, although they did not have the formal practices in place, nonetheless trained at least some of their core employees in the equivalent skills, raised the proportion from around one in seven to around one in three (36 per cent).

The associations with specific workplace characteristics were consistent across each of the three definitions proposed above. Workplaces were more likely to have the specified bundles of practices if they were large rather than small, if they were foreign-owned rather than domestically owned, and if they recognized trade unions. Comparing between workplaces with different types of core staff, those in which core employees were Professionals tended to be most likely to have these bundles of practices, while workplaces in which core staff were from Skilled trades or Elementary occupations tended to be least likely to do so. After controlling for the occupation of core employees, workplaces were also more likely to have bundles that met the first and third definitions where a higher proportion of staff worked with computers; the likelihood of having a bundle that met the second definition was also greater but the association was not statistically significant. These latter associations lend some support to notions of complementarity between information technology and 'high-involvement' task practices (Brynjolfsson and Hitt, 2000).

Any assessments of the extent of change in the incidence of these bundles of practices must be interpreted with caution, because of the changes in question wording that have already been noted. However, indicators that could be derived in the Panel Survey, where questions have remained unchanged, suggested small increases in the incidence of such bundles among continuing workplaces. The proportion of continuing workplaces with team-working, multi-skilling and problem-solving groups rose from 22 per cent in 1998 to 29 per cent in 2004, but the increase was smaller (from 15 per cent to 19 per cent) when this criteria was restricted to include only interdependent teams with a degree of autonomy.

Some have argued that, among the practices that are proposed as being supportive of high-involvement work organization, job security is one of the most important as it provides employees with the reassurances that may be necessary to secure their commitment to improving efficiency (Applebaum and Batt, 1994: 165). The degree of job security appeared to have risen between 1998 and 2004, with the proportion of workplaces providing job security guarantees for at least some non-managerial employees rising from 10 per cent to 14 per cent, and the proportion of employees agreeing that they felt their job was secure rising from 60 per cent to 66 per cent. However, workplaces with bundles of high-involvement management practices were no more likely to offer job security guarantees than other types of workplace, and employees in these establishments were no more likely to feel that their job was secure.

## Job influence and autonomy

Much of the discussion about changing forms of work organization focuses on their potential to enhance job influence and autonomy, as a means of securing competitive advantage (see, for example, Ichniowski *et al.*, 1996: 300–301). But job influence and autonomy are also of interest in their own right, as sources of employee well-being (Budd, 2004: 26). The Cross-Section Survey of Employees asked about the degree of influence that employees had over five aspects of their job: the tasks they performed; the pace at which they worked; how they did their work; the order in which they carried out tasks; and the time they started or finished their working day. Responses were invited on a four-point scale, ranging from 'a lot' to 'none'; the results are presented in Figure 4.1. Employees' influence was highest in respect of how they did their work and the order in which they carried out tasks: around half of all employees had 'a lot' of influence over these aspects of their job. Employees' influence was lowest in respect of start and finish times, with only one quarter (26 per cent) having 'a lot' of influence over this item and one-third (35 per cent) having no influence at all. The second and third items in Figure 4.1 were directly comparable with questions included in the 1998 Survey of Employees, and a comparison between the two surveys showed small increases in the proportion of employees with 'a lot' of influence over the pace of their work (34 per cent in 1998) and how they did their work (47 per cent in 1998).

In 2004, the degree of influence on all five aspects of employees' jobs was markedly higher among older employees than among younger employees. The degree of influence was also highest among Managers and senior officials, while

*Figure 4.1* Employees' perceptions of job influence

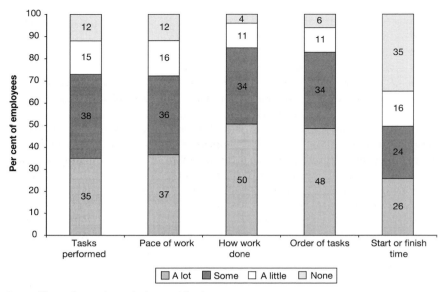

Base: All employees in workplaces with 10 or more.
Figures are weighted and based on responses from at least 21,222 employees.

Sales and customer service employees commonly reported the least influence among the nine broad occupational groups. Otherwise there was no clear hierarchy among occupations, except that those in Professional occupations, Associate professional and technical occupations and Administrative and secretarial jobs reported greater degrees of influence over the order in which they carried out tasks and start and finish times than did other non-managerial occupations. After controlling for age and occupation, men had greater influence than women over the tasks they performed in their job and over start and finish times, but women had greater influence over the order in which they carried out tasks. Employees with dependent children had slightly greater influence over their start and finish times than other employees, and there remained a statistically significant difference after controlling for gender, age and occupation. However, the overall difference was relatively small: 28 per cent of employees with dependent children had 'a lot' of influence over their start or finish times, compared with 25 per cent of all other employees.

Autonomy over the organization of work is a key element of many conceptions of team-working. By combining data about the practice of team-work from the Cross-Section Survey of Managers with data from the Survey of Employees on the degree of job influence enjoyed by core employees, it is possible to examine the nature of this autonomy in more detail. Comparisons were made between the degrees of autonomy reported by core employees in workplaces where team members jointly decided how work was to be done and their counterparts in workplaces where teams were not afforded this level of freedom. The most substantial difference was in the degree of influence over the ordering of tasks: 46 per cent of employees from workplaces with the more autonomous teams reported 'a lot' of influence over this aspect of their work, compared with 39 per cent of employees from workplaces with other forms of team-working. There were smaller differences in respect of the degree of influence over how employees went about their work, how tasks were carried out and over start and finish times. But there were no differences in the degree of influence over the pace of work.

Responses to each of the five items in Figure 4.1 were positively correlated, but many employees gave different responses on each of the items. Two-fifths (38 per cent) of all employees had 'a lot' of influence over all five items, while less than one in ten (7 per cent) had 'a little' or 'none' on all five items. Around two-thirds (64 per cent) of Managers and senior officials reported 'a lot' of influence on all five aspects of their job, compared with around two-fifths of those in Professional and Associate professional and technical occupations, around one-third of those in Administrative and secretarial occupations or Skilled trades and around one quarter of those in the remaining four occupational groups. The proportion with 'a little' or no influence on all of the five items rose to at least one in ten only among Process, plant and machine operatives (15 per cent), Sales and customer service employees (12 per cent) and those in Elementary occupations (10 per cent).

On a separate question in the Survey of Employees, respondents were asked to rate their degree of satisfaction with the scope for using their own initiative in their job, and their satisfaction with the amount of influence they had over their job. Responses were invited on a five-point scale from 'very satisfied' to 'very dissatisfied'. Overall, 71 per cent of employees were either 'satisfied' or 'very satisfied' with the scope for using their own initiative, and 58 per cent were 'satisfied' or 'very satisfied' with the amount of influence they had over their job. The proportions that were either 'dissatisfied' or 'very dissatisfied' were 10 per cent and 14 per cent respectively. There had been no change since 1998 in the proportion expressing satisfaction with the amount of influence they had over their job; satisfaction with sense of achievement was not covered in the 1998 survey and so no comparison was possible.

Employees with greater levels of influence over the various aspects of their job tended to report greater levels of satisfaction, corroborating suggestions that job influence meets a basic human need on the part of workers (Budd, 2004: 26). Among employees that had 'a lot' of influence over each of the five items in Figure 4.1, 87 per cent were satisfied with the scope for using their own initiative and 79 per cent were satisfied with the amount of influence they had over their job. Among those with little or no influence over each of the five items, in contrast, the figures were just 29 per cent and 14 per cent respectively. Such strong positive correlations between the degree of job influence and these specific elements of job satisfaction are notable not least because employees' satisfaction with these elements of their job is in turn positively correlated with the extent of their satisfaction over the sense of achievement they get from their work and their satisfaction with the work itself.

## Work intensity

While many debates about changing work processes have been primarily concerned with the prospects for increased employee autonomy, others have highlighted the prospect for work intensification (see, for example, the studies cited by Godard and Delaney, 2000: 492). In 2004, the vast majority of employees considered that their job 'required them to work very hard'. Three-quarters (76 per cent) either agreed or strongly agreed with this statement (Table 4.9), while only 5 per cent either disagreed or strongly disagreed. Employees in Managerial

*Table 4.9* Work intensity, by job and workplace characteristics

| | % of employees agreeing that . . . | |
|---|---|---|
| | *'My job requires that I work very hard'* | *'I never seem to have enough time to get my work done'* |
| All employees | 76 | 40 |
| *Occupation* | | |
| Managers and senior officials | 86 | 58 |
| Professional | 84 | 60 |
| Associate professional and technical | 77 | 45 |
| Administrative and secretarial | 74 | 39 |
| Skilled trades | 71 | 34 |
| Caring, leisure and other personal service | 78 | 34 |
| Sales and customer service | 73 | 32 |
| Process, plant and machine operatives | 70 | 27 |
| Elementary occupations | 71 | 25 |
| *Hours worked per week* | | |
| Less than 16 hours | 66 | 24 |
| 16–29 hours | 72 | 34 |
| 30–38 hours | 75 | 39 |
| 39–48 hours | 79 | 44 |
| More than 48 hours | 84 | 51 |
| *Sector of ownership* | | |
| Private | 75 | 36 |
| Public | 80 | 51 |
| *Number of competitors (private sector only)* | | |
| None | 70 | 36 |
| Few | 73 | 35 |
| Many | 76 | 36 |

Base: All employees in workplaces with 10 or more employees.
Figures are weighted and based on responses from at least 21,114 employees (13,493 in the private sector).

and Professional occupations were the most likely to strongly agree (35 per cent and 39 per cent respectively). They were followed by those in Caring, leisure and other personal service occupations (30 per cent), with around one quarter of employees in each of the other six occupational groups also being in strong agreement. The overall proportion of employees strongly agreeing that their job required them to work very hard was 28 per cent.

Two-fifths of employees considered that they 'never seemed to have enough time to get their work done', while 29 per cent either disagreed or strongly disagreed that this was the case. Again, employees in Managerial and Professional occupations were the most likely to strongly agree: the figures were 21 per cent and 28 per cent respectively. They were followed by employees in Associate professional and technical occupations (16 per cent), with the proportion in strong agreement within each of the remaining six groups standing at around one in ten. The overall proportion of employees strongly agreeing that they never seemed to have enough time to get their work done was 14 per cent.

After controlling for occupation, both indicators of work intensity were positively associated with hours worked, while employees in public sector workplaces were more likely than employees in the private sector to rate their work as intense. In both the private and public sectors, ratings of work intensity tended to be high among employees working in Education and Health and social work. Within the private sector, employees were more likely to agree that their job required them to work very hard if their workplace faced a higher number of competitors, but there was no association between the number of competitors and employees' perceptions of time pressure. While there is evidence from other sources that the level of work intensity increased during the mid-1990s (Green, 2001), the measures available in the WERS surveys of 1998 and 2004 concur with other evidence in suggesting that levels of work intensity reached something of a plateau in the late 1990s and early part of the current decade (Green, 2004). There were no substantive differences between 1998 and 2004 in the overall patterns of employees' responses on either indicator of work intensity.

## Employee well-being

Employees' affective reactions to their work and environment have been a topic of perennial interest to those concerned with employment relations. Measures of job satisfaction provide one set of indicators, and the results from questions asking employees about their degree of satisfaction with a number of facets of their job, such as training or pay, are presented at various points in this and other chapters. A further set of indicators – introduced for the first time in the 2004 Survey of Employees – measured the extent of employees' job-related well-being. The specific question set employed the six-item Job-Related Anxiety–Contentment scale proposed by Mullarkey *et al.* (1999). Figure 4.2 shows the results on each of the six items.

Correlations between the items were in line with expectations, such that the ratings on the items labelled 'tense', 'worried' and 'uneasy' were all positively

*Figure 4.2* Job-related well-being

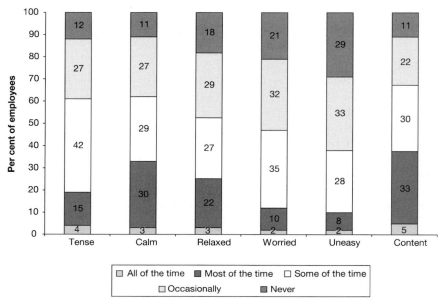

Employees were asked: "Thinking of the past few weeks, how much of the time has your job made you feel ... "
Base: All employees in workplaces with 10 or more.
Figures are weighted and based on responses from at least 21,288 employees.

correlated with each other, as were those items labelled 'calm', 'relaxed' and 'content'. These two sets of items were also negatively correlated with one another. In order to obtain an overall indication of how ratings on the set of well-being measures varied as a group across different employee characteristics, each of the six items were recoded into numerical five-point scales on which larger values indicated greater levels of contentment (less anxiety), and these were combined into a single, summated score. Scores on this overall scale were distributed approximately normally and ranged from −12 to +12, with the average (mean) score standing at 1.2.[12]

Comparing across employees from the nine occupational groups, the lowest mean scores on the overall indicator of employee well-being were found among Managers and Professionals (both having a mean of 0.1) and also among Associate professional and technical employees (0.7). The highest mean scores were found among those in Elementary occupations (2.5) and Caring, leisure and other personal service occupations (2.2), with the mean scores for the remaining four groups standing at around 1.5. There was a strong negative association between employee well-being and hours worked, which remained after controlling for occupation. After controlling for both factors, well-being was lower among women than among men and lower among employees in the public sector than among those working for private sector organizations. Returning to the themes of earlier sections, levels of employee well-being were also positively related to the degree of job influence and negatively related to the degree of work intensity. The latter association is particularly notable as it appeared to account for the lower levels of well-being among women and public sector workers. These associations disappeared after controlling for employees' perceptions of the intensity of their work.

As the questions on job-related well-being had been introduced for the first time in the 2004 survey, a comparison with 1998 was not possible. However, it was possible to compare responses to a related question which asked employees whether they worried a lot about their work outside of working hours. They were invited to respond on a five-point scale from 'strongly agree' to 'strongly disagree'. Just over one-fifth (23 per cent) of all employees in 1998 either agreed or strongly agreed that they worried a lot about their work outside of working hours. In 2004, the corresponding figure was just over one quarter (27 per cent).

## The non-employed workforce

Thus far, the chapter has focused solely on the work practices and contractual arrangements of employees, without saying a great deal about workers engaged through other means. This is natural, as the focus of the WERS surveys is primarily on the nature of the relationship between the employer and their employees. However, there are a number of other types of worker who augment the directly-employed labour force at sampled workplaces. These include temporary agency workers, freelance workers and subcontractors. Along with those practices discussed earlier in the chapter under the heading 'Working patterns', it is commonly assumed that they are deployed as means of increasing numerical (as opposed to functional) flexibility.

### *Temporary agency workers*

According to managers, 16 per cent of workplaces had some temporary agency workers. When these temporary agency workers were added to the directly-employed labour force, they comprised 2 per cent of the combined workforce. The likelihood that temporary agency workers were present rose with the size of the workplace. There was also a pronounced difference between the public and private sectors in the use of temporary agency staff, with public sector workplaces more likely to have at least some temporary agency workers (27 per cent did so, compared to 14 per cent of workplaces in the private sector). Although workplaces were more likely to make use of agency workers where a union was recognized than where there was no union recognition, this relationship disappeared when union and non-union workplaces of a similar size were compared. One quarter or more of all workplaces engaged in Electricity, gas and water, Public administration, Manufacturing and Transport and communications employed some agency workers, compared to less than one in ten workplaces in Wholesale and retail or Hotels and restaurants. Table 4.10 shows that, as with employees on fixed-term and temporary contracts, agency staff commonly worked in the core occupation within the workplace, although there was some variation in their use between occupations.

The most common reason for using temporary agency staff was to provide short-term cover for staff absences, or vacancies. Fifty-eight per cent of workplaces using temporary agency workers did so for this reason. Consistent with this, there was some evidence that workplaces were less likely to make use of agency staff where a greater proportion of the core occupational group were employed to do a job other than their own. Nearly two-fifths of workplaces (37 per cent) used agency workers to match their staffing levels to peaks in demand, while in one quarter (24 per cent) of workplaces, agency workers were used because it was not possible to fill staff vacancies. Temporary agency workers were used to cover maternity or annual leave in 17 per cent of workplaces which made use of such contracts, and around half this proportion (9 per cent) employed agency workers in order to obtain specialist skills. Four per cent of workplaces used temporary agency workers because of a freeze on permanent staff numbers. Around one-third (32 per cent) of workplaces employing agency workers cited more than one of these reasons.

## Freelance workers and homeworkers

Eleven per cent of workplaces had freelance workers. Workplaces which were part of large organizations were less likely to make use of freelance staff than

*Table 4.10* Temporary agency workers, by occupation

|  | *% of workplaces* | | |
|---|---|---|---|
|  | *All workplaces* | *Workplaces employing some staff in the specified occupation* | *Workplaces where specified occupation is the largest occupational group* |
| All occupations | 16 | – | – |
| Managers and senior officials | 0 | 0 | – |
| Professional | 3 | 8 | 13 |
| Associate professional and technical | 2 | 6 | 12 |
| Administrative and secretarial | 6 | 8 | 14 |
| Skilled trades | 1 | 3 | 5 |
| Personal service | 1 | 8 | 11 |
| Sales and customer service | 2 | 3 | 5 |
| Process, plant and machine operatives | 2 | 9 | 14 |
| Elementary | 3 | 6 | 9 |

Base: All workplaces with 10 or more employees.
Figures are weighted and based on responses from 2,062 managers.

smaller organizations. For example, 3 per cent of workplaces which were part of an organization with 10,000 or more employees employed some freelancers, compared to 15 per cent of workplaces in organizations with less than 100 employees. Workplaces which recognized at least one union were slightly less likely to employ some freelance workers than workplaces which did not recognize unions (8 per cent and 12 per cent respectively). Those in the Manufacturing, Construction, Other business services and Other community services sectors were most likely to employ some freelance workers, with around one in five workplaces doing so. By contrast, one in twenty or fewer workplaces in the Hotels and restaurants, Financial services and Public administration sectors employed any freelancers.

Six per cent of workplaces engaged people who worked for the establishment at or from their own homes, but were not employees. This was particularly common in workplaces with more than 500 employees, with 12 per cent of these workplaces using non-employed home workers. Public sector workplaces were less likely to use non-employed home workers than private sector workplaces (3 per cent and 7 per cent respectively), but there was little variation between industrial sectors. Workplaces in the Construction industry most commonly used this category of worker (15 per cent did so), while at the other end of the spectrum, around one in twenty workplaces or less used them in Electricity, gas and water, Hotels and restaurants, Public administration, Education and Health and social work.

### Subcontractors

Throughout the 1980s and 1990s compulsory competitive tendering placed a requirement on local authorities to contract out certain services such as cleaning or catering to the private sector if they could be provided for a lower cost than was feasible using in-house services. However, the Labour Government abolished these rules in favour of 'Best Value' in 2000, which allowed local authorities to contract-in services previously contracted-out where it was thought that this would result in higher standards of service. This section assesses the extent to which both public and private sector workplaces made use of subcontractors.

Managers were asked whether independent contractors provided any one of 11 services. Within 86 per cent of workplaces, at least one of these services was contracted out (Table 4.11). Generally speaking, smaller workplaces were less likely to contract-out services than larger workplaces. Also, single independent workplaces were less likely to contract-out services than workplaces which were part of a wider organization (78 and 90 per cent, respectively). A similar proportion of private and public sector workplaces contracted-out services (86 and 87 per cent, respectively). Workplaces most commonly contracted-out building maintenance (59 per cent of all workplaces) and cleaning (52 per cent).

Where the management respondent reported that some services were contracted out, they were asked whether subcontractors were doing work which

*Table 4.11* Subcontracted services and contracting-in

| | % workplaces | |
|---|---|---|
| | Service provided by independent contractors | Service brought in-house within past five years |
| Building maintenance | 59 | 1 |
| Cleaning of building and premises | 52 | 4 |
| Training | 34 | 1 |
| Transport of documents/goods | 29 | 0 |
| Security | 29 | 1 |
| Payroll | 28 | 2 |
| Computing services | 25 | 2 |
| Temporary filling of vacant posts at this workplace | 16 | 0 |
| Printing/photocopying | 15 | 1 |
| Catering | 14 | 1 |
| Recruitment | 12 | 1 |
| Any of the above | 86 | 11 |

Base: All workplaces with 10 or more employees.
Figures are weighted and based on responses from 2,057 managers (column 1) and 2,043 managers (column 2).

was done by employees of the workplace or organization five years previously. This was the case in 19 per cent of these workplaces, or 16 per cent of all workplaces. Managers in 18 per cent of the workplaces where the subcontractors were carrying out tasks which were formerly provided in-house said that at least some of the subcontractors were former employees. The likelihood that this was the case rose with workplace size. It was far more common for subcontracting public sector workplaces to employ former employees as subcontractors than subcontracting private sector workplaces (38 per cent and 13 per cent respectively did so).

Managers were asked why they had contracted-out services which were previously carried out by employees. The most common reason was to produce a cost saving (47 per cent), while 43 per cent contracted out to gain an improved service. Thirty per cent of managers said that services were contracted out in order to focus on core business activities, and 10 per cent of workplaces cited greater flexibility. Only 2 per cent of workplaces mentioned compulsory competitive tendering or government regulations.

WERS 2004 introduced new questions to investigate the extent to which both public and private sector workplaces had contracted-in services which were previously provided by subcontractors. Eleven per cent of workplaces had brought some, formerly outsourced services in-house within the five years prior to the survey, and there was little difference in this proportion between the public and private sectors. Contracting-in was more common in larger rather than smaller workplaces and varied across industries. Around one-fifth of workplaces in the Manufacturing sector and Electricity, gas and water had contracted-in some services, compared to only 2 per cent of workplaces in Financial services. The service most likely to be brought in-house was cleaning (4 per cent of all workplaces).

One of the most common reasons for deciding to provide a service in-house rather than to continue to subcontract to another employer was because of cost savings. This was a motivation for contracting-in among 57 per cent of all workplaces that had brought at least one service in house. Improved service was another popular reason for bringing the service in house, and was a motivation in 51 per cent of workplaces. In 8 per cent of workplaces, services were contracted-in because there was sufficient in-house capacity, while union or staff pressure led to contracting-in within 1 per cent of workplaces.

## Conclusion

There has been much interest in recent years in the methods by which employees are recruited and developed, and in the ways in which work is organized. This chapter has presented evidence on a wide variety of such practices, showing how their incidence varies between different types of job and workplace, and also illustrating any changes in prevalence since the previous survey in 1998. The perceptions of employees have also been discussed, using data on the degree of job influence and work intensity, for example.

The chapter pointed to a degree of stability in the incidence of practices that are often cited as indicators of sophisticated human resource management. There was no marked increase in the prevalence of team-working, multi-skilling or problem-solving groups, for example, indicating that the diffusion of so-called 'high involvement management' practices has been rather muted in recent years.[13] Nor was there much change in the use of selection tests – one potential indicator of a sophisticated approach to recruitment. The provision of training became more extensive, however, as did the extent to which formal performance appraisals were used to identify training needs. These patterns suggest that skills are an increasing priority in British workplaces, although the large proportion of 'over-skilled' employees also suggests that there may be opportunities to better use the skills that employees already possess.

Differences were clearly apparent between occupations in recruitment methods, training provision, working patterns and work organization, with those in higher-skilled occupations tending to be subject to more formal arrangements. They also received greater levels of training and enjoyed more extensive levels of influence over their jobs. However, the *quid pro quo* was that such workers also reported higher levels of work intensity, which fed through into lower levels of employee well-being. Further investigation of the relationships between job characteristics and workplace practices will undoubtedly be an important avenue for future research, not least feeding into debates about the quality of working life.

# 5 Representation, consultation and communication

## Introduction

Mechanisms for employee representation, consultation and communication have always been of interest to those concerned with employment relations. The traditional form of employee representation in Britain is representation via a trade union. Earlier surveys in the WERS series have traced the decline of union membership and influence in British workplaces over the course of the 1980s and 1990s (Millward *et al.*, 2000), but there are signs that the speed of the descent has slowed in recent years (Grainger and Holt, 2005). There is now legislative support for union recognition, introduced in the period between the last two surveys, and a marked increase in the number of voluntary recognition agreements has been recorded over this period (Gall, 2004). There are also indications that managers' attitudes toward trade unions may have become less hostile (Poole *et al.*, 2005). Nevertheless, some still predict further decline in union representation, as a result of the continued shift towards private sector service activities, the substantial outflow from union membership and the displacement of certain union activities through enhanced individual rights (Metcalf, 2005).

Some argue that legislation in the area of information and consultation may provide new opportunities for unions to gain a foothold in workplaces they have previously found difficult to organize.[1] Yet the legislation allows for a broad range of arrangements, and so has equally highlighted the prospects for representative forms of voice that do not necessarily involve unions, such as joint consultative committees, and for direct forms of communication between managers and employees. Arrangements for direct communication, in particular, became more common in the 1990s as employers managed increasingly without unions (Forth and Millward, 2002a).

In the light of these various issues, this chapter considers the incidence and operation of a variety of arrangements for employee representation, consultation and communication, along with changes since 1998. The chapter begins with trade union representation. It then moves on to consider employee representation through consultative committees, and the incidence of stand-alone non-union representatives. A variety of arrangements for direct communication are then considered. The chapter concludes by investigating the effectiveness of different arrangements, as seen from the perspective of employees.

## Trade union membership density

Employees' membership of trade unions or independent staff associations is perhaps the most familiar indicator of collective labour organization. In 1998 and 2004, the WERS Survey of Employees obtained a first-hand account of the membership of trade unions and independent staff associations from individual employees. The Cross-Section Survey of Managers also obtained an estimate of the total number of employees at each surveyed workplace who were members of trade unions or independent staff associations. Together, these data enable one to examine the extent to which various demographic, job and workplace characteristics are associated with union or staff association membership, and also to investigate the degree to which membership is concentrated within particular workplaces in a given sector.

The Survey of Employees indicated that 34 per cent of employees covered by WERS belonged to trade unions or independent staff associations in 2004.[2] A further 17 per cent of employees were no longer union members, although they had belonged to a union in the past, leaving almost one half (49 per cent of employees) who were not, and had never been, a member of a union. Aggregate membership density had fallen slightly since 1998, when 37 per cent of employees were union members. This decline was accompanied by a similar decrease in the proportion of employees who had previously been union members (19 per cent in 1998) and a corresponding rise in the proportion who had never belonged to a union (45 per cent in 1998). Thus, the rise in 'never-membership' among employees in Britain throughout the 1980s and 1990s, documented by Bryson and Gomez (2005), appears to have continued into the current decade.

In keeping with official statistics on union membership density among all employees, the likelihood of belonging to a union in workplaces with 10 or more employees showed no significant difference by gender in 2004, although women were more likely than men never to have been members of a union (53 per cent compared to 46 per cent). Union density rose with age, but reached a peak among employees aged between 50 and 59 and then fell back among older workers. Density was also higher among full-time employees (35 per cent) than among those working part-time (27 per cent), and higher among permanent employees (35 per cent) than among those on fixed-term appointments (29 per cent) or temporary contracts (17 per cent).

Continuing to utilize membership data from the Survey of Employees, and turning to examine how membership density varies across different types of workplace, the first column of Table 5.1 shows that density was much higher in larger workplaces than in smaller establishments. It was also higher in larger organizations, in the public sector and, correspondingly, in those industry sectors with greater degrees of public ownership (cf. Table 2.2).

*Table 5.1* Trade union membership density, by workplace characteristics

| | % employees | % workplaces | | |
|---|---|---|---|---|
| | Aggregate union density | Workplace-level union density (%) | | |
| | | Zero | 1–49 | 50 or more |
| All workplaces | 34 | 64 | 18 | 18 |
| *Workplace size* | | | | |
| 10–24 employees | 18 | 75 | 13 | 12 |
| 25–49 employees | 30 | 55 | 21 | 24 |
| 50–99 employees | 26 | 54 | 23 | 22 |
| 100–199 employees | 38 | 32 | 35 | 32 |
| 200–499 employees | 37 | 24 | 46 | 31 |
| 500 or more employees | 47 | 22 | 45 | 33 |
| All workplaces with 25 or more employees | 37 | 49 | 25 | 25 |
| *Organization status* | | | | |
| Stand-alone workplace | 20 | 84 | 12 | 4 |
| Part of a larger organization | 37 | 55 | 21 | 24 |
| *Organization size* | | | | |
| 10–99 employees | 8 | 86 | 10 | 3 |
| 100–999 employees | 24 | 62 | 27 | 11 |
| 1,000–9,999 employees | 42 | 52 | 21 | 26 |
| 10,000 or more employees | 47 | 34 | 24 | 41 |
| *Sector of ownership* | | | | |
| Private | 22 | 77 | 15 | 8 |
| Public | 64 | 7 | 31 | 62 |
| *Industry* | | | | |
| Manufacturing | 31 | 73 | 17 | 11 |
| Electricity, gas and water | 66 | (5) | (30) | (66) |
| Construction | 25 | 78 | 16 | 7 |
| Wholesale and retail | 15 | 86 | 11 | 3 |
| Hotels and restaurants | 6 | 98 | 2 | 0 |
| Transport and communication | 54 | 41 | 21 | 38 |
| Financial services | 32 | 32 | 12 | 56 |
| Other business services | 13 | 81 | 14 | 5 |
| Public administration | 64 | 1 | 30 | 70 |
| Education | 57 | 7 | 35 | 58 |
| Health and social work | 44 | 47 | 31 | 22 |
| Other community services | 30 | 62 | 26 | 12 |

Base (column 1): All employees in workplaces with 10 or more.
Base (columns 2–4): All workplaces with 10 or more employees.
Figures are weighted and based on responses from 21,540 employees (column 1) and 1,973 managers (columns 2–4).

The remaining columns of Table 5.1 use data on workplace union density from the Cross-Section Survey of Managers to show the proportion of workplaces with no union members, and the proportions where members made up either a minority or majority of the workforce. Around one in every thirty managers (3 per cent) were unable to estimate what proportion of their employees were members of a trade union. The remainder underestimated aggregate union membership density by six percentage points, when compared with employees' own accounts.[3] Managers underestimated membership to a greater degree in large workplaces, where they are less likely to have personal knowledge of employees' membership status and may have had to rely on records of the numbers of employees for whom union subscriptions are deducted via the payroll (commonly referred to as 'check-off' procedures). The practice of check-off became less common in the 1990s as managers withdrew support for unions (Millward *et al.*, 2000) and unions sought to collect their subscriptions via direct debit so as to maintain contact with members when they changed jobs. Three-fifths (61 per cent) of workplaces with union members operated check-off in 2004, compared with two-thirds (66 per cent) in 1998. But whatever the role of check-off procedures, it appears that, in large workplaces, some managers had a tendency to consider that membership was less extensive among the workforce than was the case in practice.

Although managers were not always aware of the full complement of union members at their workplace, the estimates of aggregate union density correspond sufficiently for the managers' accounts to provide a meaningful picture of the extent of membership concentration at workplace level. According to managers, almost two-thirds (64 per cent) of workplaces had no union members. In a fifth of workplaces (18 per cent), union members comprised a minority of all employees and in a further fifth (also 18 per cent) they comprised the majority. The proportion of workplaces without union members had risen from 57 per cent in 1998. However, among the subset of workplaces with 25 or more employees, the substantial rise in 'no-member workplaces' that had been witnessed in the latter part of the 1980s and much of the 1990s (Millward *et al.*, 2000: 85) was checked between 1998 and 2004: the incidence among this subset of workplaces was 49 per cent in both years.

The likelihood that a workplace had at least some union members was unsurprisingly associated positively with the size of the workplace. Only one quarter of workplaces with between 10 and 24 employees had any union members, compared with 78 per cent of those with 500 or more employees. However, unions appeared to find it no easier to achieve majority membership in very large workplaces than in medium-sized ones, possibly reflecting constraints on organizing brought about by increasing occupational diversity. A strong positive association was also apparent between workplace-level union density and the size of the organization to which the establishment belonged. Workplaces belonging to organizations with less than 100 employees were unlikely to have any union members at all (just 14 per cent did so), whereas establishments belonging to very large organizations with 10,000 or more employees were likely both to have at least some members and for these members to form the majority of the workforce. This association held irrespective of the size of the workplace itself.

The private and public sectors formed polar opposites in respect of the pattern of union density at workplace level. In the private sector, just over three-quarters (77 per cent) of workplaces had no union members, and less than one in ten (8 per cent) had majority membership. By stark contrast, less then one in ten public sector workplaces were without members, and in three-fifths (62 per cent) a majority of employees belonged to unions. This public sector effect was sufficient to explain the relatively high rates of majority membership in Public administration and Education. But it did not account for the varied pattern of workplace density within Transport and communication or Financial services. Here, there were distinct differences within each industry sector: relatively low density in Transport, but higher density in Communication; and typically high density in banks and building societies, but low density among workplaces engaged in other financial activities, such as insurance.

Overall, one in twenty workplaces (5 per cent) had at least 90 per cent of their employees belonging to trade unions, but the proportion reached one in five (19 per cent) in the public sector, compared with just one in fifty (2 per cent) in the private sector. Indeed, over two-thirds (69 per cent) of workplaces with a density of at least 90 per cent were in the public sector, although they were not concentrated in any particular areas of activity.

In most cases where union members were present at an establishment, these members belonged to only one or two different trade unions. In just over one half (53 per cent) of workplaces with members, these all belonged to a single union, and in a further fifth (21 per cent) they were divided between two unions. This left 27 per cent where three or more unions were represented among the workforce. The presence of members from multiple unions was particularly common in the public sector, where two-thirds (66 per cent) of all workplaces had members of more than one union among their workforce; the equivalent figure in the private sector was just 5 per cent.

There was no clear evidence of a concentration of membership into fewer unions between 1998 and 2004. The small decline in the proportion of all workplaces with members from more than one union (from 19 per cent in 1998 to 16 per cent in 2004) was not statistically significant and could be wholly attributed to the overall decline in the proportion of workplaces with any union members.[4]

## Management support for trade union membership

While employees in Britain are free to decide whether to belong to a trade union, the extent of management support for union membership nonetheless exerts a powerful influence over the propensity of employees to become (or remain) union members. In 2004, one-fifth of managers (21 per cent) were in favour of union membership among employees at their workplace, one in six

(17 per cent) were not in favour of it, and the remainder (62 per cent) expressed neutrality on the issue. In 1998, the figures were 25 per cent, 18 per cent and 57 per cent respectively, the only statistically significant change being the increase in the percentage of managers taking a neutral stance.

The first four surveys in the WERS series also asked whether managers required employees to join a trade union, either before or shortly after starting work. This phenomenon (usually referred to as a 'closed shop') became almost non-existent in the 1990s (Millward *et al.*, 2000: 146) after finally being out-lawed in 1991. Therefore WERS 2004 took a broader approach and, alongside the traditional question about managers' general attitude, also asked, in follow-up questions, whether managers did anything actively either to support or dis-courage union membership. It is then possible to distinguish active encourage-ment from passive support, and similarly to distinguish active discouragement from passive opposition.

Managers actively supported union membership in 13 per cent of all work-places, while in just 3 per cent of workplaces they took active steps to dis-courage it (Table 5.2).[5] Data from the Survey of Employee Representatives indicated that active support might involve managers personally encouraging employees to join the union, or providing union representatives with an opportunity to speak to new recruits during their induction, while active dis-couragement might involve managers dismissing the union as ineffectual, or inferring that membership would harm employees' career prospects. Active support was much more common in the public sector (40 per cent) than the private sector (7 per cent), and more prevalent among large workplaces than small ones (30 per cent among workplaces with 500 or more employees, compared with

*Table 5.2* Management attitudes towards union membership

| | % workplaces | | | | |
|---|---|---|---|---|---|
| | *Actively encourages* | *In favour* | *Neutral* | *Not in favour* | *Actively discourages* |
| All workplaces | 13 | 10 | 60 | 14 | 3 |
| *Workplace size* | | | | | |
| 10–24 employees | 9 | 8 | 62 | 17 | 4 |
| 25–49 employees | 16 | 13 | 58 | 10 | 2 |
| 50–99 employees | 18 | 10 | 59 | 10 | 2 |
| 100–199 employees | 20 | 17 | 52 | 10 | 0 |
| 200–499 employees | 23 | 20 | 43 | 14 | 0 |
| 500 or more employees | 30 | 18 | 38 | 12 | 2 |
| *Sector of ownership* | | | | | |
| Private | 7 | 5 | 67 | 17 | 3 |
| Public | 40 | 33 | 24 | 3 | 0 |

Base: All workplaces with 10 or more employees.
Figures are weighted and based on responses from 2,047 managers.

9 per cent among workplaces with less than 25 employees). Around three-quarters of those workplaces which actively discouraged union membership were family-owned establishments with fewer than 50 employees.[6] In aggregate, 6 per cent of small, family-owned establishments actively discouraged membership of trade unions. Overall, 5 per cent of those managers who actively supported union membership took steps to find out whether potential recruits were union members – presumably following this with some encouragement to join. Among the small proportion of those who actively discouraged membership, one quarter (1 per cent of all managers) took steps to establish whether new recruits belonged to trade unions.

Managers' responses to the initial question as to whether they were in favour of union membership, not in favour or neutral towards it, were compared with the modal response among employees at their workplace, who were asked the same question in the Survey of Employees. In one-third of workplaces, the modal employee response comprised a less positive report of their managers' attitude towards union membership than had been given by the management respondent, but in a further sixth employees were more sanguine than their managers. Responses were most closely aligned when managers backed up their attitudes with actions to encourage or discourage membership among their employees.

Table 5.3 indicates clearly the strength of the relationship between managers' attitudes and employees' propensity to belong to a trade union. Where managers held a positive attitude towards union membership, around three-fifths of employees were union members, whereas the proportion stood at just one in twenty where managers' views were negative. In aggregate, the level of union membership among employees did not differ between workplaces where managers actively encouraged union membership and those where managers gave only passive support. Equally, there was no difference between workplaces where managers actively discouraged membership and those where managers passively opposed it. However, there were differences in small workplaces, where one

*Table 5.3* Union density, by management attitudes towards union membership

|  | % employees | % workplaces | | |
|  | Aggregate union density | Workplace-level union density (%) | | |
|  |  | Zero | 1–49 | 50 or more |
|---|---|---|---|---|
| Actively encourages | 58 | 3 | 35 | 62 |
| In favour | 61 | 13 | 36 | 51 |
| Neutral | 21 | 77 | 15 | 8 |
| Not in favour | 5 | 92 | 7 | 1 |
| Actively discourages | 5 | 100 | 0 | 0 |

Base (column 1): All employees in workplaces with 10 or more.
Base (columns 2–4): All workplaces with 10 or more employees.
Figures are weighted and based on responses from 21,432 employees (column 1) and 1,959 managers (columns 2–4).

might expect the attitudes of a senior manager and the behaviour of individual workers to be more closely connected. Here, active encouragement was associated with a greater likelihood that the majority of employees in a workplace would belong to trade unions when compared with passive support, and levels of union membership were lower in workplaces where managers actively discouraged membership than in those where managers passively opposed it. Indeed, workplaces where managers actively discouraged membership were extremely unlikely to have any union members at all. These broad relationships were also apparent from the pattern of workplace-level union density, which is more heavily determined by behaviour in small establishments.

The Cross-Section Survey of Managers further investigated managers' views of trade unions by asking two attitudinal questions to gauge managers' opinions about the utility of unions in facilitating consultation and improving workplace performance. When asked whether they would rather consult directly with employees than with unions, three-quarters of managers (77 per cent) agreed, while just one in ten (8 per cent) disagreed and 15 per cent expressed no firm opinion either way. When asked whether unions help find ways to improve workplace performance, one quarter (23 per cent) agreed, almost two-fifths (37 per cent) disagreed and a similar proportion (40 per cent) expressed no firm view. Neither pattern had changed since 1998.

Managers' attitudes towards union membership were broadly indicative of their views about the utility of trade unions. Nevertheless, it was apparent that, even among those managers who were in favour of union membership, there was a degree of scepticism as to whether collaboration with unions was the most effective means of managing the workplace. Among managers who were not in favour of union membership, 91 per cent agreed that they would rather consult directly with employees than with unions; the figure stood at 55 per cent among managers who were in favour of union membership. Similarly, only 4 per cent of managers who were not in favour of union membership agreed that unions helped to find ways to improve workplace performance, compared with 53 per cent of those in favour of membership.

A corresponding pattern was found when comparing workplaces that recognized unions and those without recognition. In workplaces that did not recognize trade unions, 86 per cent of managers agreed that they would rather consult directly with employees, compared to 56 per cent of managers where unions were recognized. And, in the absence of recognition, only 12 per cent of managers agreed that unions helped to find ways to improve workplace performance, compared with 49 per cent of managers in workplaces with union recognition.

## Union recruitment activity

In an attempt to address declining membership levels, unions have in recent years placed a greater emphasis on membership recruitment by full-time officials and lay representatives (Waddington, 2003). In view of these efforts, it is noteworthy that the vast majority of non-members (83 per cent) had never been asked to join a union or staff association at their workplace. For many, this is explained by the absence of union members or representatives at their establishment. However, the proportion was two-thirds (67 per cent) among non-members working in establishments where at least some colleagues belonged to a union, and three-fifths (60 per cent) where unions were recognized. It remained above one half (55 per cent) where an on-site union representative was present. This may be indicative of occupational unionism, or of representatives with limited time targeting only those employees whom they consider likely to join. Certainly, it appeared from the Survey of Employee Representatives that most union representatives were actively seeking out recruits.

Three-quarters (77 per cent) of trade union representatives said that they, or other representatives of their union, had attempted to recruit new members at their workplace in the 12 months prior to the survey. Around one-fifth (22 per cent) did not specify whether this involved attempts to recruit non-members who already had their pay and conditions negotiated by the representative's union (so-called 'infill' recruitment) or employees who were not covered by such negotiations ('expansion'). But among those who did specify (58 per cent of all union representatives), over four-fifths (85 per cent) had attempted infill and two-fifths (39 per cent) had attempted expansion. One quarter (24 per cent) had attempted both. Almost all of those attempting infill (94 per cent) were successful in recruiting at least some new members; the success rate was slightly lower (83 per cent) among those attempting expansion. However, successful recruitment provided no guarantee of rising membership density at the workplace. Density had risen in only half (48 per cent) of those workplaces where representatives had recruited new members over the past two years; in 39 per cent density had remained stable and in 13 per cent it had gone down.[7] The two main reasons given for falling density were that union members had left the workplace or that new employees had not wished to join; a third common reason was that employees had left the union.

Some have suggested that legislation providing paid time off for union representatives who sit on information and consultation bodies may assist unions' organizing efforts, by affording representatives more time to approach non-members (Labour Research, 2004: 18). There were suggestions from the Survey of Employee Representatives that those who spent greater amounts of time each week on union activities were both more likely to attempt recruitment, and more likely to succeed, but the differences were not statistically significant. More relevant was the assistance received from managers in informing union representatives about new recruits, and the assistance received from unions in training lay representatives to recruit and organize. Just under half (46 per cent) of union representatives said that managers normally informed them, or other representatives of their union, when a new recruit joined the workplace. In these workplaces, four-fifths (81 per cent) of representatives had tried to recruit and almost all (97 per cent) had been successful, whereas in workplaces where managers did not provide this information, the rates of attempted and successful recruitment were somewhat lower (72 per cent and 86 per cent, respectively). Although representatives received such assistance from only a minority of managers, most (88 per cent) had received some assistance from their union in the form of advice or assistance from a full-time official, posters or training. Training of lay representatives was the route most likely to bring success in the recruitment of new members: almost all (99 per cent) of the one-third of union representatives that had been trained in recruitment or organizing reported that their recruitment attempts had been successful in the past year.

Despite union representatives' efforts, most workplaces where representatives were present (80 per cent) still had at least some non-members who would be eligible to join the representatives' union. The proportion of workplaces with potential for further recruitment was highest in private sector manufacturing (91 per cent), followed by private sector services (84 per cent) and lowest in the public sector (76 per cent). In one quarter of workplaces, there was potential for both infill and expansion, while in 49 per cent the potential was limited to infill and in 5 per cent it was limited to expansion. Most of these workplaces had received some form of assistance from the wider union in respect of recruitment in the past 12 months, but in less than half (43 per cent) had the union developed a formal recruitment plan.

## Trade union recognition

While retaining and recruiting members is a fundamental objective for unions as a means of establishing legitimacy and cohesion, membership is of little import if it does not also bring influence in dealings with management. A union's ultimate goal in their relations with managers is likely to be the joint regulation of the employment relationship, covering terms and conditions, work rules and employment procedures, such as those relating to the resolution of disputes. However, the formal recognition of trade unions by management for the purposes of collective bargaining has become less common over recent decades, reflecting changes in the composition of the economy and the difficulties of obtaining negotiating rights in new workplaces (Millward *et al.*, 2000: 95–108).

The granting of recognition rights has traditionally been the gift of employers, but the introduction of a statutory recognition procedure (via the Employment Relations Act 1999) has provided a new lever to those unions that can demonstrate sufficient levels of support for recognition among employees. Research indicates that the procedure itself has had a rather limited direct impact, in terms of the numbers of recognition agreements awarded through statutory means, but the indirect impact on the extent of voluntary recognition appears to be more extensive, with the balance of de-recognitions and new recognitions having altered in favour of the latter (Gall, 2004; Blanden *et al.*, 2005). The evidence from WERS also indicates that something substantive has changed since the late 1990s although, in common with other studies, the precise effect of legislation is difficult to untangle.

Managers were asked whether any trade unions were recognized for the purposes of negotiating the pay and conditions of any sections of the workforce at the establishment. The negotiations themselves may take place at the workplace, or alternatively at a higher level in the organization, or at industry level through an employers' association. Accordingly, some establishments may be covered by recognition agreements although none of the employees working there belong to the signatory unions. It should also be acknowledged that the formal recognition of a union or unions does not necessarily imply that active negotiations take place over the full range of terms and conditions, or even at all – case studies have provided ample evidence of both partial and dormant recognition agreements. Such issues are examined in Chapter 7; here the discussion focuses on the formal status of recognition rather than the detail of everyday practice.

Overall, 30 per cent of workplaces recognized at least one trade union for the purposes of negotiating pay and conditions. However, Table 5.4 shows that the incidence of union recognition was much higher among large workplaces than small ones: two-thirds (67 per cent) of workplaces with 500 or more employees recognized trade unions, compared with just one-fifth (21 per cent) of those with between 10 and 24 employees. Accordingly, the proportion of employees working in establishments with recognized unions was considerably higher than the workplace-level incidence of recognition, standing at one half.

Union recognition was also positively associated with the size of the organization to which the workplace belonged. Workplaces belonging to organizations with fewer than 100 employees were very unlikely to recognize unions: only 6 per cent did so. The equivalent figure among workplaces belonging to organizations with 10,000 or more employees was 62 per cent. Simple multivariate analysis showed that the associations with workplace and organization size were independent of one another, indicating that both contribute to managers' decision-making in respect of recognition.

The most striking relationship shown in Table 5.4, however, was with sector of ownership. The recognition of trade unions was almost universal (90 per cent) among public sector workplaces, with a few schools and medical practices accounting for most of the small minority of public sector establishments without recognition. In the private sector, by contrast, union recognition was a characteristic shared by only one in every seven workplaces (16 per cent). And so, although the private sector accounted for around four-fifths of all establishments (see Chapter 2), it accounted for a minority (45 per cent) of all workplaces that recognized trade unions.

Stark contrasts were also apparent between recognition rates in different industry sectors. Many could be explained by contrasting degrees of public ownership, although the almost universal absence of recognition from the Hotels and restaurants sector set this industry apart, even within the private sector. Electricity, gas and water and Financial services stood out as the only industry sectors in which recognition was the norm among private sector employers, although recognition was also reasonably common among larger, private-sector workplaces engaged in Manufacturing, Transport and communication and Education.

Given the continual decline in the incidence of trade union recognition during the 1980s and 1990s (Millward *et al.*, 2000: 95–108), and the notable change in the attitude of the state towards engagement with trade unions, evident not least from the introduction of a statutory union recognition procedure, it is naturally of great interest to examine how the incidence of union recognition

*Table 5.4* Trade union recognition, by workplace characteristics

| | % workplaces | | % employees | |
|---|---|---|---|---|
| | All workplaces | Private sector | All workplaces | Private sector |
| All workplaces | 30 | 16 | 50 | 33 |
| *Workplace size* | | | | |
| 10–24 employees | 21 | 11 | 22 | 11 |
| 25–49 employees | 36 | 21 | 36 | 21 |
| 50–99 employees | 36 | 16 | 36 | 17 |
| 100–199 employees | 52 | 38 | 53 | 40 |
| 200–499 employees | 64 | 53 | 66 | 55 |
| 500 or more employees | 67 | 52 | 76 | 59 |
| *Organization status* | | | | |
| Stand-alone workplace | 7 | 6 | 26 | 19 |
| Part of a larger organization | 40 | 23 | 57 | 52 |
| *Organization size* | | | | |
| 10–99 employees | 6 | 5 | 7 | 5 |
| 100–999 employees | 28 | 17 | 36 | 25 |
| 1,000–9,999 employees | 45 | 23 | 66 | 47 |
| 10,000 or more employees | 62 | 43 | 71 | 57 |
| *Sector of ownership* | | | | |
| Private | 16 | – | 33 | – |
| Public | 90 | – | 95 | – |
| *Industry* | | | | |
| Manufacturing | 23 | 21 | 51 | 50 |
| Electricity, gas and water | (95) | (95) | (97) | (97) |
| Construction | 16 | 13 | 33 | 24 |
| Wholesale and retail | 10 | 10 | 24 | 24 |
| Hotels and restaurants | 0 | 0 | 5 | 4 |
| Transport and communication | 43 | 22 | 68 | 58 |
| Financial services | 72 | 72 | 56 | 56 |
| Other business services | 11 | 7 | 17 | 13 |
| Public administration | 100 | * | 100 | * |
| Education | 81 | 37 | 83 | 69 |
| Health and social work | 41 | 16 | 69 | 23 |
| Other community services | 35 | 23 | 54 | 33 |

Base: All workplaces with 10 or more employees.
Figures are weighted and based on responses from 1,992 managers (1,422 in the private sector).

has changed since 1998. In order to make such a comparison, it is necessary to move to a slightly more restrictive measure of union recognition, since the measure available in the first four surveys in the WERS series is confined to unions with at least some members at the workplace. WERS 2004 was the first in the series to break the link between membership and recognition by asking whether managers recognized any trade unions that did not have members at the workplace. This may occur if the employer is party to an industry-wide agreement or, more commonly, if the workplace is part of a larger organization that automatically extends recognition to all of its sites.

In 2004, 8 per cent of all workplaces recognized trade unions that were without members at the workplace. Around two-thirds of these also recognized other unions with a membership presence at the establishment. But the remainder, which together accounted for 3 per cent of all workplaces, or one-tenth of those with recognized unions, would not have been identified as recognizing unions in earlier surveys in the series.

Under the more restrictive measure used in those earlier surveys, the percentage of workplaces that recognized unions in 2004 stood at 27 per cent (Table 5.5). These workplaces employed 48 per cent of all employees. The equivalent figures in 1998 were 33 per cent and 53 per cent respectively, indicating a small decline in the incidence of recognition over the intervening period. There was a notable divergence between the private and public sectors, however. In the private sector, the proportion of workplaces recognizing unions fell from one-fifth to around one in seven (15 per cent), whereas the proportion remained stable in the public sector at just over four-fifths.

Data from the 1998–2004 Panel Survey indicated that, within the private sector, the incidence of recognition remained stable among continuing workplaces, and there was little difference between workplaces falling out of scope and those growing into scope. Thus it was the lower rate of recognition among new

*Table 5.5* Trade union recognition, 1998 and 2004

|  | 1998 | | 2004 | |
| --- | --- | --- | --- | --- |
|  | *% workplaces* | *% employees* | *% workplaces* | *% employees* |
| All workplaces | 33 | 53 | 27 | 48 |
| Private sector | 20 | 39 | 15 | 32 |
| Public sector | 83 | 91 | 82 | 92 |
| *Workplace size* | | | | |
| 10–24 employees | 28 | 28 | 18 | 18 |
| 25 or more employees | 41 | 58 | 39 | 54 |

Base: All workplaces with 10 or more employees.
Figures are weighted and based on responses from 1,994 managers in 2004 and 2,150 in 1998.
Note:
    Uses a more restricted measure of union recognition than Table 5.4, concerning only those recognized unions with members at the workplace (see text for further details).

private sector workplaces (10 per cent) when compared with those that had closed between 1998 and 2004 (26 per cent) which accounted for much of the aggregate decline. Small shifts in the composition of the population towards the private sector and in favour of 'joiners' (both discussed in Chapter 2), served to accentuate the decline observed in the economy as a whole.

Workplace size is another factor that is closely associated with the incidence of recognition and, here too, a divergence was apparent over the period. The rate of recognition among small workplaces with between 10 and 24 employees fell from 28 per cent in 1998 to 18 per cent in 2004. However, it remained stable among workplaces with 25 or more employees (41 per cent in 1998 and 39 per cent in 2004). A similar picture was apparent in the private sector, where the rate of recognition fell from 17 per cent to 9 per cent among work-places with 10–24 employees, but remained approximately stable among workplaces with 25 or more (25 per cent in 1998 and 23 per cent in 2004).

The stability in the rate of recognition among private sector workplaces with 25 or more employees between 1998 and 2004 marked a substantial departure from the experience of the late 1980s and 1990s, when the rate of recognition among private workplaces with 25 or more employees fell proportionately by around 3 or 4 per cent per annum, on average (Millward *et al.*, 2000: 97). This begs the question of what might have altered among this subset of private sector workplaces with 25 or more employees to bring about such a change.

One apparent difference was identified in the behaviour of private sector workplaces that continued in operation with 25 or more employees between 1998 and 2004, when compared with their equivalents in the period 1990–1998. In the earlier period, the rate of recognition among continuing private sector workplaces was stable at 34 per cent, since the small proportion of workplaces (5 per cent) that ceased to recognize unions were balanced out by the similarly small proportion (4 per cent) that began to recognize unions for the first time.[8] Between 1998 and 2004 however, the rate of recognition among continuing private sector workplaces with 25 or more employees rose by eight percentage points, from 24 per cent to 32 per cent. Only 2 per cent of workplaces ceased to recognize unions, whereas 10 per cent began to recognize them for the first time. This represents a substantial shift in behaviour when compared with the earlier period, but one which is broadly consistent with the data collected by Gall (2004) that indicates a five-fold increase in the number of new recognition agreements and a similar proportionate decrease in the number of cases of de-recognition over the same time period. And while a panel survey can be expected to accentuate the extent of change between one period and the next because of the cumulative effect of measurement error (Freeman, 1984: 5), there seems no obvious reason why the degree of error might change over time.[9] Consequently, it seems safe to conclude that there has been a substantive change in behaviour since 1998 among continuing private sector workplaces with 25 or more employees. Without such a change, the rate of recognition would have continued to decline among this subset of the population.

It is far from straightforward to ascertain what role the statutory recognition procedure may have played in bringing about this change. It seems safe to assume that the direct effect of the legislation has been relatively small, given that most of the new recognition agreements reported by trade unions have been secured through voluntary means. Indeed, it is widely accepted that the primary impact of the legislation has been to prompt activity in the 'shadow' of the law, by encouraging unions to step up and target their campaigning efforts, and by encouraging employers to give greater consideration to unions' requests. In this regard, it is perhaps notable that the rate of recognition among new private sector workplaces with 25 or more employees that were established between 1999 and 2004 was no higher than the rate observed among equivalent workplaces established in the five years prior to the 1998 survey. This suggests no step change in behaviour among fledgling workplaces and accords with the suggestion that a union must first build up a relatively high level of membership at a workplace before a campaign will prove successful (Gall, 2004: 261–263). Yet whatever the mechanisms – and these are not easy to discern in WERS – it does seem clear, both from the survey data and other sources, that the period since 1998 has seen a change in the pattern of union recognition in Britain.

The prospects for further increases in recognition activity would appear to rely on further organizing efforts by trade unions. Only 1 per cent of private sector workplaces had turned down a request for recognition since 1998 – all such requests observed in the survey coming in workplaces that already recognized unions. A further 1 per cent of private sector workplaces had a majority of union members but no recognized unions, and 4 per cent had membership density of at least 10 per cent without any recognition; together, these workplaces employed 6 per cent of all employees in the private sector. Nevertheless, if recognition is to be granted at these workplaces in the future, it is clear that the decision will often be taken at a higher level. Only half of all managers said that they were able to make a decision about the recognition of trade unions at their establishment without consulting with managers at another workplace in the organization.

### Bargaining arrangements

In the preceding discussion, union recognition has been treated as a single decision on the part of managers. But, as was demonstrated earlier in the chapter, it is often the case that a number of unions may be represented at an establishment; managers may then opt to recognize all of these unions, a selection or just one. The recognition of multiple unions may prove expedient in accommodating diverse groups of workers, but it has often been associated with higher wage settlements, as unions compete against each other to obtain the most favourable settlements for their own members, and with lower levels of workplace performance (see Bryson *et al.*, 2005, for a review).

Among the 30 per cent of workplaces that recognized trade unions, around half (49 per cent) recognized a single union, just under one-third (29 per cent) recognized two unions and one-fifth (21 per cent) recognized three or more. Smaller workplaces were more likely than larger ones to recognize only a single union. The recognition of a single union was also more likely in the private sector than in the public sector. However, in both cases, the differences were due to union members in smaller workplaces and in private sector establishments being more likely to all belong to the same union. Where employees were grouped into two or more unions, larger workplaces and those in the public sector appeared no more likely to adopt a selective approach to recognition than smaller workplaces and those in the private sector.

In two-fifths (43 per cent) of workplaces where a single union was recognized, this was the result of a formal agreement to recognize only that union. Such 'single-union deals' were the subject of much comment and debate in the late 1980s and early 1990s, as they were seen to offer the prospect of more harmonious relations and simplified bargaining arrangements. They were welcomed by many managers, but eschewed by most unions because of thoughts that they would render the union ineffectual (Gall, 1993: 74). An alternative arrangement that also offers the prospect of streamlining the process of management–union negotiations is 'single-table bargaining', whereby all of the recognized unions negotiate with managers as one unit. Single-table bargaining took place in 60 per cent of workplaces that recognized more than one union. Fragmented bargaining arrangements therefore accounted for around one-fifth (19 per cent) of all establishments that recognized unions; these establishments in turn accounted for 5 per cent of all workplaces.

## Trade union representatives

As a collective activity, workplace unionism necessarily entails that some form of representative arrangement is established, if members are to be consulted, their views articulated and their energies marshalled, in a coherent and organized way. For most union members this role is fulfilled, not by a paid official of their trade union, but by a lay union representative: an employee of the workplace, appointed from among the union members there to represent them in dealings with managers. The roles and activity of lay union representatives are discussed in Chapter 6; here the concern is with the overall prevalence of such representatives.

Union representatives were present on-site in two-fifths (38 per cent) of workplaces with union members.[10] Combining data obtained from managers on the presence of on-site union representatives with data obtained from employees on union membership, just over three-quarters (77 per cent) of all union members worked in establishments with at least one on-site union representative. However, three-fifths of these union members worked in workplaces with multiple unions, and it is possible that only some of those unions may have had representatives on-site; the figure of 77 per cent is therefore an upper-bound estimate of the percentage of union members with access to an on-site representative from their trade union. It nonetheless indicates that a sizeable minority of union members had no on-site representative available to them at their workplace.

In most cases, the lack of access to an on-site representative was seemingly due to the total number of union members at the workplace being too low either to necessitate, or to give rise to, a local representative. Examining the relationship between the presence of on-site union representatives and the number of union members at the workplace, it appeared that a critical mass of around 15 union members was required in order to offer at least a 50:50 chance of there being a union representative on-site. Once the number of union members reached 30 or more, the chances rose to 75:25 and with at least 60 members it was almost certain that an on-site rep would be present (90:10).

The number of local union representatives is noted to have diminished during the 1980s and 1990s (Terry, 2003: 259) but, while the 1980s provided evidence of a 'thinning out' of representation where unions remained recognized, in the 1990s any further decline merely reflected the continued decline in union recognition at workplace level (Millward *et al.*, 1999: 242–243). The period between 1998 and 2004 saw the return to the earlier pattern. In 1998, 55 per cent of workplaces with recognized trade unions had an on-site representative from at least one of these unions. In 2004, the equivalent figure was 45 per cent. The decline in on-site representatives of recognized unions was greatest among small workplaces and in the public sector. Overall, lay union representatives were present in 13 per cent of workplaces in 2004, compared with 17 per cent of workplaces in 1998.

The decrease between 1998 and 2004 in the incidence of on-site union representatives of recognized unions was compensated by an increase in the extent of access to lay representatives located elsewhere. The vast majority (90 per cent) of workplaces where recognized unions did not have an on-site representative were nonetheless part of a larger organization, and in two-fifths (42 per cent) of such workplaces, members had access to a lay representative at another site in that organization. If these off-site representatives are included in a composite measure of the availability of union representation among workplaces with recognized unions, this indicates that in almost half of workplaces with recognized unions (45 per cent), members had access to a lay representative on-site; in a further fifth (21 per cent) they relied upon a lay representative at another site in the workplace; and in almost one third (31 per cent), members had no access to a lay representative.[11] The corresponding figures in 1998 were 55 per cent, 14 per cent and 29 per cent respectively. Accordingly, the overall percentage of unionized workplaces at which members of recognized unions had access to a representative did not differ significantly in 1998 and 2004, though it became more likely that representatives were located at another establishment within the organization.

Among the many topics that are of concern to union representatives, training and learning is one that has attracted increasing interest over the past two decades (Munro and Rainbird, 2004). Indeed, rights to time off have recently been introduced for designated Union Learning Representatives via the

Employment Act 2002. Managers who reported that union representatives were present at their establishment were asked whether any of these representatives had specific responsibility for promoting training or learning among employees at the workplace: 12 per cent reported that at least some on-site union representatives did have such a role. The figure was much higher in workplaces with two or more on-site representatives than in workplaces with a sole on-site representative (20 per cent and 4 per cent respectively). In aggregate, 6 per cent of union representatives were reported to have specific responsibility for promoting training or learning. The characteristics and activities of senior Union Learning Representatives will be considered in more detail in Chapter 6.

## Stand-alone non-union representatives

A further avenue of representative voice may be provided by non-union employee representatives: employees whose constituency is not determined by union membership, but who nonetheless perform some general, representative function on behalf of their colleagues in dealings with managers. One forum in which non-union representatives are commonly found is the joint consultative committee – discussed more broadly in the following section. However, there are also a minority of workplaces (5 per cent) with 'stand-alone' non-union representatives.

Stand-alone non-union representatives were not only found in non-union workplaces. In fact, they were no less likely to be found in workplaces with union members than in workplaces without unions. And they were just as common among workplaces where managers were in favour of union membership as they were among workplaces where managers were not in favour. But where stand-alone non-union representatives were present in unionized workplaces, union membership density tended to be at a relatively low level, indicating a low degree of attachment to those union structures that were in place.

Aside from the associations with unionism, the characteristic most obviously associated with the prevalence of stand-alone non-union representatives was the size of the workplace. Some 4 per cent of workplaces with between 10 and 49 employees had at least one stand-alone non-union representative, but this rose to 6 per cent among workplaces with between 50 and 249 employees and 11 per cent among those with 250 employees or more. Stand-alone non-union representatives were present to similar extents among private and public sector workplaces (5 per cent and 3 per cent respectively). Their prevalence also varied little across industry sectors, with stand-alone non-union representatives found in between 3 and 7 per cent of workplaces in each of the twelve broad industry sectors. The role of stand-alone non-union representatives is discussed further in Chapter 6.

## Joint consultative committees

The final avenue for employee representation to be discussed here concerns committees of managers and employees that are primarily concerned with consultation rather than negotiation. These may be referred to as works councils, representative forums or joint consultative committees; the latter is used hereafter as the generic label.

Joint consultative committees (JCCs) have been found to exist both as a complement to, and as a substitute for, union representation (Terry, 1999). Union representatives often feature among the membership of committees that exist in unionized establishments, but JCCs also constitute the most common form of representative voice in workplaces where there are no union members. In this respect, there are debates as to whether they can adequately fill the representation gap left by the decline of workplace unionism. Some disagree, emphasizing the weaknesses of arrangements that exist primarily for the purposes of consultation rather than collective bargaining, and arguing that the establishment of consultative committees or works councils may be harmful to any potential recovery in union organization (Kelly, 1996). Others are more sanguine, seeing consultative bodies as offering unions the opportunity for formal engagement with managers in situations where negotiation is not yet possible (Hyman, 1996). The weight of opinion appears to have come down in favour of the latter position (Heery *et al.*, 2004a: 31), with many now seeing the introduction of statutory support for employee consultation as potentially beneficial to union activity. Nonetheless, questions remain about the incidence and operation of existing arrangements, and about their effectiveness in providing a role for employees and their representatives in consultation over developments at the workplace.

Joint consultative committees were present in 14 per cent of workplaces in 2004 (Table 5.6). The incidence varied markedly according to the size of the workplace: JCCs were rarely present in workplaces with fewer than 25 employees, where managers may find it easy to consult directly with staff, but they were a normal feature of establishments with 200 or more employees. Committees were also more common in the public sector than among private sector workplaces, although the difference was most apparent among smaller establishments. Around one-fifth (22 per cent) of public sector workplaces with less than 50 employees had a consultative committee, compared with just 6 per cent of private sector workplaces in the same size group. Among workplaces with 50 or more employees, the figures were 45 per cent and 37 per cent respectively. Within the private sector, the two industry sectors with above average incidence of consultative committees were Manufacturing (19 per cent) and Transport and communication (18 per cent).

There had been a decline in the incidence of consultative committees at workplace level since 1998, when one-fifth of establishments had such arrangements for consulting their staff. The decline was primarily evident among workplaces with less than 100 employees, where the percentage of workplaces with on-site committees fell from 17 per cent in 1998 to 10 per cent in 2004. Among workplaces with 100 or more employees, the incidence remained stable (56 per cent in 1998, compared with 54 per cent in 2004). The decline was also concentrated within workplaces that did not recognize trade unions, where the incidence of a workplace-level consultative committee fell from 14 per cent in 1998 to 8 per cent in 2004. Among workplaces that did recognize unions, the proportion with a workplace-level committee remained unchanged (32 per cent in 1998; 29 per cent in 2004). The proportion of all employees working in an establishment with an on-site committee fell from 46 per cent in 1998 to 42 per cent in 2004.

*Table* 5.6 Joint consultative committees, by workplace characteristics

| | % workplaces | | |
|---|---|---|---|
| | Workplace-level committee | Higher-level committee only | No committee |
| All workplaces | 14 | 25 | 62 |
| *Workplace size* | | | |
| 10–24 employees | 4 | 26 | 70 |
| 25–49 employees | 16 | 24 | 59 |
| 50–99 employees | 26 | 27 | 47 |
| 100–199 employees | 47 | 16 | 37 |
| 200–499 employees | 59 | 13 | 28 |
| 500 or more employees | 73 | 9 | 18 |
| *Organization status* | | | |
| Stand-alone workplace | 6 | – | 94 |
| Part of a larger organization | 18 | 36 | 46 |
| *Organization size* | | | |
| 10–99 employees | 5 | 1 | 94 |
| 100–999 employees | 18 | 29 | 53 |
| 1,000–9,999 employees | 22 | 44 | 35 |
| 10,000 or more employees | 21 | 50 | 30 |
| *Sector of ownership* | | | |
| Private | 11 | 20 | 69 |
| Public | 28 | 46 | 26 |
| *Industry* | | | |
| Manufacturing | 21 | 4 | 75 |
| Electricity, gas and water | (52) | (35) | (14) |
| Construction | 8 | 5 | 87 |
| Wholesale and retail | 11 | 31 | 58 |
| Hotels and restaurants | 4 | 28 | 68 |
| Transport and communication | 16 | 29 | 55 |
| Financial services | 5 | 57 | 38 |
| Other business services | 10 | 16 | 74 |
| Public administration | 42 | 40 | 18 |
| Education | 30 | 31 | 40 |
| Health and social work | 13 | 25 | 62 |
| Other community services | 14 | 23 | 62 |

Base: All workplaces with 10 or more employees.
Figures are weighted and based on responses from 2,020 managers.

In addition to the 14 per cent of establishments with a workplace-level consultative committee, a further 25 per cent were without an on-site committee but had a multi-issue consultative committee that operated at a higher level than the establishment, for instance, at regional, divisional or head office level (Table 5.6). The equivalent figure in 1998 was 27 per cent. Higher-level committees did not therefore appear to be covering the gaps left by the withdrawal of workplace-level committees. Indeed, around three-fifths (62 per cent) of workplaces were not covered by a joint consultative committee in 2004, compared with just over half (53 per cent) in 1998.

Focusing on consultative arrangements at the apex of the organization, managers in workplaces that were part of private-sector, transnational companies were asked whether the organization of which they were part operated a European Works Council (EWC). Around one in eight managers in such workplaces were unable to answer but, among the remainder, the proportion replying positively was 27 per cent. Overall, 5 per cent of all workplaces were covered by EWCs. Neither figure had changed since 1998.

Returning to the establishment level, most workplace-level committees covered a range of issues although a minority covered a single issue such as staffing or health and safety. The incidence of specific arrangements for consultation over redundancies and health and safety is discussed further in Chapter 7. Hereafter, the focus is primarily on committees covering a range of issues. Such committees were present in 12 per cent of workplaces in 2004, compared with 18 per cent in 1998.

The incidence of on-site multi-issue committees fell in the private and public sectors, among workplaces with and without recognized unions and among workplaces with and without on-site personnel specialists. However, the decline was seen primarily among smaller workplaces, with the incidence of on-site multi-issue committees falling from 15 per cent in 1998 to 9 per cent in 2004 among establishments with fewer than 100 employees. In contrast, the incidence remained stable among workplaces with 100 or more employees (47 per cent in 1998, compared with 49 per cent in 2004). One consequence was that the proportion of employees working in establishments with on-site multi-issue committees also saw little change between 1998 (38 per cent) and 2004 (40 per cent).

### The operation of workplace consultative committees

Managers were asked a number of questions about the operation of workplace-level consultative committees.[12] One feature that has been highlighted by earlier WERS surveys is the irregularity with which some committees meet (Millward *et al.*, 2000: 108–109). In 2004, three-quarters of committees had met at least four times in the previous 12 months (e.g. quarterly). A further fifth (21 per cent) had met twice or three times, while the remaining 4 per cent had met only once in the year or not at all. In 1998, 83 per cent of committees had met on at least four occasions, 14 per cent had met twice or three times and 4 per cent met only once or not at all.

The types of issues discussed by consultative committees are categorized in Figure 5.1. The spirit of the new regulations on information and consultation was broadly reflected in the range of topics discussed, with most committees addressing financial issues, employment issues, work organization or future plans. Financial issues were, however, less commonly discussed than employment issues, work organization and future plans. The lower ranking of financial issues may reflect some reluctance on the part of managers to share financial information with employee representatives on consultative committees. Indeed, only three-fifths of managers said that they shared commercially-sensitive information with representatives on the committee. A further quarter (27 per cent) said that they did not share such information, while 13 per cent said that it was not relevant to the committee in question. The proportion sharing commercially-sensitive information rose only marginally, to 70 per cent, in cases where the committee discussed financial issues.

The likelihood of each issue being discussed had changed little since 1998, except in respect of pay, employment and health and safety. Pay issues were discussed by around half of all committees (47 per cent) in 1998, rising to two-thirds (66 per cent) in 2004. The figure had risen both in workplaces with and without recognized unions. Employment issues were also more commonly discussed in 2004 (78 per cent, compared with 71 per cent in 1998), but health

*Figure 5.1* Issues discussed by workplace-level joint consultative committees

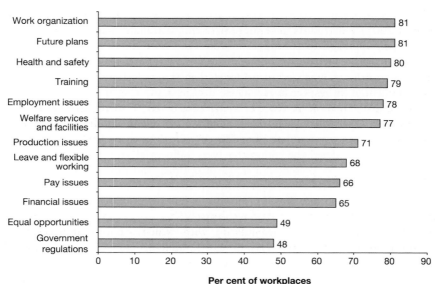

**Per cent of workplaces**

Base: All workplaces with 10 or more employees and an on-site multi-issue consultative committee.
Figures are weighted and based on responses from 729 managers.

and safety issues were less commonly dealt with (80 per cent in 2004, compared with 88 per cent in 1998). Further discussion on the range of issues that are subject to consultation is presented in Chapter 7.

Turning to the manner in which issues are dealt with, managers were presented with three statements and asked to state which of these best described managers' usual approach when consulting members of the committee. The statements were designed to identify whether consultative committees were involved at an early stage in developing solutions to a problem (so-called 'options-based consultation'), or whether they were more likely to be used as a sounding board once managers had decided upon their preferred course of action. The results showed that there were two dominant approaches: 43 per cent said that their usual approach was to look to the committee to provide solutions to problems, while a further 45 per cent said that they usually sought feedback from the committee on a range of options put forward by management. The remaining 11 per cent said that they usually sought feedback on a preferred option. The same question was put to non-union committee representatives interviewed as part of the Survey of Employee Representatives, enabling a comparison to be made between the perceptions of managers and representatives in the same workplaces. Responses were obtained from around three-quarters of representatives, among whom three-fifths (58 per cent) gave the same response as the management respondent, one quarter (25 per cent) gave a response indicating a greater degree of involvement in identifying solutions and one-fifth (18 per cent) gave a response indicating a lesser degree of involvement.[13]

It has been argued that managers must be committed to consulting early in the decision-making process if consultation is to be effective (Dix and Oxenbridge, 2003). The results gave support to this notion, as managers reporting a more open approach to consultation were also more likely to report that the committee had a substantive influence over managerial decision-making. Overall, one quarter of managers considered that the consultative committee was 'very influential' in respect of managers' decisions affecting the workforce at the establishment, three-fifths (62 per cent) considered it 'fairly influential' and one-tenth (12 per cent) considered that it was 'not very influential'. However, where the committee was invited to identify solutions to problems, 35 per cent of managers considered the committee 'very influential', compared with 19 per cent where managers presented a range of options, and just 11 per cent where managers only invited feedback on their preferred option. The percentages of managers reporting that the committee was 'not very influential' were 12 per cent, 11 per cent and 25 per cent respectively.

The proportion of managers viewing the consultative committee at their workplace as 'very influential' had decreased markedly since 1998, when 41 per cent gave this response. The proportion viewing their committee as 'fairly influential' rose by the same degree as a result. It is not possible to ascertain whether this may have resulted from a change in managers' general approach to consultation over the period, as the questions on that topic were new to the 2004 survey.

## *Employee representation on consultative committees*

It has also been argued that the strategies for appointing employee representatives to consultative committees should be fair and transparent (Dix and Oxenbridge, 2003). Possible mechanisms for ensuring fairness and transparency include the provision of elections, or other procedures that allow individuals to be selected or nominated by the employees they will represent, rather than being appointed by managers.

Managers were asked whether elections were usually held among employees to appoint representatives to the committee. This was the case for almost three-fifths (57 per cent) of committees. For a further 15 per cent of committees, representatives were selected by employees without recourse to an election. For 10 per cent of committees, representatives were selected by managers, in 8 per cent they were selected by unions and in 10 per cent managers said that they appointed anyone who would volunteer for the role. The likelihood that representatives were appointed by election increased with the size of the workplace, just as the likelihood that representatives were simply selected decreased. Equally, in workplaces with larger numbers of employees, representatives were more likely to have been selected by unions and less likely to have been appointed by managers.

Representatives on fewer than half (44 per cent) of all committees were provided with training or instruction to help them in their role. Where training was provided, this routinely covered the structure and format of committee meetings (83 per cent of workplaces providing training to committee representatives) or behaviour at meetings (70 per cent of such workplaces). It was less likely to comprise problem-solving skills (48 per cent) or presentation skills (45 per cent), and even less frequently covered the interpretation of financial data (26 per cent). Only one in seven consultative committees that considered financial issues (16 per cent) provided training to employee representatives in the interpretation of financial data.

Returning to the broad composition of the consultative committee, it was possible to distinguish between employee representatives who also served as union representatives at the establishment and those who operated independently of trade unions (referred to here and in Chapter 6 as 'non-union JCC representatives'). Overall, 11 per cent of consultative committees were composed wholly of union representatives, 67 per cent were composed wholly of non-union representatives and 22 per cent were so-called 'mixed constituency' committees. The prevalence of non-union committees partly reflects the predominance of non-union workplaces, however. In workplaces where at least some union representatives were present on site, 25 per cent of consultative committees comprised wholly of union representatives, 23 per cent were wholly non-union and 52 per cent were 'mixed constituency'.

Some have suggested that, without union involvement, consultative structures may be limited in both their resources and effectiveness (Terry, 1999: 28; Gollan, 2000: 444). In support of this contention, it was apparent that consultative committees which featured union representatives among their members were more likely than wholly non-union committees to have discussed many of the issues presented in Figure 5.1. Some of the greatest differences were apparent in respect of employment issues (discussed by 88 per cent of committees with at least some union representatives, compared with 74 per cent of non-unionized committees), financial issues (discussed by 75 per cent and 61 per cent respectively) and equal opportunities (64 per cent and 41 per cent respectively). However, committees including union representatives were no more likely than non-union committees to have access to commercially-sensitive information and were no more likely to have been provided with training or instruction from managers in respect of representatives' role on the committee. What is more, committees including union representatives were just as likely to be treated as a sounding board for managers' preferred solutions, rather than as a problem-solving body and, consequently, were no more influential than non-union committees, on average.

One possible explanation for these findings is that, although committees including union representatives were better able to ensure that certain issues were brought onto the agenda of committee meetings, a lack of trust inhibited managers from yielding autonomy and influence to such committees. Indeed, some have indicated that trust is a particularly important factor in determining the effectiveness of such arrangements (Gollan, 2000: 444; Dix and Oxenbridge, 2003: 73). This specific hypothesis is not tested here. However, the issue of trust is examined in some detail in Chapter 6.

## Summary of arrangements for employee representation

In order to provide a broad overview of the availability of representative arrangements, a measure was compiled to identify workplaces with any of the arrangements discussed hitherto, namely recognized unions, joint consultative committees (whether at the workplace or at a higher level), lay union representatives or stand-alone non-union representatives. In 2004, around one half (49 per cent) of all workplaces had at least one of these arrangements (Table 5.7). As one might expect from the preceding discussion, this proportion had fallen since 1998, when it stood at just under three-fifths (57 per cent). And in keeping with the patterns of decline witnessed in respect of union recognition and joint consultation, the overall availability of representative arrangements was seen to have fallen primarily among small workplaces and in the private sector. This did mean, however, that the proportion of employees working in establishments with some form of representative structure saw a less precipitous decline, falling from 74 per cent in 1998 to 71 per cent in 2004.

Assessing the extent of change across industry sectors, it was apparent that those industries witnessing the largest declines in the availability of representative structures tended to be those with the highest proportions of small, private sector workplaces. However, two sectors – Wholesale and retail and Financial services – provided exceptions to this rule. Both sectors are dominated by small,

*Table* 5.7 Broad incidence of arrangements for employee representation, by workplace characteristics

| | Any arrangement for employee representation[a] | | | |
| | % workplaces | | % employees | |
| | 1998 | 2004 | 1998 | 2004 |
|---|---|---|---|---|
| All workplaces | 57 | 49 | – | – |
| All employees | – | – | 74 | 71 |
| *Workplace size* | | | | |
| 10–24 employees | 50 | 38 | 50 | 40 |
| 25–49 employees | 61 | 55 | 61 | 56 |
| 50–99 employees | 67 | 66 | 69 | 67 |
| 100–199 employees | 77 | 76 | 77 | 77 |
| 200–499 employees | 86 | 86 | 86 | 87 |
| 500 or more employees | 92 | 90 | 94 | 92 |
| Workplaces with 25 or more employees | 67 | 63 | 79 | 77 |
| *Organization status* | | | | |
| Stand-alone workplace | 29 | 14 | 47 | 37 |
| Part of a larger organization | 71 | 65 | 82 | 80 |
| *Organization size* | | | | |
| 10–99 employees | 29 | 14 | 33 | 19 |
| 100–999 employees | 53 | 55 | 64 | 62 |
| 1,000–9,999 employees | 80 | 73 | 83 | 86 |
| 10,000 or more employees | 84 | 87 | 94 | 94 |
| *Sector of ownership* | | | | |
| Private | 47 | 39 | 65 | 61 |
| Public | 96 | 93 | 99 | 98 |
| *Industry* | | | | |
| Manufacturing | 52 | 37 | 76 | 71 |
| Electricity, gas and water | (100) | (95) | (100) | (97) |
| Construction | 32 | 20 | 52 | 43 |
| Wholesale and retail | 44 | 47 | 66 | 67 |
| Hotels and restaurants | 58 | 36 | 60 | 46 |
| Transport and communication | 57 | 57 | 80 | 80 |
| Financial services | 88 | 85 | 79 | 80 |
| Other business services | 42 | 34 | 52 | 49 |
| Public administration | 100 | 100 | 100 | 100 |
| Education | 84 | 86 | 92 | 94 |
| Health and social work | 66 | 49 | 82 | 77 |
| Other community services | 63 | 42 | 73 | 65 |

Base: All workplaces with 10 or more employees.
Figures are weighted and based on responses from 2,169 managers in 1998 and 2,029 managers in 2004.
Note:
[a] Denotes the presence of at least one of the following: a recognized union, a joint consultative committee (whether at the workplace or at a higher level), a lay union representative or a stand-alone non-union representative.

private sector establishments, but the incidence of representative arrangements was stable in the two sectors between 1998 and 2004. The preponderance of large *firms* in either sector provides a likely explanation. Indeed, the incidence of representative arrangements fell sharply among workplaces belonging to organizations with fewer than 100 employees (from 29 per cent in 1998 to 14 per cent in 2004), while remaining steady within larger organizations (74 per cent in both years). It is possible that the introduction in April 2005 of regulations supporting information and consultation in organizations with 150 or more employees may have served to prevent any notable decline in the incidence of arrangements for employee representation among larger organizations, although it is difficult to establish any direct association with the available data.

## Direct communication methods

Thus far, the chapter has considered arrangements for representation which rely on employee representatives as intermediaries. The focus now turns to direct methods of communication between managers and employees. The mechanisms vary according to whether the communication is face-to-face or written, and also according to whether there is an opportunity for dialogue. Following these themes, the mechanisms discussed here are categorized into three groups, beginning with face-to-face, two-way communication through workforce meetings and team briefings. The second group comprises written methods that might permit upward communication from employees to managers, namely e-mail, suggestion schemes and employee surveys. The final category comprises methods that are primarily, if not wholly, concerned with downward communication, specifically use of the management chain, newsletters, notice boards and company intranets. Past research has shown substantial growth in the use of direct communication methods, especially in the private sector, and particularly among those arrangements allowing for two-way communication or dialogue (Forth and Millward, 2002a). Changes in the incidence of the various methods since 1998 are discussed where possible.

### Workforce meetings

One of the most common forms of direct communication between managers and employees are face-to-face meetings between senior managers and the whole workforce. Such meetings took place in four-fifths (79 per cent) of all workplaces (Table 5.8). There was little variation in the incidence of meetings by workplace size, but it is likely that, where the workforce was particularly large, practicalities may have meant that senior managers met with employees on a departmental basis, rather than gathering all staff together for a single meeting.[14] The incidence of workforce meetings was slightly higher in the public sector than among private sector workplaces. And in the private sector, the incidence was positively associated with the size of the organization to which the establishment belonged.

*Table 5.8* Arrangements for direct communication, by sector of ownership

| | % of workplaces | | | | | |
|---|---|---|---|---|---|---|
| | 1998 | | | 2004 | | |
| | *Private sector* | *Public sector* | *All workplaces* | *Private sector* | *Public sector* | *All workplaces* |
| *Face-to-face meetings* | | | | | | |
| Meetings between senior managers and the whole workforce | – | – | – | 77 | 89 | 79 |
| Team briefings | – | – | – | 68 | 81 | 71 |
| Any face-to-face meetings | 82 | 96 | 85 | 90 | 97 | 91 |
| *Written two-way communication* | | | | | | |
| Employee surveys | – | – | – | 37 | 66 | 42 |
| E-mail | – | – | – | 36 | 48 | 38 |
| Suggestion schemes | 29 | 35 | 31 | 30 | 30 | 30 |
| Any written two-way communication | – | – | – | 62 | 84 | 66 |
| *Downward communication* | | | | | | |
| Notice boards | – | – | – | 72 | 86 | 74 |
| Systematic use of management chain | 46 | 75 | 52 | 60 | 81 | 64 |
| Regular newsletters | 35 | 59 | 40 | 41 | 63 | 45 |
| Intranet | – | – | – | 31 | 48 | 34 |
| Any downward communication | – | – | – | 80 | 97 | 83 |

Base: All workplaces with 10 or more employees.
Figures are weighted and based on responses from at least 2,189 managers in 1998 and at least 2,057 managers in 2004.

Managers were asked how often such meetings took place. In one quarter of cases (24 per cent), workforce meetings took place at least once a week, in 31 per cent they took place at least once a month, in 26 per cent they occurred at least once every three months, leaving one-fifth (20 per cent) of workplaces where such meetings took place less than quarterly. Meetings tended to occur less often in larger workplaces than in smaller ones, perhaps in acknowledgement of the practicalities outlined above. The proportion of time made available in workforce meetings for employees to ask questions of senior managers, or offer their views, was also lower in larger workplaces. On average, 87 per cent of meetings made at least 10 per cent of the meeting time available for employees' questions or views, and 59 per cent offered at least one quarter of the time. But among workplaces with 500 or more employees, the figures were 78 per cent and 32 per cent respectively.

Combining information about the regularity and openness of meetings showed that, overall, almost two-fifths (38 per cent) of workplaces had workforce meetings at least monthly at which at least 10 per cent of the meeting time was made available for employees' views or questions. The incidence was unsurprisingly lower among larger workplaces, but was positively associated with the size of the wider organization. Such meetings were also considerably more likely in public sector workplaces (57 per cent) than in the private sector (34 per cent), although this was largely a function of differences in workplace and organization size between the two sectors. Education was the industry sector most likely to hold such meetings (62 per cent), with Construction the least likely (18 per cent) – features that remained after controlling for workplace size, organization size and sector of ownership.

A variety of issues were discussed in workforce meetings, with the most popular being future plans and matters that were either directly or indirectly related to production or service delivery (Figure 5.2). Terms and conditions such as pay or leave arrangements were much less likely to be covered.

## Team briefings

The second form of face-to-face meetings considered in WERS 2004 was meetings between line managers or supervisors and all the workers for whom they are responsible. These are sometimes referred to as briefing groups or team

*Figure 5.2* Issues discussed at face-to-face meetings

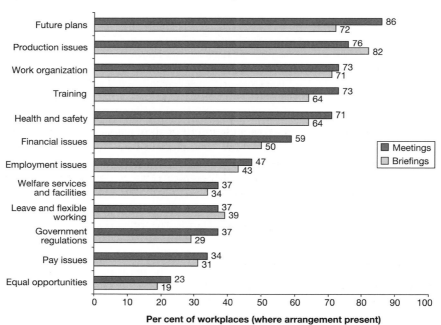

Base: All workplaces with 10 or more employees.
Figures are weighted and based on responses from at least 1,603 managers (meetings) and 1,730 managers (briefings).

briefings. Briefings took place in 71 per cent of all workplaces (Table 5.8), but their incidence was positively related to the size of the workplace; they took place in three-fifths (59 per cent) of workplaces with fewer than 25 employees, but in four-fifths (82 per cent) of workplaces with 25–49 employees and higher proportions of larger workplaces. In common with workforce meetings, team briefings were more common in the public sector than among private sector establishments. Briefings were slightly more likely than workforce meetings to focus directly on issues relating to production or service delivery, and were less likely to cover issues that pertain to the organization as a whole, such as future plans and financial issues (Figure 5.2).

Briefings tended to take place on a frequent basis: in almost half (46 per cent) of all instances, they took place at least once a week and in a further third (35 per cent) they took place at least once a month. They also commonly offered time for employees to ask questions or offer views, with only one-tenth (11 per cent) making less than 10 per cent of the meeting time available for this purpose, and two-thirds (64 per cent) making available at least one quarter of the time. Half of all workplaces reported team briefings that occured at least monthly and at which at least 10 per cent of the meeting time was made available for employees' views or questions. Such briefings took place in 47 per cent of private sector workplaces and 66 per cent of those in the public sector.

### Changes in the incidence of face-to-face meetings

Changes in the management questionnaire mean that it is not possible to separately chart changes in the incidence of workforce meetings and team briefings between 1998 and 2004, since the distinction made between the two forms of meeting in 2004 is not directly replicated in the 1998 questionnaire. However, it is possible to reliably chart the growth of face-to-face meetings as a whole, and this shows that there has been a small growth in the use of face-to-face meetings since 1998. Most workplaces (85 per cent) made some use of face-to-face meetings in 1998, but by 2004 the figure had risen to 91 per cent. The growth took place exclusively in the private sector and, continuing a trend observed in the 1990s (Forth and Millward, 2002a: 5), primarily occurred among workplaces without a personnel specialist on site. An increase in the proportion of workplaces that did have a personnel specialist on site also made a small contribution to the growth in face-to-face meetings.

### Written forms of upward communication

A number of arrangements provide the opportunity for upward communication from employees to managers, in written form. These include the use of e-mail, suggestion schemes and employee surveys. Managers in just over two-fifths (42 per cent) of workplaces said that they, or a third party, had conducted a formal survey of their employees' views or opinions during the two years that preceded the WERS interview (Table 5.8). Employee attitude surveys were more likely to have taken place in larger workplaces than smaller ones, and were more likely to have been conducted in workplaces belonging to large organizations. They were almost twice as common in the public sector (66 per cent) as in the private sector (37 per cent) although, as in the case of workforce meetings, this was largely a function of differences in workplace and organization size between the two sectors. In most cases (80 per cent), the results of the survey had been fed back to employees in written form.

A slightly smaller proportion of workplaces (38 per cent) made regular use of e-mail to communicate or consult with employees at their workplace. Naturally, the use of e-mail was strongly associated with the use of computers among staff. But it appeared that, in some cases, there was a risk that a substantial minority of employees may have been excluded by virtue of their lack of regular access to a computer. In around one-third of workplaces (32 per cent) where e-mail was used to communicate or consult with staff, at least one-fifth of all employees did not use computers as part of their normal work duties.

Finally, just under one-third (30 per cent) made use of suggestion schemes, a proportion that had not changed since 1998. Unlike many of the other forms of direct communication, the incidence of suggestion schemes did not vary between the private and public sectors. Suggestion schemes were slightly more common, however, in workplaces that used problem-solving groups as a means of identifying improvements to production processes or service delivery. Two-fifths (41 per cent) of workplaces with problem-solving groups also made use of suggestion schemes, compared with around one quarter (27 per cent) of other workplaces.

### Arrangements for downward communication

The third and final category of mechanisms for direct communication concerns arrangements that function primarily as a means of conveying information in a single direction, from managers to employees. WERS asked about the use of notice boards, newsletters, intranets and systematic use of the management chain. Each of the four practices was more common in larger workplaces and in the public sector. Overall, however, notice boards were the most common of the four arrangements, being used in three-quarters (74 per cent) of all workplaces (Table 5.8). Least common was the posting of information on a company intranet (34 per cent) where, again, a substantial minority of employees may have found access difficult; 37 per cent of workplaces using an intranet to disseminate information reported that at least one-fifth of their staff did not make use of computers in the course of their normal work duties.

There were increases since 1998 in the use of the management chain and newsletters, although these were the only two arrangements for which such a comparison was possible. In both cases, the increase was proportionately larger in the private sector than in the public sector but, in contrast to the increase in face-to-face meetings, the greater diffusion was not confined to workplaces without personnel specialists.

## Summary of arrangements for direct communication

To provide a summary of formal arrangements for direct communication, workplaces were hierarchically coded onto a four-category variable indicating (in order of preference): (1) the presence of face-to-face meetings that took place at least once a month and offered at least 10 per cent of the available time for employees' views and opinions; (2) the presence of other face-to-face meetings or written forms of upward communication; (3) the use of downward methods of communication only; or (4) the absence of formal arrangements for direct communication. Table 5.9 indicates that just under two-thirds (63 per cent) of all workplaces provided regular meetings with a substantive opportunity for employee feedback. These workplaces employed 67 per cent of all employees. A further 30 per cent of workplaces did not provide meetings of this type, but did provide meetings on a less regular basis or with less opportunity for feedback, or provided written forms of upward communication. A further 4 per cent of workplaces had formal arrangements for downward communication only, while 2 per cent had no formal arrangements for direct communication with employees. Many of the workplaces in the latter two categories were small private sector establishments.

## Employees' perceptions of arrangements for information-sharing and representation

Much of the preceding discussion has pointed to the further decline in arrangements for employee representation, with managers and employees seemingly becoming more reliant on direct methods of communication, such as face-to-face meetings. In order to make some initial assessment of what these trends might imply for the conduct of employment relations, the chapter concludes by looking at employees' perceptions of the utility of different arrangements for

*Table 5.9* Summary of direct communication arrangements, by sector of ownership

|  | *% workplaces* | | | *% employees* | | |
|---|---|---|---|---|---|---|
|  | *Private sector* | *Public sector* | *All workplaces* | *Private sector* | *Public sector* | *All employees* |
| Regular meetings with feedback | 59 | 81 | 63 | 64 | 77 | 67 |
| Other meetings, or written, two-way communication | 33 | 17 | 30 | 32 | 22 | 30 |
| Downward communication only | 5 | 1 | 4 | 3 | 1 | 2 |
| No formal arrangements | 3 | 0 | 2 | 1 | 0 | 1 |

Base: All workplaces with 10 or more employees.
Figures are weighted and based on responses from 1,463 (columns 1 and 4), 554 (columns 2 and 5) and 2,017 (columns 3 and 6) managers.
Note:
   Arrangements hierarchically coded where more than one type of arrangement present (see text for details).

information-sharing and representation. These data merit more detailed investigation than is possible within the confines of this volume. However, the initial results point to some of the potential strengths and weaknesses of different arrangements.

In order to gauge employees' views on the adequacy of information-sharing by managers, the Survey of Employees asked how good managers at the employee's workplace were at keeping them informed about: changes to the way the organization is run; changes in they way the employee does his/her job; changes in staffing; and financial issues. The results are presented in Figure 5.3. In respect of each of the four items, at least two-fifths of employees considered that managers were 'good' or 'very good' at keeping employees informed about the matter at hand although, in each case, less than one in seven considered their managers to be 'very good' and at least one-fifth considered them 'poor' or 'very poor'. Employees were least likely to give managers a positive rating in respect of financial issues, reflecting a relatively lower degree of openness about financial matters on the part of managers (see Figures 5.1 and 5.2 and Kersley *et al.*, 2005, Table 5). Combining responses across the four items, one quarter (23 per cent) of all employees rated managers as being at least 'good' on every item, and one in ten (11 per cent) rated them as no better than 'poor' in each area. There were no strong associations between employees' ratings and workplace characteristics,

*Figure 5.3* Employees' ratings of managers' information-sharing

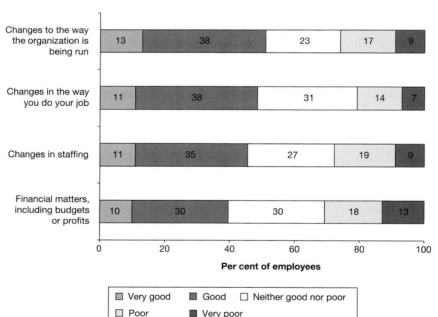

Base: All employees in workplaces with 10 or more.
Figures are weighted and based on responses from at least 20,013 employees.

such as size or sector. But it was noticeable that employees in white-collar occupations (Professionals, Associate professional and technical employees, Administrative and secretarial staff and Sales and customer service employees) were more likely to rate managers as 'good' or 'very good' on each item than were employees in blue-collar jobs (Skilled trades, Caring, leisure and other personal service occupations, Process, plant and machine operatives and Elementary occupations). One quarter (25 per cent) of the white-collar group gave managers 'good' or 'very good' ratings across all four items, compared with 18 per cent of the blue-collar group.

This contrast may partly reflect a greater level of day-to-day contact with managers among white-collar employees than among blue-collar employees. It might also partly reflect differential access to information communication technologies (ICTs). Employees were asked whether they found different arrangements helpful in keeping them informed about their workplace. Table 5.10 shows that e-mail and company intranets were among the most likely arrangements to be considered helpful. Just under nine-tenths (86 per cent) of employees who recorded the use of e-mail at their establishment considered it helpful in keeping them informed, while the same was true of four-fifths of employees with access to an intranet.

Notably, only three-fifths (60 per cent) of employees recording the presence of union or other employee representatives found that such channels helped to keep them informed about their workplace. Even among union members, the proportion rose to only 64 per cent, with higher proportions of members saying that each of the other five mechanisms was helpful.

Nevertheless, other data indicated that many employees preferred to rely on union representatives when dealing with matters of direct personal interest, such as pay. Employees were asked who they thought would best represent them in dealing with managers if they wanted to get increases in their pay, gain access to training or make a complaint, or if managers wanted to discipline them. Possible response options were: myself; a trade union; an employee representative (non-union); another employee; or somebody else. Figure 5.4

*Table 5.10* Employees' perceptions of the helpfulness of different communication arrangements

|  | All employees (%) | | | If used (%) |
| --- | --- | --- | --- | --- |
|  | Helpful | Not helpful | Not used here | Helpful |
| E-mail | 59 | 9 | 31 | 86 |
| Workplace intranet | 49 | 13 | 39 | 80 |
| Meetings between managers and employees | 70 | 17 | 13 | 80 |
| Workplace newsletter or magazine | 51 | 16 | 33 | 76 |
| Notice boards | 62 | 24 | 14 | 72 |
| Union or other employee representatives | 29 | 20 | 51 | 60 |

Base: All employees in workplaces with 10 or more.
Figures are weighted and based on responses from at least 15,965 employees (columns 1–3) and at least 8,502 employees (column 4).

*Figure 5.4* Employees' perceptions as to who would best represent them

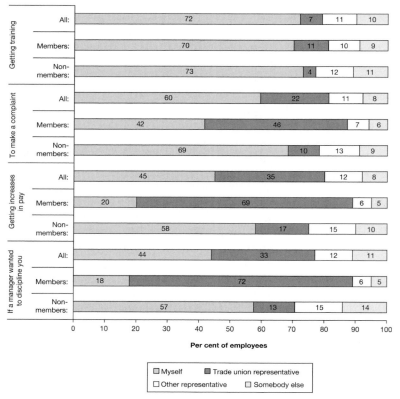

Base: All employees in workplaces with 10 or more.
Figures are weighted and based on responses from at least 21,019 employees (at least 7,929 union members and at least 13,052 non-members).

presents the results, combining the last two categories for simplicity. Figure 5.4 also distinguishes between union members and non-members in view of the obvious differences of opinion between these two groups. In summary, a minority of employees considered that they would benefit from assistance in gaining access to training or making a complaint, while the majority preferred help in getting pay increases or responding to disciplinary charges. Trade union representatives were thought to be the most effective form of assistance in respect of each issue apart from training.

Some 72 per cent of employees considered that they would best represent themselves in respect of training. This figure varied little between members and non-members, and only 11 per cent of union members identified union representatives as their preferred agent, despite unions having devoted much attention to the learning agenda in recent years. Three-fifths of employees considered that they would best represent themselves when making a complaint, as did 45 per cent of employees when seeking a pay increase and 44 per cent of employees when responding to a disciplinary charge. But union representatives were considered the most effective channel by around one-fifth of employees in respect of raising complaints, and by around one-third in respect of pay and discipline. Here, the differences between union members and non-members were more striking, particularly in relation to pay and discipline where most (although not all) union members considered that they would benefit from the assistance of union representatives. Moreover, there were also a number of non-members who believed that they would be best served by a union. This presumably indicates a small additional demand for union representation, if these workers could be organized.

## Conclusion

Earlier surveys in the WERS series comprehensively documented the changing arrangements for representation, consultation and communication in British workplaces throughout the 1980s and the 1990s. The decline of union representation and growth of direct methods of communication were principal among these changes. The results from WERS 2004 indicated a continuation of these broad trends, although there were some notable differences with what had taken place in earlier periods.

Union membership, recognition and lay representation all declined between 1998 and 2004. At the same time, however, there were signs that trade unions had begun to steady their ship, with the scale of the declines in membership and recognition being much smaller than had been seen throughout the 1980s and 1990s. Indeed, trade union representation remains a reality for substantial proportions of employees and employers in Britain.

Nevertheless, some predict that the true turning point towards better fortunes for trade unions may still be some way away (Metcalf, 2005). Nor are there many indications of expansion in other forms of employee representation, such as joint consultative committees or stand-alone non-union representatives. The proportion of all workplaces with any form of employee representation fell from almost three-fifths to around one half between 1998 and 2004. Arrangements for direct communication, on the other hand, were widespread and, where it was possible to chart changes since 1998, seemed to have generally become more prevalent over the period.

Data on employees' perceptions of the utility of different arrangements showed that employees were clearly more likely to consider that methods of direct communication were helpful in keeping them informed about changes at their workplace, when compared with representative structures. But the analysis also indicated that employee representatives – particularly union representatives – continue to play a valued role in assisting employees in gaining pay increases, raising grievances and responding to disciplinary charges. The next chapter focuses in more detail on this role, looking at the characteristics of employee representatives, the breadth of their role, and the nature of their interaction with managers on behalf of the employees they represent.

# 6    Employee representatives

## Introduction

The previous chapter documented a decline in the incidence of arrangements for employee representation between 1998 and 2004, including reductions in the proportions of workplaces with recognized unions, on-site union representatives and workplace-level joint consultative committees. It also reported increases in the prevalence of certain types of direct communication between managers and employees. Yet despite an apparent continuation in the shift towards direct mechanisms for employee participation, there remains significant interest in the role played by employee representatives at workplace level. Indeed, more than half (53 per cent) of all employees still work in establishments with some form of on-site employee representation. The aim of this chapter is to explore the characteristics of employee representatives and their function within workplaces.

Traditionally, research on employee representation in UK workplaces has been dominated by studies of trade union shop stewards, who previously played the principal role in workplace representation (Terry, 2003: 257). In recent years, some workplace managers have become increasingly proactive in setting up representative structures to communicate with or consult with the work-force, either as the sole mode of communication with employees or, in work-places where trade unions have a presence, as new mechanisms running alongside established union representative structures. Whereas the *raison d'être* of union representative structures was historically that of acting as a mechanism for negotiations to take place between managers and representatives, the focus of many new representative structures is that of 'consultation' with employees, whereby managers seek employees' views, via representatives, as part of the management decision-making process. This, alongside the growth of non-union workplaces, has led to increasing interest in different types of representatives, including those who sit on consultative committees, or who play more the role of an 'advocate' in dealing with employee problems and concerns (see Dundon *et al.*, 2005). Yet Terry (1999: 16) writes that, in the UK, formal systems of non-union representation have rarely been investigated, in part because of a general assumption that such structures are largely cosmetic and relatively ineffective. WERS 2004 provides an opportunity to examine the similarities and differences between the roles and activities of union and non-union representatives in a way that has not previously been possible.

Permission to interview employee representatives was sought as part of the Cross-Section Survey of Managers. Interviews were conducted with union and non-union employee representatives, where they were present. Interviews with union representatives were conducted with the senior lay representative of the recognized union with the most members at the workplace or, where no recognition agreement was present, with the senior representative of the largest non-recognized trade union.[1] Interviews with non-union representatives were conducted with the senior non-union representative sitting on the workplace-based joint consultative committee (JCC) that dealt with the widest range of issues or, where non-union JCC representatives were not present, with the senior non-union 'stand-alone' employee representative.[2]

A total of 964 interviews were conducted in 875 workplaces with 10 or more employees. In 89 workplaces, two employee representatives – one union and one non-union – were interviewed. Given the low numbers of interviews with representatives of non-recognized unions and with non-union stand-alone representatives, comparisons are largely made hereafter between all trade union representatives and all non-union representatives.[3] However, where interesting differences emerge between non-union JCC and stand-alone representatives, these data are also reported. Findings for representatives of recognized unions are also highlighted where comparisons are possible with data collected in 1998. Finally, it should also be noted that the results presented in the chapter pertain to *senior* employee representatives in workplaces with 10 or more employees; the features described are not necessarily typical of more junior representatives or of those few representatives that may be present in smaller workplaces.

This chapter begins by profiling the characteristics of different types of employee representative. It then goes on to describe their roles and activities, including the amount of time spent on representative duties, the issues that they dealt with, and the facilities and training that are available. An analysis of the nature of representatives' constituencies, and the extent to which representatives mirror their constituents' characteristics is also presented. The chapter also examines the extent of representatives' interactions with employees, managers, other representatives and external organizations, as well as focusing on the quality of relationships between managers and employee representatives.

## Characteristics of representatives

Traditionally, the popular conception of an employee representative was based on union representatives, most prominently those working in Manufacturing industries. However, given the growth of the service sector and the concentration of union organization in the public sector, both of which contain large concentrations of female and 'non-standard' workers, one might expect to see some change in the make-up of the population of representatives, reflecting this increasingly diverse workforce. Certainly, Terry (2003: 261) observes that the gender gap among representatives now appears to be closing. This section reports on the gender, age and ethnicity of representatives and also examines the extent to which characteristics often viewed as stereotypical are still in evidence. It also describes the occupational composition of representatives and assesses the level of experience among representatives of different types.

In summary, the 2004 survey identified a number of differences in the characteristics of the three types of representatives (Table 6.1). Union representatives and non-union JCC representatives were fairly evenly divided by gender (56 per cent of union representatives were male, as were 53 per cent of non-union JCC representatives). In contrast, only a minority of stand-alone representatives were male (27 per cent). The proportion of senior representatives of recognized unions that were male decreased from 64 per cent in 1998 to 57 per cent in 2004. The age profile of trade union representatives and non-union stand-alone representatives was similar, with non-union JCC representatives, on average, slightly younger. The average age of non-union JCC representatives was 40 years, compared with 44 years for non-union stand-alone representatives and 46 years for union representatives.[4] The vast majority of representatives (97 per cent) indicated that they belonged to a white ethnic group. The remaining four categories (mixed background, Asian or Asian British, Black or Black British, Chinese or other ethnic groups) each accounted for no more than 1 per cent of representatives. Turning to hours worked, the majority of representatives (90 per cent) worked full-time (30 or more hours) in their job each week. Eight per cent of union representatives, and 6 per cent of non-union JCC representatives worked part-time hours, but the proportion was much higher (28 per cent) among non-union stand-alone representatives. The majority (87 per cent) of representatives who worked part-time hours were female.

*Table 6.1* Characteristics of employee representatives

|  | % representatives | | | |
|  | Union representative | Non-union JCC representative | Non-union stand-alone representative | All representatives |
|---|---|---|---|---|
| Male | 56 | 53 | 27 | 52 |
| Aged 40 or older | 78 | 56 | 65 | 73 |
| Ethnic group: White | 96 | 97 | 100 | 97 |
| Work full-time hours (30+) | 92 | 94 | 72 | 90 |
| Combination of each of the above characteristics | 38 | 24 | 18 | 33 |

Base: All senior employee representatives in workplaces with 10 or more employees.
Figures are weighted and based on responses from at least 716 union representatives, 169 non-union JCC representatives, and 60 non-union stand-alone representatives.

Research has documented the aspiration within the union movement for greater diversity among representatives, in order to reflect a more diverse workforce. Healy *et al.* (2004b), for example, recount the efforts of British trade unions to promote greater involvement among black female union representatives, while Heery *et al.* (2004a) assess union attempts to represent 'non-standard' (part-time, freelance, temporary and fixed-term contract) workers. In light of this research, it was of interest to examine the proportion of senior representatives who displayed the combined – perhaps stereotypical – characteristics of being male, from a white ethnic group, aged 40 or older, and working full-time hours. Almost two-fifths of union representatives (38 per cent) fitted this profile in 2004 compared with around one quarter (24 per cent) of non-union JCC representatives and one-fifth (18 per cent) of stand-alone representatives (Table 6.1).[5] When analysed by sector, the differences among union representatives were stark. In the private Manufacturing sector, almost three-quarters (72 per cent) of union representatives matched the profile, compared with one-third (35 per cent) of union representatives in the public sector and a similar proportion (36 per cent) in private services.

Turning to the occupational classification of representatives, respondents were asked to indicate which of the nine Major Groups of the *Standard Occupational Classification (2000)* they belonged to. Both trade union and non-union representatives were fairly evenly spread across the nine occupational groups. However, a higher proportion of union representatives than non-union representatives worked in Professional occupations (25 per cent compared to 15 per cent), and a lower proportion worked in Sales and customer service occupations (7 per cent compared to 17 per cent). Additionally, non-union stand-alone representatives were more likely to report their occupation as belonging to the Managers and senior officials category (20 per cent) than union representatives and non-union JCC representatives (11 per cent of each). This may mean that these stand-alone representatives are seen as less independent from management.

There were some differences between representatives in terms of how long they had been in post. Union representatives had held their position as representatives for eight years on average, compared with an average of five years for non-union stand-alone representatives, and three years for non-union JCC representatives. The longer tenure of union representatives and stand-alone representatives was largely a function of their longer tenure in their current job, and reflected their older age in comparison to non-union JCC representatives. The average non-union stand-alone representative and union representative had each spent similar proportions of their current job tenure as representatives (64 and 60 per cent, respectively). Non-union JCC representatives differed, having been in post for 45 per cent of the time spent in their current job. The shorter 'representative tenure' of JCC representatives may also reflect more frequent turnover of JCC representatives due to fixed term appointments on committees, or alternatively, the temporary nature of some committees. The average tenure for representatives of recognized unions was slightly higher in 2004 (eight years) than it was in 1998 (six years).

## What do representatives do?

### *Time spent on representative duties*

The amount of time spent by representatives on their representative duties provides a measure of the extent and importance of representatives' role within workplaces. Union representatives spent, on average, a much higher number of hours per week on their duties than non-union JCC or stand-alone representatives. Union representatives were more likely to be full-time representatives (13 per cent) compared with non-union JCC representatives (2 per cent) and stand-alone representatives (3 per cent). Part-time union representatives also spent, on average, twice as long on their representative duties as part-time non-union representatives (6.3 hours per week compared with 2.5 hours per week). Among part-time non-union representatives, JCC representatives spent an average of 3.1 hours per week on duties, and stand-alone representatives devoted an average of 1.8 hours per week to their representative role. Within workplaces where both union and non-union part-time representatives were present, part-time union representatives spent an average of 5.7 hours on representative activities, while part-time non-union representatives spent an average of 2.9 hours.

Considering the distribution in hours spent on representative activities, around one-third of representatives (34 per cent) reported spending one hour or less per week on representative duties; just under one-third (31 per cent) spent between two and four hours per week, and just over one-third (35 per cent) spent five hours or more. Over one quarter (28 per cent) of those who spent five hours or more per week on representative duties were full-time representatives. Among union representatives, around one quarter (24 per cent) spent one hour or less per week on representative duties, one-third spent between two and four hours per week and over two-fifths (43 per cent) spent five hours or more per week. In contrast, only one-fifth (19 per cent) of JCC representatives and one-tenth (9 per cent) of stand-alone representatives spent five or more hours in their role as a representative. Most non-union JCC and stand-alone representatives spent one hour or less per week on representative duties (53 and 66 per cent respectively).

For non-union representatives – both JCC and stand-alone – there was no straightforward relationship between constituency size and hours spent on representative duties. Most non-union representatives spent one hour or less on representative duties, regardless of the number of employees they represented at the sampled workplace. For union representatives, however, the greater the number of union members they represented, the greater the proportion spending five or more hours per week on duties. Representatives in the public sector also tended to spend longer hours on representative duties than those in the private sector, even after excluding full-time representatives.

A higher proportion of representatives of recognized unions were spending five or more hours per week on representative duties in 2004 than in 1998 (44 per cent in 2004, compared with 24 per cent in 1998). This was not explained by the increase in the proportion of representatives based away from the sampled workplace (who might potentially have larger constituencies than on-site representatives); an increase in time spent was also apparent among on-site representatives.

### Payment for time spent on representative duties

Statute provides employee representatives in specific circumstances with legal rights to reasonable paid time off to carry out their representative duties.[6] Outside of these circumstances, management may show support for representatives by paying them for time spent on representative duties. The vast majority of trade union representatives (89 per cent) were paid by their employer to carry out representative duties; the figure was 91 per cent among representatives of recognized unions. The proportions of paid non-union JCC representatives and paid stand-alone representatives were lower (83 per cent and 74 per cent respectively), but the differences were not statistically significant.

There was no straightforward relationship between the likelihood of being paid for time spent carrying out representative duties and constituency size. However, the greater the number of hours spent on representative duties, the greater the likelihood that representatives would be paid by the employer for this time. All full-time representatives were paid by their employer for representative work, as were most part-time representatives (85 per cent). Part-time representatives in the Education sector were the most likely to be unpaid and spent the fewest hours on representative duties each week. Conversely, part-time representatives in the Public administration sector spent the longest weekly hours on representative work and were the most likely to be paid. Three-quarters (77 per cent) of representatives who spent one hour or less per week on representative duties were paid for this work. This rose to 95 per cent of representatives spending five hours or more on representative duties.

There appeared to be an association between management attitudes towards trade unions and whether the most senior union representative was paid for hours spent on representative duties. Managers who agreed with the statement 'We would rather consult directly with employees than with unions' were less likely to pay for time spent on representative duties than those who disagreed, although the difference was not substantial (84 per cent compared with 95 per cent).

### Issues that representatives spent time on

Employee representatives were asked which of 12 specific issues they had spent time on in their role as representatives in the previous year, and which of those issues they felt had been the most important in the workplace over this period. Figure 6.1 summarizes the results by grouping the 12 specific issues asked about (and two further issues mentioned spontaneously by a number of respondents during interviews) into four categories, with a fifth category encompassing other infrequently cited or poorly specified issues. Trade union

*Figure 6.1* Issues dealt with by employee representatives

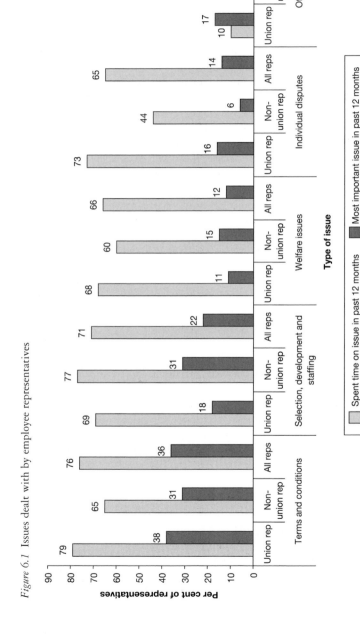

Base: All senior employee representatives in workplaces with 10 or more employees.

Figures are weighted and based on responses from 681 union representatives and 222 non-union representatives. 'Terms and conditions' comprises rates of pay, hours of work, holiday entitlements and pension entitlements. 'Selection, development and staffing' comprises recruitment or selection of employees, training, staffing levels, performance appraisals and working practices. 'Welfare issues' comprises equal opportunities, health and safety, and absence or staff sickness. 'Individual disputes' comprises disciplinary matters and grievances.

representatives were somewhat more likely than non-union representatives to have spent time on terms and conditions (comprising rates of pay, hours of work, holiday entitlements and pension entitlements), and were much more likely than non-union representatives to have spent time on disputes (comprising disciplinary matters and grievances). Differences between union representatives and non-union representatives in respect of selection, development and staffing issues (comprising recruitment or selection of employees, training, staffing levels, performance appraisals and working practices), welfare issues (comprising equal opportunities, health and safety, and absence or staff sickness) and other unspecified issues were not statistically significant.[7]

Looking at particular issues within these categories, union representatives were significantly more likely than non-union representatives to have spent time on hours of work, pensions and equal opportunities, while non-union representatives were more likely than union representatives to have spent time on issues relating to training. Around half of all representatives had spent time on staffing levels, including 52 per cent of stand-alone representatives. This did not indicate, however, that stand-alone representatives were primarily playing the role of representatives during redundancy processes (during which employers are sometimes legally required to consult with the workforce): of those stand-alone representatives who had spent time on staffing levels, only one quarter (26 per cent) were located in workplaces where redundancies had occurred in the previous year. Where representatives spent time on only one of the 12 individual issues asked about, no single issue dominated among any of the three types of representative, again demonstrating that non-union stand-alone representatives in particular were not 'single issue' representatives. In particular, very few representatives had spent time solely on health and safety. Where union representatives spent time on only one group of issues, these tended to be traditional 'bread and butter' issues, with almost half (48 per cent) having spent time on terms and conditions only.

Employee representatives were asked which issue they felt to have been the most important in the 12 months prior to the survey. Union and non-union representatives were each most likely to cite issues relating to terms and conditions (Figure 6.1). Within this, rates of pay were cited as the single most important issue by 23 per cent of each type of representative (union, non-union JCC and non-union stand-alone representatives). Non-union representatives were more likely than union representatives to consider selection, development and staffing to be the most important, while the reverse was true in respect of individual disputes.

The breadth or span of issues that representatives engaged with was analysed by looking at how many of the four groups of specific issues presented in Figure 6.1 representatives had spent time on. This provides some indication of the extent to which the representative's role is embedded in the workplace. Union representatives were more likely than non-union representatives to spend time on all four areas (44 per cent compared with 23 per cent) and these proportions varied little when excluding full-time representatives. Among union representatives, off-site representatives were also more likely to deal with a wider range of issues than their on-site counterparts. Considering the 12 specific issues, almost all full-time representatives (91 per cent), half of union representatives and less than a third (30 per cent) of non-union representatives reported having spent time on six or more. The survey data also allowed assessment of how many representatives spent time on a combination of traditional areas of representative involvement: namely terms and conditions and individual disputes. The majority of trade union representatives – almost two-thirds (65 per cent) – had spent time on both groups of issues. However, fewer non-union JCC representatives and stand-alone representatives had spent time on both sets of issues (32 per cent and 29 per cent respectively).

Union representatives were more likely to have been involved in all four categories of issues where they viewed managers as not supportive, where they rated the management–representative relationship as poor, and where some form of collective conflict had taken place. This may suggest that poor relations give rise to problems across a range of different areas and lead to union representatives' involvement across a broader range of issues than in situations where relationships are more collaborative. A similar comparison could not be undertaken for non-union representatives because of the small numbers of workplaces where relationships between managers and non-union representatives were not rated positively.

Another way of examining the activities of employee representatives is to consider the nature of representatives' engagement with workplace managers over a range of different topics. Chapter 7 reports on the scope of negotiation and consultation between unions and management, either at the workplace or at a higher level in the organization. Here, the focus is on the nature of the interviewed representatives' specific involvement. Representatives were asked whether management normally negotiated, consulted, informed or did not involve them in respect of a range of workplace issues. Figure 6.2 reports the results for union representatives (a questionnaire error having prohibited the collection of equivalent data from non-union representatives). The figure shows that the sampled union representatives were most likely to have been involved in *negotiations* with managers at the workplace level over pay, hours, holidays and procedures for resolving individual disputes. At least three-tenths of union representatives had been involved in negotiations over each of these issues. A further third of union representatives had been involved in *consultations* over disputes procedures, with representatives also commonly reporting having been consulted over health and safety, equal opportunities and employee training. At the other end of the spectrum, union representatives were least likely to report having been involved in negotiations or consultations over employee recruitment, pension entitlements, performance appraisals and staffing plans.

Due to changes in the questionnaire, comparisons with the extent of involvement reported by representatives of recognized unions in 1998 is possible on only a small number of items, namely: equal opportunities, performance appraisals, staffing plans, employee recruitment or selection, and training.

*Figure 6.2* Negotiation, consultation and information-sharing with union representatives

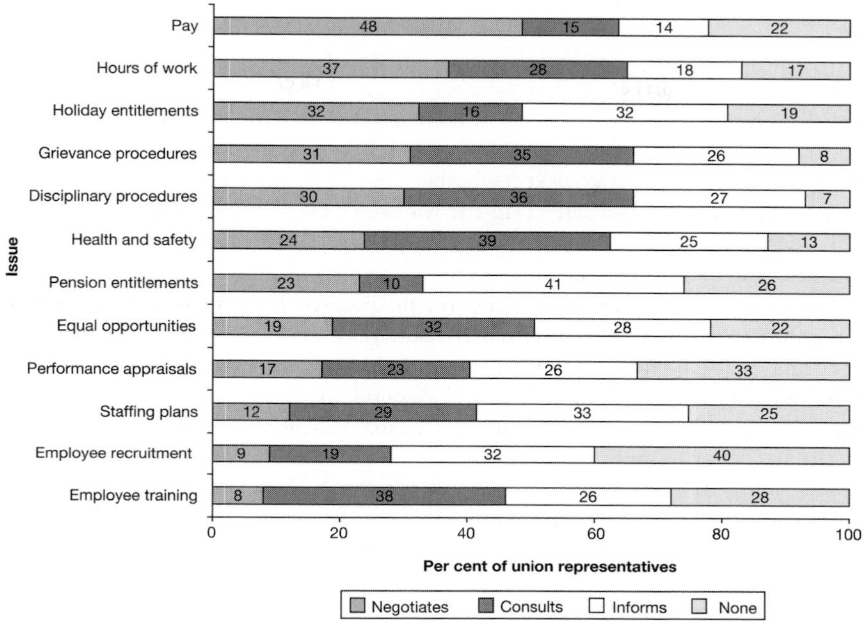

Base: All senior employee representatives in workplaces with 10 or more employees.
Figures are weighted and based on responses from at least 706 union representatives.

In 2004, union representatives were more likely than in 1998 to report that workplace managers negotiated or consulted with them over each of these issues, with the exception of health and safety where no difference was apparent.

One in seven senior trade union representatives (14 per cent) reported that they were designated Union Learning Representatives (ULRs).[8] Analysis of the tenure and duties of these representatives indicated that many were likely to have added the role of ULR to their existing responsibilities, and thus they did not constitute a random sample of ULRs, some of whom will be dedicated solely to this role. Indeed, while ULRs are a relatively recent innovation, over half (55 per cent) of those identified in the Survey of Employee Representatives had been in their post as a union representative for five or more years. Equally, the role of most ULRs interviewed as part of the survey was not restricted to training and development issues and instead encompassed a broader range of issues and functions, with most having spent time on a wide range of issues over the preceding twelve months. Even so, only 29 per cent of ULRs had spent time on training in the previous 12 months (compared with 37 per cent of other union representatives). This low figure might have arisen because the sampled representatives may not have been designated as ULRs for sufficient time to have engaged in this role, although data on their tenure as a ULR were not available to enable this hypothesis to be tested.

### Contact with external organizations

Representatives may, in the course of their job, be required to seek help or advice from the trade unions they represent, or from other external organizations. Trade union representatives were asked whether they had contacted paid trade union officials to discuss matters affecting the workforce over the preceding 12 months. This contact may have occurred through special or routine meetings, or telephone conversations. Almost three-quarters (72 per cent) of union representatives had contacted a paid official at least once over the preceding 12 months. In the main, this contact appeared to occur fairly frequently, at least once every three months.

For most union representatives, contact with officials primarily related to representation of individual members' rights. Around one half of union representatives had made contact either to obtain legal advice (55 per cent), to gain assistance in the handling of individual grievances (53 per cent) or to seek assistance in the handling of disciplinary actions (46 per cent). Fewer union representatives sought assistance relating to 'collective' issues: almost one quarter (23 per cent) contacted officials to seek assistance in pay bargaining, while 19 per cent sought information before commencing pay bargaining; and 17 per cent sought assistance relating to industrial action. As noted earlier, many union representatives were not themselves directly involved in determining or negotiating pay. Among those who were, over half had contacted paid officials for assistance in pay bargaining (57 per cent) or for information prior to pay bargaining commencing (51 per cent), indicating that many representatives engaged in bargaining without seeking assistance from union officials.

All representatives (both union and non-union) were asked if they had sought information or advice from a list of external bodies – either in person, over the telephone, or through a website – in the preceding 12 months. Considering first the responses of union representatives, almost one-fifth had made contact with either a trade union body such as the TUC or General Federation of Trade Unions (19 per cent), or with the Advisory, Conciliation and Arbitration Service (Acas) (18 per cent). Around one in seven union representatives had either contacted a lawyer (15 per cent), the DTI (12 per cent), or some other government department (12 per cent); and 6 per cent each had made contact with Citizens Advice Bureaux (CABx) or had sought information or advice from some other professional body. In total, around three-fifths of union representatives (61 per cent) had contacted at least one body for information or advice. Overall, non-union representatives were less likely than union representatives to seek advice, with one-fifth (22 per cent) having had contact with an external body. Bodies contacted by non-union representatives included Acas (9 per cent), trade unions (7 per cent), and government departments or agencies other than the DTI (5 per cent). Four per cent had contacted each of the DTI, the CABx and professional bodies of some kind; 3 per cent contacted lawyers.

# Representatives' access to facilities and training

The provision of paid time off for employee representatives to carry out their representative duties was discussed earlier in the chapter. However, analysis of the extent of representatives' access to a range of facilities, and the extent to which they have access to training, also give some indication of management support for representatives at the workplace, as both can determine the extent and efficacy of representatives' dealings with their constituents.

## *Access to facilities*

Employee representatives were presented with a list of eight specific facilities and were asked which ones were provided by management for use as part of their representative duties at that workplace. Some differences were evident when comparing access to facilities across the three different types of representative (Figure 6.3). For example, similar proportions of all three types of representative were provided with office or other equipment (one or more of a telephone, photocopier or computer) and with office space (either an office specifically for representative duties, or one that is also used for other purposes). However, non-union stand-alone representatives were less likely than both trade union and non-union JCC representatives to be provided with rooms for meetings, access to e-mail and space on their organization's intranet. Non-union JCC

*Figure 6.3* Facilities available to employee representatives

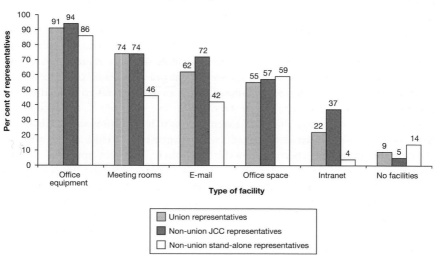

Base: All senior employee representatives in workplaces with 10 or more employees.
Figures are weighted and based on responses from 722 union representatives, 178 non-union JCC representatives, and 61 non-union stand-alone representatives.

representatives were more likely than union representatives to have space on an intranet.

Access to certain individual items was compared between 1998 and 2004 among representatives of recognized unions, where changes in question wording did not prohibit it. The comparison indicated no significant differences in access to meeting rooms (81 per cent in 1998; 74 per cent in 2004), office space (54 per cent in 1998 compared with 55 per cent in 2004), or use of a telephone (83 per cent in 1998 compared with 87 per cent in 2004). Representatives of recognized unions in 2004 were, however, more likely to have access to photocopiers (71 per cent in 1998; 81 per cent in 2004) and computers (39 per cent in 1998; 67 per cent in 2004).

The survey also enables one to examine the range of facilities provided to union and non-union representatives *in the same workplaces*. In around one-fifth (21 per cent) of workplaces where both union and non-union representatives were present, both had access to the same number of facilities. The remaining 79 per cent of workplaces with both types of representatives were broadly evenly split into those where union representatives were provided with fewer facilities than non-union representatives (45 per cent of workplaces) and those where union representatives had access to a greater number of facilities than their non-union counterparts (34 per cent). Looking across all non-union representatives, these were more likely to have access to a greater number of facilities where there was a union representative also present in their workplace. Whereas 60 per cent of non-union representatives were provided with four or more of the listed facilities in workplaces with no union representatives, this rose to 80 per cent of non-union representatives who worked alongside union representatives.

The number of facilities available to representatives appeared to be positively associated with the number of hours spent on representative duties. Representatives who were paid for the time they spent on representative duties also had access to a greater number of facilities than unpaid representatives. In addition, there was some variation according to workplace size, such that representatives were more likely to have access to a wider range of facilities in larger workplaces.

It might be expected that the extent to which facilities are available to representatives is partly determined by management attitudes and support for representatives and their role in the workplace. The data appeared to confirm this. In workplaces where union representatives described management as being in favour of union membership, managers provided those representatives with a wider range of facilities than in establishments where management were not considered to be in favour of membership. Equally, where union representatives agreed that management was 'supportive of the role played by representatives', the range of facilities provided was higher than where managers were not considered supportive. The numbers of non-union representatives were too small to permit the equivalent analysis among that group.

## Access to training

Union representatives were asked whether they or any of the workplace representatives of their union had received training or instruction for their role as an employee representative, either in the preceding 12 months or at any time previously. Similarly, non-union representatives were asked if they or other non-union representatives they worked with had received training for their role as an employee representative. Almost two-thirds (63 per cent) of all representatives reported that either they or their colleagues had received at least some training during their time as representatives. One-third of all representatives said that training had been received in the previous 12 months. Trade union representatives were significantly more likely to have received training than non-union representatives. Almost three-quarters (74 per cent) of trade union representatives reported that either they, or their colleagues, had received training at some time in the past (76 per cent among representatives of recognized trade unions). The same was true of just under half (45 per cent) of non-union JCC representatives and only one-fifth (21 per cent) of stand-alone representatives. Union representatives were also more likely than non-union representatives to have received training in the previous 12 months. Two-fifths of union representatives reported that either they, or their colleagues, had been trained in the preceding 12 months, compared with one quarter of non-union JCC representatives and 5 per cent of stand-alone representatives. This suggests that union representatives receive training on a more frequent or regular basis than non-union representatives throughout their tenure.

The larger the workplace, the more likely both union and non-union representatives were to report that they or their colleagues had received training. Conversely, representatives who had never received training were present in high proportions in single independent establishments, and workplaces which were part of organizations with less than 100 employees. This was the case for both union and non-union representatives. For union representatives, the presence or absence of a recognized union also made a difference: only 29 per cent of representatives had received training in non-recognized workplaces, compared with 76 per cent of representatives in workplaces with a recognized union. Data indicated little association between union and non-union representatives' perceptions of management support, and whether they or their colleagues had received training.

Due to changes in the questionnaire, it was only possible to assess changes in the provision of training over time among the two-thirds of union representatives who were the *sole representative* of a recognized union at the sampled workplace. Among this subset of union representatives, the percentage receiving training in 2004 (29 per cent) was no different to that observed in 1998 (27 per cent). There was also no significant difference in the degree to which union representatives were given paid time off to attend training. In 2004, 82 per cent of sole union representatives who attended courses in work time reported that managers paid for time off to attend training all of the time (compared with 87 per cent of union representatives who attended courses in work time in 1998). In 2004, a further 3 per cent were sometimes given paid time off (compared with 4 per cent in 1998); and 15 per cent of sole union representatives were not paid for time off for training (compared with 9 per cent in 1998).

Focusing on the topics of training courses delivered to representatives in the year prior to the survey, around two-fifths of representatives reporting training said that they, or their colleagues, had participated in induction training for representatives (46 per cent), or training related to health and safety (45 per cent), employment law (38 per cent) and negotiating/collective bargaining/pay (36 per cent). One in seven (13 per cent) cited training in grievance and disciplinary matters. Similar proportions of union and non-union representatives reported that they and their colleagues had received training on health and safety or had taken part in an induction course, but union representatives were more likely than non-union representatives to have received training relating to employment law, negotiating/collective bargaining/pay, and grievance and discipline issues. Among union representatives, 30 per cent of those reporting training said that they, or their colleagues, had received training on trade union recruitment.

A small proportion of union representatives (2 per cent) and non-union representatives (3 per cent) engaging in training in the previous year had done so outside of work hours. The vast majority of the remainder (86 per cent of union representatives and 93 per cent of non-union representatives) reported that their employer always paid them for the time taken to attend courses. A further 5 per cent of union representatives, and 4 per cent of non-union representatives, indicated that managers had sometimes paid for time spent in training. The remaining 8 per cent of union representatives indicated that management had not paid for the time taken to attend courses.

For many union representatives who had received training in the previous 12 months, this training had been delivered either by their union (77 per cent), by a union organization such as the TUC or General Federation of Trade Unions (34 per cent), by an external training provider (15 per cent), or by the representatives' employing organization (10 per cent). Most non-union representatives who had received training in the previous year had been trained either by their organization (61 per cent), or by an external training provider (35 per cent).

## The nature of representatives' constituencies

The chapter now turns to look at the nature of the constituencies served by employee representatives of different types. The section begins by looking at whether representatives operated alone or as part of a group, and at the number of constituents they were serving. It then moves on to look at the mode of appointment, and examines the extent to which representatives were typical of their constituents.

### Constituency size

Representatives were asked whether any colleagues worked alongside them at the workplace performing the same type of representative role.[9] Around two-thirds (65 per cent) of union representatives worked alone, as did the vast majority of stand-alone representatives (81 per cent). In contrast, and as a consequence of their function, JCC representatives all worked as part of a larger group: indeed, the median number of JCC representatives was six (Table 6.2).[10] It might be assumed that JCC representatives are present in greater numbers than other forms of representatives because JCCs are seen to require a certain number of representatives in order to function effectively.

Not only did JCC representatives tend to be more numerous, but where they were present they also collectively represented a greater number of constituents in each workplace. Together, the representatives on the most important JCC represented a median of 28 employees. By contrast, union representatives collectively represented a median of 18 members, and non-union stand-alone representatives collectively served an average of 17 employees. When expressed as a proportion of all employees at the workplace, union representatives represented one half of the workforce (51 per cent) on average, non-union JCC representatives represented around two-thirds (65 per cent) and stand-alone representatives represented almost all employees (93 per cent). Computing the average number of employees represented by each individual representative, it was found that each union representative and non-union stand-alone representative represented a median of 15 employees, while the average constituency

*Table 6.2* Constituency size by type of employee representative

|  | Union representative | Non-union JCC representative | Non-union stand-alone representative |
| --- | --- | --- | --- |
|  | *Median* | *Median* | *Median* |
| Number of representatives of similar type at workplace | 1 | 6 | 1 |
| Number of constituents[a] represented by all representatives of similar type at workplace | 18 | 28 | 17 |
| Proportion of all employees represented by all representatives of similar type at workplace | 51 | 65 | 93 |
| Number of constituents represented per representative | 15 | 6 | 15 |

Base: All senior employee representatives in workplaces with 10 or more employees.
Figures are weighted and based on responses from 724 union representatives, 179 non-union JCC representatives and 61 stand-alone non-union representatives.
Note:
[a] Employees in the case of non-union JCC representatives and stand-alone representatives; members of the representative's union in the case of union representatives.

size for each non-union JCC representative was six employees. The lower number of employees per JCC representative was largely a function of the greater numbers of JCC representatives present in the average workplace.

Looking in detail at union representatives of recognized unions, the median number of union members per representative appeared to have risen only slightly from 13 members per representative in 1998 to 15 members in 2004. The mean was also similar (22 in 1998, compared with 24 in 2004), but these means were not significantly different at the 5 per cent level. While constituency size had not increased since 1998, the hours spent by union representatives on duties, as reported earlier, had increased. This may perhaps indicate that the issues dealt with by representatives in 2004 were more complex and time-consuming than in 1998, or it may be that they were simply dealing with a greater number or range of issues than in 1998.[11]

Some trade union representatives additionally represented other employees at the workplace who did not fall within the boundaries of their constituency. Specifically, around one-eighth (12 per cent) of union representatives represented employees who were members of another union and almost one-third (30 per cent) represented employees who were not members of any union. The relatively large minority of union representatives acting on behalf of non-members may be as a result of union representatives bargaining on behalf of non-members in their bargaining units, or accompanying non-members in discipline and grievance cases. It may also stem from managers consulting with union representatives on behalf of mixed groups of both union and non-union workers, over issues such as redundancy or transfers of undertakings. A small minority (7 per cent) represented both members of other unions and non-members. Similarly, one quarter (26 per cent) of non-union JCC representatives indicated that they represented employees who were union members, as did around one-tenth (11 per cent) of stand-alone representatives.

### Method of appointment

While constituency sizes varied to some degree between the different types of representative, so too did their mode of appointment, with union representatives and non-union JCC representatives usually elected to their positions while stand-alone non-union representatives were commonly appointed without an election. Almost two-thirds of union representatives (64 per cent) were elected, compared with over half (55 per cent) of non-union JCC representatives and one quarter (24 per cent) of non-union stand-alone representatives.

The remaining non-elected representatives had been appointed through a variety of means. One quarter of non-union JCC representatives (26 per cent) and a majority of non-union stand-alone representatives (56 per cent) had been selected by managers, compared with 3 per cent of union representatives. Similar proportions of all three types of representatives had volunteered for the role without election (19 per cent of union representatives; 17 per cent of non-union stand-alone representatives and 14 per cent of non-union JCC representatives).

The remainder had either been selected for the role by union members (7 per cent of union representatives) or employees (4 per cent of non-union JCC representatives and 3 per cent of non-union stand-alone representatives), or selected by existing union representatives or officials (8 per cent of union representatives) or existing non-union representatives (1 per cent of non-union representatives).

As in 1998, male union representatives were much more likely than female union representatives to be elected (73 per cent compared with 50 per cent) and female representatives were more likely than male representatives to have volunteered for the post without having gone through a selection process (28 per cent compared to 12 per cent).

### How 'typical' are representatives?

By comparing information on the gender of each representative and their hours of work with data they provided on the composition of their constituencies, it was possible to examine the extent to which representatives were characteristic of their constituents on these two specific dimensions. In general, the gender composition of constituencies was reflected in the gender of representatives. Taking a female-dominated constituency to be one in which at least 60 per cent of the constituents were women, and a male-dominated constituency to be one in which at least 60 per cent were men, most female-dominated constituencies (72 per cent) were represented by female representatives and, likewise, most male-dominated groups (91 per cent) were represented by male representatives. A slight majority of 'balanced' constituencies (58 per cent) were represented by male representatives. Overall, just over four-fifths (83 per cent) of senior representatives were typical of at least 40 per cent of their constituents in terms of gender. Where representatives were not typical of at least 40 per cent of their constituents, this tended to be a result of male representatives representing female-dominated constituencies, as most of those representatives who were not 'typical' of their constituents were male (85 per cent). Overall, female representatives were more likely to reflect their constituents' gender than male representatives (95 per cent of female representatives represented constituences where at least 40 per cent of members were female, while 72 per cent of male representatives represented constituences where at least 40 per cent of members were male). Non-union representatives were also more likely to be typical of their constituents by gender than union representatives (89 per cent of non-union representatives compared with 80 per cent of union representatives).

The hours worked by the representative also reflected the composition of the constituency, albeit to a lesser extent than in the case of gender. Full-time representatives represented almost all (96 per cent) of constituencies in which at least 60 per cent of employees worked full-time. But they also represented most of the constituencies that enjoyed a balance of full and part-time workers (83 per cent) and the majority of those dominated by part-time workers (64 per cent). Overall, more than four-fifths (86 per cent) of senior representatives were typical of at least 40 per cent of their constituents in respect of hours worked. But this was primarily due to the relatively small proportion of constituencies dominated by part-time employees.

The method of appointment seemed to have little bearing on the extent to which representatives – both union and non-union – reflected their constituencies in terms of gender and hours worked. In other words, representatives were no more likely to be 'typical' of their constituencies in terms of gender or hours worked where constituents had elected them, than where they had been appointed by other means.

## Contact with constituents and managers

The nature of the representatives' role is such that they are likely to seek frequent contact with their constituents, both to inform them of developments at the establishment or to collate views and opinions which might then be distilled and passed on to managers. The survey asked what methods were used by representatives to communicate with their constituents; the results are shown in Figure 6.4. Personal discussions were the most frequently mentioned method of communication, used by 79 per cent of union representatives and 88 per cent of non-union representatives. These were followed by notice boards and general meetings. Union representatives were more likely than non-union representatives to use general meetings, newsletters, and telephone contact, reflecting the fact that almost one quarter (24 per cent) were based off-site. Non-union stand-alone representatives were less likely than both JCC representatives and union representatives to use almost all of the communication methods above,

*Figure 6.4* Employee representatives' communication channels with constituents

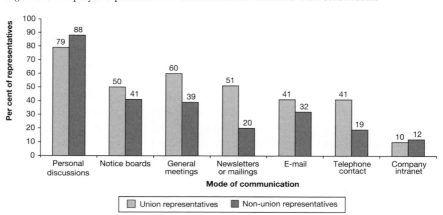

Base: All senior employee representatives in workplaces with 10 or more employees.
Figures are weighted and based on responses from 722 union representatives and 240 non-union representatives.

with the great majority preferring to communicate through personal discussions or meetings.

Thus far, the discussion has focused on the roles and activities of representatives without much consideration of the means by which representatives engage with managers. The incidence of regular, planned meetings, or *ad hoc* meetings and discussions, provides an indication of the degree to which managers accept the legitimacy of representatives at their workplace and, equally, of the opportunities available to representatives to raise issues of concern to their constituents and to participate in workplace decision-making. Table 6.3 summarizes the incidence of representatives' contact with management. Looking first at union representatives, half of all union representatives had regular, planned meetings with managers at their workplace at which managers negotiated or consulted with them about issues concerning the establishment. The incidence was similar among both on-site representatives of recognized unions and those situated at another site within the organization (54 per cent and 46 per cent, respectively). But it was comparatively low (19 per cent) among the small number of representatives of non-recognized unions, reflecting the less institutionalized nature of the union/management relationship in such cases.

Outside of formal meetings, representatives often have contact with managers on a day-to-day, possibly informal, basis. Over three-quarters of union representatives had contact with managers (above supervisor level) in the previous 12 months, outside of planned negotiation or consultation meetings, in order to discuss matters affecting the employees they represented (Table 6.3). The majority (55 per cent) had at least monthly contact with managers. Over two-fifths (44 per cent) of union representatives had both regular, planned meetings and *ad hoc* meetings with managers at their workplace, one-third (34 per cent) relied on *ad hoc* meetings only and 6 per cent relied only on planned meetings. One in six

*Table 6.3* Employee representatives' contact with management

| | % representatives | | |
| --- | --- | --- | --- |
| | Union representatives | Non-union JCC representatives | Non-union stand-alone representatives |
| Regular planned meetings with management | 50 | 100[a] | 53 |
| *Ad hoc* management contact in previous 12 months | 78 | 88 | 93 |
| No contact of any sort with management in previous 12 months | 16 | 0[a] | 2 |

Base: All senior employee representatives in workplaces with 10 or more employees.
Figures are weighted and based on responses from 721 union representatives, 179 JCC representatives and 61 stand-alone non-union representatives.
Note:
[a] These percentages follow by virtue of the representative's presence on an active JCC.

union representatives (16 per cent) had not met with managers at all during the previous 12 months. Most of these representatives were found in workplaces with recognized unions (95 per cent) but close to half (44 per cent) spent one hour or less on representative activities each week.

The incidence of planned negotiation or consultation meetings was higher among non-union representatives than among union representatives: 77 per cent of non-union representatives had regular, planned meetings of this nature with managers at their workplace. However, this figure includes attendance of at least one joint consultative committee meeting by all non-union JCC representatives, and so a more direct comparison with the union case is arguably provided by non-union stand-alone representatives, just over half of whom (53 per cent) reported regular planned meetings with management. It seemed, however, that for stand-alone representatives, *ad hoc* meetings with management comprised the dominant form of communication with managers. Almost all (93 per cent) of stand-alone representatives had met management outside of these meetings in the previous 12 months. Stand-alone representatives may be more likely to have informal contact with management because they are more likely to work in close proximity to managers or to be working in management roles themselves. The great majority (88 per cent) of non-union JCC representatives also had contact with managers in the previous 12 months outside of meetings of the consultation committee that they sat on, in order to discuss matters affecting the employees they represented.

Meetings with employee representatives to discuss matters affecting the workforce is one fundamental means by which managers may show their support for representative arrangements. In workplaces where union representatives agreed that managers were supportive of their role, most (88 per cent) reported either planned or *ad hoc* meetings with managers. But this proportion was lower (70 per cent) where representatives did not consider managers supportive.

Looking at the nature of regular planned meetings in which managers negotiated or consulted with representatives (or meetings of JCCs), it was apparent that, where they took place, such meetings were often frequent and typically covered a wide range of issues. For almost three-fifths of union representatives attending such meetings (58 per cent) and a similar proportion of stand-alone non-union representatives (60 per cent), planned meetings took place at least once a month. For a further third of either group, they took place at least once every three months. Meetings of JCCs were less regular, with 36 per cent of non-union JCC representatives reporting that their committee met monthly and 56 per cent reporting that it met at least once a quarter. For only a minority of representatives were meetings relatively infrequent: 9 per cent of union representatives, 8 per cent of non-union JCC representatives and 5 per cent of stand-alone non-union representatives attended regular, planned meetings less than once every three months.

Table 6.4 shows the proportion of representatives of each type who reported discussing each of a range of specific issues during planned meetings. High proportions (in most cases between two-thirds and three-quarters) of all three

*Table 6.4* Issues discussed at meetings between employee representatives and management

| | % representatives | | |
| --- | --- | --- | --- |
| | Union representatives | Non-union JCC representatives | Non-union stand-alone representatives |
| Production issues | 37 | 61 | (40) |
| Employment issues | 68 | 75 | (52) |
| Financial issues | 65 | 53 | (14) |
| Future plans | 78 | 84 | (49) |
| Pay issues | 61 | 70 | (44) |
| Leave and flexible working arrangements/working time | 63 | 60 | (48) |
| Welfare services and facilities | 51 | 69 | (43) |
| Government regulations | 48 | 53 | (22) |
| Work organization | 76 | 67 | (70) |
| Health and safety | 76 | 76 | (81) |
| Equal opportunities | 46 | 44 | (21) |
| Training | 71 | 68 | (61) |
| Other/anything that arises | 7 | 8 | (0) |

Base: All senior employee representatives in workplaces with 10 or more employees, who attended planned meetings with managers in the past 12 months.
Figures are weighted and based on responses from 529 union representatives, 179 non-union JCC representatives and 39 stand-alone non-union representatives.

groups of representatives discussed health and safety, work organization, and training. However, smaller proportions of non-union stand-alone representatives discussed most of the other listed issues when compared with union and non-union JCC representatives, who were significantly more likely than stand-alone representatives to discuss future plans, government regulations and equal opportunities. Non-union JCC representatives were more likely than union representatives to discuss production issues and welfare services and facilities, while union representatives were not significantly more likely than JCC representatives to discuss any of the listed issues.

One means through which managers can facilitate meaningful discussions at such planned meetings is by providing representatives with all the information that they require before the meeting commences. Around three-fifths (62 per cent) of representatives reported that managers did so, with no substantial differences evident across the three types of representative. More striking, however, was the extent to which the provision of information prior to meetings was related to the perceived degree of management support for the representatives' role. Full information was usually provided in advance of meetings in around 68 per cent of workplaces where representatives considered that managers were supportive of their role, but in only 18 per cent of workplaces where managers were not considered supportive, again with little difference across the three types of representative. The approach taken by managers in respect of access to information appears, therefore, to constitute a reasonably clear expression of their broader attitude towards employee representatives.

Representatives who reported having had informal contact with managers were asked whether such contact was more likely to relate to issues affecting individual employees or groups.[12] Union representatives and non-union JCC representatives were evenly split; 53 per cent of union representatives and 46 per cent of non-union JCC representatives reported that such contact was most likely to relate to issues affecting groups of employees, with the remainder of either group reporting that it was more likely to relate to individuals. In comparison, non-union stand-alone representatives were less likely to bring collective concerns to managers. Only 31 per cent reported that *ad hoc* contact with managers was most likely to relate to issues affecting groups of employees. This may support the notion of stand-alone representatives acting as 'advocates' for individual employees, for example when work-related problems arise.

Representatives were asked to indicate which of one or more types of manager they would normally approach to discuss a matter affecting the employees they represented. Most representatives (72 per cent) reported that issues would normally be raised with the most senior manager at the workplace, or the proprietor where present, implying that most representatives have access to, and regular contact with, the top level of management in their establishments. The most senior manager was the usual point of contact for almost all non-union stand-alone representatives (92 per cent), compared with 68 per cent of union representatives and 70 per cent of non-union JCC representatives. However, this appeared to reflect the smaller size of workplaces in which non-union stand-alone representatives were located – such workplaces typically having fewer intermediate levels of management – rather than any preferential access on the part of such representatives. Other common points of contact for union representatives and non-union JCC representatives were employee relations, personnel or human resources (HR) managers, and managers or supervisors of affected employees, with around one quarter of both union representatives and non-union JCC representatives indicating that they would contact the HR manager, or would contact a supervisor. But even where an HR manager was present at the workplace or at a higher level, the majority of representatives of all three categories still indicated that they approached the most senior manager at the workplace.

## Contact with other representatives

Table 6.5 reports the extent to which employee representatives work alongside other union or non-union representatives, the degree of contact between them and the quality of their relationships. Looking first at contact between union representatives, one quarter (26 per cent) of union representatives reported working alongside representatives from other unions. Of these, over half reported that they held meetings with these representatives (not attended by managers) to

*Table 6.5* Employee representatives' contact with other representatives

| | % representatives | | | |
|---|---|---|---|---|
| | *Union reps reporting presence of reps of other unions* | *Union reps reporting presence of non-union reps* | *Non-union JCC reps reporting union reps* | *Non-union stand-alone reps reporting union reps* |
| Work alongside other reps of given type | 26 | 9 | 34 | 14 |
| Hold meetings with other reps of given type | 56 | 46 | 39 | (49) |
| Report good relationship with other reps of given type | 81 | 88 | 75 | (64) |

Base: All senior employee representatives in workplaces with 10 or more employees.

Row 1: Figures are weighted and based on responses from 708 union representatives (columns 1 and 2); 120 non-union JCC representatives (column 3); and 60 stand-alone non-union representatives (column 4).

Rows 2 and 3: Figures are weighted and based on responses from 333 union representatives (column 1) and 135 union representatives (column 2); 62 non-union JCC representatives (column 3); and 21 stand-alone non-union representatives (column 4).

discuss issues relating to the workplace, and four-fifths reported that they had a 'good' or 'very good' relationship with the other union representatives. The larger the workplace, the more likely that multi-union meetings were held. Of the 9 per cent of union representatives in workplaces where *non-union* representatives were present, almost nine in ten deemed relationships with these representatives as 'good' or 'very good' and only 4 per cent reported 'poor' relationships. Almost half of union representatives in workplaces with non-union representatives had meetings with them (not attended by managers) to discuss workplace issues.

One-third (34 per cent) of non-union JCC representatives reported that union representatives were also present in their workplace.[13] In most of these workplaces (75 per cent) union representatives sat on the JCC. And two-fifths (39 per cent) of non-union JCC representatives in these workplaces met to discuss issues with union representatives in representative-only meetings. The views of JCC representatives in these workplaces towards union representatives were favourable, with three-quarters describing the relationship as 'very good' or 'good', and the remaining quarter rating it as 'neither good nor poor'. These views on the relationship were unaffected by whether the JCC representative was a union member or not. Looking finally at non-union stand-alone representatives, one in seven (14 per cent) worked in workplaces in which union representatives were also present. Around one half reported meeting with union representatives to discuss issues, and almost two-thirds reported having a 'good' or 'very good' relationship with these union representatives.

## Relationship with management

### *The quality of the management–employee representative relationship*

The nature of representatives' interactions and relationships with managers has been the focus of a wealth of research both in the past (Batstone *et al.*, 1977) and more recently in the context of employee or trade union 'partnership' relationships with management (see Bacon and Storey, 2000; Terry and Smith, 2003; Wills, 2004) and the role of non-union representatives in workplaces (see Dietz *et al.*, 2005). Much research indicates that the nature of such relationships can determine the legitimacy of representatives in the workplace, their degree of involvement in workplace decision-making and their access to facilities and other forms of support.

Employee representatives were asked to provide a general indication of the quality of the relationship with managers at their workplace by rating that relationship on a five-point scale ranging from 'very good' to 'very poor'. Most representatives reported that they had a 'good' or 'very good' relationship with managers at their workplace and very few rated it as 'poor'. Among union representatives, 76 per cent rated it as either 'very good' or 'good'; a further 18 per cent indicated that it was 'neither good nor poor' and 6 per cent rated it 'poor' or 'very poor'. In 1998, the proportion of union representatives who reported their relationship with managers as either 'good' or 'very good' was slightly lower (71 per cent) but the difference was not statistically significant.

Non-union representatives, however, had better relationships with managers than union representatives. A higher proportion of non-union representatives (92 per cent) said the relationship was 'very good' or 'good'. And among non-union representatives, stand-alone representatives perceived that they had better relationships with managers than non-union JCC representatives, with four-fifths (80 per cent) of stand-alone representatives rating the relationship as 'very good', compared with over one half of non-union JCC representatives (53 per cent).

There was considerable consistency in views between representatives, with around half (51 per cent) of union representatives and non-union representatives in the same workplaces giving the same rating of the relationship. In another 18 per cent of workplaces where there were both union and non-union representatives, the former rated the relationship more favourably than the latter; and in 31 per cent, non-union representatives rated it more favourably than union representatives. In 49 per cent of workplaces where union representatives and non-union representatives were interviewed, both rated the relationship as 'very good' or 'good'.

It may be that management–representative relationships are worse in workplaces where conflict has taken place, and thus the incidence of conflict might explain overall differences in union representatives' and non-union representatives' perceptions of relationships with managers. One might also expect that union representatives will be more likely than their non-union counterparts to encounter instances of workplace conflict – individualized or collective – in the course of their work as representatives, and that this may affect their views of relationships with managers. The data seemed to bear this out. The quality of the relationship was lower in the 38 per cent of workplaces where there had been a collective dispute, industrial action or threatened industrial action in the previous 12 months: 33 per cent of representatives rated the relationship 'very good' where there had been some collective conflict, compared with 51 per cent where there had been no such conflict. Conflict was more common in workplaces where union representatives were present (43 per cent) than in workplaces where non-union representatives were present (25 per cent). However, this did not wholly explain the differences between union representatives and non-union representatives. Union representatives gave considerably lower ratings of the relationship than non-union representatives, even in workplaces without any overt conflict.

Management support can be very important in determining the effectiveness of representatives and their capacity to fulfil their role to members' expectations. Terry (2003: 266–267), for example, links the decline in the incidence of union workplace representation since the mid-1980s to a withdrawal of management support for union representatives. In 2004, where representatives remained in place, most (78 per cent) agreed that management was supportive of the role that they played. Non-union representatives were more likely than union representatives to consider management supportive: almost all (90 per cent) agreed that managers were supportive, compared with around three-quarters (73 per cent) of union representatives. There had been a small increase since 1998 in the proportion of representatives of recognized unions who considered management supportive (up from 66 per cent). Union representatives were also more likely to disagree that management was supportive (14 per cent) than non-union representatives (2 per cent). Non-union stand-alone representatives were particularly likely to *strongly* agree that management was supportive (42 per cent, compared with 18 per cent of non-union JCC representatives and 17 per cent of union representatives).

One might postulate that managers were less supportive of union representatives because they preferred to deal with other types of representatives, such as non-union representatives. Alternatively, some managers may simply be less disposed towards representation. A comparison of how union representatives and non-union representatives rated management support in the same workplace indicated a slight tendency for managers to be viewed as more supportive by non-union representatives than union representatives in such workplaces, but this was by no means the norm. In two-fifths of workplaces, managers (39 per cent) were considered equally supportive by union representatives and non-union representatives. In one-third (35 per cent), non-union representatives indicated a higher level of support than union representatives, and in one quarter the situation was reversed.

### Collaborative working

Collaborative or cooperative working between management and employee representatives has been much discussed in recent years in the context of 'partnership' relationships, a key feature of which is the involvement of employees or their representatives in workplace change initiatives to bring about improvements in performance (Marks *et al.,* 1998; Martinez Lucio and Stuart, 2004). Representatives were asked three questions to gauge the extent to which they worked in collaboration with managers. They were asked to respond on three five-point scales ranging from 'strongly agree' to 'strongly disagree' as to whether: managers involved representatives when changes took place; valued representatives' opinions; and shared information only when representatives requested it. Figure 6.5 shows that non-union representatives generally reported a greater level of collaboration than union representatives. For instance, when asked whether employee representatives worked closely with management when changes were being introduced, over three-quarters of non-union representatives agreed, compared with two-thirds of union representatives. However, compared with 1998, union representatives in 2004 were more likely to agree that they worked closely with management on workplace change (52 per cent in 1998 compared with 66 per cent in 2004). Non-union representatives were also significantly more likely than union representatives to agree that management valued their opinion. But yet again, there was an increase in the proportion of union representatives who agreed that managers valued their opinion since 1998 (56 per cent in 1998, compared with 64 per cent in 2004). Consistent with their other responses on questions relating to collaborative working,

*Figure 6.5* Collaborative working between employee representatives and management

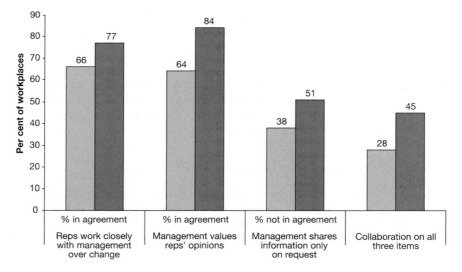

Base: All senior employee representatives in workplaces with 10 or more employees.
Figures are weighted and based on responses from 720 union representatives and 240 non-union representatives.

non-union representatives were also more likely to perceive greater access to management information than union representatives. Around one half (51 per cent) of non-union representatives disagreed that management only shared information with employee representatives when they requested it, compared with two-fifths (38 per cent) of union representatives.

Collating data relating to the extent of agreement across all three items provided an overall measure of collaborative working. One-third of all representatives indicated that there was collaboration on each of the three items. The figure was higher for non-union representatives (45 per cent) than union representatives (28 per cent). This is consistent with findings reported earlier which indicated that non-union representatives were also more likely to rate their relationships with managers as 'very good' or 'good'. One might expect that where union representatives have greater power and legitimacy in the workplace – by merit of high union membership density – employers are more likely to be compelled to engage in collaboration with them. However, the analysis indicated that there was no relationship between density levels and agreement by union representatives on all three items of collaborative working, combined.

Given differences in views on collaborative working among union representatives and non-union representatives, one might expect the extent of collaborative working to differ between union representatives and non-union representatives in the same workplace. This appeared to be the case. In 23 per cent of workplaces where both types of representative were present, they both rated managers as collaborative on the summary variable. In a further 37 per cent, neither representative rated managers as collaborative. But, consistent with data relating to the component aspects of collaborative working, where the representatives' views differed, it was more common for the non-union representative to report collaboration than the union representative. The non-union representative was the only representative to report collaboration in one-third (32 per cent) of workplaces where both representatives were present, whereas the union representative was the only representative to report collaborative working in just 8 per cent of workplaces where both types were present.

### Trust between employee representatives and management

Mutual trust between managers, employees and employee representatives has been proposed as the foundation for collaborative relationships (see Dietz, 2004). In their study of 54 partnership organizations, Guest and Peccei (2001) found that a 'high trust' form of partnership, based in part on significant representative participation, was associated with positive outcomes for employers, employees, and employee representatives. Data from the 2004 survey are able to further illuminate the links between trust, collaborative working, and employment relationships more generally. To assess the degree of trust in their relationships, managers and representatives were asked to rate each other on three dimensions of trust: (1) whether the other party could be relied upon to live up to the commitments they had made; (2) whether the other party was sincere in their attempts to understand the repondent's point of view; and (3) whether the other party could be trusted to act with honesty and integrity.[14] Responses were given on a five-point scale from 'strongly agree' to 'strongly disagree', with agreement taken to indicate trust of the other party.

Figure 6.6 shows the extent of shared and one-sided trust between managers and employee representatives. Where both parties agreed that they trusted the other on a particular dimension, this is labelled 'mutual trust'. The extent of mutual trust between managers and union representatives was reasonably high, with a shared view of trust held by around half of each set of respondents, on each of the three individual items. At least three-quarters of managers said that they trusted their union representatives, and at least three-fifths of union representatives said they trusted their managers. However, the extent of trust between managers and non-union representatives was much higher: very few managers said they did not trust their non-union representatives (no more than 15 per cent on any of the three items). In respect of union representatives, on each of the three items, one-sided trust was more likely to result from a lack of trust on the part of representatives than a lack of trust on the part of managers, with managers more likely to trust representatives than *vice versa*. The reverse was true in the case of non-union representatives, at least in respect of the first two items, where one-sided trust was more likely to result from a lack of trust on the part of managers. And for all three items, an absence of trust (where both parties had given a low rating to each other on each item) was more prevalent between union representatives and managers than it was in relationships between managers and non-union representatives.

The three items were combined to produce a summary indicator of trust, whereby agreement on all three dimensions indicated trust of the other party. Again, this showed a marked difference between management relationships with union representatives and non-union representatives. The incidence of mutual trust between managers and union representatives was low (31 per cent of workplaces with union representatives) but it was much more prevalent between managers and non-union representatives (64 per cent of workplaces with non-union representatives). Looking at the proportion of workplaces where there was a lack of trust on both sides (where neither party agreed that they could trust each other across all three dimensions, labelled 'no trust'), this was much higher in respect of management–union representative relations (23 per cent) than management–non-union representative relations (7 per cent).

Relaxing the condition for mutual trust and defining it on the basis of workplaces where managers and representatives agreed on two items of trust, rather than three, many of the broad patterns remained the same. Overall levels of mutual trust did, however, increase to 52 per cent of workplaces in which union representatives and managers were present, and 82 per cent of workplaces where non-union representatives and managers were present.

The different levels of trust in management between union and non-union representatives are of considerable interest. Three lines of enquiry were followed

*Figure 6.6* Trust between employee representatives and management

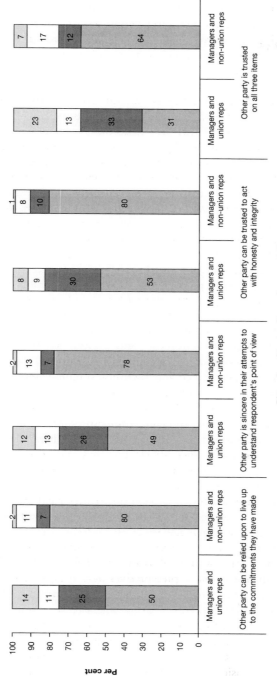

Base: All workplaces with 10 or more employees and on-site employee representatives.
Figures are weighted and based on responses from 808 managers, 656 on-site union representatives, and 238 non-union representatives.

in an attempt to shed further light on the possible reasons for these differences. The first examined whether lower levels of trust among union representatives were simply a function of their location in certain sectors where a culture of low trust relations may be more common. However, an analysis of the workplaces where both union representatives and non-union representatives were present (89 workplaces in total) showed that the incidences of mutual, one-sided and no trust were broadly the same for union representatives taken as a group within these workplaces, and for all union representatives. The same results were evident for non-union representatives. This indicated that the levels of trust exhibited by union representatives overall were not lower simply because of any potential concentration of union representatives in 'low trust industries' or 'low trust workplaces'.

A second possible explanation is that union representatives, with their longer average tenure, may be less trusting of management as a result of mistrust between the parties built over many years. However, no significant association was found between union representatives' tenure in the representative's role and whether they trusted managers on all three items. A third possible explanation for union representatives' lower levels of trust may lie in the fact that they deal with more activities related to individual or collective disputes than their non-union counterparts, and here a relationship was apparent. Conflict was measured by representatives' involvement in grievance or disciplinary issues in the previous 12 months ('individual conflict') or the presence of some form of collective conflict at the workplace over the last 12 months. The data showed that conflict, whether individual or collective, was associated with lower levels of trust for both union and non-union representatives; however, the occurrence of conflict had a much greater association with union representatives' assessment of trust than it did among non-union representatives.

Further analysis, summarized in Figure 6.7, suggests that trust is a prerequisite for collaborative working and good relationships more generally, although it is not always sufficient to ensure collaboration. Where trust was more extensive, representatives were more likely to agree that managers and representatives worked collaboratively. Where managers and representatives trusted each other, the vast majority of representatives agreed that they worked closely with management when changes were being introduced, and that management valued their opinions. They were also more likely to disagree that management only shared information when requested. Collaboration across all three items occurred in the majority of workplaces where there was mutual trust (55 per cent), but in only one-fifth of workplaces where trust was one-sided (21 per cent) and one-tenth of workplaces where there was no trust (12 per cent). This would suggest that trust contributes to a climate that is conducive to collaboration, as just one in ten workplaces had collaboration where trust was absent. Yet it is not a sufficient condition, as indicated by the 45 per cent of workplaces in which mutual trust was evident, but where collaboration was not extensive.

The results also indicated that, although mutual trust appears to be synonymous with good relationships and management support, it is less of a prerequisite.

*Figure 6.7* Trust and collaborative working between employee representatives and management

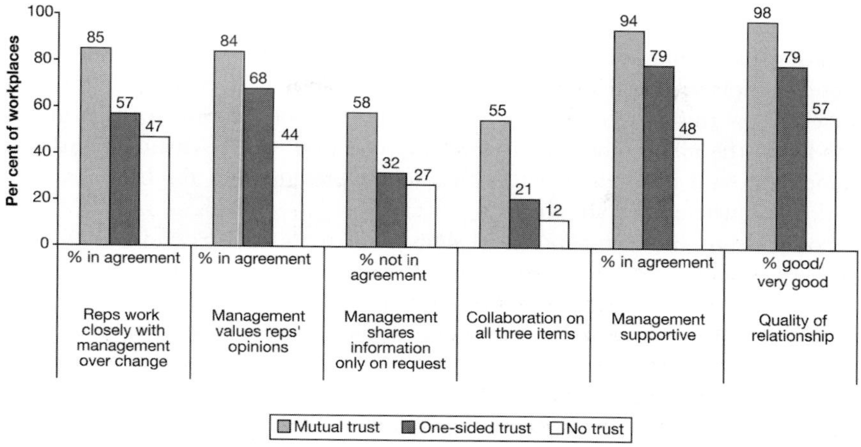

Base: All workplaces with 10 or more employees and on-site employee representatives.
Figures are weighted and based on responses from at least 892 employee representatives.

Almost all representatives in workplaces where mutual trust was evident reported that management was supportive of the role played by representatives, and rated the relationship as 'very good' or 'good'. It seems then that management was very likely to be supportive, and the quality of the relationship was almost certain to be good, where there was mutual trust. However, even where trust was not mutual, a large proportion of representatives still reported a high level of support and good relationships. It may be that some representatives may regard the relationship as 'good' but at the same time may subscribe to a pluralist view of the employment relationship (Clegg, 1975), in which they view a difference of interests, conflict, and thus a lack of trust, as inevitable. Finally, a positive association was also identified between the degree of trust and managers' views that unions helped find ways to improve workplace performance, although the direction of causality is not clear. Managers' views of union utility may be driven by a pre-existing relationship of trust; alternatively, a constructive relationship with unions could, over time, generate trust.

## Conclusion

This chapter provides new insights into the characteristics, roles and activities of the three principal groups of employee representatives in British workplaces. To date, much research into non-union representation has been based upon qualitative, case-study data (see Lloyd, 2001; Bonner and Gollan, 2004). However, WERS 2004 provides an opportunity to build a representative picture of non-union representation at an aggregate level across workplaces, and to set this alongside up-to-date information about the changing roles and activities of trade union representatives. Hall and Terry (2004: 214) speculate that legislative-based systems of employee representation such as the Information and Consultation of Employees Regulations (2004) will have the greatest impact in those workplaces where no trade union is recognized. If this is so, the data presented in this chapter may provide invaluable information to help understand how the role of non-union representatives may evolve within a legislative framework, and how union and non-union representatives might co-exist in workplaces where both are present.

Comparisons between union and non-union representatives identified both similarities and differences; some of the latter are highlighted here by way of a summary. In terms of their personal characteristics, union representatives were more likely to fit the profile of the 'stereotypical' or traditional representative, but they were also more likely to have been elected to their positions by their constituents, while substantial proportions of non-union representatives had been selected by managers. Union representatives also differed from non-union representatives in respect of the longer hours they spent on representative duties each week. In terms of the scope of involvement in workplace matters, the data pointed to a broad range of interests, although the focus was different for union and non-union representatives. Union representatives commonly focused on traditional concerns such as terms and conditions and individual disputes, while non-union representatives were more likely to focus on issues relating to staffing and training.

Looking at access to training and facilities, union and non-union JCC representatives had access to a wider range of facilities than stand-alone representatives. This may be related to the scope of representatives' roles, as stand-alone representatives were seemingly more likely to act on behalf of individual employees, rather than groups, in dealings with management. For union representatives, access to facilities was linked to their assessment of both management support and the extent of collaborative working, as well as to the character of their relationship with management. Trade union representatives were more likely to have received training for their role than non-union representatives. This issue may take on greater prominence as the Information and Consultation of Employees Regulations bed in, as inequalities in expertise between union and non-union representatives may come to light where both are present in workplaces. A key issue is whether employers will be willing to provide training to non-union representatives, to address this shortfall.

Representatives of all types had regular formal and informal contact with managers, although non-union representatives reported more contact with managers than union representatives. There was evidence that union and non-union representatives got along well, where they were both present. Many representatives also met regularly with other types of representative in their workplace, and most reported that their relationships with these representatives were good. However, a key difference between union representatives and non-union representatives related to the tenor of their relationships with management.

Union representatives were less likely than non-union representatives to feel that they had a good relationship with management, to see management as supportive of their role, to consider that they worked collaboratively with managers and to have relationships that were characterized by mutual trust. Further analysis indicated that, where mutual trust was present, collaborative working was more likely to occur, management was more likely to be supportive, and management–representative relationships were more positive. But while trust was not a prerequisite for good relations, it did appear to be more of a requirement for collaboration. The role of trust in facilitating employee involvement in decision-making is likely to be a fruitful area for future research. But it will be of equal interest to examine the extent to which trust proves important in determining the character of any outcomes.

# 7 The determination of pay and other terms and conditions

## Introduction

Perhaps there is nothing in industrial relations that has occasioned quite so much comment in the past 20 years as the decline of trade unionism as a force in the workplace. This is often equated with a diminution in the scope and depth of joint regulation, that is, the extent to which employees have a say in the way their jobs and the workplace are organized, and the way they are rewarded for their efforts. Certainly, the reach of trade unionism has diminished in the 1980s and 1990s and, as Chapter 5 illustrates, has continued to decline since the late 1990s. Some maintain that, even where unions are present, they have become a 'hollow shell' with little or no real influence on the decision-making process. One commentator, reflecting on the evidence from surveys and case studies, was led 'to the inescapable conclusion that workplace trade unions no longer negotiate to any significant extent on behalf of their members' (Terry, 2004: 205). He went on to conclude: 'The concept of "joint regulation" as the normative cornerstone of British industrial relations [which was] clear evidence of unions' capacity to shape . . . the policies and practices of employers, has to be set aside' (ibid.).

But is it really the case that the time for 'joint regulation' has passed? Managers have become less hostile to unions in the last quarter of a century and seem more prepared to entertain a role for unions that goes beyond a concern with pay and conditions alone (Poole et al., 2005: 126–127). Even if unions have lost the capacity to regulate the workplace jointly, it is possible that non-union forms of representation, or direct two-way forms of communication between management and employees, can form the basis for joint regulation at work. Indeed, there are some policy developments that are predicated on the assumption that this is the case. For instance, the 1996 Health and Safety (Consultation with Employees) Regulations permit employers to discharge a new duty to consult with employees on health and safety matters in a timely fashion through direct communications. The Information and Consultation of Employees Regulations (2004) applies to non-union and union workplaces, opening up further possibilities for joint regulation through structures that are not exclusively dependent on trade unionism.

This chapter considers the way in which pay and non-pay terms and conditions are being set in the light of this shift away from union-based joint regulation. The chapter covers four broad areas. First, it considers the incidence of pay determination methods, the proportion of employees covered by these methods, and the use of contingent pay. The second area is the involvement of employees in the determination of non-pay terms and conditions. Third, it explores the effects of pay determination methods on the pay distribution, fringe benefit provision and pay satisfaction. The fourth topic covered is workplace regulation in two spheres where employees have statutory rights to consultation, namely health and safety and collective redundancies.

## Methods of pay determination

Methods of pay determination are central to understanding industrial relations in Britain since they are linked to employee pay levels, the distribution of wages between and across workplaces, and the ways in which employers seek to recruit, retain and motivate employees. Information on pay determination methods was collected in the Cross-Section Survey of Managers for each of the nine occupational groups that were present at the workplace. Managerial respondents were asked to identify which of seven pay determination methods 'most closely characterizes the way that pay is set for [the occupation]'. A showcard was presented to managers that distinguished between collective bargaining for more than one employer (e.g. at industry-level), bargaining at an organization level, or bargaining at the sampled workplace; pay setting by management, either at a higher level in the organization, at the sampled workplace or through individual negotiation with employees; or pay determination by an Independent Pay Review Body. By far the most common form of pay determination in 2004 was unilateral pay setting by management, either at the workplace or at a higher level in the organization. Seventy per cent of workplaces set pay for at least some of their employees in this way. Around one quarter (27 per cent) of workplaces set pay for at least some of their employees through collective bargaining with unions (Table 7.1).[1] The percentage of workplaces with any collective bargaining and the percentage of employees covered by collective bargaining both rose with workplace size. One-fifth (19 per cent) of workplaces with fewer than 25 employees used collective bargaining to set the pay of at least some of their employees, with one-sixth (17 per cent) of employees in these smallest workplaces having their pay set in this way. Almost two-thirds (65 per cent) of workplaces with 500 or more employees set some pay through collective bargaining, with two-thirds (68 per cent) of employees covered in these largest workplaces. The greater prevalence of collective bargaining in larger establishments meant that the percentage of employees who had their pay set through collective bargaining was much higher (40 per cent) than the percentage of workplaces with at least some collective bargaining.

In the public sector, collective bargaining was the dominant form of pay setting – it was present in around four-fifths (83 per cent) of public sector workplaces and covered 82 per cent of public sector workers. In contrast, only

*Table 7.1* Incidence and coverage of collective bargaining, by workplace characteristics

|  | Workplaces with any collective bargaining | Employees covered by collective bargaining |
|---|---|---|
|  | % workplaces | % employees |
| All workplaces | 27 | 40 |
| *Workplace size* |  |  |
| 10–24 employees | 19 | 17 |
| 25–49 employees | 33 | 26 |
| 50–99 employees | 31 | 27 |
| 100–199 employees | 48 | 42 |
| 200–499 employees | 57 | 52 |
| 500 or more employees | 65 | 68 |
| Workplaces with 25 or more employees | 37 | 45 |
| *Organizational status* |  |  |
| Stand-alone workplace | 7 | 22 |
| Part of a larger organization | 36 | 45 |
| *Organization size* |  |  |
| 10–99 employees | 6 | 5 |
| 100–999 employees | 26 | 29 |
| 1,000–9,999 employees | 40 | 55 |
| 10,000 or more employees | 53 | 56 |
| *Sector of ownership* |  |  |
| Private sector | 14 | 26 |
| Public sector | 83 | 82 |
| *Industry* |  |  |
| Manufacturing | 20 | 39 |
| Electricity, gas and water | 96 | 87 |
| Construction | 17 | 26 |
| Wholesale and retail | 9 | 17 |
| Hotels and restaurants | 2 | 5 |
| Transport and communication | 43 | 63 |
| Financial services | 63 | 49 |
| Other business services | 10 | 12 |
| Public administration | 93 | 90 |
| Education | 67 | 58 |
| Health and social work | 36 | 60 |
| Other community services | 32 | 46 |
| *Trade union recognition* |  |  |
| No union recognized | 2 | 1 |
| At least one union recognized | 86 | 82 |

Base: All workplaces with 10 or more employees.
Figures are weighted and based on responses from 2,037 managers.
Note:
    See endnote 1 of Chapter 7 for details of the derivation of collective bargaining coverage.

14 per cent of private sector workplaces used collective bargaining, with around one quarter (26 per cent) of private sector employees having their pay set through collective bargaining. Industry differences in the use and coverage of collective bargaining were very marked: it dominated Public administration and the Electricity, gas and water sector, but was almost non-existent in Hotels and restaurants where union recognition was also very low.[2]

Table 7.2 focuses on collective bargaining in the private sector. The percentage of workplaces with any collective bargaining and the percentage of employees covered by collective bargaining rose with workplace size, as was the case for the whole economy. However, collective bargaining was less evident than in the whole economy, even among the largest workplaces. Workplace ownership was strongly associated with collective bargaining. The incidence and coverage of collective bargaining were lower where the workplace was family-owned, compared to circumstances where no individual or family had a controlling interest, and they were lower in stand-alone workplaces than in workplaces belonging to larger organizations. Although the workplace incidence of collective bargaining was similar across domestically-owned workplaces and those with some foreign-ownership, the percentage of employees with pay set through collective bargaining was much higher in foreign-owned workplaces (32 per cent compared with 23 per cent). Collective bargaining was more in evidence where a higher percentage of employees were union members. Nevertheless, one in ten private sector workplaces with 90–99 per cent union density had no collective bargaining for any of their employees.

While three-quarters (73 per cent) of workplaces had no collective bargaining at all, in one-sixth (17 per cent) of workplaces, all employees had their pay set through collective bargaining (Table 7.3). There were relatively few workplaces (10 per cent) where some but not all employees were covered by collective bargaining. In the smallest organizations, stand-alone workplaces and industries such as Hotels and restaurants, the percentage of workplaces with no collective bargaining coverage ranged between 93 per cent and 98 per cent, so that union negotiation over pay was virtually unheard of. Conversely, *all* employees had their pay set through collective bargaining in around one-third of workplaces in the largest organizations (with 10,000 or more employees), the Electricity, gas and water sector, and Transport and communication. In the public sector, Financial services, workplaces recognizing unions, and those workplaces with union density of 50 per cent or more, the percentage of workplaces with 100 per cent bargaining coverage ranged between 51 and 78 per cent. This wide variation in the coverage of collective bargaining at workplace level is an important feature of pay setting in Britain, one that is often overlooked by those who simply dismiss joint regulation over pay and conditions as a thing of the past.

The WERS series has shown that the proportion of workplaces setting pay through collective bargaining has been in decline since the mid-1980s (Millward *et al.*, 2000: 196–199). This decline continued in the period since 1998. In tracking this change, the findings presented here are based on pay-setting variables that were consistently recorded in 1998 and 2004.[3] These time-consistent measures produce a lower estimate of collective bargaining coverage than the preferred measure available only in 2004. However, they provide a good indication of change in pay bargaining. Using the time-consistent measure, the percentage of workplaces engaging in any collective bargaining over pay fell from 30 per cent in 1998 to 22 per cent in 2004 (Table 7.4). The decline was largely confined to the private sector, where bargaining incidence fell from 17 per cent to 11 per cent.

*Table 7.2* Incidence and coverage of collective bargaining in the private sector, by workplace characteristics

|  | Workplaces with any collective bargaining | Employees covered by collective bargaining |
|---|---|---|
|  | % workplaces | % employees |
| All workplaces | 14 | 26 |
| *Workplace size* |  |  |
| 10–24 employees | 9 | 9 |
| 25–49 employees | 17 | 14 |
| 50–99 employees | 14 | 12 |
| 100–199 employees | 33 | 30 |
| 200–499 employees | 45 | 41 |
| 500 or more employees | 50 | 49 |
| Workplaces with 25 or more employees | 21 | 30 |
| *Family ownership* |  |  |
| Controlling family interest | 4 | 10 |
| No controlling interest | 22 | 33 |
| *Foreign ownership* |  |  |
| Some foreign ownership | 17 | 32 |
| UK-owned | 13 | 23 |
| *Organizational status* |  |  |
| Stand-alone workplace | 5 | 13 |
| Part of a larger organization | 19 | 30 |
| *Broad sector* |  |  |
| Manufacturing | 18 | 38 |
| Services | 13 | 22 |
| *Union membership density* |  |  |
| No union members | 2 | 2 |
| 1–24 per cent | 23 | 27 |
| 25–49 per cent | 62 | 63 |
| 50–89 per cent | 78 | 81 |
| 90–99 per cent | 89 | 94 |
| 100 per cent | (94) | (60) |

Base: All private sector workplaces with 10 or more employees.
Figures are weighted and based on responses from 1,468 managers.
Note:
    See endnote 1 of Chapter 7 for details of the derivation of collective bargaining coverage.

*Table 7.3* Collective bargaining coverage at workplace level

| | % of workplaces | | |
|---|---|---|---|
| | Percentage of employees covered by collective bargaining | | |
| | *100* | *1–99* | *Zero* |
| All workplaces | 17 | 10 | 73 |
| *Organization size* | | | |
| 10–99 employees | 3 | 2 | 95 |
| 100–999 employees | 17 | 9 | 74 |
| 1,000-9,999 employees | 23 | 16 | 61 |
| 10,000 or more employees | 37 | 16 | 47 |
| *Broad sector* | | | |
| Private manufacturing | 6 | 12 | 82 |
| Private services | 9 | 4 | 87 |
| Public sector | 56 | 27 | 17 |
| *Organizational status* | | | |
| Stand-alone workplace | 4 | 3 | 93 |
| Part of a larger organization | 23 | 13 | 64 |
| *Industry* | | | |
| Manufacturing | 8 | 11 | 81 |
| Electricity, gas and water | 35 | 60 | 5 |
| Construction | 5 | 12 | 83 |
| Wholesale and retail | 5 | 4 | 91 |
| Hotels and restaurants | 2 | 0 | 98 |
| Transport and communication | 32 | 10 | 58 |
| Financial services | 59 | 4 | 37 |
| Other business services | 8 | 2 | 90 |
| Public administration | 77 | 16 | 7 |
| Education | 22 | 44 | 34 |
| Health and social work | 28 | 8 | 64 |
| Other community services | 25 | 7 | 68 |
| *Trade union recognition* | | | |
| No union recognized | 2 | 2 | 96 |
| At least one union recognized | 58 | 29 | 13 |
| *Union membership density* | | | |
| No union members | 2 | 1 | 97 |
| 1–24 per cent | 18 | 12 | 70 |
| 25–49 per cent | 39 | 32 | 29 |
| 50–89 per cent | 51 | 29 | 20 |
| 90–99 per cent | 66 | 29 | 5 |
| 100 per cent | 78 | 18 | 4 |

Base: All workplaces with 10 or more employees.
Figures are weighted and based on responses from 2,037 managers.
Note:
    See endnote 1 of Chapter 7 for details of the derivation of collective bargaining coverage.

In the private sector, no single pay determination method replaced collective bargaining. Rather, there was some movement away from 'mixed methods' of pay determination towards the use of a single pay determination method within the workplace, though this single method varied across workplaces. The biggest change has been the growth in the percentage of workplaces where all pay was set by management at workplace level: this was the sole method of pay determination in over two-fifths (43 per cent) of private sector workplaces in 2004, compared with one-third (32 per cent) in 1998.

The pattern of change was somewhat different in the public sector. The incidence of collective bargaining has remained broadly constant, with 77 per

*Table 7.4* Pay determination methods (workplaces), 1998 and 2004

| | % workplaces | | | | | |
| --- | --- | --- | --- | --- | --- | --- |
| | *1998* | | | *2004* | | |
| | *Public sector* | *Private sector* | *All* | *Public sector* | *Private sector* | *All* |
| *Single method of collective bargaining* | | | | | | |
| Only multi-employer | 28 | 2 | 8 | 36 | 1 | 7 |
| Only single-employer | 19 | 4 | 7 | 12 | 4 | 5 |
| Only workplace-level | 0 | 1 | 1 | 1 | 1 | 1 |
| *Single other method* | | | | | | |
| Only set by management, higher level | 9 | 24 | 21 | 7 | 23 | 20 |
| Only set by management, workplace | 1 | 32 | 25 | 1 | 43 | 35 |
| Only set by individual negotiations | 0 | 6 | 5 | 0 | 5 | 4 |
| Only other methods[a] | 4 | 3 | 3 | 1 | 1 | 2 |
| Pay Review Body[b] | – | – | – | 1 | 0 | 1 |
| *Mixture of methods* | 39 | 28 | 31 | 41 | 23 | 26 |
| *All methods* | 100 | 100 | 100 | 100 | 100 | 100 |
| Any collective bargaining | 79 | 17 | 30 | 77 | 11 | 22 |
| Any set by management | 21 | 81 | 69 | 28 | 79 | 70 |
| Any individual negotiations | 1 | 16 | 13 | 2 | 15 | 13 |
| Any other methods[a] | 39 | 8 | 14 | 32 | 2 | 7 |
| Pay Review Body[b] | – | – | – | 32 | 0 | 6 |

Base: All workplaces with 10 or more employees.
Figures are weighted and based on responses from 2,125 managers in 1998 and 1,994 managers in 2004.
Notes:
    [a] In 2004 many responses coded as 'Other methods' in the interview were subsequently back-coded to specific methods, thereby lowering the incidence of 'Other methods' in comparison with 1998.
    [b] In 1998, pay determination via Independent Pay Review Bodies was given as an example of 'Other methods', whereas in 2004 it was separately coded. The figures provided for Pay Review Bodies in 2004 are also counted in the figures provided for 'Only other methods' and 'Any other methods'. Endnote 3 of Chapter 7 provides details of the derivation of time-consistent estimates of collective bargaining coverage.

cent of public sector workplaces using collective bargaining in 2004 compared with 79 per cent in 1998. Among workplaces only setting pay through a single method of collective bargaining, there has been a shift away from single-employer bargaining to multi-employer bargaining. There has also been an increase in the incidence of unilateral pay setting by management: the percentage of public sector workplaces where some employees' pay was set unilaterally by management rose from 21 per cent in 1998 to 28 per cent in 2004. This has also been accompanied by a decline in the incidence of 'other' pay methods attributable, in part, to the diminished role played by Independent Pay Review Bodies in settlements within the National Health Service.

Using time-consistent measures, the proportion of all employees who had their pay set through collective bargaining fell from 38 per cent in 1998 to 35 per cent in 2004, though this difference is not statistically significant (Table 7.5). Coverage remained stable among single independent establishments, but fell among workplaces that were part of a larger organization. It also remained stable in establishments with 25 or more employees, the shift from 41 per cent in 1998 to 39 per cent in 2004 being statistically non-significant.[4]

Where employees were covered by collective bargaining, negotiations were a little more likely to take place at sectoral or national level in 2004 than they were in 1998. However, this trend was largely accounted for by change in the public sector: in the private sector, fewer employees were covered by pay bargaining in 2004 than 1998, whether at national, sectoral, organizational or workplace level. There was a significant rise in the percentage of all employees whose pay was set unilaterally by management at the workplace or a higher level (up from 49 per cent to 57 per cent). This rise was largely confined to the private sector and to workplaces that did not recognize trade unions for pay bargaining. By 2004, almost three-quarters (72 per cent) of private sector employees had their pay set unilaterally by management, a figure that rose to nine in ten (88 per cent) where unions were not recognized for pay bargaining.

The picture of change in collective bargaining coverage differed markedly across industrial sectors of the economy (Table 7.6). In private manufacturing, one-third (34 per cent) of employees had their pay set through collective bargaining in 2004, down from 43 per in 1998. Coverage was relatively stable in private services as a whole (20 per cent in 1998, compared with 18 per cent in 2004), although the annual rate of decline was particularly steep in Hotels and restaurants and Wholesale and retail.[5] However, coverage rose in the public sector from 66 per cent to 75 per cent. This was largely because, at the time of fieldwork, many health professionals whose pay was previously set by Independent Pay Review Bodies had a bargained settlement under the Agenda for Change. Consequently, coverage in the Health and social work sector rose proportionately more than in any other sector (from 40 per cent in 1998 to 55 per cent in 2004). Collective bargaining coverage rose in the public sector, even though the percentage of public sector workplaces engaging in any pay bargaining did not change (Table 7.3), because of a return to collective bargaining in larger public sector workplaces, such as hospitals. This rise in collective bargaining coverage in the public sector

*Table 7.5* Pay determination methods (employees), 1998 and 2004

| | All workplaces | | Sector of ownership | | | | Organization status | | | | Unions recognized[c] | | | | 25 or more employees | |
| | | | Public | | Private | | Stand-alone Workplace | | Part of larger organization | | At least one | | None | | | |
| | 1998 | 2004 | 1998 | 2004 | 1998 | 2004 | 1998 | 2004 | 1998 | 2004 | 1998 | 2004 | 1998 | 2004 | 1998 | 2004 |
|---|---|---|---|---|---|---|---|---|---|---|---|---|---|---|---|---|
| *Collective bargaining* | | | | | | | | | | | | | | | | |
| More than one employer | 14 | 18 | 40 | 58 | 5 | 4 | 10 | 12 | 16 | 19 | 24 | 36 | 3 | 2 | 15 | 20 |
| At organization level | 16 | 11 | 21 | 16 | 13 | 10 | 0 | 0 | 20 | 15 | 28 | 25 | 1 | 0 | 17 | 13 |
| At workplace | 8 | 6 | 4 | 2 | 9 | 7 | 7 | 5 | 8 | 6 | 14 | 12 | 1 | 1 | 9 | 7 |
| *Any of the above* | 38 | 35 | 66 | 75 | 27 | 21 | 17 | 17 | 44 | 40 | 66 | 73 | 5 | 3 | 41 | 39 |
| *Other methods* | | | | | | | | | | | | | | | | |
| Set by management higher in organization | 19 | 22 | 8 | 8 | 24 | 27 | 0 | 0 | 25 | 28 | 11 | 12 | 29 | 30 | 17 | 21 |
| Set by management at workplace | 30 | 35 | 3 | 5 | 40 | 45 | 65 | 71 | 19 | 25 | 10 | 8 | 52 | 58 | 29 | 32 |
| Negotiation with individual employees | 3 | 4 | 0 | 0 | 4 | 5 | 9 | 8 | 1 | 3 | 1 | 1 | 6 | 6 | 2 | 3 |
| Some other way[a] | 9 | 4 | 22 | 10 | 5 | 1 | 9 | 2 | 10 | 3 | 11 | 4 | 7 | 2 | 10 | 3 |
| Pay Review Body[b] | – | 3 | – | 10 | – | 0 | – | 1 | – | 3 | – | 4 | – | 1 | – | 4 |
| *Any of the above* | 62 | 65 | 34 | 25 | 73 | 79 | 83 | 83 | 56 | 60 | 34 | 27 | 95 | 97 | 59 | 61 |

% workplaces

Base: All workplaces with 10 or more employees.

Figures are weighted and based on responses from 2,113 managers in 1998 and 2,001 managers in 2004.

Notes:

[a] In 2004, many responses coded as 'Other methods' in the interview were subsequently back-coded to specific methods, thereby lowering the incidence of 'Other' methods in comparison with 1998.

[b] In 1998, pay determination via Independent Pay Review Bodies was given as an example of 'other' methods, whereas in 2004 it was separately coded. The Figures provided for Pay Review Bodies in 2004 are also counted in the figures provided for 'Some other way'.

[c] To retain comparability between 2004 and 1998, union recognition is confined to unions with members on site. Endnote 3 of Chapter 7 provides details of the derivation of time-consistent estimates of collective bargaining coverage.

accounted for most of the rise in coverage in workplaces recognizing trade unions. Coverage in the unionized private sector rose from 64 per cent to 66 per cent, a change that is not statistically significant.

Reflecting on the findings from WERS 1998, Millward *et al.* predicted 'that collective bargaining will continue to contract' (2000: 235). Coverage has contracted, but how does the rate of change compare to the 1980s and 1990s? WERS contains data going back to the early 1980s for the population of workplaces with 25 or more employees. Among these workplaces, aggregate

*Table* 7.6 Aggregate collective bargaining coverage, 1998 and 2004

| | % employees | | *Average annual change[b] (%)* |
|---|---|---|---|
| | *1998* | *2004* | |
| All workplaces | 38 | 35 | −1.1 |
| *Broad sector* | | | |
| Private manufacturing | 43 | 34 | −3.5 |
| Private services | 20 | 18 | −1.4 |
| Public sector | 66 | 75 | +2.1 |
| *Industry* | | | |
| Manufacturing | 43 | 35 | −3.0 |
| Electricity, gas and water | 90 | 86 | −0.6 |
| Construction | 32 | 24 | −4.2 |
| Wholesale and retail | 21 | 13 | −7.2 |
| Hotels and restaurants | 12 | 4 | −16.2 |
| Transport and communication | 58 | 61 | +0.9 |
| Financial services | 49 | 35 | −5.0 |
| Other business services | 12 | 9 | −3.7 |
| Public administration | 83 | 80 | −0.6 |
| Education | 44 | 49 | +1.9 |
| Health and social work | 40 | 55 | +5.1 |
| Other community services | 36 | 40 | +2.0 |
| Any recognized unions[a] | 66 | 73 | +1.4 |
| *Workplaces with 25 or more employees* | | | |
| All | 41 | 39 | −0.7 |
| Private manufacturing | 46 | 38 | −2.6 |
| Private services | 23 | 21 | −1.1 |
| Public sector | 66 | 77 | +2.5 |

Base: All workplaces with 10 or more employees, except the last four rows which are confined to workplaces with 25 or more employees.

Figures are weighted and based on responses from 2,113 managers in 1998 and 2,001 managers in 2004.

Notes:

[a] To retain comparability between 2004 and 1998, union recognition is confined to unions with members on site.

[b] The method of calculation is outlined in endnote 6. Endnote 3 provides details of the derivation of time-consistent estimates of collective bargaining coverage.

collective bargaining coverage fell by 0.7 per cent a year on average over the period from 1998 to 2004, from 41 per cent to 39 per cent (Table 7.6). This compares with an average of 3.3 per cent per year for the whole economy between 1990 and 1998 and an average of 2.9 per cent per year over the period 1984–1990 (ibid.: 197).[6] Thus, the rate of decline in aggregate collective bargaining coverage in the economy as a whole has slowed since 1998 compared to the 1990s and 1980s. The picture is more mixed in the private sector. In private manufacturing, aggregate collective bargaining coverage fell at twice the rate over the period 1998–2004 compared with 1990–1998 (the annual rates of decline being 2.6 per cent and 1.3 per cent, respectively). The rate of decline in the most recent period was identical to that experienced over the period 1984–1990. In private services, on the other hand, the rate of decline in aggregate collective bargaining coverage slowed from an average of 4.7 per cent per year between 1990 and 1998 to an average of 1.1 per cent per year between 1998 and 2004. However, in 1998, levels of aggregate bargaining coverage were already much lower in private services than private manufacturing so that, in a sense, bargaining coverage had further to fall in manufacturing.

## *Quantifying the effect of declining union recognition on aggregate collective bargaining coverage*

Tables 7.5 and 7.6 show there was a small decline in the percentage of employees who had their pay set via collective bargaining between 1998 and 2004, with the percentage falling in the non-union sector and rising among employees in workplaces recognizing unions, while the unionized sector shrank overall. Of interest, then, is the share of declining bargaining coverage that is attributable to declining union recognition and the share due to changes in bargaining coverage *within* the unionized and non-unionized sectors. These shares can be identified using shift-share analysis – Forth (2000) provides an explanation of the method using WERS data. The analysis shows that, across the whole economy, if the percentage of workplaces recognizing trade unions had remained unchanged over the period, and only aggregate coverage had changed within unionized and non-unionized workplaces, bargaining coverage would have *risen* by over two percentage points instead of falling by over two percentage points. If, on the other hand, coverage within the union and non-union sectors had remained constant and the only change had been in the relative size of the two sectors, aggregate bargaining coverage would have *fallen* by four percentage points. Thus, the rise in coverage in the unionized sector mitigated what would have been an even larger decline in coverage due to the falling rate of union recognition.

The situation was somewhat different in the private sector where four-fifths (81 per cent) of the decline in aggregate bargaining coverage was due to declining union recognition, 11 per cent was due to falling coverage within the union sector, and the remaining 8 per cent was accounted for by an interaction between these two factors.

*The role of compositional and behavioural change in collective bargaining coverage*

How much of this change in aggregate collective bargaining coverage is accounted for by compositional change in the population of workplaces, and how much of it is accounted for by behavioural change within those workplaces that remained in existence over the period 1998 to 2004? Across the economy as a whole, the slower rate of decline since 1998 indicated by the comparison of cross-sectional data was due to two factors. First, bargaining coverage was fairly stable among those establishments which existed in both 2004 and 1998: 38 per cent of employees in continuing establishments had their pay set by collective bargaining in 2004 compared with 41 per cent in 1998. Second, workplaces which were set up or had grown into scope between 1998 and 2004 had similar coverage rates to those which closed or fell out of scope – 28 per cent in both cases.

## Variable pay schemes

One source of pay variation across and within workplaces is variable pay schemes. These are used to reward worker effort or performance through performance-related payments, or because employers wish to share some of the returns to improved workplace performance in the form of share options or profit-related payments. Although fairness considerations feature in employers' decisions to deploy variable payment systems, they are often used to extract greater effort from employees, and to increase employees' motivation and commitment to the goals of the organization.[7] It is often maintained that employers are increasingly likely to adopt performance-oriented reward systems in preference to a 'standard rate' or 'common rate' for the job which characterizes a joint regulation approach to pay (Marsden, 2004: 130–131). This change, it is argued, is motivated by employers' desire 'to make their organizations more responsive to more competitive and faster changing markets' (ibid.) by devolving decision-making and relying more heavily on employee initiative. We might, therefore, expect an increased incidence of variable payment systems since 1998.

This next section maps the incidence of variable payment systems across workplaces in 2004 and considers how their usage has altered since 1998. It is not possible to measure the changing incidence of variable pay methods through a comparison of the 2004 and 1998 Cross-Section Surveys of Managers because the format and wording of the relevant questions have changed. However, it is possible to explore change among continuing workplaces with the 1998–2004 Panel Survey, where consistent measures have been retained.

The survey covered three types of variable pay schemes: performance-related payment systems, profit-related payments or bonuses, and employee share schemes. Although these three schemes were positively and significantly correlated,[8] analysis of previous WERS suggests they 'have different sets of determinants and are associated with different outcomes' (Millward *et al.*, 2000: 212). They are, therefore, discussed separately below.

### *Performance-related payment systems*

Performance-related pay systems – also known as incentive pay schemes – comprise payment by results (PBR), in which the level of pay is determined objectively by the amount of work done or its value, and merit-based systems, in which pay is related to a subjective assessment of performance by a supervisor or manager.[9] Two-fifths (40 per cent) of workplaces had incentive pay schemes: merit pay alone was used in 9 per cent of workplaces, PBR alone was used in nearly one quarter (23 per cent) of workplaces, and a further 7 per cent used both PBR and merit pay to reward employees. Where incentive payments were made, they were paid to both managerial and non-managerial employees in more than half (56 per cent) of cases, to managerial employees only in 10 per cent of cases, and to non-managerial employees only in 34 per cent of cases. Where workplaces had incentive payments in place, employees in Sales and customer service occupations were most likely to receive them, while those in Caring, leisure and other personal service occupations and Elementary occupations were least likely to receive them.

Incentive payments were more common in the private than the public sector: 44 per cent of private sector workplaces had incentive payments, compared with one-fifth (19 per cent) of public sector workplaces. With four-fifths (82 per cent) of its workplaces using incentive payments, the Financial services sector was more likely to have them than any other sector. Incentive payments were less common where workplaces recognized trade unions: 32 per cent of unionized workplaces used them compared with 43 per cent of non-unionized workplaces. However, this was due to the higher incidence of unionized workplaces in the public sector where incentive payments were less common. Within private services, the incidence of incentive payments was similar across unionized and non-unionized workplaces (47 per cent and 45 per cent respectively). Within private manufacturing, incentive payments were actually more prevalent in unionized than non-unionized workplaces (51 per cent versus 33 per cent).

A further factor associated with the presence of incentive payments was the degree of product market competition faced by the workplace. In the trading sector, incentive payments were more common where product market competition was more in evidence. Thus, half (50 per cent) of those who assessed the degree of competition in their market as 'very high' had PBR or merit pay, compared with a little over one-third (36 per cent) of those perceiving market competition to be 'very low'. Similarly, nearly half (47 per cent) of those workplaces saying they had 'many competitors' had incentive payments compared with 28 per cent of those who said they dominated their product market and had no competitors. The basis on which workplaces competed was also associated with the use of incentive payments. Incentive payments were most likely to be used in workplaces where demand for goods or services was highly dependent upon price but not quality, and were least likely to be used where managers said demand was not highly dependent on either price or quality.

In 1998, 19 per cent of workplaces had 'individual or group performance-related schemes'. However, this measure of incentive payments is not comparable to the 2004 measure, so it is not possible to infer whether performance-related payments have become more common since 1998.[10] It is possible, however, to infer whether there has been a change in the incidence of incentive payment schemes among workplaces in the 1998–2004 Panel Survey since the 2004 questions replicate those asked in 1998.[11] In 2004, 32 per cent of continuing workplaces had performance-related pay schemes, up from 20 per cent in 1998. It appears, therefore, that there has been a substantial increase in the incidence of performance-related pay schemes since 1998. There is further support for this proposition from a comparison of leavers and joiners with continuing workplaces in the 1998 and 2004 Cross-Section Surveys. In 1998, 17 per cent of leavers and 19 per cent of continuing workplaces used individual or group-based performance-related pay. In 2004, 37 per cent of continuing workplaces and 44 per cent of joiners used incentive payments. Even if one accepts that some of the difference is accounted for by differences in question wording in the two cross-section surveys, these figures provide further evidence that workplaces in 2004 were much more likely to use incentive payments than workplaces in 1998.

## Share ownership schemes

Managers in all trading sector establishments (all private sector workplaces and those that were part of government-owned trading corporations) were asked whether they operated any employee share ownership schemes (ESOSs). Respondents were prompted with a show card listing Share Incentive Plans (SIP), Save As You Earn (SAYE or Sharesave), Enterprise Management Incentives (EMI), Company Share Option Plans (CSOP) and 'Other employee share schemes'. Twenty-one per cent of workplaces had at least one of these schemes. The most common scheme was SAYE, operated by 13 per cent of workplaces, followed by SIP (8 per cent), CSOP (6 per cent) and 'Other' employee share ownership schemes (4 per cent). Less than 1 per cent of workplaces operated EMI. Eight per cent of workplaces operated more than one type of scheme.

Where ESOSs were operated, eligibility extended to non-managerial employees in 85 per cent of cases, suggesting that they are not simply a mechanism for rewarding and retaining managerial staff. Furthermore, in three-quarters (76 per cent) of the cases where non-managerial staff were eligible for ESOSs, *every* non-managerial employee was eligible. Where they were eligible, non-managerial employees generally tended to participate in ESOSs. For instance, in workplaces where all non-managerial employees were eligible for ESOSs, they all participated in 44 per cent of cases and, in two-thirds (67 per cent) of cases, participation rates were at least 40 per cent.

Whether or not an establishment operated an ESOS was largely determined by the size of the organization to which it belonged. Whereas 2 per cent of workplaces in organizations with fewer than 50 employees operated ESOSs, this rose to 8 per cent among those with 50–249 employees, and 44 per cent among those with at least 250 employees. Over three-fifths (63 per cent) of the largest organizations with 10,000 or more employees had ESOSs. Their incidence also varied with broad sector, with private service workplaces more than twice as likely to operate ESOSs as private manufacturers (23 per cent and 10 per cent respectively). They were particularly prevalent in Financial services, where four-in-five establishments (82 per cent) operated ESOSs. Foreign ownership was also associated with a higher incidence of ESOSs: 41 per cent of workplaces with some foreign ownership operated ESOSs, compared with 16 per cent of workplaces that were wholly UK owned. As in the case of performance-related payments, the incidence of ESOSs was also higher where product market competition was more in evidence. Those who assessed the degree of competition in their market as 'very high' were twice as likely to operate ESOSs as those who perceived less market competition (30 per cent versus 15 per cent respectively). Similarly, the incidence of ESOSs was twice as high among workplaces who said they had 'many competitors' compared to those who said they dominated their product market and had no competitors (22 per cent versus 11 per cent respectively).

A simple comparison of the incidence of ESOSs across unionized and non-unionized workplaces indicates that ESOSs were more than three times more prevalent where unions were recognized (48 per cent versus 15 per cent). However, the higher incidence of ESOSs in unionized workplaces was only apparent in organizations with at least 1,000 employees. In smaller organizations, ESOSs were equally rare in unionized and non-unionized establishments.

The incidence of ESOSs in the 2004 Cross-Section Survey of Managers was similar to that in the 1998 survey, when 15 per cent of all workplaces and 19 per cent of private sector workplaces had an ESOS. However, such a comparison should be treated with caution as the wording and format of the question have changed.[12] However, a reliable comparison can be drawn from the 1998–2004 Panel Survey which repeated the 1998 question. This indicated that 15 per cent of workplaces that continued to operate over the period had ESOSs in 1998, and the same proportion had them in 2004. Together, these figures suggest little change in the incidence of ESOSs over the period.

### Profit-related payments

All workplaces were asked 'Do any employees at this workplace receive profit-related payments or profit-related bonuses?' Across the economy as a whole, this was the case in 30 per cent of workplaces. However, profit is only a meaningful concept in the trading sector, so the analysis in the remainder of this section is confined to trading sector workplaces. In the trading sector, 36 per cent of workplaces answered 'yes' – 37 per cent in the private sector, and 15 per cent in the public sector.

The sectors with the highest incidence of profit-related payments (PRP) were Financial services (67 per cent) and Electricity, gas and water (59 per cent).

Foreign-owned workplaces had a greater tendency to use PRP than domestically-owned workplaces (50 per cent compared to 34 per cent). Although PRP was less common among the smallest organizations and establishments, there was no simple linear relationship between workplace size and the incidence of PRP. As noted in earlier surveys, PRP was less common where unions were recognized for pay bargaining: one-third (35 per cent) of unionized workplaces had PRP, compared with two-fifths (43 per cent) of non-unionized workplaces. However, as in the case of incentive payments, this association was due to the higher concentration of unionized workplaces in the public sector. In private services, the incidence of PRP was higher in unionized workplaces than in non-unionized workplaces (47 per cent versus 35 per cent). It was also a little higher in private manufacturing (41 per cent in unionized workplaces compared with 37 per cent in non-unionized workplaces).

As with incentive payments, a link was apparent between variable pay schemes and product market competition: 42 per cent of those who perceived competition as 'very high' had PRP schemes, as did 35 per cent of those with 'many' competitors, whereas PRP was present in 24 per cent of workplaces where competition was 'very low' and only 14 per cent where the respondent to the managerial interview said they had no competitors and dominated the market.

Workplaces belonging to multiple-establishment organizations were asked how PRP was calculated. In nearly half (48 per cent) of cases a workplace-based measure of profits was used; in 40 per cent of cases, an organization-based measure was used; in 8 per cent, profits were calculated at division or subsidiary level; 4 per cent used some other method.

In two-thirds (63 per cent) of cases – 22 per cent of all trading sector workplaces – the PRP scheme covered non-managerial employees. In the 12 months prior to the survey, payments had been made to non-managerial employees in all but 16 per cent of the establishments where non-managerial workers participated in the scheme and, in 49 per cent of establishments, *all* non-managerial participants had received payments.

In 1998, 39 per cent of trading sector workplaces had PRP schemes. However, changes in the question format mean that, again, this figure is not comparable with the 2004 figure reported above. A reliable comparison among continuing workplaces is possible using the 1998–2004 Panel Survey where the 1998 questions are replicated. Forty-one per cent of trading sector workplaces in the panel had a PRP scheme in 2004, identical to the figure in 1998. Thus, as in the case of ESOSs, it seems there has been little change in the incidence of PRP since 1998.[13] This is despite the fact that payments made under PRP schemes have been fully taxable since 2000.

## Determination of employees' terms and conditions

What, then, of the fate of joint regulation in determining the setting of terms and conditions of employment generally? WERS 2004 asked managers whether they normally negotiated with, consulted, or informed union or non-union representatives over the 12 terms and conditions of employment – including pay – that are listed in Table 7.7. These data are not directly comparable with those collected in 1998 and so an analysis of change in joint regulation is not possible.[14] In two-thirds of workplaces (67 per cent) management did not engage with employees on any of the 12 listed items. If one considers individual items, this absence of engagement with staff was most pronounced with respect to staff selection and least apparent in the case of disciplinary and grievance procedures and health and safety matters. Management were most likely to negotiate over pay, hours and holidays, and least likely to negotiate over staffing plans, training and staff selection.

The joint regulation of pay and conditions was far more common where a union was recognized. Sixty-one per cent of workplaces which recognized unions normally negotiated over pay, one half negotiated over hours and holidays, more than one-third negotiated over pensions and over one quarter negotiated grievance and disciplinary procedures (see the figures in parentheses in Table 7.7). Currently, the statutory recognition procedure stipulates that bargaining occurs over pay, holidays and hours worked. The concern has been to ensure that the statutory underpinning to collective bargaining does not stray into areas that are not commonly covered under voluntary arrangements.

*Table* 7.7 Joint regulation of terms and conditions

|  | % of workplaces | | | |
|---|---|---|---|---|
|  | *Nothing* | *Inform* | *Consult* | *Negotiate* |
| *Issue* | | | | |
| Pay | 70 (16) | 6 (10) | 5 (13) | 18 (61) |
| Hours | 71 (18) | 5 (10) | 8 (20) | 16 (53) |
| Holidays | 71 (19) | 9 (17) | 5 (13) | 15 (52) |
| Pensions | 73 (22) | 11 (25) | 6 (16) | 10 (36) |
| Staff selection | 78 (42) | 10 (26) | 9 (23) | 3 (9) |
| Training | 75 (36) | 10 (24) | 13 (31) | 3 (9) |
| Grievance procedure | 69 (15) | 9 (20) | 14 (36) | 9 (28) |
| Disciplinary procedure | 69 (15) | 9 (21) | 13 (35) | 8 (29) |
| Staffing plans | 75 (33) | 11 (26) | 12 (34) | 3 (7) |
| Equal opportunities | 72 (22) | 10 (23) | 14 (40) | 5 (15) |
| Health and safety | 69 (17) | 9 (19) | 17 (49) | 5 (15) |
| Performance appraisal | 75 (33) | 9 (20) | 12 (33) | 4 (14) |

Base: All workplaces with 10 or more employees.
Figures are weighted and based on responses from at least 2,007 managers.
Notes:
  Managerial respondent was asked 'whether management normally negotiates, consults, informs or does not involve unions' on 12 items. The question was also asked with respect to non-union employee representatives. Figures in parentheses relate to workplaces with recognized trades unions and are based on responses from at least 1,004 managers. Each item is hierarchically coded so that, if the respondent says 'consults' this takes priority over 'informs', whereas 'negotiates' takes priority over 'consults'.

However, recent research indicates that, in over half of all new voluntary recognition agreements, the scope of bargaining is defined broadly in terms of 'pay and conditions' (Moore *et al.*, 2004). This might conceivably extend to issues such as pensions and training. Negotiation over these issues occurs in a sizeable percentage of establishments recognizing unions, but is less common than in the case of the three issues currently included in the statutory list. However, in nearly one-third (31 per cent) of workplaces recognizing unions, managers maintained that they negotiated on none of the 12 issues. If analysis is confined to union workplaces where negotiation occurred on at least one item, negotiation over pensions occurred in over half of unionized workplaces (52 per cent) – 43 per cent in the private sector and 60 per cent in the public sector. Negotiation over training occurred in 14 per cent of unionized work-places where negotiation over one or more issues took place.

In the absence of a recognized union, management only negotiated, consulted or informed employees on one of the 12 items, on average. In unionized work-places, managers negotiated, consulted or informed employees on an average of nine out of 12 items. Negotiations were almost exclusively confined to union-ized workplaces. Negotiations over any of the 12 items only occurred in 2 per cent of workplaces without recognized unions, and in all these cases it was over a single item. Where a union was recognized, negotiations occurred on three of the 12 items, on average. There was substantial variance in the scope of bar-gaining in unionized workplaces, however. In 31 per cent of cases where unions were recognized for bargaining, the manager said negotiations did not normally occur on any item; in a further 7 per cent, negotiations normally occurred on one item; in 35 per cent negotiations occurred on two, three or four items; and in 27 per cent of cases negotiations normally occurred over five or more items. There were also marked differences across the public and private sectors: the scope of collective bargaining was broader in the public sector than the private sector, the mean number of items subject to negotiation being 3.5 and 2.9 respectively.

There were clear patterns of pay bargaining in workplaces recognizing unions across the 12 items. These were revealed using factor analysis, which identified three factors; together they accounted for 74 per cent of the variance in nego-tiation across items. The first factor, which consisted of substantive terms and conditions of employment, included negotiation over pay, hours, holidays and pensions; the second dealing with procedural matters grouped negotiation over grievance procedures, disciplinary procedures, equal opportunities and health and safety; the third focused on staff development issues and grouped negotia-tion over staff selection, staffing plans and training.[15] Performance appraisals were not strongly associated with any of the three factors.

Joint regulation over terms and conditions was more common where employees had a representative on-site. Furthermore, the type of joint regula-tion varied with the nature of that representation. In workplaces having only on-site union representatives, management was more likely to negotiate over terms and conditions and less likely to simply inform representatives about decisions taken than in cases where the only representatives were non-union.

Some degree of engagement with employee representatives over terms and conditions was most common where there were both union and non-union representatives on-site, although this engagement was more likely to take the form of information and consultation, as opposed to negotiation, than in the cases where the only representatives present were union representatives.

### Pay negotiation in workplaces recognizing trade unions

The emergence of workplaces that recognized unions for pay bargaining, yet reported no pay determination via collective bargaining, was first identified in the WERS data in 1998 (Millward *et al.*, 2000: 160–166) and was interpreted as evidence consistent with recognized unions becoming 'hollow shells'. An alternative proposition is that 'collective bargaining' is perceived by employers to be a process that is somewhat broader than one that is confined purely to *negotiation* over pay. The figures in the first row of Table 7.7 are based on the question, described above, which asked managers how they 'normally' engage with union and non-union representatives in relation to rates of pay. It is not directly comparable, therefore, to the information collected in relation to union recognition and collective bargaining coverage reported earlier. However, by examining responses to this question alongside those relating to bargaining coverage and recognition the 2004 data can further aid understanding of the relationship between recognition, collective bargaining coverage and pay negotiation.

As noted earlier, 86 per cent of workplaces recognizing unions reported pay determination through collective bargaining for at least some of their employees (Table 7.1). The question relating to what 'normally' happens in relation to rates of pay confirms that union recognition does not guarantee negotiation over pay: negotiations 'normally' occurred in three-fifths (61 per cent) of workplaces that recognized unions, and two-thirds (65 per cent) of workplaces which recognized unions and had union members on-site. In 13 per cent of unionized workplaces, the manager said management normally consulted over pay, in 10 per cent of cases they simply informed representatives of pay decisions, and in a further 16 per cent of cases managers said they did none of these things. The finding is partly accounted for by managers perceiving limited engagement with worker representatives where collective bargaining occurred above work-place-level. Managers of unionized workplaces were less likely to say that management normally negotiated over pay where there was multi-employer bargaining (63 per cent) than where the bargaining occurred at organization-level (80 per cent) or workplace-level (86 per cent). They were also more likely than managers in other unionized workplaces to say that there was no engagement with worker representatives over pay.

## The distribution of pay, fringe benefits and pay satisfaction

It is arguable that whether terms and conditions are set unilaterally by management or are the result of joint regulation only really matters if they produce different substantive outcomes. There is a sizeable literature suggesting that procedural arrangements do produce different substantive outcomes. For instance, research for the late 1990s confirmed that, in keeping with the previous literature, the pay distribution was more compressed where unions negotiated over pay (Metcalf, 2005) and union-covered workers received a fringe benefits 'premium' relative to their non-union counterparts (Forth and Millward, 2000). This section revisits this issue and explores the impact of pay determination methods, workplace-level pay dispersion and fringe benefits on employee satisfaction with pay.

The distribution of gross hourly pay among employees in 2004 is presented in Table 7.8. Figures in the first column have been compiled from the Employee Profile Questionnaire by computing the aggregate percentage of all employees in WERS workplaces that have earnings within each of the four pay bands, according to managers. They indicate that around 8 per cent of employees earned £5.00 or less per hour, almost three-quarters (72 per cent) earned between £5.01 and £14.99 per hour, and one-sixth earned £15 per hour or more.[16] In the remainder of this section, those earning £5.00 or less per hour are referred to as 'low-paid', while those earning £15 per hour or more are termed 'high-paid'. The figures in column two have been compiled by first computing, within each workplace, the percentage of employees within each pay band, and then taking the average of this percentage across all workplaces. The figures indicate that on average 12 per cent of employees in each workplace were low-paid. This figure is higher than the overall percentage of employees who were low-paid, indicating that smaller workplaces tended to have a higher proportion of employees on low wages than did larger establishments.

Column 3 presents the gross hourly pay distribution based on employees ticking one of four boxes in response to the question: 'How much do you get paid per hour, before tax and other deductions are taken out?' Although not all employees were able or willing to provide their hourly pay, the responses are more complete than those provided by managers (89 per cent of employees provided a useable response, compared with 73 per cent of workplace managers).

*Table 7.8* Distribution of gross hourly pay

| Source | Survey of Managers | | Survey of Employees |
|---|---|---|---|
| | % employees | Average % of employees within each workplace | % employees |
| Gross hourly pay (£) | | | |
| 4.50 or less | 2 | 3 | 4 |
| 4.51–5.00 | 6 | 9 | 10 |
| 5.01–14.99 | 72 | 72 | 72 |
| 15.00 or more | 18 | 15 | 13 |

Base: All employees in workplaces with 10 or more.
Figures are weighted and based on responses from 1,504 managers (columns 1 and 2) and 19,350 employees (column 3).

Furthermore, responses would not be expected to suffer from any bias that may be induced by managerial concerns at identifying the payment of low wages. Perhaps for this reason, the percentage of low-paid employees was higher on the employee measure (14 per cent) than on the employee-weighted measure given by managers. It is also similar to the percentage derived from the Autumn 2004 Labour Force Survey (12 per cent). Thirteen per cent of employees were high-paid according to the WERS employee survey, a figure that was five percentage points lower than figures derived from the managerial questionnaire and the Labour Force Survey.

Across the whole economy, workplaces with at least some employees covered by collective bargaining had a more compressed distribution of gross hourly pay than those with no collective bargaining. Without controlling for other factors, the incidence of any collective bargaining lowered the mean percentage of low-paid employees by 10 percentage points (Table 7.9). It also raised the mean percentage of high-paid employees by five percentage points, the overall effect being to increase the percentage in the middle band by six percentage points relative to workplaces with no collective bargaining. Controlling for broad sector and organizational size, the mean percentage of employees in the middle band was eight percentage points higher in covered workplaces compared to uncovered workplaces, the mean percentage of low-paid employees was six percentage points lower, and there was no statistically significant difference between covered and uncovered workplaces in terms of the mean percentage of high-paid employees. Similar effects were apparent in the private sector: controlling for organization size, the mean percentage of low-paid employees was nine percentage points lower in covered workplaces compared to uncovered ones, and the mean percentage of employees in the middle-earning band was 10 percentage points higher.

*Table 7.9* Distribution of gross hourly pay, by incidence of collective bargaining

|  | *Gross hourly pay* | | |
|---|---|---|---|
|  | *£5.00 or less* | *£5.01–£14.99* | *£15.00 or more* |
|  | *Average % of employees within each workplace* | | |
| *Any collective bargaining at workplace* | | | |
| No | 15 | 70 | 13 |
| Yes | 5 | 76 | 18 |
| Private sector only: | | | |
| *Any collective bargaining at workplace* | | | |
| No | 16 | 70 | 13 |
| Yes | 9 | 78 | 12 |

Base: All employees in workplaces with 10 or more.
Figures are weighted and based on responses from 1,488 managers (1,055 in the private sector).
Note:
    See endnote 1 of Chapter 7 for details of the derivation of collective bargaining coverage.

Further analyses explored gross hourly pay dispersion in workplaces with different mixes of pay determination methods. Pay dispersion at workplace-level was least pronounced where all pay was set through multi-employer collective bargaining. Where all pay was set through organization-level collective bargaining, or workplace-level collective bargaining, the mean percentage of low-paid employees was not significantly different from instances in which all pay was set unilaterally by management.

The links between collective bargaining and low pay can also be investigated from the perspective of the employee using data from the Employee Questionnaire in combination with managerial data on pay determination methods. Employees in workplaces with some collective bargaining were less likely to be low-paid than employees in workplaces with no collective bargaining: 8 per cent of employees in covered workplaces were low-paid, compared with 21 per cent in workplaces with no collective bargaining. Significant differences remained having controlled for broad sector and organizational size. Putting the figures the other way round, of the 14 per cent of all employees who were low-paid, four-fifths (81 per cent) were employed in workplaces with no collective bargaining. In the private sector, 10 per cent of employees in covered workplaces were low-paid compared with 21 per cent in workplaces with no collective bargaining and, again, significant differences persisted controlling for organizational size. Eighty-one per cent of the low-paid employees in the private sector were employed in uncovered workplaces.

The percentage of employees who were high-paid was identical in the covered and uncovered sectors at 13 per cent, both in the whole economy and the private sector. With controls, the probability of an employee being high-paid was significantly lower in covered workplaces. Thus, whether one considers pay dispersion within the workplace or pay dispersion among employees at large, it is clear that collective bargaining compressed pay dispersion by reducing the percentage of low-paid employees. It would appear that unions continue to wield a 'sword of justice'.

The union membership wage premium has fallen a little in recent years (Blanchflower and Bryson, 2003), with some suggesting the average membership premium is close to zero (Metcalf, 2005: 113). However, core employees in workplaces with some collective bargaining continued to receive a fringe benefits 'premium' in 2004, as they had done in 1998 (Forth and Millward, 2000). Core employees in workplaces with some collective bargaining were significantly more likely to be entitled to an employer pension scheme, and to have more than the statutory entitlement to paid annual leave and sick pay, both in the whole economy and the private sector (Table 7.10).[17] These differences persisted controlling for organizational size and, in the whole economy, broad sector. Although the evidence suggests employees in uncovered workplaces were a little more likely to have entitlement to private health insurance than covered employees and, in the private sector, were a little more likely to be entitled to a company car or allowance, these differences were not significant having controlled for organizational size.

*Table 7.10* Entitlement to fringe benefits among core employees, by incidence of collective bargaining

| | % workplaces | | | | | | |
|---|---|---|---|---|---|---|---|
| | Employer pension scheme | Company car/ allowance | Private health insurance | Over 4 weeks' paid annual leave | Extra-statutory sick pay | None of these | Average number |
| All workplaces | 64 | 15 | 16 | 59 | 54 | 19 | 2.1 |
| *Any collective bargaining at workplace* | | | | | | | |
| No | 54 | 14 | 18 | 50 | 45 | 24 | 1.8 |
| Yes | 92 | 16 | 12 | 86 | 79 | 3 | 2.9 |
| Private sector only: | | | | | | | |
| All workplaces | 58 | 14 | 19 | 53 | 50 | 22 | 1.9 |
| *Any collective bargaining at workplace* | | | | | | | |
| No | 53 | 14 | 18 | 48 | 45 | 25 | 1.8 |
| Yes | 88 | 10 | 23 | 83 | 87 | 3 | 2.9 |

Base: All workplaces with 10 or more employees.
Figures are weighted and based on responses from 2,060 managers (1,488 in the private sector).
Note:
See endnote 1 of Chapter 7 for details of the derivation of collective bargaining coverage.

It appears that having some employees covered by pay bargaining at the workplace is associated with a reduced incidence of low pay and a lower probability that an employee will be low-paid, thus compressing the pay distribution, and that collective bargaining is also associated with entitlements to more non-pay fringe benefits. But were pay determination methods, the broad pay band, the distribution of pay or fringe benefit entitlements associated with employees' pay satisfaction? Employees were asked how satisfied they were with 'the amount of pay you receive', together with other aspects of their job, with tick boxes ranging from 'very satisfied' through to 'very dissatisfied'. Pay satisfaction was lower than satisfaction with other aspects of the job, and had not changed since 1998 (Kersley *et al.*, 2005: 33). Employee-weighted multivariate analyses were run on the five-category ordered pay satisfaction variable to establish independent associations between pay satisfaction and the broad pay band, the degree of pay compression, provision of fringe benefits, and the incidence of collective bargaining.[18] Controlling for a range of individual employee characteristics and employment in the public sector, pay satisfaction rose significantly with the gross hourly pay band. Entitlements to a car or car allowance and to health insurance were associated with higher pay satisfaction, but the association with health insurance became non-significant when controlling for pay levels. This suggests that health insurance was associated with higher pay but, once this was accounted for, it had no direct effect on pay satisfaction. However, car entitlements may be a supplement to pay, or valued more highly than any cash equivalent where they were offered instead of pay. Entitlement to an employer pension scheme was associated with lower pay satisfaction, suggesting either that employees face a pay penalty in order to obtain pension rights, or else that, when offered as a supplement to pay, employees may prefer the cash equivalent.

Although union membership was associated with lower pay satisfaction, being in a workplace with some collective bargaining over pay was not. Employees were less satisfied, on average, in workplaces where pay was compressed – the measure of pay compression being the proportion of employees in the middle pay band. However, the size of this effect halved and became statistically non-significant once the employee's own pay was taken into account. This raises the issue of what is most salient in employees' minds in terms of satisfaction with their pay – is it the absolute level of their pay, or their pay relative to other employees at their workplace? To explore the effect of low pay, an indicator of whether an employee was paid £5.00 or less per hour was interacted with the percentage of employees in his or her workplace paid £5.00 or less per hour. Being low-paid was associated with lower pay satisfaction, but the percentage of low-paid employees at the workplace was not statistically significant. Nor was the interaction between an employee's own low pay and the incidence of low pay at the workplace. This suggests that, for low-paid employees, what mattered was their own pay level, rather than the percentage of other employees at the workplace who were also low paid. However, pay relativities did affect pay satisfaction for medium-paid and high-paid, as their degree of pay satisfaction was higher in workplaces where the median worker was low-paid than in workplaces where the median worker was medium-paid or high-paid. This suggests that, in low-paying workplaces, higher-paid employees are even more satisfied with their pay than they would be in other workplaces.

## Consultation over redundancies

As a result of EU requirements, employee representation with respect to consultation over collective redundancies has been statutorily regulated for some time. Following a European Court of Justice ruling in the mid-1990s, requirements for employers to consult over redundancies were extended to representatives elected by employees, whether representatives of recognized unions or not. The regulations were amended in 1999 to ensure that, where recognized unions were present, employers could not by-pass them by consulting solely with elected non-union representatives (Hall and Edwards, 1999). These changes are significant because they introduced statutory employee representation mechanisms 'to fill the increasingly wide gaps left by reliance on employer recognition of trade unions' (Dickens and Hall, 2003: 142).

In 2004, 13 per cent of workplaces reported redundancies in the previous 12 months. In a further 2 per cent of workplaces, redundancies had been proposed but were later withdrawn. There were 1.3 redundancies per hundred employees.[19] The rate of redundancies was highest in Manufacturing (3.1) and lowest in Health (0.1); it was four times higher in the private sector than the public sector (1.6 versus 0.4), and it was higher in non-unionized workplaces than in workplaces recognizing trade unions (1.5 compared with 1.1). Redundancy was a little more common in 1998 when 17 per cent of workplaces reported making redundancies and the redundancy rate was 1.6 per 100 employees, although this was not statistically different from the rate in 2004.[20]

Managerial respondents were provided with a list of factors and asked to identify the reasons for making redundancies in 2004. They were allowed to identify more than one reason. 'Reorganized working methods' was the most common reason, cited by over one-third (37 per cent) of those who had made redundancies in the previous 12 months, followed by 'lack of demand for products/services' (28 per cent) and 'improving competitiveness/efficiency/cost reduction' (19 per cent). The other major reason given was 'reduction in budget/cash limits' (16 per cent). Reasons for redundancy differed across private services and private Manufacturing: 'reorganized working methods' was more likely to be cited as a reason for redundancies in services than manufacturing (48 per cent compared with 39 per cent) whereas 'improving competitiveness/efficiency/cost reduction' was more likely to be cited in Manufacturing than services (37 per cent versus 29 per cent).

Employers consulted with employees or their representatives in three-quarters (75 per cent) of cases where redundancies were made or proposed. Where redundancies had actually occurred, there was consultation in 77 per cent of workplaces (Table 7.11). Consultation was less likely where unions were absent and, where it did occur in non-unionized workplaces, it was usually direct with the employees concerned, rather than through elected representatives. Where unions were recognized, consultation was undertaken through union representatives in more than half (55 per cent) of cases. In workplaces where union and non-union representatives were both present on-site, this rose to two-thirds (67 per cent).

*Table 7.11* Redundancy consultation arrangements, by union recognition

|  | *% workplaces* | | |
|---|---|---|---|
|  | *All workplaces* | *No union recognition* | *At least one recognized union* |
| Trade union representative/ shop steward | 18 | 4 | 55 |
| Joint consultative committee/ Works Council/other consultative committee | 14 | 8 | 29 |
| Other employee representatives | 10 | 6 | 19 |
| Directly with employees | 69 | 71 | 63 |
| No consultation | 23 | 26 | 14 |

Base: All workplaces with 10 or more employees where redundancies occurred in the previous 12 months.
All figures are weighted and based on responses from 609 managers (254 managers where no union recognition; 331 where at least one recognized union).
Note:
Managers could identify more than one arrangement so column percentages do not sum to 100.

Nevertheless, where redundancies were made in unionized workplaces, the employer consulted employees directly in 63 per cent of cases, consulted with non-union representatives in one-sixth of cases and used a consultative committee in over one quarter of cases. These figures clearly demonstrate that 'dual channel' arrangements for consultation over redundancies were well entrenched in unionized workplaces by 2004.[21]

The number of redundancies was another factor affecting whether consultation occurred and, if so, with whom. Employers are not required by statute to consult with employees unless 20 or more redundancies at a single establishment are proposed within a 90-day period. The survey does not contain information on the number of redundancies made in the previous 90 days. Instead, the survey provided information on the number of redundancies made among the employees on the payroll 12 months previously. In 8 per cent of workplaces that had made at least some redundancies in the year prior to the survey (1 per cent of all workplaces), 20 or more redundancies had been made. No consultation occurred in 12 per cent of these workplaces. Consultation was more likely when unions were present (94 per cent compared with 83 per cent in non-union workplaces). Furthermore, where unions were recognized, consultations took place with union representatives in 88 per cent of cases. Together these findings suggest unions retained a pivotal role in consulting over redundancies, particularly where they may have been able to fall back on statutory support for their role.

The 2004 survey pursued the suggestion made in previous research that consultation over redundancies gives employees an opportunity to influence the handling of job losses (Hall and Edwards, 1999). Where consultation had occurred with union or non-union employee representatives, managers were asked what issues the consultation covered. In most cases (86 per cent) it covered criteria for selection; and in over half (59 per cent) consultations covered redundancy payments. In two-thirds of cases, there had been consultation regarding options for reducing the number of redundancies. Managers were then asked whether the consultation with representatives had led to any changes in managers' original proposals. In three-quarters (78 per cent) of cases, it had not. However, in 10 per cent of cases it had led to reductions in the numbers made redundant, in 6 per cent changes in the selection criteria had occurred and in 5 per cent redundancy payments had increased. Outcomes appeared, therefore, to be a little more favourable from the employee perspective where representatives were engaged in the consultations. In addition, there was a reduction in the number of redundancies in 19 per cent of cases where union representatives were involved, compared to 12 per cent in the case of consultation through consultative committees and 14 per cent in the case of non-union representatives. However, these differences were not statistically significant.[22]

## Consultation over health and safety matters

Engagement between employers and employees over health and safety at work has been statutorily regulated under the Health and Safety at Work Act for three decades. Over most of that period, the requirement for employers to consult with their employees over such matters was confined to instances in which the employer recognized a trade union. For the first time, the 1996 Health and Safety (Consultation with Employees) Regulations required employers to consult employees who are not covered by union-appointed safety representatives. The regulations also permit employers to discharge this duty to consult through direct communications with employees, rather than employee representatives (James and Walters, 1997). Since the change in legislation, consultation through representative channels – joint committees or free-standing worker representatives – has declined markedly, whereas direct consultation over health and safety has become more prevalent (Table 7.12, columns 1 and 3).[23] The 1998–2004 Panel Survey did not include questions on health and safety arrangements. However, it is possible to compare continuing workplaces and joiners and leavers using the 1998 and 2004 Cross-Section Surveys of Managers. This provides an indication of the extent to which the change is driven by behavioural change among continuing establishments, on the one hand, and on the other hand, compositional change arising as 'leavers' leave the population, some establishments 'grow' into scope for WERS, and new establishments join. There is clear evidence that the shift to direct communication was due to compositional change in the population of workplaces, not behavioural change among continuing establishments. Continuing establishments were more likely to deal with health and safety through committees and worker representatives than both joiners and leavers, and they were a little more likely to use representative mechanisms in 2004 than they were in 1998. Joiners (those new establishments with 10 or more employees and those older workplaces growing

*Table 7.12* Health and safety consultation arrangements, 1998 and 2004

| | % workplaces | | | |
|---|---|---|---|---|
| | 1998 | | 2004 | |
| | All workplaces | At least one recognized union[b] | All workplaces | At least one recognized union[b] |
| Single or multi-issue joint consultative committees | 26 | 39 | 20 | 41 |
| Free-standing worker representatives | 25 | 32 | 22 | 22 |
| Direct methods[a] | 47 | 29 | 57 | 37 |
| No arrangements | 2 | 0 | 1 | 0 |

Base: All workplaces with 10 or more employees.
All figures are weighted and based on responses from 2,159 managers in 1998 (1,195 with recognized unions) and 2,043 managers in 2004 (1,195 with recognized unions).
Notes:
   [a] 'Direct methods' include newsletters/notice board/e-mail, management chain/cascade, staff meetings and consultation directly with the workforce.
   [b] Concerns only those trade unions with members at the workplace.

into the population of establishments with at least 10 employees) were much more likely to use direct communication methods than leavers.

Unlike the regulations governing collective redundancies, those relating to health and safety do not require unionized employers to engage with the recognized union over health and safety. It is therefore possible for employers to by-pass union representatives and to opt for direct communication with employees instead. As the figures in columns 2 and 4 of Table 7.12 indicate, among workplaces recognizing trade unions there was little change in the incidence of joint committees dealing with health and safety. However, there was a rise in direct consultation accompanied by a marked decline in health and safety representation by free-standing worker representatives. In the non-union sector, an increase in direct consultation of a similar scale (57 per cent to 65 per cent) was accompanied by a decline in the use of joint committees (from 19 per cent to 12 per cent) but relative stability in the incidence of free-standing representatives (22 per cent in 2004 compared with 21 per cent in 1998).

It is apparent from the penultimate row in Table 7.7 that, even in unionized establishments, management 'normally' does nothing to engage with representatives over health and safety in one-sixth (17 per cent) of cases and, in another fifth (19 per cent), management simply informs union representatives about these matters. However, workplaces with managers who said they 'normally' did nothing to engage with worker representatives over health and safety nevertheless had arrangements in place for health and safety matters. In workplaces recognizing unions where the manager said the norm was not to engage with representatives on health and safety, two-fifths (41 per cent) actually had a joint committee dealing with health and safety matters, 16 per cent had free-standing worker representatives dealing with health and safety, another two-fifths (42 per cent) used direct consultation methods for health and safety, and only 1 per cent appeared to do nothing at all. Similarly, in the non-union sector, among those saying 'normally' they did nothing to engage with employees on health and safety issues, 8 per cent had joint committees dealing with health and safety, 22 per cent had free-standing health and safety worker representatives, 69 per cent used direct communications, and only 1 per cent had no arrangements at all.

For the first time, the 2004 survey asked managers to identify what issues were discussed at regular meetings between senior management and the whole workforce, and at team briefings. Health and safety issues featured prominently in both settings: 70 per cent of workplaces with regular workforce meetings covered health and safety issues in such meetings, and a little under two-thirds (63 per cent) of establishments with team briefings covered health and safety issues in that forum. In both cases health and safety issues were the fifth most commonly cited issue from among the 12 issues presented as potentially being discussed at meetings.

## Conclusion

This chapter has re-examined the oft-cited perception that employers have successfully re-established managerial prerogatives at the workplace, making joint regulation of workplace matters a minority pursuit. Certainly, there is evidence that joint regulation is by no means as common as it used to be, at least in the private sector, and the marked increase in performance-related pay since 1998 is perhaps an indication that management have been successful in making pay more contingent on how employees perform, as opposed to setting a uniform rate for the job. However, the evidence suggests that managerial engagement with workers and their representatives, either to consult or negotiate with them, is perhaps a little more widespread than is commonly imagined.

Pay determination through collective bargaining has declined since the 1998 survey, but the rate of decline has slowed considerably compared to the period before 1998, and there has even been an increase in bargaining coverage in the public sector, largely due to negotiated settlements in the Health sector.

Joint regulation of terms and conditions is the exception rather than the rule, at least according to workplace managers.[24] Nevertheless, trade unions continue to affect both the degree of joint regulation and its nature: it was more common where they were present, and weighted towards the 'negotiation end' of joint regulation compared to non-union employee representation which was more likely to be associated with information provision and consultation.

Whether pay and conditions were jointly regulated was found to affect employees' pay, non-pay conditions, and how they felt about their pay. Collective bargaining narrowed the pay dispersion by reducing the incidence of low pay, and was associated with entitlements to more fringe benefits. These factors fed through to employees' satisfaction with their pay.

Statutory provision plays an important role in determining both the likelihood and nature of consultation with employees over important employment matters, as the evidence in relation to redundancies and health and safety matters clearly illustrates. Although the survey question on the timing of redundancies does not align precisely with the legal requirements to consult, it seems employers were much more likely to consult about redundancies when required to do so by law (where 20 or more redundancies are proposed). The ability of employers to discharge their duties to consult over health and safety using direct rather than representative forms of engagement with employees has coincided with an increased use of this approach, at least among new and growing workplaces. These are indications that the future of workplace joint regulation over employment matters may depend as much on the amount and form of statute in this area as upon the fortunes of trade unions, though unions are likely to play an important role in enforcing any new statutory obligations placed upon employers.

# 8  Workplace conflict

## Introduction

The employment relationship is, by its very nature, a complex interaction, comprising common and competing interests. At the heart of the relationship is an exchange of effort for money but, as it is not possible to completely specify the terms of the exchange, the employment contract inevitably carries elements of uncertainty. The benefits of the flexibility of the employment contract, together with aspects of mutuality and co-operation, are considered elsewhere in this volume. But the relationship also offers scope for divergent goals and behaviours (Edwards, 1986, 2003; Marsden, 1999). The potential for conflict is therefore considered by many to be inherent to workplace relations (see, for example, Clegg, 1975).

Such discord may manifest itself to varying degrees, being dependent not only upon the actual behaviour of employees and their managers, but also upon the culture of the workplace, methods of work organization and environmental factors, including legislative developments and competitive pressures (Earnshaw et al., 1998; Edwards, 2000). It may also take different forms of expression. Historically, attention has been focused on collective (or organized) forms of conflict, usually between unions and managers, such as strikes. However, the incidence of collective disputes has declined markedly since the late 1980s (Waddington, 2003), and the focus has shifted to unorganized and individualized expressions, such as grievances, Employment Tribunal claims and management-led sanctions including dismissals.[1] There has been a similar shift in emphasis in the policy arena, from legislation regulating industrial action to that promoting procedures for the resolution of individual disputes.

The WERS series has run alongside these debates, providing a map of the level and nature of collective and individual conflict inside the workplace (Millward et al., 1992: 185–216, 277–316; 1999: 245). It has also engaged in the growing debate on other potential indicators of employee discontent, such as absenteeism and voluntary resignations (Cully et al., 1999: 126–127). This chapter continues that tradition, providing an overview of the nature and extent of specific forms of workplace conflict in 2004, and examining the degree of change and stability since 1998. It also looks closely at workplace procedures for addressing and resolving disagreements between managers and trade unions, and managers and employees.

## Collective conflict

The discussion begins by examining the nature and incidence of disputes at the collective level. A year-on-year picture of industrial unrest can be mapped through official government statistics on stoppages of work caused by labour disputes, which include estimates of the number of workers involved and the number of working days lost (see Monger, 2005). In contrast, WERS provides a snap-shot of the incidence of disputes for the 12 months prior to the survey, allowing broad trends to be examined across the series. A unique feature of the survey is that it maps both the proportions and characteristics of workplaces involved.

Questions on industrial action, including strike and non-strike action, have remained constant throughout the series, yielding a measure of employment relations which has been subject to dramatic change. Reporting on workplaces with 25 or more employees, the 1980 survey indicated that 22 per cent of workplaces had experienced strike or non-strike action in the 12 months prior to interview; the equivalent figures for 1984 and 1990 were 25 per cent and 12 per cent respectively (Millward *et al.*, 1992), while in 1998 only 2 per cent of workplaces had been affected. These same measures of industrial action were used in the 2004 survey, with managers asked to report on the incidences of actual and threatened strike and non-strike action, the latter including overtime bans, work to rule and 'blacking' of work. Balloting of union members for industrial action was also explored.

### Industrial action

In 2004, the incidence of industrial action was broadly the same as in 1998, with 3 per cent of workplaces with 10 or more employees reporting that industrial action had taken place in the past year (Table 8.1). Among managers recording some form of industrial action, around three-fifths (57 per cent) reported a strike of some kind, varying from one day to a week or more. In workplaces where strike action had taken place (2 per cent of all workplaces), 46 per cent reported more than one strike, with the mean number of strikes standing at 2.5. This had remained largely stable since 1998 when the mean rate was 1.9.[2]

Three-fifths (61 per cent) of workplaces experiencing industrial action reported events other than strikes. In these workplaces (2 per cent of all establishments), about three-tenths (28 per cent) reported 'working to rule' and the same proportion said there had been action in the form of 'overtime bans' or 'restrictions initiated by employees'. 'Go slows' were recorded in 13 per cent of such workplaces and 'blacking of work' in 3 per cent. One per cent reported action in the form of a 'work in' or 'sit in', while 2 per cent reported other, unspecified forms of action.[3]

*Table 8.1* Collective conflict, by sector of ownership, 1998 and 2004

| | % of workplaces | | | | | |
| | 1998 | | | 2004 | | |
| | Public sector | Private sector | All | Public sector | Private sector | All |
|---|---|---|---|---|---|---|
| Any industrial action | 5 | 1 | 2 | 11 | 1 | 3 |
| *Of which:* | | | | | | |
| Strike action | 4 | 0 | 1 | 8 | 0 | 2 |
| Non-strike action | 1 | 1 | 1 | 5 | 1 | 2 |
| Threatened action | 8 | 2 | 3 | 11 | 3 | 4 |
| Any industrial action, threatened or taken | 9 | 3 | 4 | 16 | 3 | 5 |
| Picketing | 2 | 0 | 1 | 5 | 0 | 1 |
| Ballots | 20 | 3 | 6 | 22 | 2 | 5 |
| Collective disputes | 7 | 5 | 6 | 12 | 4 | 5 |

Base: All workplaces with 10 or more employees.
Figures are weighted and based on responses from at least 2,197 managers in 1998, and at least 1,913 managers in 2004.

The scope for detailed cross-tabular analysis of the incidence of industrial action, whether or not involving strikes, is limited by the relatively low proportion of workplaces reporting action of any kind. Nonetheless, it was apparent that collective unrest was most common among workplaces in the public sector. Almost one in ten public sector workplaces (8 per cent) had experienced a strike and one in twenty (5 per cent) reported non-strike action, whereas in the private sector only 1 per cent of workplaces had experienced any form of action. Those parts of the public sector most likely to have been affected were Public administration and Education. Within the public sector, an association was also apparent between the incidence of industrial action and the level of union membership at the workplace. Among public sector workplaces where less than half of the employees were union members, only one in twenty (4 per cent) had experienced industrial action, compared with one in ten (11 per cent) where membership density was between 50 and 89 per cent and one quarter (26 per cent) where at least 90 per cent of employees were union members. The incidence of action in the private sector varied little according to union membership levels.

Four per cent of managers reported that there had been one or more occasion in the previous 12 months on which employees had *threatened* industrial action (3 per cent in 1998).[4] In almost half of these cases (49 per cent), the threat was that employees would go on strike. Threats did not always result in a stoppage of work, and so the total proportion of workplaces having had actual or potential experience of industrial action in 2004 stood at one in twenty. As would be expected, in view of the patterns discussed above, the figure was considerably higher in the public sector (16 per cent) than in the private sector (3 per cent).

Picketing represents a further indicator of employee action in the workplace, established largely to reinforce strike action. Picketing is lawful where it takes place at or near the pickets' own place of work. In 2004, managers in 1 per cent of workplaces reported that their establishment had been picketed in the past year (the same proportion as in 1998); and of those reporting industrial action, 28 per cent reported that there had been a picket. In WERS 2004, picketing was exclusive to public sector establishments (5 per cent of which had been picketed), and was most common in Public administration (16 per cent).

For industrial action to be lawful, trade unions must, among other things, carry out a postal ballot of their members and, via the ballot, gain a majority in support of action. One in twenty workplaces (5 per cent) reported that unions had balloted their members at the establishment in the 12 months prior to the survey interview in order to establish the level of support for industrial action (6 per cent in 1998). It was not uncommon for workplaces to have had more than one ballot in the year: 25 per cent (1 per cent of all establishments) reported two or more. Nearly half (47 per cent) of all ballots resulted in a majority support, up from 34 per cent in 1998. The design of the survey meant that it was not possible to explore directly the linkages between the balloting process and any subsequent action. Nevertheless, only three-fifths (58 per cent) of those workplaces reporting some industrial action in the previous year reported that union members had been balloted in the period, and just two-fifths (42 per cent) reported a ballot in favour of action.[5] It was also noteworthy that around half (47 per cent) of those workplaces reporting a ballot in favour of action appeared to have averted this eventuality, reporting no such action in the year.

The preceding discussion covers the incidence of industrial action, but the questions on specific forms of action do not provide information on the various causes. Instead, WERS does provide information on the overall incidence of collective disputes concerning one general area: pay and conditions. In 2004, managers in 5 per cent of workplaces reported some collective dispute over pay or conditions during the 12 months prior to the survey (6 per cent in 1998). Such disputes had taken place in 11 per cent of workplaces with recognized unions and in 4 per cent of other workplaces in 2004. Not all such disputes result in industrial action, or even threatened action, but 45 per cent of workplaces reporting a collective dispute over pay and conditions in the year preceding the survey also reported some instance of actual or threatened industrial action in the same period. And in 3 per cent of all workplaces, managers reported that the size of the most recent pay settlement for core employees had been influenced by actual or threatened industrial action. In official statistics, pay issues account for the vast majority (84 per cent) of working days lost to work stoppages (Monger, 2005: 246).

## Employee representatives' account of collective conflict

Managers' reports of industrial unrest provide one important insight into the degree of conflict within workplaces, but WERS also provides a unique opportunity to examine the same issues from the perspective of employee representatives in the sub-section of workplaces where both parties were interviewed. Linking managers' responses to those of employee representatives in the same workplaces, the findings showed that both parties reported broadly the same incidence of industrial action. Ten per cent of managers reported some form of industrial action in the 12 months prior to the survey, compared with 11 per cent of employee representatives; in 91 per cent of workplaces their accounts coincided. There was, however, notably less agreement about the incidence of threatened action. Eleven per cent of managers and 16 per cent of employee representatives said that there had been threatened action in the 12 months prior to the survey, with their accounts coinciding in 83 per cent of workplaces. The discrepancy was still greater in relation to collective disputes over pay or conditions. Ten per cent of managers reported that there had been at least one dispute in the past year, compared with 29 per cent of employee representatives (32 per cent of union and 20 per cent of non-union representatives). Managers and employee representatives' accounts of whether there had been a collective dispute over pay and conditions coincided in only three-quarters of workplaces (73 per cent).

### *Disruption caused by industrial action in other organizations*

Industrial action within a workplace is usually intended to disrupt the activities of that establishment, as a means of persuading managers to enter into negotiations about the matter in dispute. However, disruption may also be caused in other workplaces, if those establishments rely on the affected workplace to provide supplies of raw materials, or to deliver or purchase their own products or services. WERS 2004 asked managers whether their workplace had suffered significant disruption in the past 12 months as a result of industrial action in another organization. The precise causes of disruption in supply or delivery chains may not always be apparent. However, managers in one in every twenty-five workplaces (4 per cent) reported that they had suffered disruption in the past year as a result of industrial action in another organization. The incidence was similar among workplaces in the private and public sectors (3 per cent and 5 per cent respectively). But there were greater variations across industry sectors, disruption most commonly affecting workplaces in Financial services (11 per cent) and Public administration (10 per cent). Across the remaining ten industry sectors, the proportion of workplaces reporting disruption did not exceed 5 per cent.

## Collective disputes procedures

The formalizing of procedures to manage disputes between employees and managers has been a feature of workplace change in the past 25 years, with a growth in arrangements to respond to individual and collective conflict. Procedures may not provide a mechanism for preventing disputes – on the contrary, they may provide a vehicle for voicing concerns – but they may help to promote fair treatment in the handling of disagreements, and help move parties towards a resolution in a timely fashion. In 2004, 43 per cent of managers reported that a formal procedure was in place for dealing with collective or group disputes raised by any group of non-managerial employees. The incidence of such procedures was therefore similar to that observed in 1998, when they were present in 47 per cent of all workplaces.

The first two columns of Table 8.2 illustrate the presence of collective disputes procedures by a number of workplace characteristics. As Table 8.2 shows, their presence was positively associated with the size of the workplace: just less than two-fifths (38 per cent) of workplaces with between 10 and 24 employees had a collective disputes procedure in place compared with three-quarters (74 per cent of workplaces) with at least 500 employees. As a consequence, the majority of employees (58 per cent) worked in an establishment with a collective disputes procedure. Collective disputes procedures were also more prevalent in public sector workplaces (77 per cent) than in the private sector (36 per cent), and they were more prevalent in workplaces having a recognized union (78 per cent) than in workplaces without recognition (29 per cent). Although workplace size, sector and recognition are associated with one another, multivariate analysis confirmed that each had an independent association with the likelihood of a workplace having a collective disputes procedure.

The vast majority of workplaces (92 per cent) had a single procedure. However, 4 per cent reported separate procedures for different workers and 6 per cent reported separate procedures for different issues. Workplaces that belonged to large organizations and those with recognized unions were more likely to have different procedures for different groups of workers. However, there was little variation across such characteristics in the extent to which procedures covered single or multiple issues.

In most cases (93 per cent), the procedures in place covered all non-managerial employees. Managers were also asked whether their collective disputes procedures covered four of the most commonly disputed issues, listed on a showcard. Over four-fifths of procedures covered pay and conditions (86 per cent), and similar proportions covered health and safety (84 per cent) and work organization (82 per cent). A slightly lower proportion (72 per cent) covered redundancy. The small proportion of procedures that did not cover disputes over pay and conditions tended to cover the organization of work or health and safety issues, and tended not to cover redundancy situations. Overall, 54 per cent of workplaces with procedures had arrangements that covered all non-managerial employees and which covered all four of the cited issues. These establishments comprised 23 per cent of all workplaces and employed 30 per cent of all employees.

Some collective disputes procedures include a provision for the issue to be referred to a body or person outside the establishment in situations when managers and employees fail to agree. WERS 2004 asked managers at workplaces with collective disputes procedures covering pay and conditions whether such a provision existed within their procedure; managers in around three-fifths (63 per cent) of such workplaces indicated that it did. One quarter of these were

*Table 8.2* Collective and individual disputes procedures, by workplace characteristics

|  | Collective disputes procedure | | Individual grievance procedure | | Disciplinary procedure | |
|---|---|---|---|---|---|---|
|  | % of workplaces | % of employees | % of workplaces | % of employees | % of workplaces | % of employees |
| All workplaces | 43 | 58 | 88 | 96 | 91 | 97 |
| *Workplace size* | | | | | | |
| 10–24 employees | 38 | 37 | 83 | 83 | 86 | 87 |
| 25–49 employees | 46 | 45 | 93 | 93 | 97 | 97 |
| 50–99 employees | 52 | 52 | 99 | 99 | 99 | 99 |
| 100–199 employees | 61 | 61 | 100 | 100 | 99 | 99 |
| 200–499 employees | 61 | 63 | 99 | 99 | 99 | 99 |
| 500 or more employees | 74 | 79 | 100 | 100 | 100 | 100 |
| All workplaces with 25 or more employees | 51 | 62 | 96 | 98 | 98 | 99 |
| *Organization status* | | | | | | |
| Stand-alone workplace | 28 | 39 | 76 | 87 | 81 | 91 |
| Part of a larger organization | 51 | 63 | 94 | 98 | 95 | 99 |
| *Organization size* | | | | | | |
| 10–99 employees | 28 | 30 | 75 | 81 | 81 | 87 |
| 100–999 employees | 44 | 45 | 96 | 98 | 97 | 99 |
| 1,000–9,999 employees | 53 | 66 | 99 | 100 | 99 | 100 |
| 10,000 employees or more | 63 | 76 | 98 | 100 | 98 | 99 |
| *Sector of ownership* | | | | | | |
| Private | 36 | 48 | 86 | 94 | 89 | 96 |
| Public | 77 | 84 | 99 | 100 | 99 | 99 |
| *Industry* | | | | | | |
| Manufacturing | 37 | 59 | 79 | 95 | 85 | 96 |
| Electricity, gas and water | (94) | (88) | (100) | (100) | (100) | (100) |
| Construction | 30 | 36 | 68 | 82 | 83 | 94 |
| Wholesale and retail | 40 | 54 | 89 | 95 | 92 | 97 |
| Hotels and restaurants | 16 | 26 | 73 | 84 | 81 | 89 |
| Transport and communication | 51 | 72 | 87 | 96 | 90 | 97 |
| Financial services | 61 | 48 | 99 | 99 | 98 | 99 |
| Other business services | 32 | 33 | 90 | 96 | 88 | 95 |
| Public administration | 91 | 86 | 100 | 100 | 100 | 100 |
| Education | 64 | 68 | 100 | 100 | 98 | 99 |
| Health and social work | 58 | 76 | 96 | 99 | 96 | 99 |
| Other community services | 44 | 61 | 96 | 98 | 95 | 98 |
| *Trade union recognition* | | | | | | |
| No union recognized | 29 | 34 | 83 | 91 | 87 | 94 |
| At least one union recognized | 78 | 83 | 100 | 100 | 99 | 100 |

Base: All workplaces with 10 or more employees.
Figures are weighted and based on responses from 2,036 managers (collective disputes procedures), 2,061 managers (grievance procedures) and 2,059 managers (disciplinary procedures).

establishments in which the procedure provided solely for the matter to be referred to a higher level in the same organization. In the remaining cases (all single independent establishments and 71 per cent of those belonging to a larger organization), there was provision for the matter to be referred to a body outside of the organization. The outside bodies commonly cited included Acas, whether for conciliation (41 per cent of workplaces referring outside the organization) or arbitration (35 per cent), higher levels within the union (45 per cent) and employers associations (15 per cent). Fifteen per cent included referral to an independent mediator or arbitrator. Where provision for referral was made, one half of procedures prohibited industrial action from taking place before the issue had been referred outside the establishment.

Table 8.1 indicated that one in twenty workplaces had experienced at least one collective dispute over pay and conditions in the 12 months prior to the survey. Just over half of these workplaces (55 per cent) had a collective disputes procedure that covered pay and conditions, and in most of these cases (78 per cent), managers reported that the procedure had been used to resolve the most recent dispute.[6] This left around one-fifth that had not invoked their procedure to resolve the most recent dispute. The number of cases was too small, however, to permit a reliable investigation of the types of workplaces that were more or less likely to invoke their procedures.

Workplaces with collective disputes procedures were more likely than those without procedures to report industrial action, whether threatened or taken, and were also more likely to report collective disputes over pay and conditions. However, this association was explained by the greater prevalence of both procedures and collective unrest in workplaces with recognized unions. After controlling for the presence of recognized unions, the differences between workplaces with and without procedures were no longer statistically significant. This tabular analysis therefore provides no clear-cut indication as to the nature of the connection between the presence of collective disputes procedures and levels of collective unrest.

## Individual disputes procedures

Disputes between managers and individual employees are considerably more prevalent than collective disputes. Differences between managers and individual workers may take the form of grievances, raised by employees because they feel aggrieved by their work environment, terms and conditions or workplace relations, or because they feel that a decision has had a direct, adverse effect upon them or even infringed their rights. Alternatively, differences may take the form of disciplinary actions initiated by the employer in response to problems of employee performance, capability or conduct. In the more extreme situations, such actions may lead to dismissal. For the purposes of reporting, findings on the incidence and nature of grievance and disciplinary procedures are presented alongside one another. This is not an entirely artificial construct since both types of procedures seek to promote a fair and timely approach to handling problems as well as a degree of consistency in the way managers respond to situations that are potentially conflictual.

The formalization of procedures for handling individualized conflict in the workplace represents one of the hallmarks of contemporary employment relations arrangements, a development which gathered pace during the 1980s (Millward *et al.*, 1992: 190). One explanation for the importance of rules in the handling of disciplinary and grievance issues is the growth and significance of the law. The framework for employment rights has expanded considerably since the 1970s, and in recent years in particular (Dickens and Hall, 2003). In this context, it is of interest to examine whether the trend in the formalization of procedures has continued since the previous survey was conducted in 1998. A further area of enquiry is whether the content of procedures has altered. Until October 2004, tribunal judgments on what constitutes the reasonable handling of dismissal situations were commonly based on the Acas Code of Practice. The Employment Act 2002 has brought about a change in this area, creating a new prescribed framework for internal procedures. While a large part of the WERS fieldwork period pre-dates the implementation of this legislation, it is of interest to explore the extent to which workplace arrangements comply with the new legal provisions.

This section draws on managers' accounts to describe the nature of arrangements found in workplaces and also where and how employees are accompanied in grievance and disciplinary situations. The section also reports on managers and employee representatives' views of the effectiveness of different arrangements. Data on the incidence of grievances and disciplinary sanctions are reported later in the chapter.

## *The presence of formal procedures*

Procedures for dealing with both grievances and disciplinary situations were widespread in 2004. Some 88 per cent of workplaces had a formal procedure for handling individual grievances, while 91 per cent had a formal procedure for dealing with disciplinary issues.[7] Table 8.2 shows that the incidence of both types of arrangements varied in similar ways across different workplace characteristics. Formal grievance procedures were less likely in small establishments (83 per cent in workplaces with less than 25 employees compared with almost 100 per cent among workplaces with 50 or more); were less likely in the private sector (86 per cent compared with 99 per cent in the public sector); and, varied considerably in prevalence across different industries. While around three-tenths of workplaces in the Construction and Hotels and restaurants sectors were without formal grievance procedures, they were universal in many other service sector industries, particularly those with a high degree of public ownership. Broadly the same picture was found in respect of disciplinary arrangements. Grievance and disciplinary procedures were also more common in workplaces with recognized unions: relationships that held in both the private and public sectors of the economy.

In 1998, the proportion of workplaces with a grievance procedure was similar (86 per cent), but the incidence of disciplinary procedures increased over the six-year period from 85 per cent in 1998. Much of this increase in the prevalence of disciplinary procedures was due to the increased adoption of formal disciplinary procedures by small, non-union firms in the private sector. The incidence of disciplinary procedures among private sector workplaces that were part of organizations with fewer than 100 employees, and which did not recognize trade unions, increased from 65 per cent in 1998 to 80 per cent in 2004. Among all other workplaces, the incidence increased from 95 per cent to 98 per cent. Colvin (2003a) suggests that the increasing adoption of dispute resolution procedures among non-union firms in the United States is being driven by a rise in employment rights litigation, union avoidance and the sophistication of human resource strategies. Each of these potential explanations seems plausible in the British case, where recent changes in the law (cited above) may equally have played a role. However, the precise causes merit further investigation.

## *The nature of procedural arrangements*

The reporting of a formal procedure might have symbolic importance, but the detailed requirements that are placed on managers and employees when raising issues are perhaps a more meaningful indicator of the practical significance of any arrangement. The Cross-Section Survey of Managers was designed to explore the roles and responsibilities of both employees and employers in both grievance and disciplinary situations. Three dimensions were considered: whether the employee (or the employer, in the case of a disciplinary situation) is required to put their concerns in writing; next, whether employees are asked to attend a formal meeting in either instance; and, finally, whether the employee has the right to appeal against the final decision. It may be that the level of formality is adjusted according to the gravity or complexity of the issues in question and, to reflect this, distinctions were made in respect of the first two of these three dimensions between requirements that were universal, and those that were contingent upon the issues in question. Figure 8.1 shows the incidence of individual elements in relation to handling employee grievances and disciplinary arrangements.

The opportunity for an employee to appeal against a decision, whether on the grounds of procedural unfairness or perceived inappropriateness of the outcome, is broadly considered essential to 'natural justice'. The right to appeal was the single most widespread feature, being present in more than nine in ten workplaces in their handling of grievances and disciplinary situations (Figure 8.1). The provision for appeals was universal in the public sector and, within the private sector, it was also generally pervasive. However, among private sector organizations with fewer than 50 employees, around one in eight workplaces did not provide a right of appeal in grievance or disciplinary situations. Good practice would suggest that an appeal is best heard by a senior manager not

*Figure 8.1* Procedures for handling grievances and disciplinary actions

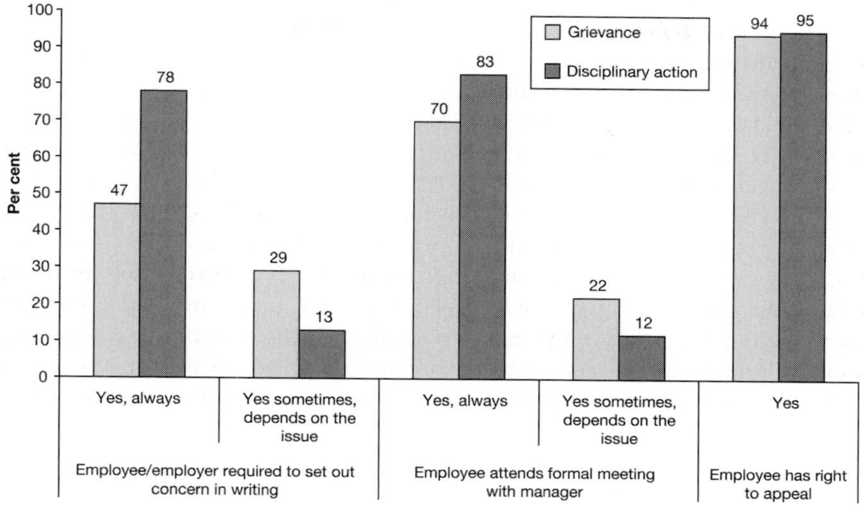

Base: All workplaces with 10 or more employees.
Figures are weighted and based on responses from at least 2,045 managers.

previously involved in the hearing of a case. Clearly, in smaller organizations this is logistically more problematic than in larger enterprises, and may go some way to explaining a lower incidence of appeals in smaller firms.

The use of formal meetings was widespread for both discipline and grievance procedures (95 per cent and 92 per cent of workplaces respectively), though in reasonable proportions of workplaces, the use of meetings was dependent upon the issue involved. This was particularly true in respect of grievances, where 22 per cent of workplaces said that formal meetings were held only for certain issues. The requirement to put matters in writing was marginally less wide-spread than the use of formal meetings, at least in disciplinary situations. On matters relating to discipline, employers in 78 per cent of workplaces were required always to set out their case in writing, and in a further 13 per cent this requirement applied in respect of certain issues. The requirement to put matters in writing was considerably less common in respect of grievances, however, with employees being required always to put grievances in writing in fewer than half of all workplaces (47 per cent). Analysis of the individual components revealed much the same distribution as found in relation to formal procedures with a slightly higher prevalence of each element in workplaces in the public sector, in larger workplaces and in workplaces with recognized unions.

Data on these three aspects of the handling of grievances and disciplinary matters illustrate the stark differences between formal procedures and informal arrangements for dispute resolution. Among workplaces with a formal proce-dure for handling grievances, around one half (52 per cent) always required the employee to set out the grievance in writing, close to three-quarters (75 per cent) always required a formal meeting to discuss the grievance and 97 per cent offered employees a right of appeal against any decision (Table 8.3). In contrast, among those few workplaces without a formal grievance procedure, one in ten (9 per cent) required the employee always to set out their grievance in writing, 32 per cent always required a formal meeting and 71 per cent offered a right of appeal. The pattern was similar in respect of disciplinary actions. Among workplaces with a formal procedure, 83 per cent of workplaces always set out the issue in writing, 87 per cent always required a meeting and 97 per cent offered a right of appeal. Among establishments without a procedure, the figures were 29 per cent, 42 per cent and 74 per cent respectively.

Less than 3 per cent of all workplaces reported operating *none* of the three arrangements shown in Figure 8.1 (2 per cent in respect of handling grievances and 1 per cent in relation to dealing with disciplinary situations). These were almost all small, single-site establishments in the private sector. This is not to say that some workplaces may not have arrangements containing features other than those explored in the survey. However, the three components explored in the Cross-Section Survey of Managers are of particular significance since they reflect the new legal framework – the so-called 'three-step' statutory procedure – which came into effect in October 2004. Many workplaces had arrangements that provided recourse to all three of these steps, but it was also apparent that, in a number of workplaces, the nature of the issue determined whether all three of the steps would be used.

*Table 8.3* Nature of formal procedures and informal arrangements for handling grievances and disciplinary actions

| | % of workplaces | | | | | |
|---|---|---|---|---|---|---|
| | Grievances | | | Disciplinary actions | | |
| | Formal procedure | No formal procedure | All workplaces | Formal procedure | No formal procedure | All workplaces |
| | | | | | | Cell % |
| Employer/employee always required to set out concern in writing | 52 | 9 | 47 | 83 | 29 | 78 |
| Employee always required to attend a formal meeting | 75 | 32 | 70 | 87 | 42 | 83 |
| Employee has right to appeal | 97 | 71 | 94 | 97 | 74 | 95 |
| | | | | | | Column % |
| All three elements cited above | 47 | 9 | 43 | 76 | 19 | 71 |
| All three, but depends upon the issue | 31 | 12 | 29 | 17 | 9 | 16 |
| One or two elements only | 22 | 63 | 27 | 7 | 60 | 12 |
| None of the three elements | 0 | 16 | 2 | 0 | 12 | 1 |

Base: All workplaces with 10 or more employees.
Figures are weighted and based on responses from at least 2,042 managers (grievance procedures) and at least 2,051 managers (disciplinary procedures).

In handling grievances raised by employees, 43 per cent of workplaces reported that all three elements always applied (Table 8.3). A further 29 per cent of workplaces practised all three elements, but required concerns to be set out in writing or formal meetings to take place only for particular issues. Another 27 per cent practised at least one of the three elements, with two-fifths of these (39 per cent) offering a meeting in every case alongside the right to appeal. The incidence of the full 'three-step' arrangements in relation to disciplinary action was somewhat higher: 71 per cent of workplaces had each step in place, irrespective of the issues in question, and a further 16 per cent replicated the three steps, but only on certain issues. Workplaces with formal procedures for handling grievances or discipline were much more likely to operate all three steps than workplaces having only informal arrangements, possibly because those implementing formal procedures may have taken advice on the recommended components. However, it is equally clear from Table 8.3 that the presence of a formal procedure provided no guarantee that all three steps would be followed in any particular grievance or disciplinary situation.

Again, arrangements matching the 'three-step procedure' were more prevalent in larger workplaces. Accordingly, just over half (53 per cent) of all employees worked in establishments applying all three steps in relation to grievances, and four-fifths (82 per cent) worked in establishments applying all three steps in respect of disciplinary action. Arrangements matching the three-step procedure were also more likely in the public sector and in workplaces with a recognized union, although the difference between the private and public sectors could be explained by the differing rate of union recognition in the two sectors. After controlling for workplace size, sector of ownership and union recognition, 'three-step' procedures in respect of both grievances and discipline were also found to be more likely in workplaces with a personnel specialist either at the workplace or at a higher level in the organization.

As the fieldwork for WERS 2004 began before the introduction of the statutory three-step dispute resolution procedure on 1 October 2004 and continued after the legislation was enacted, it is possible to make some assessment of the impact of the legislation on workplace procedures. The assessment is necessarily crude because the sample was not issued in a random manner throughout the fieldwork period. Specifically, sampled workplaces were categorized into one of two 'waves', with those belonging to large organizations that had more than one establishment in the sample generally being classified as 'wave two' and issued to interviewers later in fieldwork after some initial contact had been made with senior managers at head office.[8] After controlling for the 'sample wave', the incidence of arrangements matching the three-step procedure in relation to disciplinary actions and grievances appeared to be around four to six percentage points higher among workplaces interviewed after 1 October 2004 than among those interviewed prior to this date; however, the differences were not statistically significant, and so the analysis is somewhat inconclusive.[9] It is, of course, likely that some establishments will have brought their dispute resolution procedures into line with the regulations prior to 1 October 2004, thus reducing the apparent impact of the legislation in this analysis. Nonetheless, it is also apparent that, after the regulations came into force, there remained substantial proportions of workplaces that did not profess to operate the three steps proposed by statute. Among workplaces interviewed after 1 October 2004, 80 per cent operated all three steps in respect of disciplinary actions and just 52 per cent operated all three steps in respect of grievances.

To summarize, the data are indicative of a level of formality in the handling of concerns raised by employees and employers in a sizeable proportion of workplaces. Most establishments operated a formal procedure for resolving grievances and handling disciplinary situations, and many of these procedures incorporated each of the three steps promoted in the new legal framework for dispute resolution. However, it was also apparent that requirements to set out concerns in writing and to attend formal meetings often depended upon the issue under consideration. Moreover, around one in ten workplaces had no formal procedures for resolving individual disputes, and sizeable proportions omitted at least one of these three components within those formal or informal arrangements that were in place.

## The right to accompaniment

Since 1999 employees have had a statutory right to be accompanied by a fellow worker or trade union official at grievance or disciplinary meetings.[10] Of those workplaces reporting that a formal meeting was part of their procedural arrangements, almost all allowed employees to be accompanied. In around three-tenths, the employee had the freedom to choose who should accompany them at a meeting (27 per cent in relation to grievance meetings and 30 per cent in respect of disciplinary meetings). In a further two-thirds, trade union representatives or work colleagues were cited among the permitted companions (67 per cent in grievance meetings and 62 per cent in disciplinary meetings). Just 1 per cent of workplaces with formal grievance meetings did not allow employees to be accompanied; the equivalent figure among workplaces with formal disciplinary meetings was 2 per cent. These workplaces were generally small, private sector establishments without recognized unions.[11]

Employee representatives were also asked about employees' rights to be accompanied and, matching their responses to those of managers in the same workplaces, there was widespread consensus between the two parties in respect of employees' rights to be accompanied. In workplaces where both a manager and an employee representative were interviewed, all managers and employee representatives were of the view that at least some accompaniment would be allowed at grievance or disciplinary meetings. In around one-sixth of these workplaces, managers and employee representatives concurred that the employee was free to choose any companion (16 per cent in respect of grievances; 17 per cent in respect of disciplinary matters) and in a further half they concurred that the list of permitted companions included either union representatives or work colleagues (51 per cent and 54 per cent). The remaining workplaces, where managers and representatives did not share the same view, were split evenly between those in which the manager considered that anyone could accompany the employee, but the employee representative considered that there were restrictions (14 per cent in the case of both grievances and disciplinary matters) and those in which the representative thought the employee was free to choose but the manager reported restrictions (17 per cent and 15 per cent). The views of union representatives were more likely to tally with those of managers than were the views of non-union representatives, possibly reflecting union representatives' greater level of involvement in individual disputes (see Chapter 6).

What role might the companion play in supporting an employee? The legislation defines the companion's role as presenting the worker's case and supporting their position, though the companion is not entitled, by statute, to answer questions put directly to the worker. This distinction was to some extent reflected in the practices reported by managers, as a greater proportion described the role of the companion as representing the views of the employee, rather than responding on his or her behalf. In instances where companions were allowed at grievance meetings, 78 per cent of managers described the role as asking questions on behalf of the employee; this was the case in 81 per cent in relation to disciplinary meetings (Table 8.4). However, a substantial proportion

*Table 8.4* Role of companions in grievance and disciplinary meetings

|  | % of workplaces | | |
|---|---|---|---|
|  | Ask questions | Answer questions | Confer |
| *Grievance meetings* | | | |
| All workplaces | 78 | 47 | 95 |
| Private | 75 | 43 | 94 |
| Public | 91 | 66 | 99 |
| No union recognized | 76 | 43 | 93 |
| At least one union recognized | 85 | 55 | 99 |
| Employment relations specialist at workplace or higher level | 75 | 40 | 95 |
| No specialist | 85 | 56 | 94 |
| *Disciplinary meetings* | | | |
| All workplaces | 81 | 49 | 95 |
| Private | 78 | 45 | 93 |
| Public | 92 | 66 | 100 |
| No union recognized | 79 | 47 | 93 |
| At least one union recognized | 85 | 54 | 99 |
| Employment relations specialist at workplace or higher level | 76 | 41 | 95 |
| No specialist | 88 | 61 | 94 |

Base: All workplaces with 10 or more employees.
Figures are weighted and based on at least 1,908 workplaces with grievance procedures that allow accompaniment, and 1,964 workplaces with disciplinary procedures allowing accompaniment.

of workplaces allowed the companion to play a fuller role than that defined by the legislation: in relation to grievance hearings, 47 per cent said that companions were permitted to answer questions on behalf of the employee and the same was true of a similar proportion (49 per cent) of those accompanying employees at disciplinary meetings. The survey also asked whether companions were allowed to confer with the employee, either in the meeting room or outside. There was widespread acknowledgement of this as a legitimate role, with 95 per cent supporting this in grievance meetings and the same proportion supporting it in disciplinary meetings.

Using multivariate analysis to control for size, sector of ownership, union recognition and the presence of a personnel specialist, either at the workplace or at a higher level, the findings showed that public sector workplaces were more likely than private sector workplaces to permit the companion to ask and to answer questions on behalf of the employee. They were also more likely to allow the companion to confer privately with the employee, although this association was only statistically significant in respect of grievance meetings. These same analyses also showed that the recognition of trade unions was not significantly associated with the opportunity to ask or answer questions, but it was positively associated with the opportunity to confer privately with the employee. Conversely, workplaces with a personnel specialist were less likely to allow the companion to ask or answer questions; there was no association with the provision of opportunities to confer.

Employee representatives were also asked about the role of companions. Comparing their responses with those of managers in the same workplaces, the patterns of agreement and disagreement were very similar in respect of grievances and disciplinary meetings. In workplaces where both a manager and an employee representative were interviewed, there was widespread consensus as to whether companions could ask questions (around four-fifths of managers and employee representatives agreed on this item) and whether companions could confer with the employee in private (around 95 per cent agreed). But there was less consensus as to whether companions could answer questions on behalf of the employee: around three-fifths of managers and employee representatives agreed on this item. In a further third of cases, employee representatives considered that a companion would be permitted to ask questions but managers said they would be denied this role, and in the remaining tenth managers reported that companions could ask questions but employee representatives did not agree. As in the case of who might be allowed to accompany employees at grievance and disciplinary meetings, the views of union representatives were more likely to tally with those of managers than were the views of non-union representatives.

*Effectiveness of arrangements*

It is in the interests of all parties to ensure that procedures are effective and acceptable to those who are required to operate them, and equally to those whose concerns they address. In this respect, it may be helpful to involve employees – either directly or through their representatives – in the formulation and implementation of arrangements, and to ensure that they are made fully aware of them through information provision. This section explores both of these issues, alongside information on employee representatives' satisfaction with those procedures that were in place.

In the vast majority of workplaces where managers reported a formal grievance or disciplinary procedure, information about the procedures was made personally available to employees in written form (93 and 94 per cent respectively). Almost two-thirds cited the contract of employment as the means of conveying details of both disciplinary and grievance procedures (64 per cent each); around three-fifths cited the staff handbook (63 per cent in respect of grievance procedures and 61 per cent in respect of disciplinary procedures); and just under one-fifth had set out information in the letter of appointment (16 per cent in respect of grievance procedures and 18 per cent in respect of disciplinary procedures). The other main method for conveying information on grievance arrangements was via an induction programme, used in around two-fifths of workplaces (40 per cent in respect of grievance procedures and 37 per cent in respect of disciplinary procedures). In around one quarter of workplaces information was conveyed by supervisors or line managers, and in around one-tenth it was displayed on a notice board.

Management collaboration with employee representatives on the design of procedures was discussed in Chapter 7 and it was found that, for around four-fifths of all workplaces, grievance or disciplinary procedures had not been subject to consultation or negotiation with employee representatives, either at the workplace or at a higher level in the organization (Table 7.7). Beyond formulating arrangements, a further measure is how embedded representatives are in the operation of arrangements. The Survey of Employee Representatives asked representatives whether they were routinely notified by management when an employee they represented raised an issue through the grievance procedure. This was the case in almost half (48 per cent) of the workplaces where the employee representative reported a procedure. The results showed no significant difference between the involvement of union and non-union representatives (46 per cent and 52 per cent respectively). Where representatives were not routinely notified, they were asked at what stage they became involved with individual grievances. Most (91 per cent) said that they became involved when the employees asked them to (83 per cent in respect of non-union representatives and 94 per cent in respect of union representatives). Almost one-fifth (16 per cent) said that they were notified when the grievance could not be resolved (a similar proportion in respect of union and non-union representatives). Two per cent of those not routinely notified of grievances said that they never got involved in such matters; these were exclusively non-union representatives.

Finally, the survey also posed questions to employee representatives regarding their overall satisfaction with grievance and disciplinary procedures. Of those with formal grievance procedures at their workplace, 73 per cent were 'satisfied' with the working of the procedure (including 10 per cent who were 'very satisfied'), 17 per cent were 'neither satisfied nor dissatisfied', and 10 per cent were 'dissatisfied'. A similar pattern was found in relation to disciplinary arrangements, where 76 per cent of representatives were 'satisfied' (including 21 per cent 'very satisfied') and 8 per cent were 'dissatisfied'. For both types of procedure, union representatives were more likely to express dissatisfaction than non-union representatives: 13 per cent of union representatives were dissatisfied with grievance procedures and 10 per cent were dissatisfied with disciplinary procedures. The equivalent figures for non-union representatives were 1 per cent and 2 per cent respectively. Representatives who had reported that grievances had been formally raised by employees through the grievance procedure in the previous 12 months were also more likely to be dissatisfied with the procedure (20 per cent) than those who had reported that the procedure had not been used in the past 12 months (4 per cent); this broad association held among both union and non-union representatives. Employee representatives were not asked about the use of the disciplinary procedure and so an equivalent analysis is not possible.

## The incidence of individual disputes

Having considered the detail of arrangements that employers have in place to manage grievances and discipline, the chapter now moves on to consider the incidence of such individualized expressions of conflict. A host of factors within a workplace will influence the incidence of grievances and disciplinary actions. The presence and nature of formal dispute resolution procedures are, of course, two such factors. However, contrary to some expectations, it is possible that workplaces with grievance procedures may report relatively high rates of grievances, because the presence of formal procedures may promote confidence among employees that their complaints will be given proper consideration (Colvin, 2003b). The culture of a workplace may also be important, as some employees may have a realistic fear of retribution (Lewin and Peterson, 1999). Similarly, the presence of disciplinary procedures may give rise to greater use of formal sanctions (Earnshaw *et al.*, 1998), while the presence of other factors that may promote greater levels of self-discipline, such as team-work, may also have a bearing on the incidence of disciplinary sanctions within an establishment (Edwards, 2000; Colvin, 2003b). A number of these issues are considered here.

The section begins by looking at the incidence of employee grievances and the types of issues raised in this way. Looking beyond the workplace, it also reports on the incidence of claims made by employees to an Employment Tribunal as an external recourse for dispute resolution. Turning the table, the final section considers the extent to which employers use workplace procedures to raise disciplinary issues via a range of sanctions.

### Individual grievances

While no question was asked about the actual number of grievances raised at the workplace, the survey did ask whether *any* grievances had been raised in the past year, whether formally or otherwise. Grievances had been raised in just under half of all workplaces (47 per cent) (Table 8.5). This represented a marked decrease since 1998, when grievances had been raised in just under three-fifths (56 per cent) of workplaces.

The probability that at least one employee will raise a grievance can be expected to rise with the number of employees at the workplace. The results confirmed this: 36 per cent of workplaces with 10–24 employees reported that a grievance had been raised in the previous year, compared with 93 per cent of workplaces with 500 or more employees. Grievances were also more commonly raised where unions were recognized, but this association no longer held after controlling for workplace size. There was also some variation by industry (Table 8.5). Grievances were most likely to be raised in the Electricity, gas and water sector and in the Construction sector (61 per cent and 58 per cent respectively) and least likely in the Financial services sector (34 per cent).

Turning to consider the role of formal procedures in resolving grievances, it was apparent that almost all (92 per cent) of those workplaces in which a grievance had been raised had a formal grievance procedure. However, less than half of these workplaces (45 per cent) noted that their procedure had been used

*Table 8.5* Indicators of individual conflict and potential indicators of discontent, by industry

| | *Any grievances* | *Employment Tribunal claims* | *Disciplinary sanctions*[a] | *Absenteeism* | *Voluntary resignations* |
|---|---|---|---|---|---|
| | *% of workplaces* | *Claims per 1,000 employees* | *Sanctions per 100 employees* | *% of working days lost (workplace average)* | *Resignations per 100 employees* |
| All workplaces | 47 | 2.2 | 5.7 | 5.0 | 13.7 |
| *Industry* | | | | | |
| Manufacturing | 57 | 3.0 | 5.7 | 3.7 | 9.7 |
| Electricity, gas and water | (61) | (1.6) | (3.1) | (2.9) | (5.8) |
| Construction | 58 | 2.8 | 5.2 | 5.1 | 14.5 |
| Wholesale and retail | 42 | 1.8 | 8.6 | 3.8 | 20.3 |
| Hotels and restaurants | 40 | 0.8 | 8.7 | 4.3 | 34.0 |
| Transport and communication | 57 | 2.1 | 7.4 | 5.9 | 10.3 |
| Financial services | 34 | 1.7 | 2.9 | 5.2 | 12.2 |
| Other business services | 47 | 4.1 | 9.1 | 4.4 | 13.6 |
| Public administration | 57 | 2.7 | 2.1 | 5.8 | 5.7 |
| Education | 38 | 0.9 | 0.9 | 7.3 | 7.2 |
| Health and social work | 52 | 1.3 | 2.5 | 6.4 | 12.4 |
| Other community services | 42 | 2.1 | 5.4 | 6.2 | 14.8 |

Base: All workplaces with at least 10 employees.
Figures are weighted and based on responses from 1,959 managers (grievances); 1,951 (tribunal claims); 1,980 (disciplinary sanctions); 1,697 (absenteeism); and 1,890 (voluntary resignations).
Notes:
[a] Disciplinary sanctions comprise formal verbal warnings, formal written warnings, suspensions with or without pay, deductions from pay, internal transfers and dismissals.

in the past year. It follows that a formal grievance procedure had been invoked on at least one occasion in only 41 per cent of workplaces where a grievance had been raised. In keeping with the proposition noted above, workplaces that had formal grievance procedures were more likely to have seen a grievance raised in the year preceding the survey than workplaces without a formal procedure: grievances had been raised in 49 per cent of workplaces with a formal procedure, and in 34 per cent of those without. However, no statistically significant difference remained after controlling for workplace size.

In workplaces where grievances had been raised, but in which the grievance procedure had not been called upon during the year, managers were asked for their opinions as to why the procedure had not been invoked. The vast majority cited good management-employee relations (73 per cent), while many also noted that disputes had been resolved informally without recourse to the procedure (46 per cent). Small proportions of managers considered that employees may not have used the procedure because of fears about the consequences (2 per cent) or because the procedure was ineffective (also 2 per cent).

Managers were asked what types of grievance had been raised in the 12 months prior to the survey. The responses are presented in Table 8.6. It was most common for grievances to have been raised in respect of pay and conditions (18 per cent

*Table 8.6* Types of grievance raised, 1998 and 2004

|  | *% of workplaces* | |
| --- | --- | --- |
|  | *1998* | *2004* |
| Pay and conditions | 25 | 18 |
| Relations with supervisors/ line managers (i.e. unfair treatment, victimization) | 16 | 16 |
| Work practices, work allocation or the pace of work | 14 | 12 |
| Working time, annual leave or time off work | 13 | 10 |
| Physical working conditions or health and safety | 12 | 10 |
| Promotion, career development or internal transfers | 14 | 8 |
| Bullying at work | 3 | 7 |
| Job grading or classification | 13 | 6 |
| Use of disciplinary sanctions, including dismissal | – | 5 |
| Performance appraisal | 7 | 4 |
| Sexual harassment | 3 | 2 |
| Selection for redundancies | – | 2 |
| Relations with other employees | – | 2 |
| Sex or race discrimination | 3 | 1 |
| Racial harassment | 1 | 1 |
| Other grievances | – | 0 |
| No grievances raised formally in past 12 months | 44 | 53 |

Base: All workplaces with 10 or more employees.
Figures are weighted and based on responses from at least 2,169 managers in 1998 and 2,029 managers in 2004.

of all workplaces). This was followed by relations with supervisors and line managers (16 per cent) and working practices (12 per cent). In one-tenth of all workplaces, employees had raised issues relating to working time, annual leave or time off. In the same proportion, employees had raised grievances relating to physical working conditions. The proportions of workplaces citing grievances in respect of pay and conditions, promotion, job grading and appraisals were each lower in 2004 than in 1998. In contrast, there had been an increase in grievances relating to bullying. Changes across other items were not statistically significant.

There was some variation between the private and public sectors in the types of grievance raised in 2004. Workplaces in the private sector were more likely to have reported issues relating to pay and conditions (20 per cent, compared with 8 per cent in the public sector). In comparison, public sector workplaces were more likely to have reported issues relating to working practices (17 per cent, compared with 11 per cent in the private sector), bullying (11 per cent, compared with 6 per cent) and job grading (10 per cent, compared with 5 per cent).

## Employment Tribunal claims

Aside from raising grievances within their workplace, employees can also bring claims to an Employment Tribunal in circumstances where there is an alleged infringement of employment rights. There are now in excess of 50 jurisdictions under which an employee may bring a claim, with those relating to dismissal, wage payment, breach of contract, redundancy and discrimination being most widely invoked (Employment Tribunals Service, 2005). As in earlier WERS surveys, the Cross-Section Survey of Managers asked whether an employee or ex-employee had made an application to an Employment Tribunal in the past 12 months.

Eight per cent of managers said that their workplace had faced such a claim in the past year – broadly the same result as found in 1998 (6 per cent).[12] Thus, the vast majority of workplaces had not been subject to a claim in the past year. However, certain types of workplace were more likely to have faced a claim than others. Not surprisingly, given the greater number of employees, larger workplaces were more likely to experience claims: 3 per cent of establishments with 10 to 24 employees had one or more claim in the last year, compared with 60 per cent of workplaces with at least 500 employees. A more meaningful measure of the incidence of Employment Tribunal claims, sensitive to the size of workplaces, can be elicited by calculating the number of claims per 1,000 employees. By computing this rate among different groups of workplaces, it is possible to identify those types of establishment where employees have a greater or lesser propensity to lodge a tribunal claim.

On average, 2.2 claims were brought per 1,000 employees across all workplaces (Table 8.5). This was similar to 1998, when on average 2.0 claims were brought per 1,000 employees.[13] While it was noted above that larger workplaces were more likely than smaller workplaces to have had at least one claim brought against them, the rate of claims per 1,000 employees appeared to be lower in larger workplaces: the rate was 2.9 claims per 1,000 employees among workplaces having 25–49 employees and only 1.7 per 1,000 employees among establishments with 500 or more employees. However, the differences in rates between large and small workplaces were not significant. In addition, the smallest workplaces (those having between 10 and 24 employees) had the same rate of claims as those establishments with 500 or more employees.

The average Employment Tribunal rate per 1,000 employees was higher in workplaces without trade union recognition (2.5, compared with 1.9 in workplaces with a recognized union), but this difference was only significant at the 10 per cent level and was explained by the lower rate of claims in the public sector. Private sector workplaces saw 2.5 claims per thousand employees in the year prior to the survey, compared with a rate of 1.4 claims per thousand employees among public sector workplaces. This difference remained after controlling for workplace size and the incidence of union recognition. There was also some variation by industry (Table 8.5). Workplaces in Other business services experienced an average of 4.1 claims per thousand employees. By contrast, rates were lowest in the Hotels and restaurants sector (0.8 claims per thousand) and Education (0.9 claims per thousand). The high rate of claims in Other business services was explained by the various factors cited above, but the rate of claims remained distinctively low in Hotels and restaurants and in Education after controlling for workplace size, sector of ownership and union recognition.

Notably, the rate of tribunal claims was higher in workplaces with formal procedures for handling grievances and discipline. Workplaces with a formal disciplinary procedure experienced 2.3 tribunal claims per 1,000 employees, compared with a rate of 1.0 per 1,000 among workplaces without a procedure. The same rates were observed among workplaces with and without formal grievance procedures but, in this case, the difference was not statistically significant. Managers in workplaces that had experienced a tribunal claim in the past 12 months were asked whether their experience had resulted in any changes being made to policies or procedures at the establishment. Existing evidence indicates that the experience of defending a claim can lead employers without procedures to introduce them (Earnshaw *et al.*, 1998; Hayward *et al.*, 2004). There was limited evidence of this in WERS, but considerable proportions of employers were prompted to revise their existing procedures. Around one half (56 per cent) of workplaces experiencing claims had not made any changes to their policies or procedures. Among the remainder, 6 per cent had set up formal grievance or disciplinary procedures, 26 per cent had reviewed or redesigned their existing procedures and 52 per cent had acted to ensure that existing procedures were followed. Some 27 per cent had introduced or reviewed policies in other areas and the same proportion had revised employees' terms and conditions.

### Disciplinary sanctions

In addition to looking at the incidence of grievances, managers were also asked about their use of disciplinary measures within their workplaces. They were asked about a range of sanctions, the most severe being dismissal. Also considered were the use of formal verbal warnings, formal written warning, suspension with or without pay, deduction from pay and internal transfer (collectively referred to hereafter as 'sanctions short of dismissal'). Each represents formal actions on the part of managers as opposed to the informal, 'quiet word' approach favoured within some workplaces (Earnshaw *et al.*, 1998).

Around one half of managers (55 per cent) reported using at least one of the aforementioned sanctions in the year prior to the survey. Almost half (45 per cent) of all workplaces had issued at least one verbal warning, close to two-fifths (37 per cent) had issued a written warning and one-fifth had suspended at least one employee without pay. Smaller proportions of establishments had made deductions from pay (5 per cent) or effected internal transfers (6 per cent). Over one quarter (28 per cent) had made at least one dismissal. Each type of sanction had been applied by greater proportions of workplaces in the private sector than in the public sector, with the exceptions of internal transfers and deductions from pay which were used by similar proportions of workplaces in either sector. Where sanctions had been applied, the reasons cited by managers for taking disciplinary action were varied, but echoed the findings of earlier studies (see Edwards, 2000). Commonly cited reasons were poor performance (46 per cent of workplaces taking disciplinary action), unauthorized absence (43 per cent), poor timekeeping (39 per cent) and theft or dishonesty (25 per cent). Other reasons given included: negligence (19 per cent), abusive or violent behaviour (18 per cent), disobedience (16 per cent), health and safety breaches (14 per cent) and alcohol or drug use (11 per cent).

It is not possible to undertake a comprehensive comparison with the findings from 1998 on the use of each of these disciplinary sanctions since the previous survey asked about just three sanctions: formal written warning, suspension with or without pay and deductions from pay. Taking this same subset, the proportion of workplaces reporting use of sanctions was the same in 1998 (43 per cent) as in 2004 (42 per cent). The proportions of workplaces using each of the three types was also very similar to 2004: 41 per cent had issued written warnings, 15 per cent had suspended employees without pay and 5 per cent had made deductions from pay.

Managers in 2004 were asked to report the total number of sanctions that had been applied in the past year, thus making it possible to calculate a rate variable similar to that discussed above in relation to tribunal claims. Here, the rate is expressed as the average number of disciplinary sanctions applied per 100 employees. As Table 8.5 indicates, the overall mean rate was 5.7 sanctions per 100 employees. The sanctions rate was higher among small workplaces than among larger establishments (8.0 in workplaces with between 10 and 24 employees compared with 5.1 in workplaces with 25 or more employees), although the rate did not decrease monotonically across the standard size categories. The mean rate per 100 employees was also higher in the private sector (6.9) than in the public sector (1.9), and was somewhat higher in workplaces without recognized unions (7.2, compared with 3.9 among workplaces that did recognize unions), although the latter association was not significant after controlling for sector of ownership. There was considerable variation across industrial sectors (Table 8.5). In keeping with the pattern of tribunal claims, disciplinary sanctions were most frequent in Other business services (9.1) and comparatively infrequent in Education (0.9). However, while Hotels and restaurants had one of the lowest rates of tribunal claims, the rate of disciplinary sanctions in that sector was among the highest.

The rate of disciplinary sanctions was marginally higher in workplaces that had a formal disciplinary procedure than in workplaces without (5.7, compared with 4.9). But there was only limited support for the earlier conjecture that autonomous team-working might exert an influence over employee behaviour. The rate of disciplinary sanctions was lower (3.7 per 100 employees) in workplaces where at least three-fifths of the core group of employees worked in autonomous or semi-autonomous teams, compared with a rate of 6.4 per 100 employees in workplaces with other forms of team-working and 6.6 per 100 in workplaces with no team-working among their core employees. However, after controlling for workplace size, sector of ownership and union recognition, the only difference that remained statistically significant was the lower rate of disciplinary sanctions in the presence of autonomous or semi-autonomous teams compared with instances where other team arrangements were in place.

## Other potential indicators of discontent

In reporting the incidence of conflict, thus far the chapter has looked at manifest disputes, either of a collective or individual nature. Yet such overt actions are not the only means by which discontent may become apparent; employees' dissatisfaction with their working conditions or work relations may also be expressed through absenteeism or voluntary resignations.[14] There are inherent difficulties in using such measures as direct indicators of conflict. Naturally, absenteeism may be due to employee ill-health or may be related to caring responsibilities that cannot be accommodated through other means, such as flexible working. Similarly, the level of voluntary resignations may be affected by the availability of alternative job opportunities. Nonetheless, studies have clearly indicated how absenteeism and resignations may be used by employees as alternative means of expressing discontent when more familiar, or more organized, forms of expression are either unavailable or are less attractive (see, for example, Handy, 1968; Sapsford and Turnbull, 1994).

### Absenteeism

The Employee Profile Questionnaire collected data from managers about the proportion of work days lost through employee sickness or absence at the workplace over the past 12 months (excluding authorized leave of absence, time spent on secondment or courses and days lost to industrial action). Among workplaces where managers were able to provide an answer, the average rate of absenteeism equated to the loss of 5.0 per cent of working days per establishment; this was very similar to the rate of 4.8 per cent of working days lost that was observed in 1998.[15]

Most workplaces (94 per cent) experienced at least some absenteeism in the year preceding the survey, although there was significant variation across workplaces with those in the bottom decile experiencing absenteeism rates below 1 per cent and those in the top decile having rates of at least 11 per cent. The rate of absenteeism was higher in establishments in the public sector (7.4 per cent) than it was among establishments in the private sector (4.5 per cent). There was also significant variation in absenteeism rates by industry (Table 8.5). Average rates of absenteeism were highest in the Education and Health and social work sectors (7.3 per cent and 6.4 per cent respectively) and lowest in Electricity, gas and water supply (2.9 per cent), Manufacturing (3.7 per cent) and Wholesale and retail (3.8 per cent).

Some have argued that levels of absenteeism may be higher in larger workplaces or firms, since there are likely to be greater complementarities between employees in larger firms, thus providing 'buffer stocks' of workers (Barmby and Stephan, 2000). There was no clear association between rates of absenteeism and workplace size. However, there was a positive association between levels of absence and organization size: among workplaces belonging to organizations with less than 100 employees, the average absenteeism rate stood at 4.0 per cent of working days per year, compared with 6.6 per cent among workplaces belonging to organizations with 10,000 or more employees.

In a similar vein, it has been suggested that absence rates will be lower where employees are interdependent, as in some instances of team-working (Heywood and Jirjahn, 2004), because the high costs of absence will encourage firms to spend greater resources on monitoring or minimizing absenteeism. Others have proposed that rates will be higher where workers have access to favourable sick pay arrangements (Buzzard and Shaw, 1952). However, in cross-tabular analyses, there were no clear associations between absence rates and a variety of indicators of team-working. Also, absence rates appeared slightly lower in workplaces that provided extra-statutory sick pay to core employees. These issues merit detailed multivariate analysis which is outside the scope of this book.

## Voluntary resignations

Turning to consider the incidence of voluntary resignations, managers were asked to indicate how many of those employed at the establishment 12 months prior to the survey had left or resigned voluntarily from the establishment in the intervening year. Overall, 14 per cent of those employed 12 months prior to the survey had left voluntarily during the year (Table 8.5).[16] The average rate was more than twice as high in the private sector (15.7) as in the public sector (7.3). The rate of voluntary resignations was also negatively associated with workplace size, being highest in establishments with between 10 and 24 employees (16.3) and lowest in workplaces with at least 500 employees (11.0). Table 8.5 illustrates the variation in the average rate of resignations across industries. Some industries experienced a very high rate of voluntary resignations over the 12 months prior to the survey, in particular the Hotels and restaurants sector (34.0) and the Wholesale and retail sector (20.3).

In the light of theory and evidence about the role that unions may play in providing an alternative to employee exit, through the provision of employee voice (Freeman, 1980), it is interesting to note that the incidence of voluntary resignations was considerably lower among employees working in establishments with recognized trade unions (8.9 per cent) than it was among employees in workplaces without union recognition (17.8 per cent). This relationship persisted after controlling for workplace and organization size, sector of ownership and industry.

## Associations between indicators of conflict

It was stated earlier in the chapter that discontent may be demonstrated in different ways, depending upon the characteristics of the workplace and its environment. And so, having considered a wide range of indicators of collective and individual manifestations of conflict and discontent, it is appropriate to consider what associations might exist between these different expressions.

Considering first the associations between the various indicators of individualized conflict presented in Table 8.5, it was apparent that each of the rate variables were positively correlated with one another, with just two exceptions: the rate of Employment Tribunal claims was negatively associated with rates of absenteeism and voluntary resignations. However, none of the associations, whether positive or negative, were statistically significant. Extending the analysis to include the incidence of employee grievances, it was apparent that establishments where at least one employee had raised a grievance in the past 12 months also experienced higher rates of tribunal claims, disciplinary sanctions, absenteeism and resignations than workplaces where no grievances had been raised, but the differences were only statistically significant in respect of tribunal claims and absenteeism.

The associations between these indicators and the incidence of collective conflict were also varied. Overall, 13 per cent of establishments had witnessed at least one of the expressions of collective conflict presented in Table 8.1. The most striking differences between these workplaces and those without any collective conflict were in the incidence of grievances and in the rate of voluntary resignations. Grievances had been raised in 64 per cent of workplaces with some collective conflict, compared with 44 per cent of workplaces without. By contrast, the rate of voluntary resignations was just 9.0 employees per 100 in workplaces with some collective conflict, compared with 14.7 among workplaces without. The incidence of absenteeism was marginally higher in workplaces with collective conflict, and the incidence of disciplinary sanctions marginally lower, but here the differences did not reach statistical significance.

The significant negative association between the incidence of collective conflict and the rate of voluntary resignations echoes back to the specific point made earlier about the role that trade unions may play in providing an alternative to employee exit, and also to the more general point that conflict may take different forms depending upon the environment. Further indications of this are apparent from an examination of variations in the nature of conflict across industries. Ranking industries according to the incidence of the various expressions of conflict considered throughout the chapter, it was evident that those industries with a relatively high incidence of collective conflict generally also experienced a high level of grievances, but tended to experience comparatively low rates of disciplinary sanctions and resignations; Public administration and Electricity, gas and water provided two such examples. Equivalently, industries with low levels of collective unrest and individual grievances tended to experience higher rates of disciplinary action and voluntary resignations; Wholesale and retail, Hotels and restaurants and Other business services were illustrative of this pattern. These results support assertions that discontent will find expression in different forms, depending upon the opportunities that are available. In industries where institutional arrangements for employee voice are widespread and employees are commonly led to expect long-term employment, it appears that conflictual situations are more likely to be expressed and managed in an open manner. Where collective labour organization is uncommon and expectations about long-term employment are lower, on the other hand, there is a greater likelihood that conflict will be resolved through a severing of the ties between employer and employee.

## Conclusion

This chapter has considered a variety of issues in respect of workplace conflict, ranging from the incidence of collective and individual expressions of discontent, through the prevalence and nature of dispute resolution procedures, to the incidence of unofficial indicators of dissatisfaction. The analysis indicates that levels of conflict – whether collective, individual or unofficial – were little different in 2004 to those observed at the time of the previous survey in 1998. Workplaces experiencing collective unrest continue to comprise a very small minority of all establishments, while individual expressions were more widespread. That said, the balance between collective and individual expressions of conflict differs across workplaces, not least when comparisons are made between industry sectors. Institutional arrangements clearly play some role in helping to explain such variations, with the role of trade unions being particularly important in facilitating collective expressions of conflict and the raising of individual complaints.

The influence of trade unions is also apparent in encouraging the implementation of formal procedures for resolving disputes. The evidence from the survey indicated that procedures for resolving collective and individual disputes were widespread among larger workplaces, those in the public sector and those with recognized trade unions. It also pointed to a growth in the presence of formal disciplinary procedures since 1998, particularly within small non-union firms; a development which may have been prompted by recent changes to legislation and the growth of individual employment rights more generally. Nonetheless, while procedures for resolving collective and individual disputes were generally widespread, at least one in seven employees in the Construction and Hotel and restaurants industries worked in establishments without formal grievance procedures, and around one-tenth of those in Hotels and restaurants worked in establishments without a formal disciplinary procedure.

The existence of procedures provides the opportunity to bring consistency to the way employees and employers may raise their concerns, and can equally provide clarity in how situations of possible conflict might be addressed. And indeed, the survey evidence provided broad support for the use of such procedures. There was little evidence that employees were not using available procedures because of doubts about their effectiveness. And the majority of employee representatives were satisfied with the operation of those procedures that were in place.

# 9 Equality, diversity and work–life balance

## Introduction

The diversity of the workforce, both in the labour market, and within establishments (as indicated in Chapter 2), together with changes in the aspirations of employees, have implications for the way employers run their organizations. For example, women with pre-school age children compose a growing proportion of the labour pool (Walling, 2005: 275), while the labour force is ageing (Dixon, 2003: 67). Further to this, some employees have long experienced discrimination in the workplace, due to their gender, age, ethnicity, disability, religion, sexual orientation, trade union membership or other characteristics, and diversity challenges employers to address this discrimination. Aside from the diversity of the workforce, and the implications that this has for employment practices, there is evidence that both women and men are experiencing increasing dissatisfaction with their 'work–life' balance (White *et al.*, 2004: 102). This chapter considers WERS data on the broad area of diversity at work; especially equal opportunities policies, their presence and implementation, and the incidence of policies which potentially facilitate work–life balance. Changes in the attitudes of employees towards work–life balance are also assessed by examining the information that WERS provides on this subject.

Changes in the composition of the workforce have created considerable challenges for employers. There is some evidence to suggest that employers who implement equal opportunities practices and work–life balance arrangements have higher staff retention, reduced labour turnover, improved employee morale, higher levels of staff motivation and increased productivity (Bevan *et al.*, 1999; Dex and Scheibl, 1999; Dex and Smith, 2002; Perotin and Robinson, 2000; Woodland *et al.*, 2003). Such positive outcomes may encourage some employers to seek to enhance equality of opportunity and work–life balance within the workplace. However, there are other reasons why employers may adopt equal opportunities practices and work–life balance arrangements. They may be motivated by ethical considerations, and trade unions appear to play an important role in voicing these, providing 'social regulation' (Dickens, 1999: 14). It was shown in Chapter 7 that managers negotiated equal opportunities with trade unions in a sizeable proportion of workplaces. In addition to this, certain equal opportunities and work–life balance policies and practices are more prevalent in workplaces which recognize unions (Bewley and Fernie, 2003; Budd and Mumford, 2004). The association between union recognition and the existence of workplace equal opportunities and work–life balance arrangements is explored in this chapter.

The legislative context is also of interest since over the past 30 years successive UK governments have taken action to promote equality of opportunity via the law. Legislation has been enacted in the areas of sex, race, disability, and most recently, religion and sexual orientation, while protection against discrimination on the grounds of age is due to come into force in 2006. In addition, since 1997, the government has introduced a number of legal rights aimed at supporting employees with caring responsibilities. These include parental leave, paid paternity leave, unpaid time off to deal with a family emergency, adoption leave, and, a right for parents with young or disabled children to request flexible working. There have also been enhancements to maternity leave and pay, and legislation to protect part-time workers from less favourable treatment than that received by full-time workers.

The design of UK employment legislation owes more to Jewson and Mason's liberal conception of equality, which seeks to provide equality of opportunity, than the radical approach, which places the emphasis on securing equality of outcomes (Jewson and Mason, 1986). Indeed, positive discrimination (where employers seek to achieve equal representation in the workplace by intervening in the decision-making process), a valid course of action under the radical approach, is proscribed for all but election candidates (Sex Discrimination (Election Candidates) Act 2002).[1] As already noted, though, legislation is only one of a range of factors which affect equality of opportunity in the workplace. Webb and Liff (1988) highlight the importance of 'managing diversity', which seeks to end stereotyping through cultural change, enhancing the probability of equality of outcomes by creating 'a level playing field'. This suggests that legislation on its own can have only a limited impact on the attainment of equality, with the commitment of organizations and individuals vital to the success of the process.

The first part of this chapter looks at the incidence and coverage of equal opportunities policies. It then moves on to examine the implementation and monitoring of equal opportunities practices at the workplace, including the availability of flexible working and leave arrangements. Having assessed access to work–life balance arrangements, patterns of working hours are considered, given that these have implications for the balance between work and family life. The chapter closes by looking at attitudes towards work–life balance from both managers' and employees' perspectives. Recent legislation will be outlined in section introductions, in order to provide information on changes in the policy background which may have influenced the incidence of specific practices. Nonetheless, it is important to bear in mind that a range of more general factors, such as the changing composition and attitudes of the workforce, the need to recruit and retain staff, ethical concerns and pressure from trade unions, also shape the adoption of equal opportunities and work–life balance practices by employers.

## Promoting equality of opportunity

The Equal Opportunities Commission, the Commission for Racial Equality and the Disability Rights Commission have each established Codes of Practice which outline the practices which employers are recommended to have in place in order to avoid a breach of the law.[2] These codes suggest that employers take three steps in order to provide equality of opportunity for employees: (1) the formulation of an equal opportunities policy; (2) the implementation of the policy; and (3) monitoring the policy to ensure that it works in practice. The evidence that WERS 2004 provides on the extent to which employers have taken each of the three steps recommended in the Codes of Practice is considered in the following sections.

### *Step 1: Formulation of an equal opportunities policy*

Almost three-quarters (73 per cent) of workplaces had a formal written equal opportunities policy, or a policy on managing diversity. This compares with around two-thirds in 1998 (64 per cent). The increase in the overall incidence was due to an increase in the proportion of private sector workplaces with equal opportunities (up from 55 per cent in 1998 to 68 per cent in 2004). The proportion of workplaces in the public sector with equal opportunities policies remained unchanged (97 per cent in 1998, 98 per cent in 2004). Analysis of the 1998–2004 Panel Survey also showed an increase in the proportion of continuing workplaces with formal equal opportunities policies over the period (up from 68 per cent to 82 per cent), indicating that behavioural change had taken place. Fifteen per cent of all continuing workplaces in 2004 had adopted an equal opportunities policy since 1998 and 2 per cent ceased to have a policy in place in 2004. Analysis of the Panel Survey by sector of ownership also revealed that there was an increase in the proportion of workplaces in the private sector with an equal opportunities policy since 1998.

Most employees worked in establishments covered by a formal written equal opportunities policy (88 per cent). This is in line with Table 9.1, which shows that incidence is positively associated with the size of the workplace and organization. Chapter 3 showed that larger workplaces and organizations were also more likely to have a designated employment relations specialist at the workplace. It is possible that these specialists are more likely to be aware of the legal requirements placed on the employer. The results supported this assumption in that around nine out of ten workplaces (92 per cent) with an employment relations specialist, either at the workplace or higher in the organization, had a formal policy in place, compared to about a half of workplaces (48 per cent) without a designated specialist. This association held after controlling for workplace size.

*Table 9.1* Presence of equal opportunities policy, by workplace characteristics

| | Equal opportunities policy | |
|---|---|---|
| | *% of workplaces* | *% of employees* |
| All workplaces | 73 | 88 |
| *Workplace size* | | |
| 10–24 employees | 63 | 65 |
| 25–49 employees | 81 | 80 |
| 50–99 employees | 90 | 90 |
| 100–199 employees | 96 | 95 |
| 200–499 employees | 96 | 96 |
| 500 or more employees | 96 | 97 |
| All workplaces with 25 or more employees | 86 | 92 |
| *Organization status* | | |
| Stand-alone workplace | 47 | 67 |
| Part of a larger organization | 86 | 93 |
| *Size of organization* | | |
| Less than 100 | 46 | 52 |
| 100 to less than 1,000 | 87 | 89 |
| 1,000 to less than 10,000 | 94 | 97 |
| 10,000 or more | 97 | 98 |
| *Sector of ownership* | | |
| Private | 68 | 84 |
| Public | 98 | 99 |
| *Industry* | | |
| Manufacturing | 52 | 80 |
| Electricity, gas and water | (95) | 97 |
| Construction | 71 | 84 |
| Wholesale and retail | 71 | 84 |
| Hotels and restaurants | 50 | 71 |
| Transport and communication | 63 | 81 |
| Financial services | 96 | 97 |
| Other business services | 69 | 84 |
| Public administration | 100 | 100 |
| Education | 99 | 99 |
| Health | 89 | 95 |
| Other community services | 81 | 92 |
| *Union recognition* | | |
| No union recognized | 63 | 78 |
| At least one union recognized | 96 | 97 |

Base: All workplaces with 10 or more employees.
Figures are weighted and based on responses from 2,053 managers.

Table 9.1 also shows the incidence of a formal written equal opportunities policy by other workplace characteristics. Workplaces that were part of a larger organization were more likely to have these policies than independent sites. Most public sector workplaces were also found to have a formal equal opportunities policy. This was reflected in the variation in incidence between industries, with a formal equal opportunities policy being universal in workplaces in Public administration and least common in the Hotels and restaurants sector. Almost all workplaces with at least one recognized union had a formal equal opportunities policy. This association also held when the analysis was restricted to small (less than 100 employees) private sector workplaces. In larger private sector workplaces, the association was not significant.

There was some variation in the incidence of a formal written equal opportunities policy according to the composition of the workforce at the establishment (see Table 9.2). Formal written policies were more common in the following workplaces: those with a higher proportion of women; at least 10 per cent of the workforce from an ethnic minority; and where at least 5 per cent of the workforce were disabled. It is not apparent whether this is because having an equal opportunities policy actually increases the likelihood that women,

*Table 9.2* Presence of equal opportunities policy, by different workforce compositions

|  | Equal opportunities policy |
|---|---|
|  | % of workplaces |
| *Mostly women (over half) at workplace* | 80 |
| *Female employees* | |
| 25% or less | 64 |
| 26%–74% | 74 |
| 75% or more | 80 |
| *Ethnic minority employees* | |
| None | 66 |
| 10% or more | 82 |
| *Disabled employees* | |
| None | 70 |
| 5% or more | 81 |
| *Employees aged 16 to 21* | |
| None | 72 |
| 25% or more | 75 |
| *Employees aged 50 or over* | |
| None | 65 |
| 25% or more | 69 |

Base: All workplaces with 10 or more employees.
Figures are weighted and based on responses from at least 1,955 managers.

ethnic minorities or disabled people are employed, or whether workplaces are more likely to develop an equal opportunities policy where they already employ staff from these groups. There was no significant association between the presence of an equal opportunities policy at the workplace and the likelihood that the workplace employed higher proportions of younger or older employees.

Managers reporting that the workplace had an equal opportunities policy were also asked whether the policy explicitly referred to equality of treatment or discrimination in respect of particular grounds. Sixty-four per cent of workplaces specified particular grounds in 2004, up from 57 per cent in 1998. Among these workplaces, the grounds most commonly covered were those where legislation had been long-standing. In almost nine-tenths of workplaces with an equal opportunities policy which specified particular grounds, this policy covered sex and race (88 per cent each) while 85 per cent had an equal opportunities policy covering disability. The incidence of workplaces with formal policies covering each of these groups has remained largely unchanged since 1998. Workplaces were much more likely to have an equal opportunities policy in 2004 than in 1998 which covered the new and forthcoming statutory grounds: religion (82 per cent, up from 72 per cent in 1998), sexual orientation (71 per cent, up from 56 per cent in 1998) and age (69 per cent, up from 61 per cent in 1998). Analysis of the 1998–2004 Panel Survey also indicated that there was an increase in the proportion of continuing workplaces with an equal opportunities policy which covered the new and forthcoming statutory grounds, suggesting a change in behaviour. Sixty-eight per cent of workplaces with an equal opportunities policy reported that marital status was one of the grounds covered, a similar proportion to 1998 (65 per cent). Trade union membership was one of the grounds covered in 45 per cent of workplaces with an equal opportunities policy (47 per cent in 1998). A policy which covered trade union membership was more likely in workplaces where union density was higher.

Analysis of correlations showed that policies which covered gender were more likely to cover race, religion and disability.[3] Fifty-six per cent of workplaces had an equal opportunities policy which covered all four of these grounds, while 26 per cent of workplaces had a policy which addressed all eight of the types of discrimination. Three main factors were associated with a greater likelihood that the workplace had an equal opportunities policy which covered all eight of the grounds: whether the workplace was part of a large organization (with 1,000 or more employees) rather than one with less than 100 employees; whether it was in the public rather than the private sector; and whether there was at least one recognized union rather than no recognized union. These associations held independently of each other and after controlling for other workplace characteristics.

Workplaces without an equal opportunities policy (26 per cent) were asked their reasons for not having a policy in place. These workplaces were predominantly small, located in the private sector and did not recognize unions.

Among these workplaces, about one half (48 per cent) reported that they did not feel that they needed a policy. About one-fifth (22 per cent) considered that they had a policy but had not written it down and a similar proportion 'aimed at being an equal opportunities employer'. Five per cent of workplaces were in the process of developing a policy while a similar proportion said that they did not have a policy because they did not employ any, or had few employees, from disadvantaged groups. Sixteen per cent of establishments had not considered having a formal written policy.

### Step 2: Implementation of the policy

The Codes of Practice relating to sex, race, and disability discrimination legislation provide guidelines on how best to implement an equal opportunities policy so that it works effectively. This involves turning the intentions expressed in the policy into practice. Included in the guidelines are recommendations that the policy is covered by a collective agreement, is communicated to employees and job applicants, and that the policy is communicated by senior managers. The Cross-Section Survey of Managers provides information on the first two of these items. As Chapter 7 indicated, 72 per cent of workplaces neither negotiated, consulted or informed employee representatives over equal opportunities and 22 per cent of workplaces with recognized unions did none of these. Where the workplace did have an equal opportunities policy in place, the challenge of communicating the policy to employees arose. Managers said that employees were mostly informed about the policy through some form of written documentation (93 per cent), whether this was in a staff handbook (70 per cent), a contract of employment (43 per cent), a letter of appointment (13 per cent), via a notice board (18 per cent) or intranet or computer network (8 per cent).[4] In the 7 per cent of cases where the policy was not communicated via some written form of documentation managers most commonly said that employees were made aware of the policy as part of their induction programme (58 per cent) or were told about it by their supervisor or line-manager or foreman (36 per cent). Six per cent said that they were informed as part of training or briefing sessions and a similar proportion (5 per cent) said that they were informed as part of the job application process.

Since October 2004, all employers have been obliged under the Disability Discrimination Act (DDA) 1995 to make physical adjustments to their workplace to accommodate access for disabled employees. The Code of Practice relating to the DDA also states that it is good practice to conduct audits to establish whether access to the building should be improved in order to accommodate disabled employees. WERS 2004 showed that a formal assessment of the extent to which the workplace was accessible to employees or job applicants with disabilities had been carried out in half of all workplaces. This type of assessment was more likely to have been carried out in establishments where there was a formal written equal opportunities policy or where a higher proportion of employees were disabled. An access problem was identified in 53 per cent of workplaces where an assessment had been conducted. All managers were asked whether any adjustments were made to their building to accommodate disabled employees. Adjustments were made in around one quarter of all workplaces (28 per cent). This represented a rise in the proportion of workplaces making adjustments since 1998, when the figure was 23 per cent. In 2004, adjustments were made in three-fifths of workplaces where an access problem was identified. Managers were not asked whether a formal assessment had been carried out in 1998 and so an analysis of change is not possible in this respect.

*Recruitment practices*

There is some evidence to suggest that as people age they find it more difficult to re-enter employment. It is thought that this is because some employers discriminate on the grounds of age, although this is difficult to quantify (Cabinet Office, 2000). However, by the end of 2006, discrimination in recruitment on the grounds of age will be unlawful. As indicated previously in Chapter 4, managers were asked to state which factors were important when recruiting new employees. In 16 per cent of workplaces age was considered important. This proportion was lower than in 1998, when age was thought important in 22 per cent of workplaces. The 1998–2004 Panel Survey also showed a fall in the proportion of continuing workplaces where age was an important factor in recruitment, from 18 per cent in 1998 to 12 per cent in 2004.

As might be expected, workplaces that did not have a formal written equal opportunities policy were more likely to cite age as a factor in recruitment. Indeed, one quarter (25 per cent) of workplaces without a formal equal opportunities policy cited age as an important factor compared to 13 per cent of workplaces with a formal policy. Managers in smaller workplaces and organizations, the private sector and in workplaces where no union was recognized, commonly mentioned age as a factor in recruitment. There was also some variation in responses by industrial sector, with age being most often cited by managers in the Hotels and restaurants sector (33 per cent of workplaces) and less commonly mentioned in workplaces in the Financial services (6 per cent) and Construction (8 per cent) sectors.

Turning to the relationship between the likelihood that age was a factor in recruitment and the age composition of the workforce, where at least one quarter of the workforce were aged between 16 and 21, the establishment was more likely to cite age as a factor in recruitment (23 per cent) compared to workplaces with no employees in this age range (14 per cent). However, workplaces where at least one quarter of the workforce was aged over 50 were no more likely than establishments without older workers to mention age as a factor in recruitment (17 per cent compared with 20 per cent, respectively). This suggests that workplaces which used age as a factor in recruitment were more likely to favour younger workers than older workers when recruiting staff.

*Special procedures to encourage applications from certain groups*

In Great Britain, employees are protected against discrimination in recruitment as well as employment on the grounds of sex, race, disability, religion and sexual orientation. In general, the law requires that the recruitment of an individual be judged on merit, with an additional requirement that, in the case of a disabled person, employers must be prepared to make any 'reasonable adjustment' that might be necessary. This in turn means that, as mentioned in the introduction to this chapter, employers are not allowed to discriminate ('positive discrimination') in order to produce equality of outcomes. However, the law does allow employers to take 'positive action', removing barriers to free competition in the labour market. This type of action might include advertising campaigns targeted at under-represented groups, or the provision of training for certain groups to enable them to take up job opportunities. The Cross-Section Survey of Managers sought to establish whether employers were engaging in positive action by asking managers whether they had any special procedures to encourage applications from women in general, women returning to work after having children, members of ethnic minority groups, older workers, disabled people or people who had been unemployed for 12 months or more. Just over four-fifths (82 per cent) of workplaces did not have any special procedures in place, and as Table 9.3 shows, no more than 10 per cent of workplaces had any one of these procedures. Just 3 per cent of workplaces had special procedures which sought to encourage applications from each of these five groups.

Establishments with a formal equal opportunities policy were three times as likely (21 per cent) to have special procedures to encourage applications from any of the specified groups compared to workplaces without a formal policy (7 per cent). There was also some variation in the proportion of workplaces with special recruitment procedures according to the sector of ownership (see Table 9.3).

*Table 9.3* Special recruitment procedures, by sector of ownership

| | % of workplaces | | |
| --- | --- | --- | --- |
| | Sector of ownership | | |
| | Private | Public | All workplaces |
| *Special procedures to attract ...* | | | |
| Women returning to work after having children | 8 | 12 | 8 |
| Women in general | 5 | 10 | 6 |
| Members from minority ethnic groups | 6 | 21 | 9 |
| Older workers | 5 | 6 | 5 |
| Disabled workers | 5 | 29 | 10 |
| People who have been unemployed for 12 months or more | 5 | 8 | 5 |
| None of these | 87 | 63 | 82 |

Base: All workplaces with 10 or more employees.
Figures are weighted and based on responses from 2,056 managers.

Workplaces in the public sector were more likely to have special procedures to attract applications from women in general, people from ethnic minorities and disabled people. There was no significant variation according to sector of ownership in respect of the other groups.

The results also indicated that there was a positive association between the composition of the workforce and the special procedures which workplaces had in place to attract applications from different groups of employees. For example, the workplace was more likely to have special procedures to encourage applications from members of minority ethnic groups where a greater proportion of the workforce was from an ethnic minority. The exception to this was that little association was found between the incidence of special procedures to attract older workers and the age composition of the workforce.

In 1998, managers were not asked whether they had special procedures to attract applications from women in general. However, for the other groups there was comparable data in the 1998 and 2004 Cross-Section Surveys. There was a slight fall in the proportion of workplaces with procedures to attract women returning to work after having children (from 11 per cent in 1998 to 8 per cent in 2004). The decline was accounted for by a decline in the public sector (from 20 per cent in 1998 to 12 per cent in 2004) as the proportion of workplaces in the private sector with such procedures remained unchanged over the period (9 per cent in 1998 and 8 per cent in 2004). While the proportion of workplaces with procedures to attract each of the other groups remained largely unchanged over the period, the survey also recorded a decline in the incidence of procedures to attract applications from ethnic minorities or older workers in the public sector by 2004. Twelve per cent of public sector workplaces had procedures to attract older workers in 1998 compared with 6 per cent in 2004 and 27 per cent had procedures to attract applications from ethnic minorities in 1998 compared with 21 per cent in 2004. In respect of the latter procedures, this result was surprising given that the Race Relations Act was amended in 2001 placing a statutory duty on public authorities to promote race equality. This includes taking positive action and encouraging ethnic minorities to apply for work.[5] Looking at the change in incidence within the public sector, the results suggested that the decline in the incidence of special procedures to attract applications from ethnic minority groups had largely taken place in the Health sector, while there had been an increase in such procedures in Public administration.

*Job evaluation schemes*

Job evaluation schemes are used by employers to help to ensure that pay and grading systems at the workplace fairly reflect the skill requirements and responsibilities of the job. Table 9.4 reports the variation in the incidence of job evaluation schemes in workplaces with 10 or more employees by a number of workplace characteristics. Job evaluation schemes were more commonly found in larger workplaces and organizations, workplaces that were part of a

*Table 9.4* Presence of a job evaluation scheme, by workplace characteristics

|  | Job evaluation scheme |
|---|---|
|  | % of workplaces |
| All workplaces | 20 |
| *Workplace size* | |
| 10–24 employees | 17 |
| 25–49 employees | 22 |
| 50–99 employees | 23 |
| 100–199 employees | 35 |
| 200–499 employees | 36 |
| 500 or more employees | 54 |
| All workplaces with 25 or more employees | 25 |
| *Organization status* | |
| Stand-alone workplace | 7 |
| Part of a larger organization | 27 |
| *Organization size* | |
| 10–99 employees | 9 |
| 100–999 employees | 21 |
| 1,000–9,999 employees | 30 |
| 10,000 employees or more | 34 |
| *Sector of ownership* | |
| Private | 16 |
| Public | 42 |
| *Industry* | |
| Manufacturing | 14 |
| Electricity, gas and water | (43) |
| Construction | 10 |
| Wholesale and retail | 17 |
| Hotels and restaurants | 13 |
| Transport and communication | 15 |
| Financial intermediation | 42 |
| Other business services | 16 |
| Public administration | 59 |
| Education | 25 |
| Health | 28 |
| Other community services | 23 |
| *Union recognition* | |
| No union recognized | 12 |
| At least one union recognized | 41 |

Base: All workplaces with 10 or more employees.
Figures are weighted and based on responses from 2,059 managers.

wider organization, and in the public sector. Three-fifths of workplaces in Public administration had formal job evaluation schemes compared with one-tenth of workplaces in the Construction industry. The incidence of job evaluation was more prevalent in workplaces where at least one union was recognized compared to workplaces where no unions were recognized. Job evaluation schemes were also more commonly found in workplaces where women were in the majority compared to workplaces where women made up a smaller proportion of the workforce (24 per cent compared with 17 per cent, respectively). Like the other practices associated with fair treatment, a strong association was found between the incidence of these schemes and the presence of a formal written policy on equal opportunities or managing diversity. About one quarter (26 per cent) of workplaces with a formal policy had a job evaluation scheme compared to just 5 per cent of workplaces without a formal policy.

While there are a number of different types of job evaluation, they generally fall into one of two types: analytical or non-analytical. Analytical systems, such as the widely used points rating method, divide each job into factors, with points allocated to each factor. The total score then decides the job's place in the hierarchy. There are a number of advantages to this type of system, including the fact that its existence may be entered as a defence to an equal value claim. Non-analytical schemes use relatively simple techniques, such as 'job ranking', where job titles or descriptions are used to rank jobs in a league table. Managers were asked whether the scheme covering the largest number of employees was a points-rating scheme or some other scheme. Almost three-fifths of workplaces with job evaluation schemes had a points-rating mechanism in place (58 per cent), although among these workplaces, points-rating schemes were more commonplace in larger workplaces and organizations. Points-rating systems were also more common in the public sector (70 per cent) than in the private sector (52 per cent). Among workplaces with a job evaluation scheme and where at least one union was recognized, 69 per cent had a points-rating scheme in place compared with 45 per cent of workplaces where no union was recognized. This association also held in private sector workplaces. Managers in workplaces with job evaluation schemes were asked what proportion of employees were currently filling jobs covered by the largest scheme. Half of all managers in these workplaces said that all employees were covered by the largest scheme.

WERS 1998 did not contain questions on job evaluation, so it is necessary to go back to the first three surveys to observe how the incidence of job evaluation has changed over time. Between 1980 and 1990 the WERS series documented the rise in the overall incidence of job evaluation schemes in workplaces with 25 or more employees, particularly in the public sector (Millward *et al.*, 1992: 266–268). In 1980 21 per cent of workplaces with 25 or more employees had a job evaluation scheme. This rose to 26 per cent in 1990. The incidence of job evaluation in 2004 was similar to that in 1990, with 25 per cent of all workplaces with 25 or more employees reporting that these schemes were in place. Also, the rising trend in the public sector, apparent earlier in the series, continued. Forty-four per cent of public sector workplaces with 25 or more employees had job evaluation schemes in place in 2004 compared with 27 per cent in 1990. Accordingly there was a decline in the incidence of job evaluation in the private sector where it stood at around one quarter in workplaces with at least 25 employees in 1990 (27 per cent in private Manufacturing and 24 per cent in private services) falling to around one-fifth in 2004.

There appeared to have been an increase in the incidence of points-rating job evaluation schemes over time. In 2004, a points-rating system was the largest job evaluation scheme in operation in 60 per cent of workplaces with 25 or more employees, compared to 45 per cent in 1990. However, the size of the increase in incidence of this type of scheme should be treated with some caution because of changes to the question wording in 2004.[6]

## *Step 3: Monitoring equal opportunities practices*

As mentioned earlier, the Equality Commissions recommend in their Codes of Practice that in addition to formulating and subsequently implementing an equal opportunities policy, employers should monitor and review the implementation of the policy to ensure that any unforeseen outcomes which are detrimental to equality of opportunity are identified so that they can be addressed. Managers were asked whether they monitored the implementation of their equal opportunities policy. Twelve per cent of all workplaces, and 16 per cent of those with a formal written equal opportunities policy had tried to measure the impact of their equal opportunities policy on the workplace or employees. Larger establishments were more likely to measure the impact of their equal opportunities policy than smaller workplaces, and workplaces which were part of a wider organization were more likely to try to measure the impact of their equal opportunities policy than single independent establishments. Workplaces in the public sector were almost twice as likely to measure the impact of their equal opportunities policy as workplaces in the private sector (27 per cent compared to 14 per cent), and in line with this, half of all workplaces in the Public administration sector measured the impact of their equal opportunities policy, compared to just 4 per cent in Hotels and restaurants. Also, 26 per cent of workplaces where a union was recognized had sought to measure the impact of their equal opportunities policy, compared to only 12 per cent of workplaces where no unions were recognized.

Where managers did measure the impact of their equal opportunities policy on the workplace or employees, they were asked what this assessment had shown. This question was open-coded, with the code frame drawn up to reflect the common responses which emerged. In 20 per cent of these workplaces the policy had made little or no difference. However, in 17 per cent of establishments a more diverse workforce was thought to have resulted. Areas for improvement were identified, or awareness was raised in 15 per cent of workplaces while a further 10 per cent changed their procedures as a result. Four per cent of establishments were still evaluating the impact, while in 3 per cent of workplaces morale had improved as a result of introducing the equal opportunities policy.

Managers were asked whether, for gender, ethnic background, disability, or age, the establishment monitored recruitment and selection, or promotion, or reviewed recruitment and selection or promotion procedures to identify indirect discrimination (where the requirements of the job disproportionately limit access by certain groups of employees). They were also asked if they reviewed relative pay rates by these characteristics. As Table 9.5 shows, less than one quarter of workplaces carried out each of these activities. However, monitoring recruitment and selection, and reviewing recruitment and selection procedures to identify indirect discrimination were approximately twice as common as monitoring or reviewing promotions, and even more common than reviewing relative pay rates. Sixty-three per cent of workplaces did not carry out any monitoring or review activities at all, and only 3 per cent of workplaces carried out each of the types of monitoring or review by all four of the employee characteristics (gender, ethnicity, disability and age).

Establishments were generally more likely to carry out each of the forms of monitoring and review where they were larger, were part of a wider organization and recognized a union. Workplaces were also more likely to carry out each of the forms of monitoring and review in the public sector. In respect of the incidence of ethnic monitoring in the public sector, this is perhaps unsurprising given the race equality duty placed on public authorities under the Race Relations Act. This duty requires public authorities to monitor their policies and functions for any adverse impact on race equality. Workplaces were also far more likely to monitor by each of the characteristics where they had a written policy on equality of opportunity or managing diversity.

The employer was more likely to carry out each of the monitoring activities by gender where more than half the workforce was female, with the exception of reviewing relative pay rates. Workplaces were more likely to carry out monitoring

*Table 9.5* Monitoring and reviewing activities, by workforce characteristics

| | % of workplaces | | | | |
| --- | --- | --- | --- | --- | --- |
| | *Monitor recruitment and selection* | *Review recruitment and selection procedures* | *Monitor promotions* | *Review promotion procedures* | *Review relative pay rates* |
| Gender | 24 | 19 | 10 | 11 | 7 |
| Ethnic background | 24 | 20 | 10 | 11 | 5 |
| Disability | 23 | 19 | 9 | 10 | 4 |
| Age | 20 | 16 | 7 | 9 | 6 |

Base: All workplaces with 10 or more employees.
Figures are weighted and based on responses from at least 2,030 managers.

by ethnicity and disability where there were some employees from ethnic minorities, or who were disabled. However, workplaces with a high proportion of ethnic minority or disabled staff were no more likely to monitor by these characteristics than workplaces with a low proportion of these groups. Also, the proportion of employees aged 16 to 21, or 50 or more, had little bearing on the likelihood that the workplace carried out each of the monitoring activities by age.

The questions on the monitoring of equal opportunities practices in the 1998 Cross-Section Survey of Managers were less detailed than those used in 2004, as they did not distinguish between monitoring activities by different types of employee. Therefore it was not possible to assess change in monitoring activities between 1998 and 2004 using the Cross-Section data. However, consistent data items on monitoring were available in the Panel Survey. They indicated that there were significant increases in the proportion of workplaces which kept employee records with ethnic origin identified (from 30 per cent to 38 per cent), collected statistics on posts held by men and women (from 24 to 34 per cent), monitored promotions by gender or ethnicity (from 11 per cent to 20 per cent), reviewed the relative pay rates of different groups (from 17 per cent to 31 per cent) and made adjustments to the workplace to accommodate disabled employees (28 per cent to 44 per cent). By contrast, the proportion of workplaces reviewing selection and other procedures to identify indirect discrimination stayed fairly stable over this period (22 per cent in 1998 and 26 per cent in 2004).

## Work–life balance

Having looked at the incidence of employers' equal opportunities policies and practices, the chapter now turns to arrangements which potentially offer employees greater opportunity to shape their work–life balance. The gender imbalance in the domestic division of labour (see Crompton *et al.*, 2005 for evidence on the persistence of this), and the 'dual burden' that this imposes on women, mean that the provision of work–life balance arrangements by employers, and the attitude of managers towards employees who have responsibilities outside of work, have implications for gender equality within the workplace. Likewise, access to such practices may have an impact on equality for other employees who have a particular need to use them. Relevant legislative changes are briefly described in this part of the chapter, but it is important to note that, in addition to this, the range of more general factors outlined in the introduction are likely to influence the decision of employers to adopt these practices.

### Flexible working time arrangements

The Employment Act 2002 provided employees with children under the age of six or with disabled children under the age of 18 the right to request flexible working. This law placed a duty on employers to consider seriously such requests. This section presents information on a wide range of flexible working practices which 'fit ... hours to people', with the emphasis on providing flexibility to the employee, rather than mainly to the employer (White *et al.*, 2004: 109). Annual-hours contracts, which, it has been suggested, place the control over the hours of work in the hands of the employer (Gall, 1996: 49), or zero-hours contracts, which have been described as 'one-sided' given the 'high level of reliability by workers' (Leighton, 2002: 72), are not covered here.

Managers were asked whether a range of flexible working arrangements were available to at least some employees. These arrangements comprised: the ability to reduce working hours (e.g. switching from full-time to part-time employment); the ability to increase working hours (e.g. switching from part-time to full-time employment); the ability to change shift patterns; 'flexitime' (no set start or finish time, but an agreement to work a set number of hours per week or per month); 'job-sharing' (sharing a full-time job with someone else); 'homeworking' (working at or from home in normal working hours); working during school term-time only; and working 'compressed hours' (e.g. a nine-day fortnight/four-and-a-half-day week). Figure 9.1 illustrates the results.[7] It is clear from the figure that the most commonly available arrangement was the ability to reduce or increase working hours while compressed hours was the least common arrangement.

*Figure 9.1* Availability of flexible working arrangements to some employees, as reported by managers

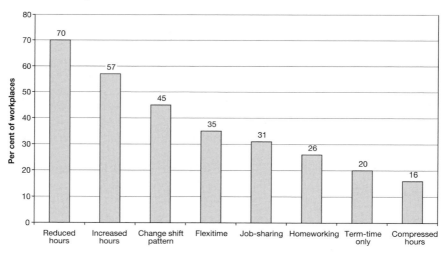

Base: All workplaces with 10 or more employees.
Figures are weighted and based on responses from at least 2,050 managers.

Generally, these arrangements were most common in the following types of establishment: larger workplaces; those which were part of a wider organization; larger organizations; public sector; and where at least one union was recognized. With the exception of home working and flexitime, workplaces where more than half the workforce were female were more likely to report that at least some employees had access to all of the listed practices.

Where workplaces provided reduced working hours and/or flexitime, managers were asked, for each arrangement, whether it was restricted to a subset of employees, or whether it was available to all. The majority of workplaces (78 per cent) providing reduced working hours did not place any restrictions on who was eligible to use this arrangement. Likewise, within 64 per cent of workplaces where flexitime was available to some employees, there were no restrictions on who could use this. Where restrictions applied, it was managerial employees who were most likely to be ineligible to take up either of these arrangements (Table 9.6), consistent with the findings of the Second Work–Life Balance Study (Woodland *et al.*, 2003: 75). There were no significant differences in the proportion of workplaces applying the restrictions listed in Table 9.6 between workplaces where unions were, and were not recognized, with the exception that non-permanent employees were less likely to be allowed to reduce their hours where a union was recognized (23 per cent of workplaces with recognized unions did not allow non-permanent staff to reduce their hours compared to 10 per cent of workplaces without recognized unions).

The Survey of Employees captured the employee perspective on the same set of flexible working arrangements, asking whether each would be available to

*Table 9.6* Groups of employees not allowed to reduce hours or work flexitime

|  | % workplaces | |
|---|---|---|
|  | *Reduced hours* | *Flexitime* |
| Employees without young children | 11 | 6 |
| Employees without other caring responsibilities | 12 | 4 |
| Part-time employees | 8 | 12 |
| Full-time employees | 16 | 12 |
| Managerial employees | 61 | 28 |
| Non-managerial employees | 5 | 12 |
| Employees with the establishment for a short period of time | 17 | 12 |
| Employees not on a permanent contract | 14 | 11 |
| Any male employees | 5 | 4 |
| Other responses: | | |
| Specific job-related criteria | 8 | 29 |
| Depends on individual circumstances | 8 | 13 |

Base: Workplaces with 10 or more employees which allow some, but not all, employees either to reduce their hours, or to work flexitime.
Figures are weighted and based on responses from at least 387 managers.

employees if individuals personally needed them. A high proportion of employees did not know whether the practices would be available (between 16 and 37 per cent). Figure 9.2 shows the proportion of employees who reported access to each of these arrangements in 2004. The 1998 Survey of Employees asked about a limited range of flexible working arrangements, so it is not possible to assess how reported access to all these practices has changed since 1998. However, the incidence of the comparable items, namely flexitime, job-sharing and homeworking, did increase from 1998 to 2004 (from 32 per cent, 15 per cent and 12 per cent respectively in 1998).

Female employees were more likely to report that each of the arrangements would be personally available to them than men, except in the case of homeworking. In fact, men were more likely than women to consider that they would be able to work at home if they needed (16 per cent compared to 12 per cent). In line with this, the likelihood that employees reported availability of all the practices except homeworking was higher in workplaces where more than half of the workforce was female. Homeworking was slightly more common in workplaces where women were not in the majority (15 per cent compared to 13 per cent).

*Figure 9.2* Availability of flexible working arrangements, as reported by employees

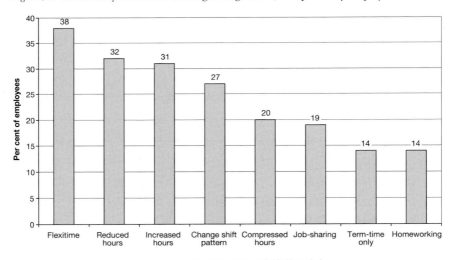

**Arrangement thought available if needed**

Base: All employees in workplaces with 10 or more employees.
Figures are weighted and based on responses from 21,655 employees.
Note:
    The percentages presented here use the total number of responses as the base, rather than just responses from employees who answered 'yes' or 'no' to the question. This is so that a reliable comparison can be made with 1998 when employees were not given the option of stating that they 'did not know' whether a practice was available.

Women with dependent children aged 18 and under were more likely to report access to each of the practices except flexitime and homeworking than women without dependent children. Men with dependent children were more likely than men without dependent children to believe that they would have access to flexitime (37 per cent compared to 33 per cent) or homeworking (18 per cent and 15 per cent respectively). They were less likely to think that they would be able to reduce (19 per cent compared to 23 per cent) or increase their hours (24 per cent compared to 27 per cent), or work termtime only (6 per cent compared to 8 per cent). Employees who cared for a family member or friend with a long-term physical or mental illness or disability were more likely to report access to flexitime (40 per cent compared to 37 per cent) and reduced working hours than employees without such caring responsibilities (35 per cent compared to 31 per cent), but were no more likely to have access to any of the other flexible working practices. However, they were less likely than employees without this type of caring responsibility to be able to work from home (12 per cent compared to 14 per cent). Employees with a long-term disability which affected the amount or type of work that they were able to do were no more likely to report access to flexible working arrangements than employees without such a disability. It is not possible to say whether the higher levels of access reported by some groups reflected their greater awareness of these arrangements or whether employers were more likely to offer flexible working arrangements where they had a greater proportion of employees likely to want to use such practices. Indeed, it is possible that some employees are attracted to workplaces which provide appropriate support.

It was shown earlier that in the 36 per cent of workplaces where flexitime was restricted to particular groups of employees, it was relatively common for managers to be excluded from flexitime schemes. Despite this, the Survey of Employees showed that managers were more likely than non-managerial employees to believe that they would have access to flexitime if needed (47 per cent compared to 37 per cent). However, within establishments where it was reported that managers were not allowed to work flexitime, results from the Survey of Employees indicated that there was no significant difference between the proportion of managerial and non-managerial employees who believed that they would have access to this practice. This perhaps indicates that managers have some informal flexibility over their hours in these workplaces. Consistent with this, 43 per cent of managers reported that they had a lot of influence over the time that they started or finished their working day, compared to 24 per cent of non-managerial employees. Managers were much more likely to think that they would be allowed to work from home than non-managerial employees (34 per cent compared to 11 per cent).

In keeping with the finding from the Cross-Section Survey of Managers that reduced working hours were often not available to managers, only 27 per cent of managers thought that they would be able to reduce their hours, compared to 33 per cent of non-managerial employees. Likewise, 15 per cent of non-managerial employees believed that they would be able to work term-time only if required, compared to just 7 per cent of managers. A similar proportion of managers and non-managerial employees thought that they would be able to increase or compress their hours, change their pattern of working hours or job-share.

A difference in the wording of the question between the 1998 and 2004 Cross-Section Surveys of Managers meant that it was not possible to report on change in the availability of flexible working practices to employees between 1998 and 2004 using these data. While in 1998, managers were asked if any non-managerial employees were allowed to use each of the flexible working practices, in the 2004 Cross-Section Survey, the wording of the question was more general, asking if any employees were allowed to use these practices. However, consistent estimates are available from the Panel Survey, making it possible to compare access to flexible working arrangements for non-managerial employees in continuing workplaces in 1998 and 2004. The results indicated that there was a significant increase between 1998 and 2004 in the proportion of workplaces allowing some non-managerial employees to work flexitime (19 per cent to 26 per cent), switch from full-time to part-time employment (46 per cent to 64 per cent), work a nine-day fortnight or four-and-a-half-day week (3 per cent to 8 per cent), use job-sharing (31 per cent to 41 per cent), term-time only contracts (14 per cent to 28 per cent) or homeworking (16 per cent to 28 per cent).

### Arrangements to support employees with caring responsibilities

As well as providing access to flexible working arrangements, employers may also provide other arrangements to employees to help them reconcile the demands of their work with their home life, including support with childcare and time off from work. As outlined in the introduction to this chapter, there are a number of reasons why employers may introduce measures to support working families, and in some cases may provide arrangements above the statutory minimum. Since 1999, the UK Government has introduced a number of legal entitlements to leave for family and caring responsibilities (Employment Relations Act 1999, Employment Act 2002). This section looks at the availability of a number of arrangements which support employees with children and other dependants.

### Childcare facilities and financial support

Managers were asked whether any employees were entitled to a number of arrangements, including a workplace nursery or a nursery linked with the workplace (henceforward referred to as a workplace nursery) or financial help with the costs of childcare, for example loans, repayable contributions to fees for childcare outside of the workplace or subsidized places not located at the establishment. Three per cent of all workplaces provided a workplace nursery, and 6 per cent of all workplaces gave financial help with childcare. Larger workplaces more commonly provided either of these arrangements. Eight per cent of all workplaces provided either one or both of these arrangements (henceforth referred to as childcare assistance). This therefore implies that workplaces tended either to provide a workplace nursery, or financial help with childcare, rather than offering both practices alongside each other. Indeed, only 1 per cent of workplaces made both of these practices available. Twenty per cent of employees worked in workplaces which offered childcare assistance to at least some employees.

Workplaces in the public sector were more likely to provide childcare assistance than those in the private sector (18 per cent compared with 5 per cent). As Figure 9.3 shows, this association held even after allowing for differences in workplace size. There was also some variation by industrial sector, with three-tenths of workplaces in Public administration and almost one-fifth of workplaces (18 per cent) in Financial services providing assistance with childcare, compared to just 2 per cent of workplaces in Construction and a similar proportion in the Wholesale and retail sectors.

*Figure 9.3* Employer provision of childcare assistance[a], by workplace size and sector of ownership

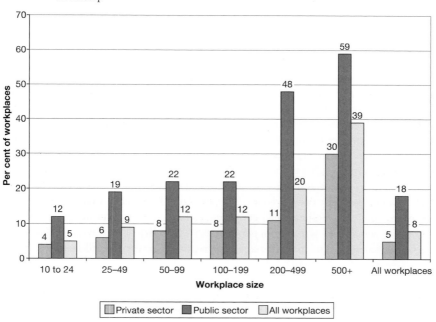

Base: All workplaces with 10 or more employees.
Figures are weighted and based on responses from 2,054 managers.
Note:
   [a] Childcare assistance covers both provision of an on-site nursery or a nursery linked to the workplace and/or financial help with childcare.

Workplaces that were part of a wider organization or where at least one union was recognized commonly provided assistance with childcare. The latter association held after controlling for sector of ownership. Workplaces with an equal opportunities policy were five times more likely to provide childcare assistance than those without such a policy (10 per cent compared to 2 per cent). Employer provision of childcare assistance was more common in workplaces with higher proportions of women, although still relatively unusual. Eleven per cent of workplaces where women were in the majority provided assistance with childcare, compared to 4 per cent of workplaces where women were not in the majority.

The Survey of Employees asked whether employees thought that childcare assistance would be available to them if they personally needed it. One-third of employees were uncertain whether childcare assistance was provided and a further 5 per cent did not provide an answer. Six per cent said that their employer provided a workplace nursery or help with childcare costs (4 per cent in 1998).

Employees working in larger workplaces, the public sector, establishments with recognized unions as well as workplaces with higher proportions of women were more likely to report access to childcare assistance than those in smaller workplaces, the private sector, and workplaces with no union recognition and with a smaller proportion of female employees. This would appear to support the account provided by managers working in workplaces with these characteristics.

Women were also slightly more likely to report that these arrangements were available than men (5 per cent compared with 7 per cent) and there were differences in responses between men and women with and without dependent children. Women with pre-school children were more likely than women without dependants to report the availability of childcare assistance (7 per cent compared with 4 per cent). However, women with older children were no more likely to believe that they would have access to childcare assistance than women without dependants (5 per cent). Similarly, men with pre-school children were more likely to report access to childcare assistance compared with men without children (12 per cent compared with 5 per cent). Men with older children were no more likely to believe that they would have access to childcare assistance compared with men without dependants (5 per cent). There was no difference between managers and non-managers in reported access to childcare assistance (7 per cent and 6 per cent).

In 1998, managers were asked whether there was a workplace nursery or whether they provided financial help with the costs of childcare for at least some non-managerial employees, rather than for employees more generally as in 2004. This makes a reliable comparison between the 1998 and 2004 Cross-Sections problematic. However, the 1998–2004 Panel Survey collected consistent estimates of the availability of childcare assistance for at least some non-managerial employees over the period. The Panel Survey recorded that the availability of childcare assistance had remained low and stable over time. Six per cent of continuing workplaces provided a workplace nursery for some non-managerial employees in 2004 compared to 4 per cent in 1998. In 2004, the proportion of continuing workplaces which provided financial help with childcare for some non-managerial employees stood at 8 per cent, compared to 5 per cent in 1998.

*Maternity leave*

Since 1999, the UK Government has made a number of enhancements to maternity leave provisions, including: extending Statutory Maternity Pay and Ordinary Maternity Leave from 18 to 26 weeks; the removal of the qualifying period for Ordinary Maternity Leave; and the right to take an additional 26 weeks' unpaid maternity leave (Additional Maternity Leave) for those meeting the qualification criteria.[8] There have also been increases since 1999 in the level of Statutory Maternity Pay.[9]

For the first time, in 2004, WERS asked employers about their provision of maternity leave in the 97 per cent of workplaces that had female employees. The focus of the questions was on extra-statutory maternity pay and leave, specifically whether employees received their normal full rate of pay for some or all of the period of maternity leave. Fifty-seven per cent of workplaces with some female employees provided full pay for some or all of the maternity leave period. Table 9.7 shows that larger workplaces and workplaces in the public sector were more likely to provide maternity leave on full pay for some or all of the maternity leave period. Workplaces with recognized unions were also more likely to provide full pay for some of the maternity leave period than those without any union recognition. This association held in workplaces in the private sector.

Managers were asked how many weeks of maternity leave on full pay were provided. Of those workplaces which did provide some weeks on full pay, a substantial number of managers were unable to state the amount of leave available (33 per cent). Among the two-thirds of workplaces where managers did provide an answer, about one-quarter (27 per cent) said that employees received full pay for six weeks or less. A further 44 per cent of workplaces provided between seven and 25 weeks of leave on full pay and almost three-tenths (29 per cent) of workplaces provided at least six months of maternity leave on full pay. Of those workplaces providing some maternity leave on full pay, the average number of weeks for which employees received full-pay was 16. The median number of weeks equated to 14. There was no difference between the mean number of weeks on full pay in the private and public sectors, although the median figure was higher for the public sector (18) compared to the private sector (13).

*Paternity leave*

Since April 2003, fathers have been legally entitled to up to two weeks' paid paternity leave, provided they qualify.[10] The law also prescribes that employees

*Table* 9.7 Extra-statutory leave arrangements, by workplace characteristics and the gender composition of the workforce

| | % of workplaces | | | | |
|---|---|---|---|---|---|
| | At least some portion of maternity leave period on full pay | At least some portion of paternity leave period on full pay | Paid parental or special paid leave for parents | Special paid (emergency) leave | Leave for carers of older adults |
| All workplaces | 57 | 55 | 25 | 49 | 6 |
| *Workplace size* | | | | | |
| 10–24 employees | 55 | 49 | 21 | 46 | 5 |
| 25–49 employees | 59 | 58 | 27 | 50 | 3 |
| 50–99 employees | 62 | 63 | 34 | 59 | 9 |
| 100–199 employees | 53 | 66 | 38 | 55 | 9 |
| 200–499 employees | 58 | 67 | 32 | 56 | 18 |
| 500 or more employees | 65 | 77 | 41 | 70 | 24 |
| *Sector of ownership* | | | | | |
| Private | 51 | 49 | 21 | 43 | 4 |
| Public | 84 | 84 | 47 | 80 | 16 |
| *Trade union recognition* | | | | | |
| No union recognized | 48 | 44 | 19 | 40 | 3 |
| At least one union recognized | 78 | 81 | 40 | 71 | 14 |
| *Proportion of female employees in the workplace* | | | | | |
| 25% or less | 53 | 43 | 18 | 42 | 3 |
| 26%–74% | 59 | 61 | 27 | 51 | 5 |
| 75% or more | 57 | 58 | 30 | 53 | 9 |

Base (column 1): All workplaces with 10 or more employees and employing some women.
Base (column 2): All workplaces with 10 or more employees and employing some men.
Base (column 3): All workplaces with 10 or more employees.
Figures are weighted and based on responses from at least 1,907 (column 1); 1,863 (column 2); 1,975 (column 3); 1,988 (column 4) and 1,985 managers (column 5).

who are legally eligible can choose to take either one week or two consecutive weeks' paternity leave, but not odd days. Managers in the 93 per cent of workplaces with some male employees were asked how fathers usually took time off around the birth. These managers were provided with a showcard listing a number of arrangements, including paternity leave, defined as 'a specific period of leave for fathers around the time of the birth'. The leave arrangement most frequently mentioned was paternity leave (either paid or unpaid), accounting for 73 per cent of workplaces with at least some male employees. This was followed by annual leave (34 per cent) and time off at the employers' discretion (26 per cent). In 7 per cent of workplaces, the situation had not arisen, and 5 per cent of managers said that fathers usually made use of some other leave arrangement. Just 2 per cent of managers said that no leave arrangements were available to fathers needing to take time off around the birth of their child. Larger workplaces and larger organizations were more likely to provide paternity leave than smaller workplaces and organizations. For example, the provision of paternity leave was almost universal (97 per cent) in workplaces with at least 500 employees compared with around three-fifths of workplaces (63 per cent) with between 10 and 24 employees. On the other hand, smaller workplaces were more likely to offer discretionary leave compared to larger workplaces. About three-tenths (29 per cent) of workplaces with between 10 and 24 employees said that fathers usually took discretionary leave compared with close to one-fifth (17 per cent) of workplaces with at least 500 or more employees. There was significant variation according to sector of ownership, with fathers usually taking paternity leave in nine-out-of-ten workplaces in the public sector (91 per cent) compared with seven-tenths of workplaces in the private sector.

Managers were asked whether any fathers taking paternity or discretionary leave received their normal full rate of pay for some or all of the leave period. Fifty-five per cent of all workplaces employing at least some male employees reported that some paternity or discretionary leave on full pay was available. Column 2 of Table 9.7 shows that larger workplaces, workplaces in the public sector and workplaces where at least one union was recognized more commonly provided new fathers with leave on full pay. The association between paid paternity leave or discretionary leave for fathers and union recognition also held after controlling for sector of ownership. Managers in workplaces where the vast majority of the workforce were women more commonly reported that some paternity leave on full pay was available compared to workplaces where women were in the minority. In addition, about twice as many managers reported the provision of paternity leave on full pay where they also reported provision of maternity leave on full pay compared to where maternity leave on full pay was not available (72 per cent compared with 35 per cent). Workplaces with a formal equal opportunities policy were also more likely to provide paid paternity or discretionary leave for fathers compared with those that did not have such a policy.

Among workplaces providing some leave on full pay for fathers, managers were also asked the number of days of paid leave provided. Managers in 15 per cent of workplaces which provided paternity or discretionary leave on full pay did not know how many days were available. Of those managers who were able to state the number of days of paternity or discretionary leave on full pay, at least ten days were available in over half (51 per cent) of establishments that made this leave available. A further 6 per cent provided between six and nine days on full pay while 44 per cent said that five days or less of leave on full pay was available to fathers. The mean number of days provided was eight while the median number was nine days. There was no significant variation in the mean or median number of days provided according to sector of ownership.

*Parental leave*

In December 1999, the UK Government introduced the right to parental leave. This entitlement allows both mothers and fathers with at least one year's continuous service to take 13 weeks of unpaid parental leave to look after their child until the age of five, or 18 weeks of leave for parents of disabled children up until their eighteenth birthday. Having asked about the availability of maternity leave, paternity leave and time off for family emergencies, managers were asked the following question: 'With the exception of maternity leave, paternity leave and time off for emergencies, how do mothers and fathers usually take time off to look after their children?' A showcard listing a number of different leave arrangements was provided and managers were permitted to give more than one response. The most commonly mentioned arrangement was annual leave (64 per cent). A third of managers said that unpaid parental leave was the usual course of action. One in ten stated that paid parental leave was the usual option and 19 per cent said that special paid leave was the norm. In 13 per cent of workplaces, parents normally took sick leave, while employees took time off and made it up later in 5 per cent of establishments. Leave was discretionary in 4 per cent of workplaces, and a further 4 per cent did not provide any specific leave provisions, so that employees had to make their own arrangements. Two per cent of managers said that the situation had never arisen.

Column 3 of Table 9.7 shows that a quarter of all managers stated that paid parental leave or special paid leave were usually taken by parents. Like the other enhanced leave arrangements discussed previously, it appeared that the incidence of paid parental leave or special paid leave for parents was more commonly available in larger workplaces, workplaces in the public sector and in workplaces with recognized unions. The association between the incidence of paid parental leave or special paid leave with union recognition also held in private sector workplaces. Workplaces with higher proportions of women were more likely to provide paid parental or special paid leave for parents than establishments where women were in the minority. Workplaces with a formal written equal opportunities policy were twice as likely to provide paid parental or special paid leave arrangements compared to workplaces without a formal written policy (29 per cent and 15 per cent, respectively).

Workplaces stating that employees took paid parental leave were also asked how many days of paid leave (not necessarily on full pay) were provided. Thirty-seven per cent were unable to provide an answer. Of those who were able to state the number of days, this was five days or less in 57 per cent of workplaces, between six and ten days in 30 per cent of establishments, and ten days or more in 14 per cent of workplaces. The mean number of days of paid parental leave was eight, while the median was five. There was some variation according to sector of ownership, with the public sector being more likely to provide a greater number of paid days of parental leave compared with the private sector (10 days compared with six days on average, whilst the median number of days were nine and five respectively).

The Survey of Employees also asked about the availability of paid parental leave. Employees were asked whether paid parental leave, defined as blocks of paid time off work to care for young children, would be personally available to them if they needed it. Around two-fifths (42 per cent) of all employees were unable to answer and 5 per cent refused to answer the question. Of those who were able to provide an answer, 19 per cent said that paid parental leave was available. In general, employees confirmed managers' accounts. Employees more commonly reported the availability of paid parental leave in larger workplaces and organizations, in the public sector and in workplaces with recognized unions.

Women were slightly more likely than men to report that paid parental leave was available to them (21 per cent compared with 17 per cent). Employees with pre-school children were more likely than employees with older children and employees without children to report that paid parental leave was available to them (26 per cent, 17 per cent and 19 per cent respectively). Managers were more likely to report that paid parental leave was available compared with non-managerial employees (25 per cent and 18 per cent respectively).

## Time off for dependants

Employees have been legally entitled to take a reasonable amount of time off work to deal with certain unexpected events or sudden emergencies and to make any necessary longer-term arrangements since 1999. The definition of a dependant is not restricted to children but also includes a husband, wife or partner, or parent of the employee. It also includes someone who lives in the same household as a member of the family, for example, a grandparent. Managers were asked how employees usually took time off at short notice to deal with an emergency involving a child or family member. Less than 1 per cent of workplaces refused to allow employees to take time off in 1998 and in 2004. Managers were able to give more than one response when asked the type of leave usually taken by employees when dealing with an emergency. The arrangement most frequently available was special paid leave (49 per cent), followed by taking time off and making it up later (45 per cent). While it was rare for managers to refuse time off, emergency leave was unpaid in a substantial proportion of workplaces (44 per cent). Almost two-fifths (39 per cent) of managers said that employees usually took annual leave in order to deal with an emergency and one in ten said that employees usually took emergency time off work as sick leave.

Column 4 of Table 9.7 shows that there was substantial variation in provision of special paid leave to deal with an emergency involving a child or family member according to sector of ownership. Four-fifths of workplaces in the public sector said that paid leave was available compared with just over two-fifths of workplaces (43 per cent) in the private sector. In general, larger workplaces and workplaces where at least one union was recognized were more likely to provide special paid leave in emergencies. The association between union recognition and the incidence of paid time off in an emergency also held in private sector workplaces. Again, workplaces with higher proportions of women were more likely to provide special paid leave in an emergency compared to those where women were in the minority.

Employees were also asked how they would usually take time off work at short notice if they needed to look after their children or family members. Figure 9.4 illustrates the types of leave commonly taken by employees in dealing with an emergency in 2004. Almost all employees said that they would be able to take time off to deal with a family emergency, supporting the accounts provided by managers. However, employees commonly reported that they took annual leave to deal with an emergency (37 per cent) rather than special paid leave (11 per cent). Women were no more likely than men to report that special paid leave was available, but were slightly more likely than men to be able to work flexibly, by taking time off and making it up later, in order to deal with an emergency. Seventeen per cent of women said that they would take time off and make it up later compared with 14 per cent of men. Men, on the other hand, were more likely to take annual leave to deal with an emergency than women (43 per cent compared to 33 per cent).

Employees with children were slightly more likely to consider that special paid time off in emergencies was provided compared with those without children. Thirteen per cent of employees with pre-school children and a similar proportion with older children said that they would take special paid leave compared with ten per cent of employees without children. Carers of family members or friends with a long-term disability or mental illness or who had problems related to old age were slightly more likely to report that special paid

*Figure 9.4* How employees take time off work at short notice

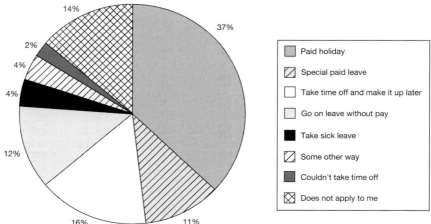

Base: All employees in workplaces with 10 or more employees.
Figures are weighted and based on responses from 20,999 employees.

leave was available compared with non-carers (13 per cent and 9 per cent, respectively). Carers were also slightly more likely to report that they would take time off in an emergency by using their annual leave compared with employees without such caring responsibilities (41 per cent compared with 37 per cent). Managers were more likely than non-managers to take time off and make it up later (24 per cent and 15 per cent respectively) but were no more likely to take up special paid leave or annual leave to deal with an emergency than non-managers.

*Change in the availability of paternity, parental and emergency leave*

It is not possible to examine change in the availability of paternity leave, parental leave or time off for emergencies in the 1998 and 2004 Cross-Section Surveys of Managers due to changes in question wording.[11] However, the 1998–2004 Panel Survey provides comparable data regarding the number of days of paid paternity leave provided, the availability of parental leave to at least some non-managerial employees, and the availability of emergency leave in continuing workplaces. Figure 9.5 shows the distribution of the number of paid

*Figure 9.5* Availability of paid paternity leave in continuing workplaces, by sector of ownership, 1998 and 2004

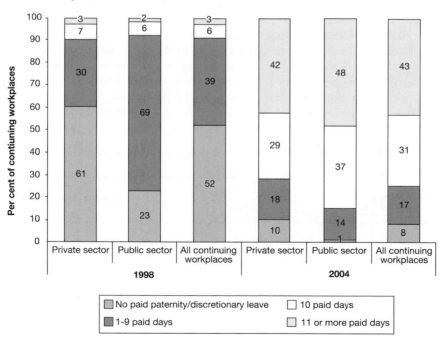

Base: All continuing workplaces with 10 or more employees.
Figures are weighted and based on responses from 847 managers.

days of paternity leave provided in 1998 and 2004 by sector of ownership. It is clear that there has been a substantial increase in the proportion of workplaces providing some paid paternity or discretionary leave for fathers since 1998, with around one half of all continuing workplaces providing paid leave for fathers in 1998 and most (92 per cent) continuing workplaces providing paid leave for fathers in 2004. In workplaces where leave was provided, the mean number of days provided rose from six days in 1998 to ten days in 2004. Considering parental leave, the proportion of workplaces providing this arrangement to at least some non-managerial employees also rose between 1998 and 2004 (from 38 per cent in 1998 to 73 per cent in 2004). These increases are perhaps unsurprising given the introduction of the right to unpaid parental leave in December 1999 and the right to paid paternity leave in April 2003.

Turning to emergency leave, Table 9.8 shows that the proportion of continuing establishments offering special paid leave increased from about one quarter in 1998 to about three-tenths in 2004 and the proportion of workplaces where employees dealt with an emergency by taking annual leave fell from 26 per cent to 22 per cent. The statutory provision is for unpaid emergency leave. The incidence of other ways of taking time off to deal with an emergency has remained relatively stable over time.

Workplaces in the public sector were more likely than those in the private sector to provide paternity, parental or special paid leave, in 1998 and 2004, according to the Panel Survey of Managers. However, the gap in provision between the two sectors for each of these arrangements has closed substantially since the late 1990s. Figure 9.5 illustrates the increase in the provision of paid paternity leave for fathers in continuing private sector workplaces between 1998 and 2004. As for the provision of parental leave for both mothers and fathers, 27 per cent of continuing workplaces in the private sector reported that parental leave was available compared with 68 per cent of public sector workplaces in 1998. By

*Table 9.8* Employer provision of time off work at short notice in continuing workplaces, 1998 and 2004

|  | *% of workplaces* | |
| --- | --- | --- |
|  | *1998* | *2004* |
| Take time off but make it up later | 21 | 20 |
| As leave without pay | 15 | 16 |
| As sick leave | 4 | 3 |
| As special paid leave | 24 | 31 |
| As annual leave | 26 | 22 |
| Not allowed | – | 0 |
| Never asked | 0 | 0 |
| Other/multiple combinations | 10 | 9 |

Base: All continuing workplaces with 10 or more employees.
Figures are weighted and based on responses from 936 managers.

2004, the gap had closed significantly so that 71 per cent of continuing private sector workplaces provided parental leave compared with 78 per cent of those in the public sector. Special paid emergency leave was available in 16 per cent of continuing private sector workplaces in 1998, compared to 46 per cent of public sector workplaces. By 2004, one quarter of private sector establishments provided special paid leave compared with one half of public sector workplaces.

## Support for carers of older adults

There has been growing policy and academic interest in the experience of carers, other than those with dependent children, particularly given the ageing profile of the population (Agree *et al.*, 2003; Hindess, 2003). For the first time in 2004, managers were asked whether any employees were entitled to a specific period of leave for carers of older adults (in addition to time off for emergencies). Managers were also asked whether any financial help with the care of older adults was provided. Six per cent of workplaces provided leave for carers, while financial help for carers was extremely rare (available in less than 1 per cent of establishments). Column 5 of Table 9.7 shows that larger workplaces and organizations were generally more likely to provide leave for carers than small workplaces or organizations. Workplaces that were part of a larger organization were also more likely to provide carers' leave (9 per cent compared to 1 per cent of single independent establishments). The public sector was four times more likely to provide leave for carers compared with the private sector. Workplaces where three-quarters of the workforce were female were about three times more likely to provide leave for the carers of older adults than workplaces where a quarter or less of the workforce was female. The incidence of leave for carers was rare among workplaces without a formal written equal opportunities policy compared to those with a formal policy (1 per cent and 8 per cent, respectively).

## Working hours

As the number of women participating in the labour market has increased in Britain over the past 30 years (Lindsay and Doyle, 2003: 472), the need for paid work to be compatible with caring responsibilities has become an important policy issue. There is evidence to suggest that a requirement to work full-time, or long hours, disadvantages employees with caring responsibilities, who are often women (see Kodz *et al.*, 2003: 207–208, for a review of the literature on this topic). Requiring employees to work long hours conflicts with the objective of creating 'a level playing field' in the workplace, in line with the 'managing diversity' agenda (Liff, 2003: 440). Within the European Union, the Part-Time Worker (Prevention of Less Favourable Treatment) Regulations (2000) and the Working Time Regulations (1998) go some way towards addressing this problem. This section looks at the hours worked by employees by their individual and workplace characteristics, as well as their personal circumstances and the characteristics of their job.

The Survey of Employees asked employees the number of hours that they worked each week, including overtime, or extra hours, but excluding meal breaks and time taken to travel to work. Overall employees worked an average of 36.1 hours a week. On average, this included 3.6 hours of overtime, with most overtime worked in the Transport and communication sector (4.9 hours). Part-time workers (defined as those working less than 30 hours a week) worked an average of 17.2 hours a week, while full-time employees worked an average of 41.6 hours a week.[12] Part-time employees were far less likely to work over-time than those who worked full-time (30 per cent did so compared to 54 per cent). Employees were more likely to work part-time hours in smaller work-places, in single independent establishments and in the public sector. The pro-portion of employees who usually worked more than 48 hours a week fell slightly between 1998 and 2004, from 13 per cent to 11 per cent, while a similar proportion worked between 39 and 48 hours a week in both years (37 per cent). However, within the Transport industry, which was excluded from the upper limit on hours under the Working Time Regulations until August 2003, working in excess of 48 hours a week was still common in 2004.[13] Thirty-one per cent of employees in the Transport industry worked more than 48 hours a week in 2004, compared to 29 per cent in 1998.

Besides asking employees the number of hours that they worked on average each week, in 2004 a new question was included in the Survey of Employees which asked the frequency with which employees had worked more than 48 hours a week over the previous 12 months. Fifty-four per cent of employees had not worked in excess of 48 hours a week at all over the previous year, while 18 per cent had done so less than once a month. Nineteen per cent of employees had worked more than 48 hours a week between one and three times a month and 9 per cent of employees had worked more than 48 hours every week over the previous year. This corresponded reasonably well with the proportion of employees reporting that they usually worked more than 48 hours a week (11 per cent).

Employees in private sector establishments tended to work more than 48 hours a week with greater frequency than those in public sector workplaces, and only around one half of employees in the private sector (51 per cent) had never worked more than 48 hours a week over the previous year, compared to three-fifths (61 per cent) of employees in the public sector. There appeared to be little difference between workplaces with and without union recognition, although where a union was recognized 8 per cent of employees had worked more than 48 hours every week over the previous year, compared to 11 per cent in work-places where no unions were recognized. Variation across industries was more dramatic. One-fifth of employees in the Transport and communication sector, and 15 per cent of those in the Education sector reported that they had worked more than 48 hours every week over the previous year. At the other end of the spectrum, two-thirds of employees in the Health sector had never worked more than 48 hours a week over the previous year, and this was also the case for more than three-fifths of employees in the Wholesale and retail (62 per cent), Financial services (61 per cent) and Public administration (62 per cent) sectors.

The fact that the concentration of part-time employees was relatively high in the Wholesale and retail and Health sectors (35 and 31 per cent of employees worked less than 30 hours a week respectively), probably explains why a small proportion of employees regularly worked more than 48 hours a week in these two sectors.

Managers were much less likely than non-managers to work part-time (7 per cent did so compared to 13 per cent of non-managerial supervisors, and 28 per cent of other employees). However, the proportion of managers working part-time did increase between 1998 and 2004 (from 3 per cent to 7 per cent), which could indicate that the Part-Time Workers (Prevention of Less Favourable Treatment) Regulations have made it easier for part-time workers to move into managerial posts, or that the expectation that it is necessary for managers to work full-time is slowly changing. Eighteen per cent of managers said that they had worked more than 48 hours every week over the previous year compared to 13 per cent of supervisors and 6 per cent of other non-managerial employees. Just 27 per cent of managers reported that they had never worked more than 48 hours a week over the previous year, compared to 41 per cent of supervisors and 63 per cent of other non-managers. The Cross-Section Survey of Managers also indicated that managers were more likely to work in excess of 48 hours a week than non-managerial employees.

Women were more likely to work part-time than men (35 per cent of women worked less than 30 hours a week, compared to 8 per cent of men), and 33 per cent of employees worked part-time in workplaces where more than half the workforce was female, compared to only ten per cent of the workforce in establishments where women did not make up the majority of the workforce. The tendency of women to work fewer hours was reflected in the fact that only 36 per cent of men reported that they had never worked more than 48 hours a week over the previous year, compared to 70 per cent of women. Similarly, employees had worked more than 48 hours a week on a less frequent basis in workplaces where more than half the workforce was female than where women did not compose the majority of the workforce. The relationship between gender, or the gender composition of the workforce, and the frequency with which employees worked more than 48 hours a week held when the analysis was restricted to full-time workers only.

Men were less likely to have worked more than 48 hours every week in workplaces where women composed more than half the workforce, compared to workplaces where a smaller proportion of the workforce was female (10 per cent compared to 17 per cent). By contrast, a similar proportion of women had worked more than 48 hours every week in workplaces where women were, and were not in the majority (5 per cent). A similar relationship was found when part-time workers were excluded from the analysis and broadly speaking, these associations held for all occupational groups, except Professionals. Within the Professional occupation, both men and women were more likely to have worked more than 48 hours every week where women made up more than half the workforce than where they did not.

There was also some variation in the hours worked by employees depending on their caring responsibilities. The gender of the respondent was an important factor in this. Women were particularly likely to work part-time if they had dependent children. While 27 per cent of women without dependent children worked part-time, almost half (49 per cent) of all women with dependent children worked less than 30 hours a week. This compared to just 4 per cent of men with dependent children, and 10 per cent of men without dependent children. In terms of the frequency with which long hours were worked, men with dependent children were more likely to have worked more than 48 hours every week over the previous year than men or women without dependent children, or women with dependent children. Women with dependent children were less likely to have worked more than 48 hours every week than any of the other groups. A similar pattern was observed when managerial employees were excluded from the analysis, suggesting that this does not simply reflect the greater likelihood that men are employed in managerial posts (noted in Chapter 2) where there is a tendency to work longer hours. It seems likely therefore that the greater frequency of working more than 48 hours a week by men with dependent children also reflects the responsibility placed on men to provide materially for the family where women do not work, work fewer hours, or receive a lower income because of relative pay disadvantage. Indeed, Kodz *et al.* (2003: 80–81) found that while the volume of work was an important factor in determining the hours worked by employees, increased pay, either because of paid overtime, or as a future reward for unpaid overtime, was also an important motivation for working long hours.

The Survey of Employees asked how much time employees spent giving help or support to family members or friends with a long-term physical or mental illness or disability, or with problems related to old age. Employees with these caring responsibilities were more likely to work part-time than those without caring responsibilities (26 per cent compared to 21 per cent). However, the proportions of employees with and without other caring responsibilities who had worked more than 48 hours every week over the previous year were very similar (9 per cent and 10 per cent respectively), although those with caring responsibilities were slightly more likely to have never worked more than 48 hours a week over the previous year than those without caring responsibilities (57 per cent and 53 per cent respectively). A similar proportion of employees with and without a long-term disability which affected the amount or type of work that they were able to do worked part-time (24 and 22 per cent respectively), and a similar proportion had worked more than 48 hours every week over the previous year (10 per cent and 9 per cent respectively). However, employees with a disability which affected the amount or type of work they did were more likely to have never worked more than 48 hours a week over the previous year (58 per cent compared to 53 per cent of those without a disability).

### Co-existence of work–life balance arrangements

The previous sections have examined employer provision of flexible working practices and arrangements to support employees with caring responsibilities. In addition, Chapter 4 reported on other arrangements which potentially allow employees to fit working around their responsibilities outside of work, namely, shift-working, night-working, temporary agency working and fixed-term and temporary contracts. This section examines the extent to which these arrangements co-exist within workplaces.

A factor analysis of the full range of 21 flexible working and support arrangements considered in this book suggested seven main categories. Table 9.9 shows the proportion of workplaces with at least one arrangement from each of these seven categories. The arrangements which make up each group are listed there. While the vast majority of workplaces provided at least one of the arrangements which allowed employees permanently to work non-standard hours, or to take extra-statutory leave on the birth of a child, very few workplaces helped any employees with the provision of care. Generally, public sector workplaces were more likely to offer at least one arrangement from any of the seven groups than private sector workplaces, but shift-working arrangements were more common in the private rather than in the public sector.

While there were no strong correlations between the seven categories of arrangements identified, a further factor analysis of the seven groups suggested that these indicated two distinct approaches by employers. The provision of

*Table 9.9* Incidence of work–life balance arrangements, by sector of ownership.

| | % of workplaces | | |
|---|---|---|---|
| | All workplaces | Public sector | Private sector |
| Extra-statutory leave at time of birth – some period of maternity or paternity leave on full pay | 82 | 98 | 77 |
| Extra-statutory leave for carers – paid parental leave, emergency leave, leave for the care of older adults | 56 | 85 | 50 |
| Provision of care – financial help with childcare, financial help with the care of older adults, workplace nursery | 8 | 18 | 6 |
| Permanent non-standard hours – any employees able to job-share, reduce, increase or compress hours, any part-time workers, term-time only contracts | 92 | 99 | 90 |
| Shift-working – any employees working shifts, able to change the shift pattern, night-working | 54 | 48 | 55 |
| Flexibility over staffing levels – any temporary agency workers, or employees on fixed-term or temporary contracts | 39 | 69 | 32 |
| Flexibility over location or hours of work – Homeworking, flexitime | 46 | 56 | 43 |

Base: All workplaces with 10 or more employees.
Figures are weighted and based on responses from at least 1,879 managers.

child or adult care, and extra-statutory leave emerged as one approach (hereafter referred to as 'the provision of caring or leave arrangements'). The other distinct approach (referred to as 'the provision of flexible working arrangements') comprised arrangements relating to shift-working, and permanent non-standard hours – arrangements which potentially offer the employee some flexibility to choose to work at times which are compatible with their family responsibilities. The practices which gave employers flexibility over staffing levels and employees flexibility over their location or hours of work did not load strongly on either of these two factors, and so were set to one side in the remainder of the analysis.

Four-fifths of all workplaces had at least one of the caring or leave arrangements, but less than 1 per cent of workplaces had all eight. The median number of caring and leave arrangements provided was two. The flexible working arrangements were more common, with almost all workplaces (95 per cent) having at least one of the nine arrangements, but again, very few workplaces (1 per cent) had all of the arrangements in place. The median number of flexible working arrangements available was four.

It could be argued that having a high number of caring or leave arrangements, or flexible working arrangements, is indicative of a comprehensive approach by an employer on either dimension. Having a variety of arrangements might also arguably benefit an employee by providing greater choice. Following this proposition, workplaces were divided about the median on the two counts described above, in order to categorize establishments into those following a more, or less, comprehensive approach to either care or leave, or flexible working. The two resulting summary variables were then tabulated against each other in order to examine the extent to which taking a comprehensive approach in one area might be associated with a comprehensive approach to the other. The analysis showed that a relatively small proportion of workplaces (14 per cent) provided a high number of both types of arrangement (more than the median number of caring or leave arrangements, and more than the median number of flexible working arrangements). A further fifth of workplaces took only a comprehensive approach to caring or leave, while the same proportion had only a comprehensive range of flexible working arrangements. The remaining 46 per cent of workplaces did not have a comprehensive approach to either of the two types of arrangement.

Public sector workplaces were more likely to provide a relatively high number of caring and leave arrangements than workplaces in the private sector (72 per cent and 25 per cent respectively), and they were also more likely to offer a wide range of flexible arrangements (51 per cent of public sector workplaces provided more than four arrangements compared to 32 per cent of private sector establishments). Workplaces in the public sector were thus more likely to have a wide range of both types of arrangement than private sector workplaces (36 per cent compared to 9 per cent). Equally, a far greater proportion of private sector workplaces did not have a comprehensive approach to caring or leave, or to flexibility (53 per cent, compared to 14 per cent of public sector workplaces).

*Managers' attitudes towards work–life balance*

Reported arrangements for flexible working and time off work provide one indicator of employer commitment to work–life balance. Another factor is management attitudes to this aspect of working life. Around two-thirds (65 per cent) of managers believed that it was up to individual employees to balance their work and family responsibilities, while 19 per cent disagreed that it was up to individual employees. Fifty-six per cent of employees worked in establishments where managers believed that it was up to the individual to manage their work and family responsibilities, and only 26 per cent of employees were in workplaces where managers disagreed with the statement. Given this, it is perhaps surprising that 58 per cent of employees found managers understanding of their family responsibilities.

More than two-thirds (69 per cent) of managers in private sector establishments thought that it was up to individuals to balance their work and family responsibilities, compared to 47 per cent of managers in public sector workplaces. In line with this, employees were more likely to find managers understanding in the public than in the private sector. However, while managers were more likely to think that it was up to the individual to balance their work and family responsibilities in smaller workplaces and in single independent establishments, employees took a very different view, being more likely to find managers understanding in such workplaces. Management views and employee experiences also differed with regard to union recognition. Managers in workplaces which recognized a union were less likely to believe that it was up to the individual to balance work and family responsibilities. However, employees working in establishments without recognized were unions more likely to find managers understanding of their family responsibilities. One explanation for this may be that unions encourage the employer to take an interest in helping employees to balance their work and family responsibilities, or that employers who recognize unions are more interested in the welfare of their employees, but the association between union membership and lower levels of job satisfaction, perhaps due to higher expectations of working life on the part of union members (Bryson *et al.*, 2004: 451), depresses employee reports.

Managers' attitudes also varied according to the gender composition of the workforce. Managers were more likely to think that it was up to the individual to balance their work and family responsibilities where women made up half or less of the workforce, compared to where they composed more than half of employees. Consistent with this, a greater proportion of employees found managers understanding of their responsibilities outside of work in workplaces where a greater proportion of the workforce was female; in addition, female employees were more likely to believe that managers were understanding of their responsibilities outside of work than male employees. Attitudes also differed depending on the gender of the management respondent, with male managers more likely to believe that it was up to the individual to balance their work and family responsibilities than female managers.

There was a strong association between the employer having a range of flexible working arrangements and management views on individual responsibility for work–life balance. Managers were less likely to believe that it was up to individuals to balance their work and family responsibilities in workplaces where some employees were allowed to work term-time only, flexitime, to reduce or increase their hours, job-share, work at home, or compress their hours, than in workplaces without these policies. This was largely verified by employees, who were more likely to report that managers were understanding where they believed that if needed, they would have access to all of these practices, but also where they thought they would be able to change their hours of work. Likewise, managers were less likely to believe that it was up to individuals to balance their work and family responsibilities where the workplace offered special paid leave for family emergencies, paid parental leave, some period of maternity or paternity leave on full pay, financial help with the care of older adults, leave for carers or older adults, a workplace nursery, or financial help with childcare. Employees were only asked if they thought they would have access to three arrangements (paid parental leave, childcare assistance or emergency leave), and they were more likely to find managers understanding in workplaces where they believed that paid parental leave or childcare assistance would be made personally available to them if it was required.

While women with dependent children were significantly more likely to find managers understanding than women without dependent children, there was no difference in the proportion of men with and without dependent children who found managers understanding. Employees with caring responsibilities but without dependent children were less likely to find managers understanding than employees with dependent children but no other caring responsibilities. This indicates that there is greater recognition by employers of the need to be understanding of the responsibilities that employees with children have outside of work than of employees with caring responsibilities more generally.

Employees who worked fewer hours each week were more likely to believe that managers were understanding of their responsibilities outside of work than employees who worked long hours. Despite this, managers, who earlier in the chapter were shown to usually work longer hours than non-managers, were more likely to report that managers were understanding of their responsibilities outside of work than non-managerial employees. Employees tended to work longer hours where managers believed that it was up to the individual to balance their work and family responsibilities. These findings suggest that the number of hours worked by the employee and their perception of whether managers are understanding of their family responsibilities are interlinked.

There was little change in employees' views on the extent to which managers were understanding about employees having to meet responsibilities outside of work between 1998 and 2004, although there was a slight increase (from 8 per cent to 12 per cent) in the proportion of employees who *strongly* agreed that managers were understanding. In 2004, 58 per cent of employees found managers understanding compared to 55 per cent in 1998. In contrast to the similarity between employee views in 1998 and 2004, there was a significant decrease in the proportion of managers who believed that it was up to the individual to balance their work and family responsibilities between 1998 and 2004 (from 84 per cent to 65 per cent). In continuing workplaces, 80 per cent of managers believed that it was up to the individual to balance their work and family responsibilities in 1998 while 67 per cent of managers took this view in 2004. An analysis of both the Panel Survey and the Cross-Section Surveys in 1998 and 2004 revealed that the reduction in the proportion of managers in continuing workplaces who believed that it was up to individuals to balance their work and family responsibilities accounted for the largest element of this change (9 per cent). However, the fact that managers in new workplaces were less likely to believe that it was up to individual employees to balance their work and family responsibilities than managers in workplaces which closed between 1998 and 2004 also accounted for a significant proportion of this change in attitudes (5 per cent). Only 1 per cent of the reduction in the proportion of managers who believed that it was up to individuals to balance their work and family responsibilities was due to managers in workplaces which fell out of scope (that is, they had ten or more employees in 1998, but less than ten by 2004) being more likely to take this view than managers in workplaces which came into scope between 1998 and 2004. The change in the attitude of managers between 1998 and 2004 seemed most pronounced in the public sector. Within 73 per cent of continuing private sector workplaces, managers believed that it was up to the individual to balance their work and family responsibilities in 2004, compared to 81 per cent in 1998. In contrast, the proportion of public sector continuing workplaces where managers took this view fell to 48 per cent from 75 per cent over this same period.

## Conclusion

WERS 2004 demonstrates that an increasing number of employers have sought to address employment inequality since 1998, although this type of activity is still more heavily concentrated in the public sector, larger workplaces and in workplaces with recognized unions. The activities of a minority of employers indicate a 'managing diversity' approach to equal opportunities, with some providing leave for the carers of older adults, and not just for employees with children. Again, this was more common in the public sector. However, very few employers monitored and reviewed the implementation of their equal opportunities policies across gender, ethnicity, disability and age. Indeed, a less systematic approach to monitoring and reviewing by some, but not all, of these characteristics was much more common across workplaces. There was some evidence that the practice of monitoring reflected the composition of the workforce. Certainly, employers may feel that there is less need to monitor or review promotions, or review relative pay rates in workplaces without a diverse workforce, although monitoring may increase awareness of the composition of the workforce where characteristics are not always visible, for example, in the case of disability.

While still the majority view, a smaller proportion of managers believed that it was up to individual employees to balance their work and family responsibilities in 2004 than in 1998, implying that employers are increasingly recognizing how the diverse circumstances facing employees impact upon their work. However, this change was not reflected in the views of employees, indicating that where management views have shifted, this is not yet manifest to employees. Despite this employee viewpoint, the incidence of a range of paid leave and some flexible working arrangements increased since 1998, as reported by both managers and employees, demonstrating that the change in management attitude has, to some extent, been backed up by action. It is possible that employee perceptions of management understanding may be driven by cultural factors, rather than purely by the policies to which they have access. For example, Liff and Ward (2001:30) found that even where formal policies are available to employees, take-up may be low if employees feel that they could be disadvantaged in terms of their future career because of management perceptions that employees using such policies are less committed to the organization. Such perceptions could take a long time to change and so are not apparent over the period since 1998.

It is also apparent that the long hours worked by some employees present a barrier to workforce diversity, and particularly diversity in managerial grades. The results indicated that a significant proportion of employees worked more than 48 hours a week. Men were more likely than women to work more than 48 hours a week, even excluding part-time workers, and managers were more likely to work more than 48 hours a week than non-managerial employees. Managers were also less likely to be allowed to reduce their hours, or work flexitime. This, coupled with the fact that women tend to take a greater responsibility for the family than men, may contribute to the under-representation of women in management grades relative to the gender composition of the workforce, as shown in Chapter 2. This suggests that cultural change, in terms of reducing the workload of managers and addressing the measurement of the contribution of employees by hours worked rather than outputs, consistent with the 'managing diversity' approach, is still needed in many workplaces in order to enhance equality in outcomes.

# 10 Workplace climate and performance

## Introduction

For much of the post-war period through to the 1980s economic observers and analysts of employment relations in Britain were primarily concerned with the way in which trade unions affected wages and productivity, and the consequential effects on workplace performance, company profits and – at the macro-economic level – inflation and shareholder confidence in British firms. How workers and managers interacted with each other collectively to create the 'climate' of employment relations was also considered important, primarily because of the role it was thought to play in mediating the link between workplace practices and productivity. How workers felt at work, and the impact that work had on their well-being more generally, was the preserve of sociologists and psychologists. This focus on unions and performance began to change in the 1980s for a number of reasons. First, the decline of trade unions in the private sector led to an increased interest in what was happening in the ever-growing non-union sector. Second, human resource analysts and advocates drew attention to the importance of management and management-initiated practices in influencing performance. Third, there was increasing acceptance of what sociologists and psychologists had been saying for a long time, namely that there were clear, albeit complex, links between how workers felt about their work and their performance at work. This led to a burgeoning literature on the relationship between worker well-being, motivation, productivity and performance. Finally, and perhaps most recently, there has been growing interest in worker well-being as an issue in its own right – regardless of its significance or otherwise for performance.

Of course, this characterization of the changing debates surrounding employment relations is broad-brush. Employment relations academics and practitioners have always shown some interest in non-union structures and practices, management practices, and the well-being of workers. But there has been a shift in the focus of the discipline such that these have become central to current debates, rather than being peripheral. This shift is reflected in the content and design of the WERS series. In particular, the 1998 survey collected information on work practices and procedures that had been largely absent from earlier surveys, which had concentrated much more on union-management practices and relations. Also, for the first time, it introduced the voice of employees through the Survey of Employees rather than relying on worker representatives' and managers' reports. This has allowed analysts to link employees (and what they are thinking and saying about their jobs and their employer) to the actual structures and practices they face at work, an approach illustrated throughout this book.

Earlier chapters have investigated employee job satisfaction and well-being. This chapter returns to what might be viewed as the more traditional concerns of employment relations. It focuses on 'outcomes' that have traditionally been central to the interests of employment relations scholars and policy-analysts, namely management-employee relations, labour productivity and workplace financial performance. Such outcomes might be regarded as primarily workplace-focused rather than employee-focused, but of course, employees care an awful lot about their relations with management and about matters that might impinge upon their pay or job security (Kersley *et al.*, 2005: 33–35).

The analysis exploits some of the unique features of the WERS data. First, following the approach adopted by the research team in 1998 (Cully *et al.*, 1999: 282–291), it compares and contrasts employee and employer perceptions of management-employee relations within and across workplaces. Second, it explores the associations between each of the outcome variables and an array of employee characteristics, workplace characteristics and workplace practices, drawing on a number of data items and indices, many of which have already been introduced in earlier chapters. Finally, the chapter takes a first step in comparing managers' subjective ratings of workplace productivity with information on output and value-added per worker provided by the new Financial Performance Questionnaire (FPQ). The findings and conclusions set out in the chapter will be of interest to a wider readership while the detail of the data analysis procedures, together with the discussion of methodological issues, will be of particular relevance to academic readers and those with an interest in further analysis of the WERS datasets.

## Management-employee relations

Relations between management and employees are one aspect of the multi-faceted concept of 'employment relations climate'. Because the climate is multi-faceted, it is best captured with validated multi-item scales (Dastmalchian *et al.*, 1989, 1991; Deery *et al.*, 1999). However, it is not practical in a multi-purpose survey like WERS to devote the survey space needed for the collection of these dedicated items. Instead, some analysts have constructed their own composite indexes of managerial relations using items that happen to be included in the WERS Survey of Employees (Guest *et al.*, 1999; Ramsay *et al.*, 2000). This analysis, on the other hand, follows Cully *et al.* (1999: Chapter 12) in focusing on a single item asked of both managers and employees in WERS, which provides an opportunity to explore perceptions of employment relations from perspective of both parties within the same workplaces, and across work-places as a whole.

Employees were asked: 'In general, how would you describe relations between managers and employees here?' Managers were asked: 'How would you rate the relationship between management and employees generally at this workplace?' Both measures have five-category response scales ranging from 'very good' to 'very poor'. The employer measure is the one used in previous studies (Fernie and Metcalf, 1995; Fernie *et al.*, 1994; Wood and de Menezes, 1998). It is sometimes described in this literature as a measure of 'employee relations climate' (Wood and de Menezes, 1998: 503). It is certainly the case that it is intended to capture what Dastmalchian *et al.* (1989: 23) describe as 'a char-acteristic atmosphere in the organization ... as perceived by organizational members'. Furthermore, as in the case of validated climate scales, it is often treated as an 'intervening variable' that is affected by structural features of the workplace but can also influence, or be influenced by, 'end result' variables such as workplace conflict. This section investigates the nature of these employment relations measures to establish the relationship between managerial and employee perceptions of climate within the same workplace and over time; whether they relate to other workplace-level outcomes as one might anticipate; and the factors associated with managerial and employee perceptions of management-employee relations in 2004.

## Comparison of employee and managerial perceptions of management-employee relations

Table 10.1 shows managers' and employees' perceptions of employee–manage-ment relations in 1998 and 2004. Across workplaces as a whole, managerial perceptions of management-employee relations appear to have improved since 1998. Analysis of the 1998–2004 Panel Survey supports this finding, as in 30

*Table 10.1* Managers' and employees' perceptions of employment relations, 1998 and 2004

|  | Managers | | Employees | |
|  | 1998 | 2004 | 1998 | 2004 |
|  | % workplaces | | % employees | |
| --- | --- | --- | --- | --- |
| Very good | 41 | 47 | 16 | 19 |
| Good | 47 | 46 | 40 | 41 |
| Neither good nor poor | 8 | 6 | 27 | 24 |
| Poor | 3 | 1 | 12 | 12 |
| Very poor | 1 | 0 | 6 | 4 |

Base (columns 1 and 2): All workplaces with 10 or more employees.
Base (columns 3 and 4): All employees in workplaces with 10 or more.
Figures are weighted and based on responses from 2,188 (column 1) and 2,045 managers (column 2), and 27,719 (column 3) and 21,278 employees (column 4).

per cent of continuing workplaces relations had 'improved a lot'. The same proportion reported that they had 'improved a little', with only 4 per cent of continuing workplaces reporting a deterioration since 1998. However, a comparison of employees' perceptions in 1998 and 2004 suggested little improvement.

Comparing managerial and employee perceptions of relations *within the same workplace*, again employees were less positive about relations than managers. Half of all employees (51 per cent) had a more negative perception of relations than their workplace's managerial respondent, whereas only 13 per cent gave a rating that was more positive than that of the managerial respondent. In the remaining one-third (36 per cent) of cases both parties agreed. These findings for 2004 resemble those for the population of establishments with 25 or more employees in 1998 reported by Cully *et al.* (1999: 283).

### Correlations between employee perceptions of management-employee relations within the workplace

It is only meaningful to talk of 'a climate' of employment relations within the workplace if there is a reasonable correlation between the perceptions of climate reported by employees within the same workplace. This can be measured using the correlation between individual employees' rating and their establishment's mean for workplaces where two or more employees responded. The correlation coefficient was reasonably high at 0.50, rising slightly to 0.51 when Managers and senior officials were excluded. Restricting the analysis to workplaces that yielded at least three employee respondents made no difference to the size of the coefficient, and it always remained above 0.42 regardless of the number of employee respondents, up to the maximum of 25. This reasonably high correlation between employees' perceptions of employment relations within the same workplace suggests the measure is indeed capturing an attribute of the workplace, and not simply an attribute of individuals.

### Correlations between employee and managerial perceptions of management-employee relations and other 'climate' indicators

Managerial and employee perceptions of employment relations were correlated with a number of features of the working environment in the way one would expect from a climate measure (Table 10.2). To explore these associations, the management and employee indicators of climate were coded so that lower values indicated poorer employment relations.[1] The correlations with binary indicators of events such as dismissals or collective disputes were then examined.[2] Perceptions of employment relations were poorer where, in the past 12 months, employees had been dismissed or made redundant, there had been a collective dispute over pay or conditions, there had been industrial action at the workplace, employees had been issued with written warnings, been suspended with or without pay, had deductions made from their pay, or been internally transferred. Employee perceptions of employment relations were also poorer

*Table 10.2* Correlations between perceptions of employment relations and other aspects of the employment relations 'climate'

|  | *Managers* | *Employees* |
|---|---|---|
| Any employees dismissed | −0.179 | −0.119 |
| Any collective dispute over pay/conditions | −0.124 | −0.082 |
| Any industrial action at the establishment | −0.144 | −0.063 |
| Any formal written warnings to employees | −0.223 | −0.147 |
| Any suspensions of employees without pay | −0.198 | −0.125 |
| Any deductions from pay | −0.082 | −0.043 |
| Any internal transfer for disciplinary reasons | −0.150 | −0.080 |
| Any redundancies | −0.164 | −0.098 |
| % days lost through employee sickness/absence | −0.041 | −0.017 |

Notes:

Sample sizes are at least 17,793 in the case of employees and at least 1,279 for managers. The data from managers exclude those workplaces where no employee questionnaires were returned.

Figures are correlation coefficients. All are statistically significant at the 1 per cent level except the correlations with the percentage of days lost, where the correlation with employee perceptions is significant at the 2 per cent level and the correlation with managerial perceptions is not significant.

The coding of the various items is described in endnotes 1 and 2 of Chapter 10.

where the percentage of working days lost through absence or sickness was higher, but this relationship, although negative, was not statistically significant in the case of managers.

## *Independent associations between managerial perceptions of management-employee relations and other factors*

To establish which factors were independently associated with managerial perceptions of management-employee relations, multivariate models were run on weighted data, using the same management indicator described above in respect of Table 10.2, such that positive coefficients indicated that the factor was associated with 'better' relations. A 'baseline' model was specified, containing respondent characteristics (gender, job tenure, and job title), structural features of the workplace (size, multi- or single-site, private/public sector, industry, age, region, ownership), and workforce composition (in terms of gender, age, ethnicity, and occupation). 'Blocks' of additional variables – relating, for instance, to high-involvement management – were then added to this baseline individually to see what relationship they bore to perceptions of climate after controlling for the variables in the baseline specification. The blocks grouped factors under the following headings: high-involvement management practices; 'voice' practices; collective bargaining structures and coverage; union recognition and density; equal opportunities policies and practices; flexible working practices and those associated with creating a work–life balance. Many of these practices have been introduced in preceding chapters, but some are new or have been combined in scales that have not been presented earlier. Full details of these groups of variables are provided on the WERS website at: http://www.dti.gov.uk/employment/research-evaluation/wers-2004/index.html.

In keeping with the rest of the book, analyses were confined to workplaces with at least 10 employees and, due to space constraints, models are reported for the whole economy only.[3] Instead of reporting all significant results, the discussion focuses on those factors that have featured prominently in the literature, or are of particular policy relevance. The objective is to identify statistically significant effects controlling for the factors included in the baseline model.[4] Full results are presented on the Routledge website at: http://www.routledge.com/textbooks/0415378133.

In the baseline model, perceptions varied with the nature of the respondent. Male employment relations managers had poorer perceptions of relations than their female counterparts, and perceptions improved with the time managers spent in the job. Analyses of the 1990 WIRS found employment relations specialists, as indicated by their job title, had poorer perceptions of management-employee relations than other managers responsible for managing workplace employment relations (Fernie *et al.*, 1994). This was still the case in 2004 for specialists with 'Human Resources' in their job title, and those with 'Employee/Staff/Industrial Relations' in their title, but the perceptions of 'Personnel Managers/Officers' were no poorer than the perceptions of proprietors/owners, Finance Managers or General Managers. The group of workplace characteristics explained a statistically significant amount of the variation in managers' perceptions of climate, with perceptions varying by industry and region, and deteriorating with establishment size. The workforce composition variables were also jointly significant.[5]

Traditionally, employment relations academics have focused on union effects on the climate of relations, with empirical evidence indicating that the presence of recognized trade unions can negatively affect managerial perceptions, especially in the presence of multiple unions or fragmented bargaining (Fernie and Metcalf, 1995). By the late 1990s, this situation appeared to have altered: union recognition was still associated with poorer managerial perceptions of climate, but the only bargaining arrangement associated with poorer managerial perceptions was the presence of single unions (Bryson, 2005). The results of the current analysis suggest that the situation may have changed once more by 2004. When added to the baseline model, neither bargaining structure nor the number of recognized unions was associated with employer perceptions of management-employee relations.

Attention has recently focused on the role performed by on-site union representatives, with evidence suggesting that full-time lay union representatives can enhance managerial perceptions of climate, performing the 'lubricating' role identified by the Donovan Commission many years ago (Bryson, 2005). This was not borne out by analyses for 2004. Analyses for the whole economy indicated that, when the nature of union representation was added to the baseline model, together with other channels of communication between management and employees, union lay representation had no significant independent effect on how managers felt about workplace relations.

One can conceive of workplace unionization as one form of employee 'voice', as discussed in Chapter 5. Voice necessarily entails opportunities for two-way communication between management and employees and can be delivered through a union or non-union employee representative, or through direct communication between management and employees. A variable identifying all eight combinations of union, non-union representative and direct voice – including 'no voice' – was added to the baseline model, together with an array of one-way communication channels such as the management chain, use of e-mail, the intranet, and so on. The only voice regime that was associated with better employer perceptions of climate than 'no voice' was a regime involving direct voice mechanisms but no representative voice. Indeed, the 'direct-voice only' regime was associated with significantly better perceptions of climate than all the other regimes, except 'union-only voice' and the combination of direct voice and non-union representative voice, where the differences were not statistically significant.[6] Breaking the typology down into its constituent practices, it was apparent that this positive association with direct voice was driven by the effects of problem-solving groups and regular meetings between senior management and the workforce.[7] These findings are reminiscent of Fernie and Metcalf's (1995) findings using WIRS 1990. However, whereas Fernie and Metcalf uncovered negative associations between management's perceptions of climate and team briefings, and a negative association with use of the management chain, neither were significant in the 2004 analyses.

Chapter 4 identified other managerial practices geared towards increasing employee involvement in their jobs and the wider working environment, sometimes labelled 'high involvement management' (HIM) practices. Usually regarded as means by which to enhance employee performance, they may also have an impact on managerial perceptions of climate. This impact may be positive where the practices are either welcomed by employees, are a source of satisfaction to managers who have taken credit for their smooth implementation, or have had demonstrable positive effects on productivity or performance. One might expect the opposite relationship if the converse happens. Although one might anticipate such effects, they have not been investigated empirically to date.

The analysis distinguished between task practices, such as team-working, and a range of supporting practices comprising: recruitment, appraisal and development practices; communication practices; welfare practices; and financial incentives.[8] These were added to the baseline model together with a variable identifying workplaces with at least one practice from all five domains. This indicator identifying workplaces that 'bundled' together all five types of practices was associated with poorer managerial perceptions of climate.

Managerial perceptions of relations were significantly better in the presence of communication practices. This effect increased with the number of practices.

Distinguishing between separate practices in this domain, the only practice that proved statistically significant in isolation was monthly meetings between senior management and the workforce. Although no single task practice was associated with managerial perceptions of employment relations, their perceptions improved as the number of task practices increased.

Where workplaces had one or more practices relating to recruitment, appraisal and development, managerial perceptions of climate were poorer than in workplaces where these practices were wholly absent. Separating the practices in this group revealed a more complicated picture: the use of personality tests in filling non-managerial posts was associated with better managerial perceptions of climate, whereas regular formal performance appraisal was associated with poorer perceptions. Finally, welfare practices and financial incentives were not associated with employer perceptions of climate. It appears that any gains in employment relations climate arising from HIM practices are uncertain, at least from a managerial perspective.

Chapter 3 showed a number of ways in which one can identify how 'strategic' an employer is in handling employment relations matters. Three measures of HR strategy were added to the baseline model: having a business strategy that covered employment relations issues; HR involvement in devising the business strategy; and Investors in People (IiP) accreditation. Having a strategy covering employment relations issues was associated with better managerial perceptions of management-employee relations. An increase in the number of these practices can be interpreted as an indicator of the degree of HR integration with the business plan. This indicator was positively associated with managerial perceptions of climate.

### Independent associations between employee perceptions of management-employee relations and other factors

The baseline model for the multivariate analyses of employee perceptions of management-employee relations contained precisely the same employer-level variables as the employer model, plus the characteristics of the individual employee (gender, age, ethnicity, academic and vocational qualifications, disability, household circumstances, and union membership) and their job (occupation, hourly wage, contractual status, tenure, training, and gender segregation of the job within the workplace). Individuals' characteristics were jointly significant: controlling for workplace characteristics and the employee's job characteristics, being male, union membership, vocational and academic qualifications and having a work-limiting disability were associated with poorer perceptions of climate, while parents living as a couple had better perceptions of management-employee relations than employees in other household circumstances. Younger and older employees had better perceptions of climate than middle-aged employees. Employees' job characteristics were also jointly significant: part-time employment, higher hourly pay, more training, and less gender segregation in the employee's job were all independently associated with better employee perceptions of management-employee relations. In contrast to managers, employees' perceptions of climate deteriorated with tenure at the workplace. Perceptions differed markedly across occupations, Managers and senior officials having the best perceptions of climate, followed by Administrative and secretarial occupations. Skilled trades had the poorest perceptions, followed by Plant and machine operatives.

Employee perceptions of climate differed with the type of manager responsible for employee relations at the workplace. 'Human Resources' and 'Employee/Industrial Relations' managers were associated with poorer employee perceptions of climate than 'Personnel Managers', 'General Managers' and owner-managers. This pattern was similar to that found among managers themselves, suggesting that the association between employment relations specialists and poorer climate was not merely an artefact of the perceptions of the sorts of managers who filled such posts. Perceptions were also better where the manager responsible for employment relations had been in post for over 10 years. However, when added to the baseline model, indicators of strategic HR management were not associated with employee perceptions of workplace relations.

Structural features of the workplace were jointly significant in explaining variation in employee perceptions of climate. As well as marked variations across industries and regions, perceptions were better in single-establishment organizations and in smaller establishments, a common finding in the literature.[9] Less well known is the extent to which the composition of the workplace appears to matter to employees when evaluating employment relations. Employees judged the climate as better where women made up a higher proportion of employees at the workplace, where there were some very young workers, and where there was little ethnic diversity in the workforce. Which occupation formed the largest occupational group within the workforce also affected perceptions.

For over two decades, commentators have maintained that what matters for the climate of employment relations and, indeed, for union effects on other outcomes such as productivity and profits, is not whether a union exists on-site, but how management responds to unions, something Freeman and Medoff (1984: 5–16) termed the 'institutional response' to unionism. Following this logic, one might anticipate a positive link between management's preparedness to engage positively with the union and the manager's perception that workplace employment relations are good. When added to the baseline model union recognition was associated with poorer employee perceptions of management-employment relations whereas, as reported earlier, it was not significant in explaining managers' perceptions. As Freeman and Medoff might have anticipated, managerial attitudes to union membership mattered to employees: perceptions of climate were poorest by far where the managerial respondent said management 'actively discouraged' union membership at the workplace. However, employee perceptions of climate were no better where an employer expressed active support for membership than in settings where the managerial respondent expressed passive support, neutrality or was simply 'not in favour' of union membership. Furthermore, the inclusion of managerial attitudes to union membership alongside union recognition had no impact on the effect of union recognition.

The early literature on perceptions of climate identified a negative association between fragmented bargaining and workplace relations (Fernie and Metcalf, 1995). Analyses for WERS 1998 found little support for this association among employers but there was evidence of such an association for employees whose perceptions of climate were poorer in the presence of multiple unionism and fragmented bargaining (Bryson, 2005). In 2004, neither multiple unionism nor the nature of bargaining arrangements had any effect on employee perceptions over and above that of union recognition *per se*. However, adding union density to the baseline model revealed that the negative association between unionization and employee perceptions of climate was confined to instances where a majority of employees at the workplace were union members.

None of the eight 'voice' regimes identified earlier were associated with better employee perceptions of climate than was the case where there were no 'voice' arrangements in place. However, union-only voice was associated with significantly better perceptions of climate than regimes in which union voice was present alongside direct voice or non-union representative voice. Similarly, direct voice-only was associated with significantly better perceptions of climate than direct voice in combination with union or non-union representative voice. These findings suggest that, at least from an employee perspective, voice channels may be substitutes for one another rather than complements.[10]

Breaking the eight-way voice typology into its constituent practices, employee perceptions of climate were poorer where unions were recognized for pay bargaining than in instances where unions were not recognized for bargaining. Climate was perceived as particularly poor where the representative of the recognized union was off-site. However, it would be wrong to assume that the 'problem' necessarily lies with types of voice that engage in pay bargaining since climate perceptions were poorer in the presence of joint consultative committees than they were in their absence (such committees do not usually bargain over pay). Furthermore, none of the direct forms of voice were positively associated with employee perceptions of climate in isolation, the only effect being the negative one of monthly meetings between the whole workforce and senior management where at least some time was devoted to employee voice (in contrast, this form of communication was positively associated with managers' perceptions of climate). It seems that, if one is looking to voice mechanisms to foster better management-employee relations, some forms of direct voice appear to 'work' for managers, but there are no easy answers when it comes to employees.

Similar conclusions can be drawn from analyses of the 'high involvement management' (HIM) practices and their relationship with perceptions of management-employee relations. Although, as in the case of managers, having at least one communication practice was linked to better employee perceptions of climate, there were no added benefits of having multiple communications practices. As in the case of managers, having at least one practice in the

'Recruitment, appraisal and development' group was associated with poorer climate perceptions. Contrary to managers, this association strengthened with the number of such practices. Unpacking the sets of practices revealed that the positive effect of job security guarantees and the negative effect of a three-step disciplinary procedure, both of which come within the set of practices labelled 'welfare' practices, tended to cancel each other out such that 'welfare' practices taken together had no significant effect on employee perceptions of climate. This was also the case with 'task' practices, the positive association with team working being off-set by the negative association with suggestion schemes. The presence of at least one practice from each of the five dimensions – the indicator of 'bundled' HIM – was not associated with employee perceptions.

In exploring the relationship between employee perceptions of climate, flexible working practices and care and leave arrangements, eight sets of practices were identified. These closely resemble the sets discussed in Chapter 9. However, they are not identical since the focus of the earlier analysis was 'work–life balance' whereas the analysis here extends a little further into flexible working practices where employers have some strategic choice in terms of how they deploy their labour force (see Chapter 4). These practices include contracting–in and out, for instance. Informed by preliminary principal components analysis, the eight domains or zones were defined in the following way using data obtained from the employer, not employees. 'Flexible hours contracts' consisted of annual hours and zero hours contracts. 'Hours flexibility' included the ability to increase or reduce hours, job-sharing, term-time working and part-time working. 'Flexible home arrangements' included home-working, flexitime and compressed hours. 'Shift and night work' included the incidence of shift working and night-working at the workplace, and the ability of workers to alter their shift patterns. 'Peripheral workers' practices consisted of the presence of fixed-term contract workers, temporary agency workers, any contracting–in and any contracting–out. Together, these five sets of practices were labelled 'flexible working practices'. The remaining three domains were labelled 'care/leave practices'. The first, which identified 'special leave arrangements', covered leave for the care of elderly people, paid or special leave for paternity or maternity, and special leave arrangements for family emergencies. The second identified payments to employees on maternity or paternity leave that exceeded the statutory minima ('extra-statutory payments'). The third related to 'financial assistance' to employees to meet their care responsibilities and included financial help with childcare, the provision of a workplace nursery, and financial help with care of the elderly.

The analysis explored the relationship between these practices and employee perceptions of climate in a number of alternative ways. First, it identified the presence or otherwise of at least one practice within each domain using zero/one indicators for the presence or otherwise of each domain. Second, it identified the number of practices the workplace had in each domain. Third, it identified 'bundles' of practices. These were defined in terms of the number of 'flexible working practices' at the workplace, a score running from zero to five depending on the number of times the workplace had at least one practice in each of the 'flexible working' domains, and a count running from 0 to 3 relating to the number of 'care/leave practice' domains in which it had practices. Fourth, the analysis also investigated the effect of each practice in isolation.

Adding variables counting the number of practices within the eight domains described above to the baseline model, practices associated with flexible hours tended to be associated with poorer employee perceptions of climate, apart from some which permitted flexibility with respect to working at home. 'Flexible hours contracts', 'flexible hours working', 'shift and night work' and 'peripheral workers' were all associated with poorer perceptions of climate. So too, perhaps surprisingly, were 'extra-statutory payments'. The one set of practices positively associated with employee perceptions of climate was 'flexible home arrangements'. Looking at each practice in isolation in the baseline model, together with count variables for the number of 'flexible working' domains and 'care/ leave' domains, the positive association between climate and 'flexible home arrangements' was driven by home-working and compressed hours; the negative association with 'hours flexibility' was due to the effect of job-sharing and the ability to increase one's hours; shift working, rather than night work, accounted for the effect of 'shift and night working'; and 'peripheral workers' combined the negative effect of temporary working and contracting–out with the positive effect of fixed-term contracts. The count of flexible working domains was negatively associated with employee perceptions of climate whereas the count of 'care/leave' domains had no significant effect. Taken together, these effects suggest a variety of flexible forms of working were associated with poorer perceptions of climate, whereas many practices which one might have anticipated as having a positive association with employee perceptions of climate had little or no effect, with few exceptions. It does appear, however, that these practices mattered to employees in terms of the way they viewed their workplace. This is in stark contrast to managers for whom they appeared to matter very little.[11]

## Labour productivity and workplace performance in the private sector

There has always been interest in the productivity of British workers, occasioned in large part by concerns about the gap between British productivity and that of Britain's competitors. Depending on the academic discipline, analysts tend to focus on different influences on productivity levels and growth, including finance markets and capital ownership, the skills base, and the role of the state. However, the perspective of the employment relations and human resource management literature, which attaches particular weight to workplace-level practices, has attracted increased attention since it raises the possibility that employers, through their labour and management practices, can make choices which have a decisive influence over labour productivity and, thus, workplace performance (see, for instance, the special edition of the *Scottish Journal of Political Economy* devoted to this issue (vol. 52, no. 3, July 2005)). In practice, it has been somewhat harder for analysts to identify practices that have an unambiguous positive influence over productivity. The elusiveness of the link between workplace practices and performance has led some to conclude that there are no 'best practices' and that 'what works' is contingent upon the circumstances in which a workplace finds itself – the nature of the production process, and product and labour markets. Others have pointed to the importance of combining practices into synergistic 'bundles' such that practices which might not work in isolation reinforce one another, clinching an improvement in performance which eludes those implementing partial changes. However, as Godard (2004) points out, if there were practices, or sets of practices, which could unambiguously enhance worker productivity, one would expect employers to be adopting these practices. And yet, as he points out, there is precious little evidence of any transformation in the set of workplace practices observed in Britain, or indeed elsewhere. Godard goes on to emphasize the costs of introducing and maintaining potentially productivity-enhancing practices, costs which may bar some employers from adopting a practice at all or, if they do so, to under-invest in its maintenance. Thus, it may be that the net benefits to HIM practices help explain their limited adoption in Britain and elsewhere. Recent evidence using WERS 1998 confirms that, whereas HIM can be productivity-enhancing, there is a wage premium paid to workers in HIM workplaces which counterbalances the productivity effect such that in 1998 there was no discernible impact on workplace financial performance (Bryson *et al.*, 2005). The authors suggested the evidence was consistent with concession wage bargaining, in which productivity enhancements were made in return for better wages, as opposed to a 'mutual gains' scenario in which HIM would have produced net benefits to the workplace as well as higher wages for the employees.

Much of the empirical analysis of labour productivity and financial performance in the workplace has relied on WERS data. The strength of these data are their ability to capture workplace-level practices and control for a range of workplace structural and workforce composition features when seeking to establish the effect of these practices on performance. However, some have pointed to the potential difficulties in relying solely on subjective measures of performance (Gunderson, 2002). The standard WERS question on labour productivity, for instance, is as follows: 'Compared with other establishments in the same industry, how would you assess your workplace's labour productivity?' with responses ranging in an ordinal fashion on a five-point scale from 'a lot better than average' to 'a lot below average'. The advantage of this type of question is that it allows the analyst to investigate an ostensibly similar measure of productivity across sectors where other measures of productivity might be difficult to compare. In addition, the judgement it elicits may draw on information that only the employer is privy to and, thus, will not be reflected in standard accounting measures.[12] Furthermore, accounting measures may simply be unavailable at the workplace level where a firm adopts a more aggregated measure, say, at the division or company level, raising the prospect of non-response or matching biases. The criticisms of subjective measures, on the other hand, might be summarized under five headings. First, these measures are often based on the assessments of employment relations managers, people who are not necessarily best-placed to make such judgements. Second, they rely upon the manager's ability to locate the workplace's performance relative to the industry average, which is itself left undefined. Third, it is not clear what measure of labour productivity the employer has in mind – sales or output per head, value-added per head, or even total factor productivity, for example. A similar problem arises with respect to the question on financial performance although, since WERS 1998, the respondent has also been asked to identify which measure of performance 'corresponds most closely' to his or her interpretation of financial performance, thus permitting the analyst to determine which workplaces are worthy of comparison.[13] Fourth, because the outcomes are ordinal rather than cardinal, it is not possible to establish just how much better or worse one workplace is than another, or quantitatively how much difference a practice might make to performance. Fifth, there is the problem of inter-rater reliability: how can one be sure that two different individuals managing identical workplaces would rate a workplace's performance in the same way?[14]

Although it has been shown that the WERS financial performance measure is a good predictor of whether a workplace will close or not (Machin and Stewart, 1996; Bryson, 2004), and that performance ratings do not appear to be systematically biased along dimensions observable to the analyst (Machin and Stewart, 1996) these are notable concerns. However, it is only very recently that it has been possible to explore these issues further by comparing subjective ratings of productivity performance with 'accounting' measures. One study compared subjective measures with accounting measures in three separate samples, finding that they were positively associated with each other and demonstrated equivalent relationships with a range of independent variables (Wall *et al.*, 2004). Another recent study compared the subjective measure of labour productivity in WERS 1998 with a relative accounting measure constructed at enterprise level from the Annual Business Inquiry (Haskel, 2005). It found a positive association, but this did not prove statistically significant.

Of course, one needs to make such comparisons with a great deal of caution. In particular, when considering these results and others presented later, it is worth bearing in mind at the outset that 'hard' financial data may contain measurement error, and that it may often be available only for units above workplace level, if at all. Equally, objective and subjective indicators of productivity and performance may measure different phenomena and, as such, should not necessarily be expected to align perfectly. Nevertheless, with these caveats in mind, it is clearly important that a robust investigation of productivity and performance using WERS data relies on a systematic assessment of how the subjective and objective measures relate to one another. The following sections add to the existing literature through analysis of the traditional subjective measures of performance and information collected through the WERS 2004 Financial Performance Questionnaire (FPQ) for a subset of workplaces responding to the 2004 survey. As discussed in Chapter 1, this FPQ is an important innovation in WERS since it obtains financial information for the workplace from the person deemed by managers at the workplace to be the best-placed person to provide that information.

The remainder of the chapter is set out as follows. First, labour productivity and financial performance are investigated using the traditional WERS subjective measures. Multivariate analyses identify independent associations between these outcomes and practices and procedures already introduced in this chapter, together with some features of market competition that did not feature in the analyses of climate. The chapter then introduces the FPQ and explains how data from the questionnaire were used in conjunction with mean industry-level data to construct accounting-based measures of WERS workplace productivity relative to industry averages. The subjective and accounting-based measures of productivity are then compared, and there is a brief exploratory analysis of their associations with a small range of workplace characteristics. Due to space constraints, and because the majority of the literature relates to the private sector, the remainder of this chapter is confined to these workplaces. In keeping with the remainder of the book, the analysis is confined to workplaces with at least 10 employees.

*Labour productivity*

As noted earlier, managers were asked: 'Compared with other establishments in the same industry, how would you assess your workplace's labour productivity?'. Choosing from an array of pre-coded answers on a showcard, 9 per cent identified productivity as 'a lot better' than average, 41 per cent said it was 'better' than average, 35 per cent said 'average', 6 per cent said 'below average' and fewer than 1 per cent said 'a lot below average'. A further 7 per cent said that 'no comparison was possible' and 3 per cent said that 'relevant data were not available'. Confining the analysis to respondents who thought a comparison was possible and collapsing the 'lot below average' and 'below average' categories, 10 per cent said productivity was 'a lot above average', 45 per cent said 'above average', 39 per cent said 'average' and 7 per cent 'below average'. It seems surprising that half of all workplaces viewed their productivity as either 'a lot better' or 'better' than average for their industry while so few regarded it as below the average, although this has been a consistent finding throughout the WERS series.[15]

For the multivariate analyses of productivity, the dependent variable was an ordered outcome where a value of one equated to productivity that was considered 'a lot below' or 'below' average and a value of four equated to 'a lot better than average', so that positive coefficients correspond to higher relative levels of productivity.[16] A baseline model was specified in a similar fashion to the baseline model for managerial perceptions of climate. The sets of independent variables are virtually identical to those used in the earlier analysis, except that the public sector indicator was omitted and a block of variables identifying the state of the product market and market competition were added. These variables relate to the following: whether the establishment produced a single product or service, or several; the geographical location of the market (local, regional, national, international); the number of competitors; the perceived degree of competition (from very high to very low); whether the workplace faced competition from overseas-based suppliers; the company's UK market share; the current state of the market (growing, mature, declining or turbulent); the proportion of a workplace's revenue or costs accounted for by labour costs; and the extent to which consumer demand for the workplace's output depended upon quality, price, both or neither. Finally, an indicator was included in this block identifying those workplaces that benchmarked against other workplaces in their industry. This might help identify those workplaces best able to make an accurate assessment of their labour productivity relative to the industry average.

Although managerial perceptions of labour productivity were higher among managers with longer tenure, respondent characteristics were not jointly significant in explaining variance in responses to the labour productivity question.[17] As one might have expected, since the question effectively conditions on industry-level productivity, the industry controls were not jointly significant. Indeed, neither the workplace nor the workforce composition blocks of variables were jointly significant. The market variables, on the other hand, were highly significant. Labour productivity was perceived to be higher where the respondent identified 'few competitors' – five or less – compared with 'many' or 'none'; and where demand was thought to be primarily dependent on quality rather than price. Productivity was perceived to be lower where the market was viewed as 'turbulent' compared with 'growing', 'mature' and 'declining' markets. Perceptions of a 'very low' degree of competition were associated with better productivity, perhaps because, having controlled for the number of competitors, this may have been indicative of the quality of these competitors. Whether the workplace benchmarked against other workplaces was not significant.

When added to the baseline model neither union density, collective bargaining coverage nor bargaining structure were jointly significant. However, a simple indicator of union recognition was associated with poorer labour productivity, a result that contrasts with recent studies of unions and productivity using earlier WERS surveys which have found little relationship between unionization *per se* and the subjective measure of labour productivity (see Bryson *et al.*, 2005, for a review of this literature). What Freeman and Medoff termed the 'institutional response' to unions also played a role since, when added to the baseline model alongside the union recognition indicator, active support for union membership was associated with higher productivity compared with a scenario in which the employer actively opposed membership.

Although none of the eight voice regimes described earlier were associated with better or worse productivity than was the case where there were no voice arrangements in place, the combination of direct and non-union representative voice was associated with better labour productivity than either direct voice-only or scenarios in which recognized unions were combined with non-union voice.[17] Breaking this typology down into its constituent parts, the combination of union recognition with lay representation was associated with particularly low labour productivity, with the effects most pronounced in the presence of an on-site full-time lay representative. In contrast, non-recognized unions with lay representation were associated with better productivity than unions recognized for bargaining purposes. No less than four direct forms of communication were associated with higher labour productivity: monthly meetings between senior management and the whole workforce in which employees have an opportunity to speak; problem-solving groups; formal surveys of employees' views and opinions; and systematic use of the management chain to cascade information.

Some high involvement management (HIM) practices were associated with higher labour productivity. Financial incentives for employee involvement were associated with higher labour productivity, the effect rising with the number of such practices. Although having at least one 'recruitment, appraisal and development' practice was associated with higher productivity, the effect did not increase with the number of these practices. Breaking the five HIM domains down into their constituent practices, the only ones with independent positive effects in isolation were regular personality tests for recruitment of non-managers and regular meetings between senior management and the workforce. The indicator for the bundling of HIM practices was not significant.

Despite much discussion about the potential costs and benefits of flexible forms of working and of practices supporting work–life balance, these sets of practices were not jointly significant when added to the baseline labour productivity model. The only practices with any independent effect were the incidence of temporary workers and term-time working, both of which were negatively associated with labour productivity. Equal opportunities policies and practices, on the other hand, were associated with productivity. An additive index identified the extensiveness of equal opportunities practices at the workplace. The index ran from zero to four with the workplace scoring one if it had an equal opportunities policy covering equal treatment or diversity, and one for each time it monitored recruitment and selection, promotions and relative pay rates by characteristics such as gender and ethnicity. This index was positively associated with labour productivity when added to the baseline model, but monitoring promotions in isolation was associated with poorer productivity.

*Financial performance*

Directly before the question on labour productivity, managers were asked: 'Compared with other establishments in the same industry, how would you assess your workplace's financial performance?' Twelve per cent thought their performance was 'a lot better than average', 41 per cent thought it was 'better than average', 33 per cent said 'average', 7 per cent 'below average' and less than 1 per cent 'a lot below average'. A further 5 per cent thought no comparison was possible, while 2 per cent did not think the relevant data were available to make a judgement. Confining the analysis to respondents who thought a comparison was possible and collapsing the 'lot below average' and 'below average' categories, 13 per cent said performance was 'a lot better than average', 44 per cent said 'above average', 35 per cent said 'average' and 8 per cent 'below average'. Asked what measure they thought most closely resembled their interpretation of financial performance, two-thirds (65 per cent) said 'profit'. However, 4 per cent cited 'value added' and 13 per cent cited 'sales', two measures that are often treated as indicators of productivity. Indeed, the subjective measures of productivity and financial performance were positively associated with one another. However, this association was equally strong when removing those cases citing 'value added' or 'sales' as their criteria for financial performance.

Multivariate analyses of financial performance were conducted in the same way as those for labour productivity. Models were run on survey-weighted data, the dependent variable being an ordered outcome where 1 = performance that was 'a lot below or below average' and 4 = 'a lot better than average'.[19] As with labour productivity, respondent characteristics were not jointly significant in explaining variance in responses to the financial performance question. Industry effects were not statistically significant, although workplace characteristics as a whole were on the borderline of statistical significance. Workforce characteristics and market variables, on the other hand, were both jointly significant. Links between financial performance and market conditions are reminiscent of those identified in the analysis of labour productivity, with performance perceived to be higher where the respondent identified few competitors compared to many or none, perceived the degree of competition to be very low, and said demand was dependent on quality but not price. Both turbulent and declining markets were associated with poorer performance than growing markets. High labour costs relative to turnover or sales were associated with perceptions of lower financial performance than the industry average, a factor that was not significant for labour productivity.

When added to the baseline model neither union density nor union recognition *per se* were associated with financial performance. However, workplaces with multiple unions had poorer performance than non-union workplaces, as did those with joint bargaining among multiple unions.[20] Employers' response to unions was also relevant, though the effect did not reflect that found in the labour productivity analysis: financial performance was perceived to be higher among employers passively opposed to union membership than it was among those who were actively supportive of membership or had no view one way or the other.

Voice regimes were associated with performance in much the same way as they were associated with productivity. None of the eight voice regimes were associated with better or worse performance than was the case where there were no voice arrangements in place, but the combination of direct and non-union representative voice was associated with better performance than most other regimes. Breaking the typology into its constituent parts, perceptions of performance were poorest where there was a combination of union recognition with a part-time on-site lay representative or an off-site representative. Three of the four direct forms of communication associated with perceptions of better than industry-average productivity were also associated with better than average performance, namely monthly meetings with senior management in which employees had the opportunity to speak or ask questions, problem-solving groups and surveys of employees' views and opinions.

The positive productivity effects of regular personality tests and regular meetings between senior management and the workforce fed through into perceptions of better financial performance. The only other HIM practice associated with performance was the receipt of profit-related payments by at least 60 per cent of non-managerial employees in the past 12 months, a factor that could either improve performance, for example by creating incentives, or else simply reflect better performance. The indicator for the bundling of HIM practices was not significant, although perceptions of performance rose with the number of communication practices.

Work–life balance and flexible working practices were not jointly significant in analyses of managerial perceptions of performance, though three practices were associated with poorer performance in isolation, namely full pay during paid paternity leave, annual hours contracts, and having part-time workers. Similarly, the full set of equal opportunities policies (having a policy, monitoring recruitment, selection and promotion, and reviewing pay) were not jointly significant when added to the baseline performance model, although having an equal opportunities policy that covered equal treatment or discrimination was associated with better perceptions of financial performance.

In summary, the pattern of results for managerial perceptions of financial performance and labour productivity were similar in a number of ways. In both sets of analyses, characteristics of the respondent, industry, structural features of the workplace, and work–life balance practices tended to play little role, whereas indicators of market competition operated in a similar way on both outcomes. A subset of direct communication practices were associated with perceptions of better productivity and performance, whereas other HIM practices, while significant in explaining variance in labour productivity, were less significant for financial performance. Perhaps the most notable differences across the two sets of results related to the role of trade unions. Union recognition was associated with poorer perceptions of labour productivity, whereas union density, bargaining coverage and bargaining arrangements played no additional part. Perceptions of financial performance, on the other hand, were not associated with union recognition in general, though they were poorer where recognized unions had on-site lay representation and where there was multiple unionism. The negative association with multiple unionism was more clear when unions bargained jointly, in contrast to the common finding in the literature that it is fragmented bargaining by multiple unions, rather than joint bargaining, that is negatively associated with financial performance (see Pencavel, 2004, for instance).

## Comparing measures of labour productivity from the management interview and the Financial Performance Questionnaire

The subjective ratings of workplace productivity and financial performance discussed above have been the mainstay of WERS-based analysis of workplace productivity and performance throughout the past 20 years. However, the introduction of the Financial Performance Questionnaire (FPQ) in WERS 2004 offers the chance to investigate the same issues using the types of data commonly seen in company accounts. The availability of these data presents many potential opportunities, not least the prospect of being able to better quantify the magnitude of any associations between practice and performance. However, these data also present a number of challenges, many of which were outlined earlier in the chapter.

In order to illustrate some of the opportunities and challenges in a practical way, the remainder of the chapter presents the results of an initial exploration of the productivity data from the FPQ. In the spirit of Wall et al (2004) and Haskel (2005), the primary focus is on comparisons between the subjective measure of workplace labour productivity relative to the industry average, as reported in some detail above, and measures of productivity relative to the industry average that have been constructed using FPQ data. The degree of convergent validity is investigated through direct comparisons of the measures, while the degree of construct validity is investigated by examining their relationships with other variables that are known to be related to workplace performance.[21] In summary, there is evidence of both convergent and construct validity, but the subjective and 'accounting' measures are not found to be intimately aligned. The initial results of analyses of productivity levels using FPQ data are also briefly discussed.

Two accounting-based measures of labour productivity can be derived using information contained in the FPQ. The first can be referred to as gross output per worker (often termed 'average labour productivity') and is derived by dividing total employment at the workplace into the total value of sales of goods and services over the past year. The second measure can be referred to as gross value-added per worker and is derived by first subtracting the total value of purchases of goods, materials and services from total sales, and then dividing this figure by total employment. The FPQ yielded a total of 1,070 responses from 2,056 establishments where a questionnaire was placed, giving an overall response rate of 52 per cent (or 47 per cent of all establishments participating in WERS 2004). However, the response rate was slightly lower among private sector workplaces than among those in the public sector, and so there were a total of 678 responses from the 1,348 private sector workplaces with 10 or more employees that accepted a questionnaire (a response rate of 50 per cent in this sub-sample). Missing values reduce this figure to a total of 586 observations on the average labour productivity measure and 547 on the value-added measure. Around three-quarters (76 per cent) of these questionnaires were completed about the sampled workplace alone and did not include other sites within the organization; the values provided in the remaining questionnaires have been adjusted by the share of turnover accounted for by the sampled workplace or, in the absence of such information, the share of employment. Around four-fifths (82 per cent) provided data relating to an accounting period ending in 2003, the remainder providing data for a period ending in 2004; all questionnaires containing data that did not derive from a full calendar year of operations were adjusted accordingly for consistency.

The measures described above indicate the simple level of labour productivity at the sampled workplace. The validity of the underlying data can be examined in one respect by comparing aggregate levels of average labour productivity and value-added per worker with the equivalent values published by the Office for National Statistics (ONS). ONS data from the Annual Business Inquiry (ABI) placed mean output per worker at £92,843 in 2003 and mean value-added per worker at £27,794. Untrimmed means computed from the WERS 2004 FPQ were markedly higher, indicating the presence of a number of very extreme values. However, after removing values exceeding the 5th and 95th percentiles, aggregate values of £112,621 and £34,035 were obtained among private sector respondents. These values are broadly in line with those found in the ABI, if one takes account of the imprecision of the WERS estimates due to sampling error and the exclusion of workplaces with fewer than five employees from the WERS sample.[22]

By comparing the values of average labour productivity and value-added per worker for each workplace with industry means published by the Office for National Statistics, it is possible to construct measures of labour productivity relative to the industry average, thus mimicking the approach adopted in the Cross-Section Survey of Managers. Since the productivity question in the management interview is not specific about the criteria used to determine relative productivity, it is possible that the responses might correspond more closely to either average labour productivity or value-added per worker. In fact, the results are not qualitatively different.

Variables were thus created to express the level of average labour productivity or value-added per worker at the workplace as a ratio of the industry mean for 2003, derived from the ABI using the most detailed level of industry data available within the publicly-available ABI data files (usually 4-digit SIC(2003), i.e. class level). Values above one indicated that the workplace was more productive than the average for its industry, while values below one indicated that it was less productive. The median values on these ratio variables were 0.91 in respect of average labour productivity and 1.02 in respect of value-added per worker, indicating that approximately half of all private sector workplaces with FPQ data were more productive than the average for their industry and that around half were less productive. However, as in the case of the variables indicating productivity levels, discussed above, there were a number of very extreme values on either ratio. Accordingly, the comparisons presented here with the subjective measure from the management interview have been computed after removing the top and bottom 5 per cent of the distributions on the respective ratio variables.

Tables 10.3 and 10.4 show the scores on both ratios within each category of the subjective labour productivity measure among private sector workplaces with 10 or more employees. The 'a lot below average' and 'below average' categories on the subjective measure were combined due to low numbers in the 'lot below' category. The first five columns of data in Table 10.3 (and the first column of data in Table 10.4) show that the number of observations on which a comparison can be made between the subjective and 'objective' measures is substantially lower than the total number of workplaces providing a rating on the subjective measure. For example, some 1,317 provided ratings between one and five on the subjective measure, but only 429 yield a ratio measure that compares average labour productivity from the FPQ with its industry average from the ABI (403 in the case of value-added). The numbers of observations are sufficiently large to permit detailed analysis. And the distributions of survey-weighted responses indicate that the subsets of respondents observed on the ratio variables did not differ substantially from the private sector as a whole in their responses to the productivity question asked in the management interview. The degree of sample attrition is still noteworthy, however. The 'lot better than average' group appears to have suffered the most, losing almost three-quarters of its observations. And, in total, the ratio measures are observed in only one-third of private sector workplaces in the overall sample, raising the prospect of non-response biases and a lack of statistical power.

The sixth column of data in Table 10.3 shows the mean values of the FPQ/ABI productivity ratio for average labour productivity, tabulated by the responses to the subjective measure obtained in the management interview. Convergent validity between the subjective measure and the FPQ/ABI ratio variable would be indicated by monotonically increasing values of the ratio variable as one moves from the 'below/lot below average' category to the 'lot better than average' category on the subjective measure. This is partly in evidence. The mean and median values on both ratio variables increase as one moves the 'below/lot below average' category, through the 'average' category to 'better than average'. And the 25th and 75th percentiles in Table 10.4 show a similar transition in most cells. However, the main discrepancies lie in the 'lot better than average' category, which appears to have a long tail of workplaces with below average values on both ratio variables. The other notable feature of Tables 10.3 and 10.4 is the wide dispersion of values within each category of the subjective measure. This indicates, for example, that those workplaces rating themselves as 'better than average' in the management interview include a fair proportion whose productivity appears below average when the FPQ data is compared with the industry mean from the ABI. Thus, the correlations between the subjective and objective measures, although positive, may not be

*Table 10.3* Comparison between the subjective measure of labour productivity and the FPQ/ABI ratio of sales per worker

| Subjective rating | All workplaces | Excluding Financial services | All with FPQ | All with FPQ, exc. Financial Services | All where FPQ/ABI ratio is available (values trimmed at 5th and 95th percentiles) | | | |
|---|---|---|---|---|---|---|---|---|
| | % of workplaces (numbers of observations) | | | | Mean | 25th percentile | 50th percentile | 75th percentile |
| Lot better than average | 9 (87) | 9 (79) | 6 (38) | 6 (34) | 5 (23) | 1.08 | 0.65 | 0.69 | 1.84 |
| Better than average | 41 (571) | 41 (522) | 42 (249) | 43 (234) | 44 (176) | 1.16 | 0.61 | 1.02 | 1.53 |
| Average | 35 (565) | 35 (521) | 35 (266) | 34 (244) | 36 (193) | 1.07 | 0.63 | 0.93 | 1.27 |
| Below average/Lot below average | 6 (94) | 6 (90) | 6 (44) | 6 (42) | 7 (37) | 1.02 | 0.43 | 0.61 | 1.39 |
| No comparison | 7 (66) | 7 (61) | 8 (32) | 8 (29) | 4 (16) | 1.13 | 0.51 | 0.78 | 1.16 |
| Data not available | 3 (35) | 3 (33) | 3 (16) | 3 (15) | 4 (13) | 0.77 | 0.31 | 1.02 | 1.15 |
| Total | 100 (1,418) | 100 (1,306) | 100 (645) | 100 (598) | 100 (458) | 1.10 | 0.60 | 0.93 | 1.35 |

Base: Private sector workplaces with 10 or more employees.
Figures are weighted; numbers of observations are as indicated in the table.

*Table 10.4* Comparison between the subjective measure of labour productivity and the FPQ/ABI ratio of value-added per worker

| | All where FPQ/ABI ratio is available *(values trimmed at 5th and 95 percentiles)* | | | | |
|---|---|---|---|---|---|
| | % workplaces *(numbers of observations)* | Mean | 25th *percentile* | 50th *percentile* | 75th *percentile* |
| *Subjective rating* | | | | | |
| Lot better than average | 5 (23) | 1.42 | 0.69 | 0.80 | 2.52 |
| Better than average | 44 (170) | 1.57 | 0.71 | 1.19 | 2.09 |
| Average | 34 (174) | 1.35 | 0.64 | 0.97 | 1.53 |
| Below average/Lot below average | 7 (36) | 1.33 | 0.57 | 0.88 | 1.55 |
| No comparison | 5 (16) | 0.94 | 0.39 | 0.69 | 1.04 |
| Data not available | 4 (14) | 1.77 | 0.53 | 1.17 | 2.63 |
| Total | 100 (433) | 1.45 | 0.64 | 1.04 | 1.70 |

Base: Private sector workplaces with 10 or more employees.
Figures are weighted; numbers of observations are as indicated in the table.

very strong. To further investigate the strength of the associations between the subjective measure and the two ratio measures, the natural logarithms of both ratios were entered separately into survey-weighted ordered-probit regressions of the subjective rating. In both cases, the association was positive but in neither case was the coefficient statistically significant. In summary, then, the subjective and objective measures of labour productivity show some degree of convergent validity, but it is clear that these measures are far from identical.

There are many possible reasons for this. One is that the management respondent was often ill-informed, but it is equally plausible that the subjective and objective measures indicate different phenomena. For example, the subjective measure may indicate a more complex conception of productivity, namely technical efficiency or total factor productivity. Equally, the comparison may be impaired by an inability to precisely match the comparison group considered by the management respondent, who may define their industry more narrowly than SIC(2003) allows. It is also possible that attrition may have yielded a sub-sample in which the differences between the two measures are particularly marked, especially among the 'lot better than average' group. It may be that those remaining in the sub-sample were the types of workplaces where managers were least able to provide an accurate subjective rating, or where the FPQ data was most prone to error.

The lack of full convergent validity between the various measures may therefore have a number of origins. It becomes more significant, however, if analyses of the subjective and objective measures of productivity do not yield consistent results. Given the differences between the subjective measure of relative labour productivity and the measures derived using FPQ/ABI data, it is unclear a priori whether workplace characteristics would be correlated with these measures in the same way. The degree of construct validity was investigated using multivariate models to estimate the independent associations between workplace features and the three relative measures of labour productivity. The models were parsimonious to aid the transparency of the results, and contained a small selection of items that are standard in productivity analyses, namely, union recognition, off-the-job training, whether the workplace was independent or part of a larger organization and foreign ownership. The models also controlled for establishment size (six dummy variables), establishment age (five dummy variables), industry (10 dummy variables) and region (12 dummy variables). The results are presented in Table 10.5 and indicate broad agreement across the various specifications, although there were also some notable differences.

The first column of data in Table 10.5 presents the results of a parsimonious model of the subjective measure of productivity, conducted on the full sample of private sector workplaces with 10 or more employees. The results are, in fact, no different to those deriving from the more complete models discussed earlier in the chapter. Column 2 presents the results of the same model as in column 1, conducted on the sub-sample of workplaces with valid data on the accounting measure of sales per worker relative to the industry mean; column 3 presents an equivalent model in which the accounting measure has replaced the subjective measure as the dependent variable. Columns 4 and 5 are similar, but refer to the value-added accounting measure. Looking across the first five columns of data in Table 10.5, it is evident that the associations with the first three independent variables – union recognition, off-the-job training and whether the workplace is independent – are of the same sign in each of the analyses, the one exception being the positive association between union recognition and the accounting measure of average labour productivity in column 3.[23] However, the precision of the estimates varies across the specifications. The union recognition indicator, for example, only proves statistically significant in the analyses of the subjective measure. It is also apparent that the association with foreign-ownership takes a different sign depending on the nature of the dependent variable, being negatively signed in the analyses of the subjective measure and positively signed (in line with prior expectations) in the analyses of the accounting measures, although it is only statistically significant in the last of the five specifications.

Columns 6 and 7 of Table 10.5 take a slightly different approach by dispensing with the comparison to the industry mean and, instead, modelling productivity levels. These models rely on the industry dummies to provide sectoral controls but also control for the value of capital per worker (the capital–labour ratio) in a manner that is traditional in analyses of accounting measures.[24] The results are broadly consistent with those seen in each of the other specifications, the principal differences being that the strength of the associations between productivity and the indicators of off-the-job training and independent establishments are more precisely estimated; and that the foreign ownership indicator is again positively signed, as it was in columns 3 and 5.

In summary, then, there are a number of similarities across the models which indicate that the subjective and accounting measures of relative labour productivity are measuring a similar underlying construct. The consistency of the

Table 10.5  Associations of subjective and objective productivity measures with workplace characteristics

| Measure | (1) Subjective rating of labour productivity | (2) Subjective rating of labour productivity | (3) Sales per worker relative to industry average (natural log) | (4) Subjective rating of labour productivity | (5) Value-added per worker relative to industry average (natural log) | (6) Sales per worker (natural log) | (7) Value-added per worker (natural log) |
|---|---|---|---|---|---|---|---|
| Union recognition | − ** | − | + | − * | − | − | − |
| Off-the-job training for at least 60% of core employees | + | + | + ** | + | + ** | + ** | + ** |
| Single independent establishment | + | + | + | + * | + | + *** | + *** |
| Foreign-owned | − | − | + | − | + *** | + ** | + *** |
| *Observations* | 1317 | 429 | 429 | 407 | 407 | 280 | 270 |
| *Model* | Ordered probit | Ordered probit | OLS | OLS | OLS | OLS | OLS |

Notes:

1. The nature of the sample for each model is outlined in the text.
2. Additional controls not reported: establishment size (six dummy variables), establishment age (five dummy variables), industry (10 dummy variables) and region (12 dummy variables). Further control for natural log of capital per worker added in models 6 and 7.
3. Key to statistical significance: * = 10 %; ** = 5%; *** = 1%

associations with union recognition and off-the-job training is also encouraging as the signs are in line with theoretical expectations. However, the results are not wholly equivalent, with the degree of confidence that can be attached to the associations varying across the specifications and the foreign ownership indicator taking a different sign depending upon the measure used. These results suggest that caution is merited when seeking to revisit some of the established analyses of workplace productivity using the new data available in WERS 2004. In the initial exploration reported here, the reduced samples available for analysis of the FPQ did not appear to introduce sample biases, but the precision of some estimates was reduced and the associations with some independent variables did differ between the subjective and accounting measures. These differences may indicate either disparities in the underlying construct being measured, or errors in measurement under either approach. It is difficult to adjudicate and so, in future work, it would seem prudent to attach most weight to results that are consistent across each of the various measures.[25]

## Conclusion

This chapter has focused on issues fundamental to employment relations and to policy, namely the climate of employment relations, labour productivity and financial performance. Identifying factors associated with these outcomes, it has illustrated the value of using more than a single 'lens' to improve understanding of what is going on within the workplace. The climate of employment relations was considered from the perspective of managers and employees in the same workplaces. In assessing workplace performance, comparisons were made between managerial perceptions and numerical 'accounting' data. Much of the analysis was exploratory in nature, and so any conclusions are necessarily cautious rather than definitive. However, a number of interesting findings did emerge.

There were substantial differences in the way in which management and employees viewed employment relations at the workplace, with managers tending to be more positive than employees, confirming analyses for WERS 1998 (Cully *et al.*, 1999; Bryson, 2005). In addition, managerial perceptions had improved since 1998, whereas employees' perceptions had not. Similarly, Chapter 9 showed that, over the period 1998–2004, employees became no more likely to view management as understanding about employees having to meet responsibilities outside work, despite management responses indicating that they had become more understanding.

There were also notable differences in the factors associated with managers' and employees' perceptions of climate. For instance, unlike analyses for WERS 1998, unionization was not associated with managers' perceptions of climate. It was, however, associated with poorer employee perceptions of climate, especially where a majority of employees were members at the workplace. The union effect was more pronounced where 'union voice' was combined with 'non-union voice', a scenario that may become more common with the Information and Consultation of Employees Regulations (2004). There were signs that, so far as managers were concerned, direct voice was associated with better climate than other voice regimes. This was not the case for employees, however. Similarly, strategic HRM was associated with better perceptions of climate among managers but not among employees. Associations with 'high-involvement management' practices were mixed for both managers and employees, with little sign that bundles worked in either case. Finally, there was evidence that various work–life balance and flexible working practices were associated with employee perceptions of climate, but they were not associated with employer perceptions. In practical terms, these findings make for difficult reading, since there was little evidence of policies or practices that were associated with better perceptions among both employers and their employees. However, it is worth recalling that Chapter 9 identified work–life balance practices that were associated with greater managerial understanding of employee responsibilities outside work, as measured by both employee perceptions and managers' stated attitudes.

The investigation of the traditional WERS measures of labour productivity and financial performance in the private sector was based on managerial perceptions relative to the industry average. Investigation of factors associated with these measures proceeded in much the same fashion as the analysis of managerial perceptions of climate, thus extending the range of factors normally considered in these analyses. Factors such as product market conditions and worker voice appeared to have very similar effects on productivity and performance. However, whereas union recognition had a negative impact on labour productivity, only the recognition of multiple unions was negatively associated with financial performance.

The investigation of workplace productivity also marked a new departure for WERS in using numerical accounting information on productivity alongside the traditional subjective measures. Numerical measures of the workplace's productivity relative to the industry average were constructed using data from the new FPQ combined with industry-level data from the ABI.

There are numerous problems in comparing the subjective and FPQ/ABI measures of productivity and performance which are worth reiterating here. First, the data are qualitatively different and thus contain different information. Second, it is not clear which numerical measure of productivity should be compared with the subjective measure, nor the industry level that is appropriate. Managers may use different measures of 'average' when framing a response to the management interview question, too, but the only ABI information at the time of writing related to mean industry performance, so it was not possible to test the sensitivity of results to the use of the median or mode. Third, there is substantial sample attrition arising from non-response to the FPQ and missing data, and the fact that the ABI does not cover Financial Services. Being 'a lot above average' on the subjective productivity measure is also predictive of being less likely to have FPQ/ABI data. All of these factors impair one's ability to make a simple comparison between the performance data from the two sources. Finally, the FPQ data appears to be subject to some measurement error, at least in the tails of the distributions.

With these caveats in mind, workplaces tended to be ordered in a similar fashion using the subjective and FPQ/ABI measures of labour productivity, with the exception of those in the 'a lot above average' category which had few observations in the matched sample. However, the overall correspondence in workplace ordering across the measures was not particularly close, as indicated by the sizeable spread in FPQ/ABI relative productivity within each category of subjective measure.

There was also mixed evidence on the factors associated with the subjective and FPQ/ABI measures of relative labour productivity. In general, factors such as union recognition were associated in a similar fashion with the subjective and FPQ/ABI productivity measures. However, foreign ownership was positively associated with the FPQ/ABI relative productivity measures, whereas it was not associated with the subjective measure.

In summary, WERS now presents a range of different measures that may be used to investigate issues of workplace performance. These include ratings of the state of employment relations provided by both managers and employees, and subjective and objective measures of workplace productivity and performance. A comparison of these different measures does not always yield consistent results, but herein lies the value of a multi-dimensional dataset. Through careful exploration of the different measures, and of their associations with workplace and employee characteristics, it is possible to gain a more detailed appreciation, not only of the measures themselves, but also of the underlying constructs they portray.

# 11 Conclusion

## Introduction

At the beginning of the twenty-first century, much of the talk in employment relations has been about the decline of trades unions (Fernie and Metcalf, 2005), the search for performance-enhancing managerial practices (Purcell and Kinnie, 2006), the quality of work and, in particular, balancing responsibilities inside and outside of work (Gospel, 2003). The value of WERS is that it enables academic and policy analysts to uncover what is actually going on inside the workplace, and identify changes over time. The analysis presented in this book and the booklet of initial findings (Kersley *et al.*, 2005) has explored the key dimensions of the employment relationship. The findings showed that unions are still in decline, though the rate of decline since the late 1990s has been somewhat slower than in the 1980s and early 1990s, and there has even been some union resurgence in parts of the public sector. Unions also continue to play an important role in pay setting and workplace performance. As in previous research, clear links between workplace practices and better performance were, for the most part, elusive, perhaps explaining why there has been no great explosion in the use of practices promoted by human resource management (HRM) advocates. Although there were signs of movement towards practices more conducive to a work–life balance, employees did not perceive such a change in managers' sympathies to work–life balance issues. Employees were also less sanguine than managers about the climate of employment relations.

Reviewing the WERS evidence for the period 1980 to 1998, Millward *et al.* (2000) posed the question: 'a transformation – but to what?' The question was prompted by a dramatic shift away from union-based forms of collective engagement due to the dominance of non-union arrangements in new workplaces, but also by the 'hollowing-out' of unionism where unions retained a foothold. The authors showed that there was, perhaps, only one clear growth area in employment relations, namely a distinct rise in the use of direct forms of communication between management and employees. The authors clearly saw a key role for government in influencing change through its labour market and social policies. However, they were then unclear about what the future might hold in this respect, especially in the context of a new Labour Government in 1997, after an absence of eighteen years. Now that the direction of the Government's approach to employment relations and social policy is much clearer, the findings from the 2004 WERS offer a new opportunity to examine the extent of change in workplace practices and in the perceptions and attitudes of managers, employees and employee representatives over the period.

This final chapter considers the evidence which WERS brings to bear on these various issues. It begins with a summary of the main findings, which largely focuses on aspects of change between the 1998 and 2004 surveys. It then considers a number of key themes highlighted in Chapter 1, including the impact of employment legislation. The chapter concludes with a look ahead to some of the design issues for a possible sixth WERS.

## Overview of main findings

Chapter 3 examined the management of employment relations. The findings indicated a continuation of the trends observed in the late 1990s, specifically the rise in the proportion of specialist employment relations managers, the 'feminization' of the personnel profession, and the fall in the amount of time spent by HR and personnel managers on employment relations issues. Work responsibilities of managers remained largely unchanged between 1998 and 2004. The findings also pointed to a decentralization of the personnel function, as there was a decline in the proportion of branch sites relying on specialists located at a higher level in the organization. However, decentralization was not always accompanied by greater levels of autonomy for local managers. The employment relations function seemed to be characterized by centralized decision-making and limited monitoring systems. There was little evidence to suggest that employment relations management became more strategic over the period.

The management of employees was also the focus of Chapter 4. The findings here showed relative stability in the incidence of practices that are often cited as indicators of sophisticated human resource management, such as team-working, multi-skilling and problem-solving groups. The use of personality and performance tests for employee selection purposes – sometimes signalling a sophisticated approach to recruitment – also remained unchanged across most types of workplace since 1998. However, age was cited less frequently as an important factor when recruiting employees. Training provision and performance appraisals became more prevalent, as did the use of formal performance appraisals as a mechanism for identifying training needs. Changing forms of people management and work arrangements can have a bearing on employees' job influence and work intensity. Here, the findings showed a small increase since 1998 in the proportion of employees with a lot of influence over the pace of their work and the way in which they went about their jobs. There was no change in employees' perceptions of work intensity.

Chapter 5 examined the incidence and operation of a variety of arrangements for employee representation, consultation and communication. The WERS series had previously charted the decline in collective labour organization between 1980 and 1998. This trend continued, with employees being less likely to belong to trade unions and workplaces being less likely to recognize unions for bargaining over pay and conditions in 2004 than in 1998. But while the overall proportion of workplaces without union members increased between 1998 and 2004, the proportion remained unchanged in workplaces with 25 or more employees. In addition, the decline in trade union recognition was confined to small, private sector workplaces, while the proportion recognizing unions remained stable among larger private sector workplaces and in the public sector. Other forms of representation, such as joint consultative committees or stand-alone non-union representatives, did not increase between 1998 and 2004 taken together, these patterns led to a fall over the period in the proportion of workplaces with any form of employee representation. On the other hand, there was an increase in the use of a number of direct communication methods (face-to-face meetings, the management chain and newsletters).

Chapter 6 explored the changing profile, role and attitudes of union representatives. Here, there was an increase in the proportion of female representatives between 1998 and 2004. While the size of their constituencies did not change substantially over this period, union representatives seemed to spend more time on representative duties in 2004 than in 1998. The data showed that managers involved and consulted union representatives to a greater degree in 2004 than in 1998 on issues outside of the traditional collective bargaining arena, such as equal opportunities, performance appraisals, staffing plans, employee recruitment or selection, and training. The picture emerging on union representatives' views on workplace relations was rather mixed. While there was no change between 1998 and 2004 in how representatives viewed their relationship with managers, or the extent to which they considered managers to be supportive, in 2004, a greater proportion of union representatives reported both working closely with management on changes taking place at the workplace and that managers valued their opinions. The findings also revealed a key difference between union and non-union representatives and their relations with managers. The extent of 'mutual trust' was found to be much higher between managers and non-union representatives than between managers and union representatives. More generally, where mutual trust was present, collaborative working was more likely to occur, management was more likely to be supportive of the role representatives played, and management–representative relationships were more positive.

The extent of joint regulation over pay and non-pay terms and conditions was investigated in Chapter 7. In 2004, the presence of collective bargaining was associated with narrower pay dispersion through a reduced incidence of low pay. It was also associated with the entitlement to a wider range of fringe benefits. These factors affected employees' satisfaction with their pay. The incidence of collective bargaining continued to fall between 1998 and 2004, as it had done over the 1980s and 1990s, though the decline was confined to the private sector. The rate of decline also slowed among workplaces with 25 or more employees relative to the earlier period. In the public sector the incidence of collective bargaining was stable between 1998 and 2004 and the percentage of employees whose pay was covered by collective bargaining increased. Managers, however, made increasing use of performance-related pay over this period.

The chapter also looked at the extent of joint regulation over a number of terms and conditions of employment. In most workplaces management did not engage at all with employee representatives on any of the 12 listed items. However, where joint regulation was a feature, managers were most likely to negotiate over pay, hours and holidays, and least likely to negotiate over staffing plans, training and staff selection. Trade unions continued to affect both the degree of joint regulation and its nature: where trade unions were present it was more common for their activities to be weighted towards negotiation whereas non-union employee representation was more closely associated with information provision and consultation.

Chapter 8 examined the nature and extent of workplace conflict as well as the procedures in place for resolving disputes both between managers and trade unions, and managers and individual employees. Comparing 1998 and 2004, the proportion of workplaces experiencing industrial action remained stable and low and the incidence of collective disputes over pay and conditions also remained unchanged. Turning to the incidence of conflict with individuals, the rate of disciplinary sanctions issued by managers (namely, written warnings, suspension with or without pay, and deductions from pay) was similar in 1998 and 2004. However, there was a marked decrease in the proportion of workplaces where employee grievances had been raised. There was also some discernible change in the types of grievances raised by individual employees, with a decrease in grievances about pay and conditions, promotion, job grading and appraisals, but an increase in grievances relating to bullying. According to WERS, there was no difference in the rate of employment tribunal claims per 1,000 employees in 1998 and 2004, although official statistics do reveal that the volume of claims in the intervening years was extremely volatile. With regards to procedures for dealing with collective conflict, the proportion of workplaces with a formal procedure for dealing with collective disputes remained stable between 1998 and 2004. The same was true of the proportion reporting that a formal grievance procedure was in place. In contrast, the proportion of workplaces with a formal procedure for handling disciplinary issues increased over this period. Much of this change in the prevalence of disciplinary procedures was due to an increase in small, non-union firms in the private sector.

Chapter 9 examined employers' equal opportunities policies and practices, including arrangements which assist employees in reconciling the demands of their job with their life outside of work. Here, the findings indicated an increase in the incidence of equal opportunities policies between 1998 and 2004, especially those covering the new and forthcoming statutory grounds of religion, sexual orientation and age. However, few workplaces systematically monitored or reviewed their policies across gender, ethnicity, disability and age. The findings from the 1998–2004 Panel Survey revealed significant increases over this period in the proportions of continuing workplaces allowing some non-managerial employees to work flexitime, to switch from full-time to part-time employment, to work a nine-day fortnight or four and a half day week, to use job-sharing, term-time only contracts or homeworking. It also showed increases in the availability of paid paternity or discretionary leave for fathers, special paid emergency leave and parental leave. However, findings from the Cross-Section Survey showed that the availability of childcare assistance provided by employers remained low in 2004.

Chapter 10 examined the factors associated with the climate of management–employee relations and workplace performance. There were substantial differences in the way in which management and employees viewed employment relations at the workplace, with managers notably more positive than employees, in keeping with patterns identified in WERS 1998. In addition, managerial perceptions of the employee relations climate improved between 1998 and 2004, whereas employees' perceptions suggested little improvement. The analysis showed that there were also notable differences in the factors associated with managers' and employees' perceptions of climate. In contrast to WERS 1998, unionization was not associated with managers' perceptions of climate, though it was associated with poorer employee perceptions of climate, especially where a majority of employees within the workplace were union members. Managers, on the other hand, viewed the climate of employment relations most positively in workplaces relying on direct methods of communication with employees. This association was not apparent in the case of employees. Similarly, workplaces employing a range of strategic human resource management practices were associated with better perceptions of climate among employers, but not among employees. The impact of individual 'high involvement' management practices was mixed for both employers and employees, with little sign that bundles of practices were positively associated with climate from either perspective. There was also evidence that various work–life balance and flexible working practices were associated with employee perceptions of climate, but they were not associated with employer perceptions.

Similar analyses were conducted in terms of the factors associated with managers' subjective assessments of labour productivity and financial performance, albeit confined to the private sector. Characteristics of the respondent, industrial sector, structural features of the workplace, and work–life balance practices tended to have little association with the productivity and financial performance measures. By contrast, strong associations were found between the different indicators of market competition and the measures of productivity and financial performance. Some direct communication practices were associated with perceptions of better productivity and performance. However, other 'high involvement' management practices, while significant in explaining variance in labour productivity, were less significant for financial performance – though there were exceptions. Perhaps the most notable differences across the two sets of results related to the role of trade unions. Union recognition was associated with poorer employer perceptions of labour productivity. While there was no general association between recognition and managers' perceptions of financial performance, a negative association did emerge in workplaces with recognized unions which had on-site lay representation and where there was multiple unionism.

## Overarching themes

The findings presented in this book covered a wide range of employment relations issues and this makes it difficult to come to simple conclusions about the current state or trajectory of workplace relations in Britain. Rather than attempting to draw sweeping conclusions about the changing system or pattern of employment relations, which risks ignoring the multi-dimensional nature of what is taking place, this section considers a few topical themes that have been addressed throughout the book and examines what the findings indicate in respect of these themes. The themes concern the impact of recent legislative reforms, whether convergence between the public and the private sectors has taken place and the experiences of employees at work.

### *The impact of legislation*

As discussed in the introductory chapter, WERS 2004 provides a unique opportunity to examine change in employers' employment relations practices across most of the areas related to the Government's employment relations reform programme since 1998. Analyses of both the 1998 and 2004 Cross-Sections as well as the 1998–2004 Panel Survey provide a valuable source of evidence to conduct an in-depth assessment of the impact of the Government's reform programme. Within the confines of this book, and the limited analysis undertaken thus far, it is only possible to provide an initial, broad assessment of the impact of legislation. Other analytical approaches may provide a more precise estimate of the impact with the data, at least in a number of the areas affected.[1] WERS does, however, provide a wealth of data not available to those who have recently evaluated the impact of legislation (Dickens *et al.*, 2005). The findings from the analysis presented in the next section aim to highlight where change has occurred and to assess the contribution of government policy to these changes. The section begins by looking at legislation that was introduced in a number of specific areas before the survey fieldwork period, namely: trade unions, equal opportunities, work–life balance and working time. Other provisions relating to disability discrimination, dispute resolution and information and consultation, all introduced after the commencement of fieldwork, are also discussed.

### *Trade unions*

Ostensibly, the most substantial legislative intervention that would have been expected to have affected union membership and union recognition was the establishment under the Employment Relations Act 1999 of a statutory procedure, which enabled a trade union to obtain recognition by the employer for collective bargaining purposes where the majority of the relevant workforce desired this. Here, the findings from the Cross-Section Survey showed that the proportion of all workplaces with union members decreased between 1998 and 2004, but remained unchanged in workplaces with 25 or more employees. And while the rate of recognition declined overall, the decline was confined to small private sector workplaces. The rate remained stable among workplaces with at least 25 employees – a notable change from the trend observed in earlier periods. The Panel Survey also revealed that new recognitions outweighed derecognitions among continuing private sector workplaces with 25 or more employees, representing a further disparity with the situation prior to 1998. Thus, the evidence from WERS appears to signal a notable change in the pattern of union recognition in Britain. Other research shows that a high proportion of recognition agreements have been concluded through voluntary means, rather than through direct recourse to the statutory procedures (Gall, 2004). This suggests that the new statutory procedure has played a more important role in setting the context in which employers and unions engage and negotiate to secure trade union recognition on a voluntary basis. It is also apparent from the content of many new recognition agreements that the default agreement provided for under the statutory recognition procedure informs union demands and employer responses to trade union claims for recognition (Moore *et al.*, 2005). In this sense, decisions about trade union recognition have been made in the 'shadow' of the law (Dickens *et al.*, 2005).

### Equal opportunities

New legislation was introduced in 2003 outlawing discrimination on the grounds of sexual orientation and religion or belief, and provisions outlawing age discrimination will be in force by late 2006. The survey results indicated that workplaces were far more likely to have equal opportunities policies covering the new and forthcoming statutory grounds in 2004 compared with 1998. The findings from both the Cross-Section Survey and the Panel also showed that the proportion of workplaces citing age as an important factor in recruitment fell over the period. In respect of age discrimination, this would suggest that many employers have made changes to their equal opportunities policies in anticipation of the forthcoming legislation.

Since 2001 public authorities have faced a statutory duty to promote race equality, by having due regard to eliminating unlawful racial discrimination; promoting equality of opportunity; and, promoting good relations between different groups. However, the findings showed that there was a decline in the proportion of public sector workplaces with special procedures to attract applications from ethnic minority groups between 1998 and 2004, suggesting that the statutory duty had not fed through to employer practice.

*Work–life balance*

Related to, but separate from the encouragement of equal opportunities, the Government has introduced a number of new legal rights since 1999 aimed at supporting employees with caring responsibilities, particularly working parents. The findings from the Panel Survey showed that, since 1998, there was an increase in the provision of a number of flexible working arrangements among continuing workplaces, which is in line with other empirical evidence on this topic (Woodland *et al.*, 2003). However, it is not easy to determine the extent to which the Government's promotion of work–life balance arrangements contributed to this trend. As Chapter 9 makes clear, there may well be other factors influencing the increasing incidence of these practices, for example, the changing composition of the workforce, the need to attract and retain staff and pressure from trade unions.

The Panel Survey also recorded an increase in the availability of paid paternity leave (a legal entitlement for fathers since April 2003) and the provision of parental leave (a legal entitlement for mothers and fathers introduced in December 1999) to at least some non-managerial employees among continuing workplaces. The right to unpaid time off for employees to deal with an emergency at short notice was enacted in December 1999. Here, the WERS findings showed that it was rare for employers to report that they refused emergency time off. While continuing workplaces in the public sector were more likely than those in the private sector to provide paternity leave, parental leave and emergency time off in both 1998 and 2004, the gap in provision has closed substantially since the late 1990s. These results are, perhaps, unsurprising given the legal environment – although as stated previously there may be a number of other factors influencing employers' decision to provide these arrangements. However, there was still a substantial minority of continuing workplaces where parental leave or paternity leave were not provided to at least some non-managerial employees (27 per cent and 8 per cent, respectively). Concurrently, there was a significant proportion of employers providing leave arrangements which went beyond the statutory minimum, for example the provision of fully paid maternity and fully paid paternity leave.[2]

It is also important to consider the extent to which employers' attitudes towards work–life balance have changed, and the influence of the law on their attitudes. The majority of managers still believed that it was up to the individual to balance their work and family commitments. But as indicated previously in the chapter, managers were more understanding of employees' outside responsibilities in 2004 than they were in 1998. Despite this, the results also indicated that employees did not perceive a change in managers' attitudes to the same degree.[3]

*Working time*

The Working Time Regulations 1998 provide workers with the right not to work more than 48 hours per week, a minimum of four weeks' paid annual leave and minimum daily and weekly in-work rest breaks. With regards to long hours working, the Survey of Employees showed that 11 per cent of employees usually worked more than 48 hours a week, a fall since 1998, when the figure stood at 13 per cent. Men were more likely to work long hours than women, even after controlling for part-time status. Managers were also more likely to work long hours than non-managerial employees. Dickens *et al.* (2005: 84) reported that the Labour Force Survey (LFS) showed average hours to be falling before the introduction of the Working Time Regulations, even for self-employed and transport workers, who were excluded from the regulations until August 2003. However, the LFS also showed that the proportion of employees working more than 48 hours a week rose slightly in the four years prior to the introduction of the Working Time Regulations, and then fell by 14.3 per cent over the period from 1998 to 2003. This led Dickens *et al.* (2005: 85) to conclude that the Working Time Regulations did have an impact on the extent of long hours working. WERS indicated a smaller decrease in the proportion of employees working more than 48 hours a week as a result of the Working Time Regulations. Within the transport industry, there was little change in the proportion of employees working more than 48 hours a week between 1998 and 2004, despite this sector being covered by the legislation from August 2003. Also, transport sector employees were more likely to work in excess of 48 hours a week than those in any other industry in 2004.

*Disability discrimination provisions*

Since October 2004, all employers have been obliged by law to make physical adjustments to the workplace to accommodate access for disabled people, under the Disability Discrimination Act (DDA) 1995. WERS 2004 asked managers whether any adjustments had been made to their building to accommodate disabled employees. Although the law came into force during the fieldwork period it is worth examining whether there has been an increase in employers making adjustments since the previous survey. The findings showed that the proportion of all workplaces making adjustments to their building to accommodate disabled employees increased over the period from 23 per cent to 28 per cent, suggesting that some employers have made changes in anticipation of the legislation.

*Individual dispute resolution*

The right to be accompanied at grievance and disciplinary meetings came into force in September 2000 and the 'three-step procedure' for handling grievances and disciplinary action came into force in October 2004. Findings from the Cross-Section Survey of Managers showed that, among workplaces where a formal meeting was part of their procedural arrangements, almost all allowed employees to be accompanied. Workplaces that did not allow employees to be accompanied were all located in the private sector or in workplaces without recognized unions. While the law provides a statutory right to be accompanied by a fellow worker or trade union official, the survey findings indicated that in around three-tenths of workplaces managers were less restrictive over whom they allowed to accompany employees.

The majority of workplaces also operated each of the three steps promoted in the new legal framework for dispute resolution. However, requirements to set out concerns in writing and to attend formal meetings often depended upon the issue under consideration. This was particularly the case for procedures for resolving grievances. While the introduction of the three-step procedure is very recent, Chapter 8 attempted an assessment of the impact of the legislation as the fieldwork period straddled the timing of its introduction. The incidence of arrangements matching the three-step procedure in relation to grievances and disciplinary actions appeared slightly higher among workplaces after 1 October 2004, when the regulations came into force, than among those interviewed prior to this date, although the results were not significantly different. The analysis did reveal, however, that in many workplaces the procedures in place at the time of the survey appeared to differ from those laid down in legislation. Among workplaces where interviews took place after 1 October 2004, 80 per cent operated all three steps in respect of disciplinary actions but just 52 per cent operated all three steps in respect of grievances.

*Information and consultation*

The Information and Consultation of Employees (ICE) Regulations (2004) give employees in larger organizations the right to be informed and consulted on a regular basis. The law came into effect in April 2005 and currently applies to organizations with 150 or more employees.[4] Given that fieldwork for WERS 2004 was almost complete when the new law came into effect, the survey provides a pre-ICE 'benchmark' against which to consider future change in information and consultation provision under the legislation. But it is also possible to assess the extent to which the impending arrival of the regulations may have affected trends in representation and communication between 1998 and 2004.

One possible impact of the regulations may have been to increase the overall prevalence of arrangements for employee representation. This was not apparent from the WERS findings which suggested, in fact, that the proportion of all workplaces with arrangements for employee representation actually fell over the period. This decline, however, was limited to workplaces that were part of small organizations (those with fewer than 100 employees). Among workplaces that were part of larger organizations, the overall incidence of representative arrangements remained stable. The impending introduction of regulations supporting information and consultation in larger organizations may therefore have served to prevent a decline in the incidence of arrangements for employee representation among such organizations, although other explanations are feasible.

The impending regulations may also have had an effect on the operation of arrangements that were already in place for informing and consulting employees. Taking the range of issues discussed, the spirit of the new regulations on information and consultation was broadly reflected in the topics discussed by joint consultative committees in 2004, with most committees addressing financial issues, employment issues, work organization or future plans. However, this had also been the case in 1998 and there was no evidence that these issues had become more commonly discussed over the period. Furthermore, fewer managers considered joint consultative committees to be influential in  2004 than in 1998. But the regulations allow for a wide diversity of practice, and so at the time of writing it is difficult to clearly anticipate how the regulations may influence practice. In this context, it is notable that the survey showed an overall increase in the use of direct methods of communication.

Regarding the more general flow of information to employees, there was an increase in the proportion of managers reporting that they regularly provided information about future staffing plans. Yet this increase was to be mostly found among workplaces that were part of smaller organizations, which are outside the immediate scope of the impending regulations. Moreover, there was a decline in the proportion of workplaces regularly sharing information about the workplace's financial position and its investment plans. Finally, although the regulations may have begun to change the attitudes of employers towards the utility of consulting their employees, the survey found no changes in the proportions of managers reporting that consultation took place with employees before changes were introduced at their workplace. Nor were there any changes among the subset of workplaces which were part of larger organizations. Here too, therefore, there is no clear evidence of any potential impact of the regulations prior to 2005.

In summary, WERS provides mixed evidence on the extent to which employer practice has changed in response to the main areas of recent legislative reform. There is evidence to suggest that some aspects of employers' practice are changing in line with the Government's legislative provisions. Most noteworthy is how employers' practices align with the reforms addressing equal opportunities and work–life balance. In respect of trade union recognition, the statutory procedure appears to have had a small direct influence, but perhaps a larger indirect effect on unions and employers. While the regulations surrounding dispute resolution are more recent, it is clear that most employers have procedures in place in line with the law. The evidence on the impact of the forthcoming regulations on information and consultation appears to be mixed at this stage.

### Convergence between the public and the private sectors?

Public sector workplaces traditionally adopted the role of 'model' employers in setting an example for private sector practice, with an emphasis on providing job security, negotiated employment policies and equality of opportunity (Winchester and Bach, 1995). They were also characterized by their commitment to collective bargaining and joint consultation both at the national and intermediary levels. The early 1980s saw the emergence of concerns over efficiency in the public sector and lack of control over the pay bill which led to a substantial pro-gramme of reform involving gradual marketization, and the privatization of some activities. Also, there was an impact on the systems of pay determination and the level at which it was determined, with the termination of collective bargaining for some staff groups – notably in the Education and Health sectors – and the increasing decentralization of pay negotiations to local level (Farnham and Horton, 1992). WERS recorded a fall in the proportion of workplaces in which pay was set by collective bargaining in both sectors between 1984 and 1998 (Millward *et al.*, 2000: 188, 191, 194). In contrast, and perhaps surprisingly, it showed that collective bargaining coverage main-tained its high levels in the previously state-owned utilities (Millward *et al.*, 2000: 198). All these trends seemed to point towards a convergence between both sectors. Nevertheless, some commentators had suggested that changes in the public sector were less comprehensive than had sometimes been portrayed (Oswick and Grant, 1996).

WERS 2004 showed that, in contrast to their position in the private sector, trade unions still had a strong footing in the public sector in 2004, with collective bargaining still the dominant form of pay determination in this sector. The proportion of workplaces setting pay through collective bargain-ing fell in the private sector between 1998 and 2004, while in the public sector there was no significant change. The proportion of private sector employees who had their pay set through collective bargaining also declined over this period. In contrast, it rose in the public sector, largely due to the re-establishment of collective bargaining in larger workplaces such as hospitals. Overall, the evidence on pay determination suggests that the gap between the sectors has widened over the period since 1998, with joint regulation con-tinuing its decline in the private sector, albeit at a slower rate than hitherto.

Management culture also seemed to differ substantially between the private and public sectors. Compared to public sector managers, the findings showed that private sector managers were more sceptical of the value of unions; were more likely to prefer consulting employees directly rather than engaging in consultation with unions; exhibited greater levels of distrust towards employees; were more of the view that decisions were best taken by senior managers; seemed to be less engaged in consultation when introducing changes and when making decisions; and, interestingly, were more likely to think that their employees expected long-term employment. In addition, the survey evidence pointed towards a widening of the gap in management attitudes, as private sector managers' distrust of their employees increased between 1998 and 2004, while the views of public sector managers remained stable. Also, public sector managers' attitudes towards unions seemed to have improved over the same period, as they increasingly agreed that unions helped find ways to improve performance. In contrast, private sector managers' attitudes about the value of unions remained unchanged.

The core management practices considered by many commentators to be covered under the umbrella of 'high involvement' management – team-working and problem-solving groups – were still more prevalent in the public sector in 2004 than they were in the private sector (see also Kersley *et al.*, 2005). In addition, some practices commonly associated with a sophisticated human resources management approach, such as the use of performance tests in employee selection, off-the-job training provision and performance appraisals, had a higher incidence in the public sector. The use of performance appraisals increased in both sectors between 1998 and 2004, but at a higher rate in the public sector, contributing to a widening of the gap between the sectors. Evidence on the incidence of job evaluation schemes also suggests that the gap may be widening, as the incidence increased since 1990 in the public sector, while in the private sector it declined.[5]

There were, however, some areas in which a degree of convergence was apparent. As mentioned earlier in this chapter, while the public sector was more likely to provide paternity leave, parental leave and time off for emergencies in both 1998 and 2004, the gap in the provision of these arrangements between the public and private sectors was reduced over this period, a change explained by the marked increase in private sector provision. In a similar way, the increase in the proportion of workplaces with formal written equal opportunities policies was confined to the private sector. In the same vein, much of the increase in workplaces with disciplinary procedures was accounted for by small private sector workplaces.

In summary, the survey evidence suggests that the two sectors remain distinct in their people management approaches, and that the gap is widening in some areas but narrowing in others. The WERS evidence suggests that policies and practice in the public and private sectors remain different, and any narrowing of the gap seems to be accounted for by moves from the private sector towards public sector practice, reflecting the 'good employer' ethos in public sector approaches.

### Employees' experiences of work

Most of the findings reported in this chapter until now have drawn heavily upon the findings from the surveys of managers. WERS is unique, however, in that it provides a valuable opportunity to examine the picture of workplace relations from two other key actors: employees and employee representatives. This section reflects on employees' experiences of work and considers whether their views have changed since 1998. The findings relating to a number of important aspects of employees' working life are reviewed, including job quality and job demands; equality and work–life balance; and the state of employment relations more generally.

The comparable indicators in WERS 1998 and 2004 suggested some improvements in particular aspects of job quality. Skills are a key focus for many, and data provided both by managers and employees indicated that the provision of off-the-job training had increased somewhat over the period. The Cross-Section Surveys of Managers and the Panel Survey showed an increase in the proportion of workplaces providing off-the-job training to core employees, while the Surveys of Employees suggested that the proportion of all employees receiving off-the-job training had also risen. Similarly, the proportion of all employees agreeing that their managers encouraged skill development increased, from around three-fifths to almost three-quarters. Employees also felt more secure in their jobs in 2004, with the proportion in agreement on this factor rising from three-fifths to two-thirds, while a greater proportion of workplaces reported having job security guarantees for non-managerial staff. In respect of the intrinsic rewards provided by their jobs, a greater proportion of employees were satisfied with the sense of achievement provided by their work in 2004 than in 1998. But employees were no more (or less) satisfied with the amount of influence they had over their jobs, despite small increases in the proportions reporting a lot of influence over the pace of their work or the way in which they did their job.

The surveys were more equivocal about changes in employees' perceptions of the demands placed on them by their work. As indicated earlier in the chapter, the proportion of employees regularly working at least 48 hours per week fell by a couple of percentage points. However, almost one-third of employees reported that they worked 48 hours or more per week at least once each month. It has also been noted that employees' perceptions of work intensity had not changed, with similar proportions of employees in 1998 and 2004 feeling that their jobs required them to work very hard and that they never seemed to have enough time to get their work done. The proportion of employees agreeing that they worried a lot about their work outside of working hours had risen slightly, from just over one-fifth to just over one quarter.

In the area of equality, the findings on employers' practices – reviewed earlier in the chapter – showed that there was a rise in the incidence of formal equal opportunities policies and that fewer employers were using age as a factor in recruitment. However, the proportion of workplaces with extensive monitoring was relatively low. And despite there being a decrease in the overall degree of horizontal job segregation by gender, there was no change in the proportion of workplaces where women were under-represented in management between 1998 and 2004. In the related area of work–life balance, this chapter has already referred to significant increases in the provision of a number of flexible working and leave arrangements. It was also noted that employees were also less positive about the change in employer attitudes, with only a small increase in the proportion agreeing that managers were understanding about their non-work responsibilities. The level of employee awareness about work–life balance arrangements was extremely variable, and employees often did not know whether specific practices were available to them at their place of work. In these areas then, developments between 1998 and 2004 looked less encouraging when viewed from the employees' perspective.

This was also partly true in respect of changes in the state of employment relations more generally, with managers tending to be more upbeat than their employees. As noted previously in the chapter, overt indicators of employee discontent were no more prevalent in 1998 than in 2004. The proportion of workplaces in which grievances had been raised by employees fell over the period – although there was an increase in the proportion reporting formal grievances about bullying. Industrial action also remained rare. And there was no change in the incidence of disciplinary sanctions against employees. But as indicated earlier, while managers were much more sanguine about the state of employment relations than they had been in 1998, there was only a slight improvement in employees' views.

In summary, the findings showed that on a number of indicators, employees' experiences of work have improved since 1998. However, it would also appear that their experiences in some areas have not changed as much as is implied by the change in either managers' attitudes or employer practices.

## Design issues for a possible sixth WERS

WERS 2004 provides a comprehensive picture of the state of employment relations in Britain in 2004 and on change since 1998. The survey attained good response rates and hence provides good quality data on a wide range of topics, some of which date back to 1980. The data also provide a comprehensive picture of changes in workplace relations in Britain. An important and successful innovation for the 2004 survey was the inclusion of the new Financial Performance Questionnaire. The survey also included some new questions. However, there is always scope for reflection and suggestions for improvement. This final section briefly reflects upon the design adopted for the 2004 survey and considers some of the design issues and challenges for any future WERS.

The first challenge will be to maintain high levels of participation in the survey. Chapter 1 highlighted that good response rates were attained across the surveys. Though the 2004 response rate for the Panel Survey was only slightly lower than in 1998, the decline was more pronounced for the Cross-Section survey. Chapter 1 suggested possible reasons for this, including the length of the interview. Interviews lasted an average of two hours (compared with an average of 108 minutes in 1998) and there is no doubt that this represents a significant commitment on the part of a senior manager. The total burden on a workplace is, of course, even larger when one adds in the Survey of Employees, the Survey of Employee Representatives and the Financial Performance Questionnaire. Given that response rates are falling across surveys over time, this problem is likely to become increasingly significant. A review of the use of questions covered in the survey might be conducted, as was the case last time (Forth, 2002), before the design of any future survey is considered. One possibility would be to cut back on some detailed data collection, for instance, by running dedicated surveys dealing with substantive areas such as pay. A second option would be to have certain modules of questions administered only among random subsets of respondents.

However, for such analysis to be useful this would involve increasing the overall sample size. It would also limit the overall value of the dataset, reducing the scope to look at the interrelations between different groups of practices. A third possibility would be to explore further linkages to other government datasets which use the IDBR as the sampling frame. Of course, these options are not mutually exclusive, nor are they exhaustive. In any event, it is hoped that the ability to augment the WERS data in this way might provide an opportunity to lessen the burden of the existing management questionnaire.

The second issue to consider is whether to bolster the geographical dimension of the WERS sample by increasing the sample size to permit more detailed analysis by country or region or, indeed, to extend the sample to include Northern Ireland. The results from the consultation exercise conducted in 2002 with policy-makers, practitioners and academics were mixed. Outside of the sponsoring bodies of WERS, there was little interest or demand from external parties for country or regional data of this nature. However, over time the interest in country and regional analysis among policy-makers has increased, not least because of the devolved administrations and the establishment of the Regional Development Agencies. Thus, there may be more interest in a geographical dimension in any future WERS. Development work by NatCen for the 2004 survey (Purdon, 2002) suggested that a significant boost to the sample would be required in a number of regions if there was not to be a loss in precision of the results. Consequently, the additional costs of a regional or country boost are likely to be substantial.

The third issue is whether it is feasible to introduce a longitudinal element into the linked employer–employee dimension of WERS. While this idea was floated by some members of the academic community in the consultation prior to WERS 2004, it was less clear how this might be operationalized and what particular analytical advantages it might bring (DTI/Acas/ESRC/PSI, 2003: 10). However, there is now even more interest among policy-makers and researchers in the opportunities provided by longitudinal linked employer–employee datasets, and more examples of how they can be constructed and analysed. With these developments in mind, there seems to be a strong argument for giving careful consideration to the practicalities and possible advantages of an innovation of this nature in the next WERS. The obvious means of achieving this objective would be to collect employee data in the second wave of the Panel Survey, adding to that collected at the same workplaces in the previous Cross-Section. The employee observations would not necessarily be collected from the same employees – indeed, many may no longer work at the establishment by the time of the return visit. But such an approach would, in theory, enable one to identify changes in the experience of work among employees at the workplace, as well as changes in managerial practice. The statistical properties of such a dataset, and the cost of undertaking two surveys of employees – one within cross-section workplaces and one within panel workplaces – would need to be carefully investigated. However, the fruits of this additional effort may prove to be considerable.

# Technical appendix

## Introduction

This technical appendix describes the design and conduct of each of the elements of WERS 2004. It also provides information about the statistical reliability of the survey results. An in-depth examination of the design and conduct of the 2004 survey is provided in *The Workplace Employment Relations Survey (WERS) 2004: Technical Report (Cross-Section and Panel Surveys)* by Chaplin *et al.* (2005). That report is available to download from the DTI website, alongside papers which arose from the consultation exercise about the design and development of WERS 2004 (www.dti.gov.uk/employment/research-evaluation/wers-2004/index.html).

A summary of the design and conduct of the 1998 WERS is provided in the technical appendix to the 1998 sourcebook (Cully *et al.*, 1999), with full information provided in the *WERS 1998 Technical Report* (Airey *et al.*, 1999).

WERS 2004 is the fifth survey in a series of surveys carried out at British workplaces. Previous surveys were conducted in 1980, 1984, 1990 and 1998. The first three cross-section surveys in the series were conducted among establishments with 25 or more employees. The scope of the fourth survey was widened to include establishments with 10 or more employees, and for WERS 2004 the scope was widened further to include workplaces with five or more employees.

One or more respondents were interviewed at each participating workplace. The management respondent was defined as 'the senior manager dealing with personnel, staff or employment relations' at the establishment. Interviews were also sought with union and non-union employee representatives at each establishment in which a management interview took place. In WERS 1998, employees were included in the remit of the survey for the first time, and a Survey of Employees was also conducted in WERS 2004. A random selection of 25 employees was made at each establishment (subject to management's agreement) and self-completion questionnaires, along with freepost reply envelopes, were left for the selected employees. At establishments with fewer than 25 employees, all employees were invited to participate.

A new element was introduced in WERS 2004: the Financial Performance Questionnaire (FPQ). The FPQ comprised a short paper questionnaire that was left after the completion of the management interview for completion by someone responsible for financial matters at the workplace.

In 1984, 1990 and 1998, re-interviews were carried out with establishments which had taken part in the previous Cross-Section Survey. This 'Panel' element of the series was repeated in 2004. Only the management respondent, defined in the same terms as above, was interviewed in the Panel Survey; there were no interviews with employee representatives and there was no employee survey. The Panel Survey was also used to trace the status of all workplaces that took part in the 1998 Cross-Section Survey but which were not selected for a re-interview in 1998. Information collected included whether the workplace was still in operation and, if so, the current number of employees at the establishment.

## The sampling frame and the sample

### Cross-Section Survey

The WERS 2004 Cross-Section Survey is based on a stratified random sample of establishments, together with a sample of employees and (where present) employee representatives at those establishments.

The sample of establishments for the WERS 2004 Cross-Section Survey was drawn from the Inter-Departmental Business Register (IDBR) in September 2003. The IDBR is maintained by the Office for National Statistics (ONS) and is the highest quality-sample frame of organizations and establishments in Britain. The IDBR also provided the sample of establishments for WERS 1998; it has its origins in the Census of Employment, which provided the samples for the first three surveys in the series.

The sampling unit was the IDBR 'local unit' which, in most instances, corresponded with the definition of an establishment used in the survey, i.e. 'the activities of a single employer at a single set of premises'.[1] The sample was drawn from the population of local units with five or more employees, operating in Sections D–O of the *Standard Industrial Classification (2003)* and located within Great Britain. However, local units meeting these criteria were exempt from selection if they could be identified as having formed part of the issued sample for the WERS 1998 Cross-Section Survey, so as to avoid duplication between the 2004 Cross-Section and 1998–2004 Panel samples.[2] A total of 1,941 of the 3,192 establishments that formed part of the issued sample in WERS 1998 were identified, by matching their IDBR local unit reference numbers to the current IDBR population, and were excluded, leaving a total of 697,055 local units from which to draw the sample.

These 697,055 local units were divided into 120 strata, formed from the cross-tabulation of IDBR-recorded industry (classified by SIC (2003) Section) and IDBR-recorded employment (10 categories). The distribution of these local units across the 120 strata is shown in Table A1. A simple random sample of local units was drawn within each stratum. Sampling fractions increased with IDBR-recorded employment to enable separate analysis by employment size group – the aim being to obtain at least 250 productive interviews in each of the size bands below 500 employees and at least 150 interviews in each of those above. The exact sampling fractions were chosen so that the standard errors for 'all establishment' estimates would be reasonably small, given this primary objective. Using larger sampling fractions for larger establishments also aids the precision of employee-based estimates in comparison with an equal probability design. Sampling fractions were also slightly higher than average within SIC (2003) Sections E, F, J and O. This was done with the aim of obtaining at least 85 productive interviews in Section E and at least 120 productive interviews in all other Sections. The sampling fractions ranged from one in 553 among local units with between five and nine employees in SIC (2003) Sections D, G, H, I, K–N to a census of local units with 1,000 or more employees in SIC (2003) Section E. The selected sample comprised 3,998 local units, as shown in Table A2. In addition, a reserve sample of 695 local units was selected so that further units could be issued in any cell of the sampling matrix if the yield of productive interviews was lower than anticipated; in practice, only local units with 5–49 employees were called up from the reserve and, among those with 10–49 employees, only units that were not part of a larger organization were approached for interview. The distribution of the reserve sample matched that of the main sample.

The WERS 2004 sample design design differs from the sample design for WERS 1998 in three key ways. First, establishments with between five and nine employees were included within the selected sample. Second, the sample size for workplaces with 10–24 employees was increased, to improve the precision of estimates for the subset of workplaces with 10 or more employees. Third, increasing sampling fractions were used among workplaces with 500–999, 1,000–1,999 and 2,000 or more employees, so as to improve the precision of employee-based estimates.

All workplaces in the selected sample were approached to participate in the Cross-Section Survey of Managers (comprising the Employee Profile Questionnaire and the management interview). Those which did participate were then asked also to participate in the Survey of Employees and to complete the Financial Performance Questionnaire. In addition, those with an eligible employee representative were asked to participate in the Survey of Employee Representatives.

If the workplace consented to participate in the Survey of Employees, questionnaires were distributed to a random sample of up to 25 employees at the sampled establishment. In workplaces with fewer than 25 employees, all were selected to participate; in larger workplaces, the sub-sample for the survey was randomly selected by the interviewer from a list of all employees provided by the employer.

The presence of eligible employee representatives was determined during the course of the Cross-Section Survey of Managers. Eligible union representatives

*Table A1* Population for the WERS 2004 Cross-Section Survey, by Standard Industrial Classification (2003) and number of employees

| SIC (2003) Section (IDBR) | Number of employees (IDBR) | | | | | | | | | |
| --- | --- | --- | --- | --- | --- | --- | --- | --- | --- | --- |
| | 5–9 | 10–24 | 25–49 | 50–99 | 100–199 | 200–499 | 500–999 | 1000–1999 | 2000 or more | Total |
| Manufacturing | 26,275 | 23,095 | 10,876 | 6,351 | 3,560 | 2,154 | 482 | 125 | 39 | 72,957 |
| Electricity, gas and water | 316 | 366 | 238 | 198 | 114 | 109 | 23 | 5 | 0 | 1,369 |
| Construction | 17,957 | 12,111 | 4,345 | 1,855 | 897 | 357 | 66 | 22 | 4 | 37,614 |
| Wholesale and retail | 87,297 | 53,823 | 15,477 | 6,863 | 2,745 | 1,824 | 340 | 34 | 8 | 168,411 |
| Hotels and restaurants | 30,603 | 24,143 | 8,041 | 3,217 | 857 | 299 | 38 | 16 | 4 | 67,218 |
| Transport and communication | 14,259 | 9,965 | 4,363 | 2,661 | 1,533 | 874 | 232 | 77 | 21 | 33,985 |
| Financial services | 11,166 | 8,520 | 2,777 | 1,298 | 667 | 515 | 209 | 76 | 34 | 25,262 |
| Other business services | 57,434 | 33,529 | 11,308 | 6,147 | 3,228 | 1,738 | 366 | 127 | 36 | 113,913 |
| Public administration | 4,246 | 6,241 | 3,340 | 2,238 | 1,332 | 1,044 | 242 | 82 | 34 | 18,799 |
| Education | 6,778 | 13,232 | 12,453 | 5,254 | 2,506 | 697 | 180 | 55 | 41 | 41,196 |
| Health and social work | 22,315 | 25,950 | 11,450 | 4,878 | 1,579 | 725 | 166 | 128 | 179 | 67,370 |
| Other community services | 25,962 | 14,306 | 4,886 | 2,421 | 952 | 347 | 56 | 25 | 6 | 48,961 |
| Total | 304,608 | 225,281 | 89,554 | 43,381 | 19,970 | 10,683 | 2,400 | 772 | 406 | 697,055 |

Note:
After excluding 1,941 of the 3,192 establishments that formed part of the issued sample in WERS 1998.

*Table A2* Selected sample for the WERS 2004 Cross-Section Survey, by Standard Industrial Classification (2003) and number of employees

| SIC (2003) Section (IDBR) | Number of employees (IDBR) | | | | | | | | | Total |
|---|---|---|---|---|---|---|---|---|---|---|
| | 5–9 | 10–24 | 25–49 | 50–99 | 100–199 | 200–499 | 500–999 | 1000–1999 | 2000 or more | |
| Manufacturing | 48 | 58 | 60 | 75 | 81 | 110 | 57 | 33 | 27 | 549 |
| Electricity, gas and water | 4 | 6 | 9 | 14 | 22 | 40 | 20 | 5 | 0 | 120 |
| Construction | 49 | 43 | 34 | 30 | 28 | 25 | 10 | 8 | 3 | 230 |
| Wholesale and retail | 158 | 131 | 85 | 74 | 60 | 91 | 33 | 13 | 7 | 652 |
| Hotels and restaurants | 58 | 59 | 43 | 36 | 19 | 15 | 5 | 3 | 2 | 240 |
| Transport and communication | 26 | 25 | 24 | 29 | 33 | 42 | 25 | 21 | 12 | 237 |
| Financial services | 26 | 28 | 21 | 19 | 19 | 34 | 25 | 22 | 19 | 213 |
| Other business services | 104 | 82 | 62 | 69 | 69 | 85 | 44 | 32 | 20 | 567 |
| Public administration | 8 | 15 | 19 | 26 | 30 | 51 | 24 | 17 | 17 | 207 |
| Education | 14 | 32 | 68 | 57 | 53 | 32 | 18 | 14 | 25 | 313 |
| Health and social work | 42 | 61 | 62 | 53 | 34 | 34 | 19 | 33 | 101 | 439 |
| Other community services | 58 | 43 | 32 | 32 | 24 | 21 | 8 | 7 | 6 | 231 |
| Total | 595 | 583 | 519 | 514 | 472 | 580 | 288 | 208 | 239 | 3,998 |

Note:
Excludes the 695 workplaces that formed part of the reserve sample.

were the senior lay representative of the largest recognized union at the establishment or, if no unions were recognized, the largest non-recognized union. Eligible non-union representatives were either the senior non-union representative on the most wide-ranging joint consultative committee, or, if there was no committee at the workplace, the senior stand-alone non-union representative. The names of these representatives were requested from managers at the end of the management interview. In workplaces where both union and non-union representatives were present, interviews were sought with both types of representative. This was a significant departure from WERS 1998 when a single interview was sought and the selection rule gave priority to interviews with union representatives.

### Panel Survey

The sample for the 1998–2004 Panel Survey was drawn as a stratified random selection from the 2,191 establishments that participated in the WERS 1998 Cross-Section Survey of Managers. Workplaces were categorized into six strata on the basis of the number of employees recorded at the establishment in 1998 (10–24 employees; 25–49; 50–99; 100–199; 200–499; and 500 or more). A sampling fraction of 0.675 was then applied within each stratum to select a sub-sample of 1,479 establishments that were to be approached for interview. Within this sub-sample, interviews were sought at all 'continuing workplaces', that is workplaces which had continued to employ at least one employee throughout the period 1998–2004 and which employed at least 10 employees at the time of the 2004 panel interview. The 2004 observation comprised a Basic Workforce Data Sheet (similar to the Employee Profile Questionnaire used in the Cross-Section) and a short Management interview. Panel workplaces were not asked to complete a Financial Performance Questionnaire, nor were they asked to participate in surveys of employees or their representatives.

The 712 establishments *not* selected for the panel were screened by telephone to establish continuity of existence and, if they continued in existence, to establish the current number of employees.

## Piloting and development work

In the summer of 2002, the potential user community was consulted on all aspects of WERS, including: its broad design; the sampling population; survey content; and, survey outputs. The consultation exercise had two distinct elements: (1) a consultation with the academic community led by the ESRC; and (2) a consultation with practitioners, think-tanks, and policy-makers and analysts across government conducted by the DTI. Sponsors considered that continuity in the design of the survey was particularly important, given the strong interest in assessing the nature and extent of change since the previous survey.

While the Sponsors considered that major revisions to both the structure and content of the 2004 survey were not necessary, it was considered that changes in a number of question areas were required. A consultation took then place with a number of academic researchers, who formed specialist teams to advise on these areas: Governance; Partnership; Skills, Job Satisfaction and Stress; Performance and Technology; Small Workplaces; and Worker Representation. These teams together with other academic researchers, lawyers and government officials made valuable contributions to the development of the survey. This work ran alongside the development work undertaken by the WERS Research Team who were responsible for designing the final instruments.

New topics were included in the Cross-Section Survey of Managers, such as trust, business strategy and computer use. Question sets were expanded in the areas of employee consultation, dispute resolution, work–life balance and equal opportunities. The Survey of Employee Representatives was completely revised, seeing a reduction in the number of questions that duplicated those asked of managers and an expansion in questions considered to be particularly relevant to non-union representatives. Questions were also added to better identify the personal characteristics of employee representatives, to better understand the activities of joint consultative committees, and to investigate the extent of union recruitment activity. In the Survey of Employees, new questions on well-being, trust and computer use were included, and questions on job satisfaction, work–life balance and consultation were revised.

Piloting of the draft questionnaires prepared by the Research Team took place between August and November 2003. The process began with the cognitive testing of the new questions which were added to the Cross-Section Survey of Managers and the Survey of Employees. This was followed by a two-stage pilot, with the first focusing on the content, comprehension, flow and length of the questionnaires and the second – 'the dress rehearsal' – used to finesse the instruments and contact procedures. The development of the Employee Representative Questionnaire and the Panel Survey involved a single-stage pilot rather than the two-stage pilot adopted for the other elements.

The main purpose of the cognitive pilot exercise was to ensure that the proposed new questions were understood consistently by respondents and that they were effective in collecting the information intended to be captured. The management questionnaire was cognitively tested on 11 managers. The exercise consisted of a face-to face interview using a paper questionnaire, followed by a cognitive interview. As a result of this exercise, questions on organizational status, employee representation and payment systems were refined. It also led to changes in the wording of questions on consultation and business strategy, and the deletion of a question on management–union partnerships. Twenty-seven employees took part in the cognitive testing of the employee questionnaire. Participants were first asked to complete the Survey of Employees questionnaire by themselves. This took around 20 minutes. Feedback was then provided on all questions. The results showed respondents' concern over confidentiality and about being asked if they had any long-standing illness. Questions relating to how employees felt about certain aspects of their job proved difficult for some respondents. The exercise resulted in a number of changes to the wording of questions and their ordering. Certain questions were deleted, including some relating to overtime or extra hours. In addition, confidentiality assurances were more strongly emphasized.

Forty-three managers were interviewed in the two-stage pilot exercise: 18 in the first stage and 25 in the second stage. The first stage showed that the questions in the Cross-Section Survey of Managers were well understood and easy to answer for the majority of respondents, including managers in small workplaces. The results from the second stage indicated that the contact procedures used in the previous survey – combining telephone and postal contact – seemed to be appropriate. Average interview length was close to the target interview duration. Computer Aided Personal Interviewing (CAPI) was used in both the first and second stages for each of the interview-based instruments, including the management questionnaire, and routing problems were identified and corrected. Following the pilot, modifications were made to the layout and wording of the introductory letters and the Employee Profile Questionnaire, and to the wording, ordering and routing of some questions in the Survey of Managers. Twenty-two of the establishments that took part in the pilot of the Cross-section Survey of Managers returned a Financial Performance Questionnaire (half in each stage), representing a response rate of 61 per cent in the first stage and 55 per cent in the second stage. One of the objectives of the piloting work was to see who would complete this instrument. In a large majority of cases the interviewer expected this to be completed by the main management respondent. This informed the design of the reminder procedures.

A total of eight employee representative interviews took place in the second stage of the pilot exercise: four union representatives, three joint committee representatives and one stand-alone non-union representative. The average interview length was found to be close to the target duration. A small number of changes were made to the wording and routing of questions.

Seventy employee questionnaires were returned in the first stage of the pilot and 219 were returned in the second stage. Informal reminder procedures were implemented to maximize the response rate, which in the second stage was 54 per cent of questionnaires placed in establishments from which any returns had been received. Overall, the pilot identified few problems with the questionnaire, and indicated that the use of the Census question on occupation could successfully yield data that could be coded to detailed levels of the *Standard Occupational Classification (2000)*. This compared well to the one-digit data obtained in the previous survey. The revisions and additions to the Survey of Employees increased its length by about one-fifth in comparison to the 1998 Survey of Employees.

Thirteen managers took part in the pilot of the Panel Survey. The pilot exercise showed that the average interview duration was well above the target length. Some questions were therefore deleted, but the instrument remained longer than originally envisaged. The target number of interviews was reduced from 1,000 to 900 to accommodate this longer interview. Following the outcome of the pilots, the Research Team finalized the research instruments in December 2003.

# Fieldwork

## *Conduct of fieldwork*

Fieldwork for the survey was conducted between February 2004 and April 2005 by the National Centre for Social Research (NatCen), who were also responsible for conducting the fieldwork for the previous surveys in the series. A total of 185 interviewers took part in a series of two-day briefing sessions run by NatCen and the research team. Most of the briefing sessions took place in February and March 2004. At these workshops interviewers were briefed on administering the Cross-Section and Panel Surveys, with an emphasis on techniques for gaining cooperation. They were also given an introduction to key concepts in employment relations.

Following the briefing, interviewers were provided with a set of sampled workplaces they were to approach. Workplaces were divided into two waves, each containing cross-section and panel addresses. 'Wave One' workplaces were either independent establishments that were not part of a larger organization or establishments for which gaining consent for participation in the survey was considered to be possible, in the view of the research team, without the workplace manager referring the decision to a higher level in the organization. These addresses were issued directly to NatCen's Telephone Unit. This Unit was given responsibility for making the first approaches with sampled establishments in order to maximize the ability of the field teams to make appointments.[3] They first telephoned the establishment to identify the name and job title of the appropriate management respondent. They then addressed a letter from the DTI to the potential respondent to explain the nature of the survey and to ask for cooperation. A further telephone call was made to arrange an interview. This information was passed on to interviewers, who, in advance of the interview, sent the Employee Profile Questionnaire (Cross-Section sample) or the Basic Workforce Data Sheet (Panel sample) and the statement of anonymity procedures, accompanied by a letter confirming the date and time of the appointment. For Panel Survey interviews the first contact was formalized into a brief telephone questionnaire used to determine whether the establishment had continued in existence since 1998. Interviewers were required to refer back to the research team all cases where difficulties were encountered in gaining cooperation. All cases where a potential respondent refused participation on the basis of being 'too busy' were sent a specific letter in response to this type of refusal, and were contacted once again two weeks after receiving this letter.

Establishments that were part of a larger organization, where there was little prospect of an interviewer obtaining an interview without prior approval from the Head Office, were classified as 'Wave Two' workplaces. Unlike previous surveys, the enterprise reference number was available for all units in WERS 2004. This reference helped in the identification of units belonging to the same organization, which resulted in a higher than usual proportion of units being classified as Wave Two. In the 1998 survey the proportion classified was 25 per cent; in the 2004 survey it was 34 per cent overall, with a slightly higher proportion (38 per cent) in the panel sample.

Gaining approval from Wave Two establishments, which was often complex and time-consuming, had always been the responsibility of the research teams, both at NatCen and the commissioning Department. A DTI letter was sent to the senior human resources or personnel director at the head office of each organization asking for a contact person at each of the establishments selected. The addressee was also sent a copy of a leaflet explaining the background to the survey, prepared by the DTI. A short summary document was prepared for organizations that requested more detailed information about the survey. Further letters or phone calls were sometimes required. Visits and presentations by the DTI and NatCen research teams proved effective in a number of organizations. In a handful of these cases negotiations led to a reduction in the number of establishments to be approached within an organization (through random sampling), or to some of the Employee Profile Questionnaire data being supplied by head office in order to reduce the burden on workplace managers. The work generated from Wave Two establishments was considerable for both NatCen and the WERS research team based at the DTI.

In establishments with 25 or more employees, and following the cross-section management interview, interviewers had to select a random sample of 25 employees. Packs were then prepared with the questionnaire, an explanatory leaflet prepared by the DTI and a freepost envelope, which were left with the manager for distribution. Also following the management interview, a letter was left with the Financial Performance Questionnaire, addressed either to the management respondent or another nominated respondent, giving guarantees of confidentiality and anonymity. Inserts were included with the questionnaires explaining that an establishment's budget could be provided for public sector workplaces in response to the question on turnover.

A three-stage reminder procedure was used for both the Survey of Employees and the Financial Performance Questionnaire.

Cross-Section management interviews averaged 118 minutes, with almost half (49 per cent) lasting two hours or longer. Union employee representative interviews lasted for 52 minutes on average, non-union employee representative interviews for 43 minutes, while the panel management interviews averaged 42 minutes. The duration of the interviews rose with the size of the establishment.

### Fieldwork outcomes

#### Cross-Section Management Questionnaire

In the Survey of Managers, 2,295 workplaces with five or more employees took part, below the intended target of 2,500. A total of 2,046 interviews were achieved with managers in workplaces with at least 10 employees and 249 interviews were achieved in workplaces with between five and nine employees.

Table A3 summarizes the overall yield for both the Cross-Section Survey of Managers and Employee Representatives and the Panel Survey. In respect of the Survey of Managers the overall yield of interviews from the total sample of 4,293 local units that were selected from the IDBR was 53 per cent. Among units with 10 or more employees the yield was 57 per cent, which was lower than the yield of 69 per cent achieved in WERS 1998. The proportion of units classified as out of scope was smaller, but the proportion of unproductive outcomes, e.g. refusals or non-contacts, was much larger. A reserve sample was issued for workplaces with between five and nine employees because of the lower than expected yield in this group. Only 36 per cent of units with between five and nine employees yielded a productive interview; 38 per cent proved to be out-of-scope, mainly because of having fewer than five employees at the time of interview.

As Table A3 shows, of the 4,293 workplaces selected from the IDBR, 706 were classified as out-of-scope. These included 263 workplaces that were found to have closed down, 229 that had fallen below the survey threshold of five employees, 116 reserve sample units of between 10 and 49 employees that belonged to a larger organization, and 32 units that were found to be vacant, at premises that had been demolished, or that had moved and could not be traced. This left 3,587 addresses within the scope of the survey. Of these, 1,292 were classified as unproductive, and these included 893 refusals to take part, a much higher number than in 1998, 354 addresses at which effective contact was not established before the end of fieldwork, also much higher than in 1998 (82 addresses), and 45 cases where the interview was postponed beyond the fieldwork period. Almost two-thirds of the establishments at which effective contact was not made were wave two establishments, because either the head offices only gave permission to contact at the end of the fieldwork period, or after the

*Table A3* Summary of fieldwork

|  | Cross-Section Survey of Managers | Cross-Section Survey of Employee Representatives | Panel Survey |
|---|---|---|---|
| Selected sample | 4,293 | 1,285 | 1,479 |
| Minus total ineligible or out of scope | 706 | | 232 |
| Total eligible and in scope | 3,587 | | 1,247 |
| *Minus* | | | |
| Refusals | 893 | 111 | 175 |
| Total non-contact/other reasons | 399 | 190 | 116 |
| Total unproductives | 1,292 | 218 | 291 |
| Total interviews achieved | 2,295 | 984 | 956 |

fieldwork was cut off; or interviewers were repeatedly asked to call back at a later date in order to arrange an interview, and eventually ran out of time.

The overall response rate for the Survey of Managers was 64 per cent, and the response rate achieved among the smallest workplaces (with between five and nine employees) was the lowest at 58 per cent. The response rate for workplaces with 10 or more employees equated to 65 per cent, which was lower than the response rate in 1998, when it was 80 per cent. A longer interview, the additional interviews with employee representatives in some workplaces, the Financial Performance Questionnaire, the overall research burden on large employers and the increased use of voicemail were all factors considered to be at play.

## Survey of Employee Representatives

In total, 1,285 eligible employee representatives were identified at 1,120 establishments and interviews were achieved with 984 of the eligible employee representatives, giving a response rate of 77 per cent. Of the 984 productive employee representative interviews, 735 were conducted with union representatives, and the remaining 249 with non-union employee representatives. The response rate among union employee representatives was 80 per cent, and among non-union representatives was 67 per cent. The most common reason for failing to obtain employee representative interviews was the refusal by management to agree to interviewers approaching the union employee representative (58 cases) or the non-union employee representative (39 cases).

## Survey of Employees

Employee questionnaires were distributed in 86 per cent of workplaces from which a management interview was obtained. Over a tenth (12 per cent) of workplaces at which questionnaires were placed did not return any, a much higher proportion than in 1998. In workplaces with more than ten employees, it seemed very unlikely that no productive questionnaires would be returned if the questionnaires had been distributed and so, for the purposes of calculating response rates, it was assumed that these workplaces had declined to participate in the Survey of Employees. A total of 22,451 employee questionnaires were completed and returned, representing a response rate of 61 per cent within workplaces participating in the survey. The response rate in workplaces with 10 or more employees was 60 per cent, slightly lower than in 1998 (66 per cent).

## Financial Performance Questionnaire

The Financial Performance Questionnaire was placed in 2,076 workplaces and 1,070 questionnaires were returned. When expressed as a proportion of those placed, this represented a response rate of 51 per cent, while the response rate expressed as a proportion of productive management interviews was 47 per cent.

*Panel Survey*

The overall yield of interviews from the total sample of 1,479 local units that were selected for the Panel Survey sample was 65 per cent. As Table A3 shows, of this sample, 232 were classified as out-of-scope, representing 16 per cent. These included 138 workplaces that were found to have closed down, 37 that had fallen below the survey threshold of 10 or more employees, and 28 units that were found to be vacant, at premises that had been demolished, or that had moved and could not be traced.

The total number of cases that were eligible and in scope was therefore 1,247. Of these, 956 cases resulted in a productive interview, giving a response rate of 77 per cent.[4] Eighty-four per cent of the establishments in the panel screening sample were found to be valid establishments, i.e. they were continuing in existence, and had 10 or more employees at the time of screening. Ten per cent of the establishments had closed down and 3 per cent were continuing with fewer than 10 employees.

*Data linking*

The majority of managers (2,166) who took part in the Cross-Section Survey agreed for authorized researchers to link the data collected from them to other surveys and datasets for statistical purposes, while in the Panel Survey 914 managers agreed to this request.

## Coding and editing

Coding and editing of the questionnaires were carried out by NatCen's data processing team, with continuous involvement from the research team of the sponsoring organizations as well as NatCen's researchers. A considerable operation was necessary to prepare the data and substantial resources were allocated from all the organizations. As in the previous survey, 'fact sheets' were the basis for editing the questionnaires. They contained information taken from the sampling frame (the IDBR in the case of the Cross-Section Survey, or the 1998 survey in the case of the Panel Survey) and data collected at the interview, as well as comments keyed in during the interview by the interviewer. The combination of CAPI, which allows the identification of error at the design and testing stage, and fact sheets resulted in a highly efficient editing process being applied to all productive cases.

The first stage of the editing procedure involved NatCen's editing team coding the semi-open questions and recording the codes on the fact sheets. The frames for coding answers to these questions were developed by the WERS Research Team from answers to 133 Cross-Section questionnaires and 248 Panel questionnaires. Coding of 'Other, please specify' text was mostly conducted by NatCen's editing team. The codes deriving from this process were stored in new variables rather than being back-coded into the originating variable. NatCen's editing team also recorded SOC and SIC codes. Any cases needing to be checked by the NatCen research team were flagged on the fact sheets. The second stage of the editing procedure involved NatCen's editing team editing the questionnaires. Here, checks on the internal consistency of the data were conducted. Again, difficult queries were brought to the attention of the NatCen research team to resolve. Finally, the third stage involved the NatCen research team and researchers from the funding organizations resolving queries which were outstanding, following the previous stages of the editing procedure.

Checks were devised to ensure that the data collected in the Employee Profile Questionnaire's grid (workforce's occupational profile by part-time or full-time status, and by gender profile) were as consistent as possible. A number of checks on the remainder of the interview data were also included in the fact sheets. There were 33 such checks on the Cross-Section Survey. Checks were devised to ensure that the interview was in scope and taking place at the selected establishment, and that its breakdown of employees had been accurately recorded. It was important to note cases where there was an apparent mismatch between the size (or SIC classification) of the sampled establishment recorded in the IDBR and the information obtained within the interview, because the interviewer might have conducted the interview at the wrong establishment. Plausible explanations for the differences were usually found by examining the nature of the industry, evidence of recent changes in workplace size, interviewer notes, the sample file or the organization's website or, in the last instance, by telephoning either the interviewer or the respondent. Further checks ensured that the ownership of the establishment had been correctly recorded, and that the joint consultative committee and unions recorded were legitimate and operated for employees at the selected establishment.

There were also a number of checks for the Survey of Employee Representatives, designed to ensure that the employee representative interview was taking place with a 'bona fide' lay representative. A check was also included to ensure that the interview took place with the correct representative. In some cases, the management respondent had led the interviewer to an employee representative that did not meet the selection criteria. These workplaces, or the interviewers who had conducted the Survey of Employee Representatives, were contacted in order to provide explanatory information. In some cases, there was no alternative but to discard the interview. Also, the interviews for union and non-union representatives differed slightly, and in some instances where an interview had been conducted with the correct employee representative, the wrong interview schedule had been used. This happened in 56 cases, where the interview had been conducted with the correct employee representative but had been conducted using the wrong interview schedule (i.e. a union representative had been interviewed as if he or she were a non-union representative). A procedure for dealing with these cases was devised, and the relevant information was transferred by members of the funding organizations to the correct schedule and retained.

The Financial Performance Questionnaire and the Survey of Employees also underwent an editing process to ensure that the data were as accurate and consistent as possible. For instance, there were a number of range checks used to ensure that any data items, such as the number of hours worked by an employee, fell inside an expected range. Editing of these questionnaires was carried out by NatCen's editing team, who checked for scanning errors or punching errors. Any outstanding queries were referred to the funding organizations' research team.

There were 11 checks on the data from the 2004 interview in the Panel Survey plus three additional checks involving comparisons between key data within the 1998 and 2004 interviews. Checks on the Panel Survey fact sheets served two purposes: firstly, to verify that the interviews had been carried out at the same establishment in both 1998 and 2004, and secondly, to identify inconsistent data within the 2004 interview. The Panel Survey data was coded to SIC 1992 and SIC 2003. Any discrepancies between the SIC 1992 codes recorded in 1998 and 2004 were given particular attention as part of the editing process. In this survey the detailed description of the work undertaken by the largest occupational group was coded to both SOC 1990 and SOC 2000. Any discrepancies between the SOC 1990 codes given for the largest occupational group in 1998 and 2004 were investigated as part of the editing process.

Overcodes were used to identify cases where a major change had been made to an interview after its completion, or where the funding organizations' research team had reason to be concerned about a particular set of responses. These overcodes were decided during the data editing and were added to the Cross-Section and Panel datasets.

## Weighting

All of the estimates presented in the main text of this book have been produced using weighted data, unless otherwise stated. The weighting factors primarily compensate for the sample-selection biases that were introduced through the application of unequal selection probabilities during sampling. The weighting factors for some elements of the survey also include adjustments to compensate for identified non-response biases.

### *Cross-Section Survey*

The weight for each establishment participating in the Cross-Section Survey of Managers was computed as the inverse of the establishment's probability of selection from the sampling frame, multiplied by an adjustment factor that post-stratified the achieved sample so that the weighted profile of establishments by industry and employment size (as measured in the WERS interview) matched the profile of the population (as indicated by the IDBR).

Where the sampled local unit corresponded precisely to an establishment (98 per cent of the achieved sample), the first element of this calculation equated to the inverse of the sampling fraction used in the stratum from which the establishment originated. However, 44 local units (2 per cent) were found to correspond only to sub-sections of a workplace; in other words, they were 'partial' units. In these instances, the establishment had a greater chance of selection than was implied by its sampling fraction, and so the true probability of selection for the establishment was calculated after having identified the stratum of each local unit that corresponded to the other parts of the establishment. The sample-selection weight was calculated as the inverse of this true probability of selection.

In some instances, the number of employees recorded on the Employee Profile Questionnaire was substantially different to the number recorded on the IDBR. This meant that establishments appearing within the same employment size category in any data analysis could have very different weights, since the employment size categories were based on interview data while the weights were computed using IDBR information. For example, an establishment in SIC (2003) Section D with 50 employees at the time of interview would have an inverse probability weight of 85 if the IDBR also recorded it as having 50 employees, but would have an inverse probability weight of 547 if the IDBR recorded it as having between five and nine employees. Although these weights provide estimates that are free from sample-selection biases, such large variation in weights within analytical categories can mean that standard errors are relatively large (thus potentially increasing the mean square error). To avoid this, the achieved sample was tabulated by interview-recorded size and industry and any sample-selection weights that were three times smaller/larger than the expected weight for each stratum were trimmed back to this limit. The trimming was not applied to any establishments for which the calculation of the inverse probability weight was non-standard (i.e. where the IDBR local unit was judged to correspond to only part of an establishment).

The post-stratification adjustment factors were calculated by applying trimmed sample-selection weights and then computing a multiplier which brought the weighted profile of the achieved sample by industry and employment size (as measured in the WERS interview) into line with the profile of the population (as indicated by the IDBR). The primary purpose of the post-stratification was to account for the comparatively low yield among local units recorded on the IDBR as having between five and nine employees. This low yield appears to have been partly caused by inaccuracies in IDBR-recorded employment for small units, leading to higher than anticipated out-of-scope rates and a large degree of migration from this size band to other size bands, exacerbated by a lower than average response rate among small units. In the absence of post-stratification, the weighted sample from WERS 2004, when tabulated using interview-recorded employment, would have appeared to under-represent workplaces with between five and nine employees, in comparison with population data from the IDBR.

Post-stratification was not applied in WERS 1998 and so, to ensure that comparisons between 1998 and 2004 are not impaired by differences in the weighting schema, new establishment weights have been computed for WERS 1998 that adjust the profile of the achieved sample in 1998 to the profile of the population by industry and employment size at the time the sample for WERS 1998 was selected. These revised weights have been employed to produce the 1998 estimates that are presented in this book.[5]

The absence of any sub-sampling for the Survey of Employee Representatives, and the high response rates achieved there, mean that no additional weights have been computed for that element of the Cross-Section Survey. Weighted estimates from the Survey of Employee Representatives are therefore computed using the main establishment weight discussed above. However, separate weighting factors have been computed for the Survey of Employees and Financial Performance Questionnaire.

The weight for each employee participating in the Cross-Section Survey of Employees was computed as the inverse of the employee's probability of selection, multiplied by adjustment factors to account for non-cooperation at establishment level and to post-stratify the achieved sample of employees by gender. The adjustment factor for establishment non-cooperation accounted for biases caused by the fact that some types of workplace were less likely to agree to participate in the employee survey, and the fact that some which consented to participate did not appear to have distributed the questionnaires, since none were returned by any of their employees. The post-stratification accounted for differential non-response among male and female employees.

An employee's probability of selection was computed as the product of the probability that their establishment was selected to take part in the Cross-Section Survey of Managers (see above) and the probability that the employee was then selected to participate in the Survey of Employees. The adjustment factor for establishment non-cooperation was computed as the inverse of the predicted odds of establishment cooperation, derived from a logistic regression model including a range of establishment characteristics taken from the management interview. Finally, post-stratification by gender was achieved by bringing the overall proportion of male and female employees in the weighted achieved sample into line with the gender distribution of aggregate employment in the WERS population indicated by summing across all Employee Profile Questionnaires.

The weight for each Financial Performance Questionnaire was constructed as the product of the establishment weight (see above) and an adjustment factor to account for differential non-response to this element of the Cross-Section Survey. Almost half of all establishments did not participate in the Financial Performance Questionnaire and there was some evidence that those that did not take part were not a random subset (e.g. a lower than average response rate was obtained among establishments with shares listed on the stock exchange). The adjustment factor was computed as the inverse of the predicted odds of participation, derived from a logistic regression model including a range of establishment characteristics taken from the management interview.

## Panel Survey

The weights applied to the 1998–2004 Panel Survey were constructed as the inverse of the probability of being selected to take part in 2004, multiplied by an adjustment to account for differential response. Since a uniform sampling fraction was applied in 2004 to select the issued sample from those workplaces participating in the WERS 1998 Cross-Section, the probability of being selected to take part in 2004 equated to the probability of a workplace participating in WERS 1998 multiplied by the sampling fraction used in 2004 (0.675). The inverse of this probability is therefore simply the 1998 Cross-Section establishment weight multiplied by 1/0.675. Despite the high response rate achieved in the Panel Survey, a non-response adjustment was computed by fitting a logistic regression model to estimate the odds of participation in 2004, with a range of independent variables being taken from the WERS 1998 Cross-Section Survey of Managers.

## Sampling errors

The use of weights in WERS 2004 ensures that estimates are unbiased: that is, free from any sample-selection biases and known non-response biases. However, in common with any other sample survey, the figures obtained from WERS remain only *estimates* of the true population parameters, since any survey estimate can be expected to vary under repeated sampling. Statistical theory allows us to quantify the degree of likely variation – labelled the 'standard error of the estimate' – and thus to construct confidence intervals around any estimate from the specific sample that has been drawn.

Standard errors can often be computed using standard formulae. However, these formulae assume that the survey has been conducted using simple random sampling. WERS 2004 includes a number of departures from this approach: stratification of the population prior to sampling; unequal sampling fractions; non-replacement of sampled units; post-stratification; and, in the case of the Survey of Employees, the clustering of observations within workplaces. While stratification prior to sampling and non-replacement of sampled units can improve the precision of survey estimates in comparison with simple random sampling, the other departures listed here tend to reduce the level of precision, and generally do so to a much greater degree. Thus, standard formulae will almost always yield standard errors that are too small.

To help identify the precision of estimates from WERS 2004, the true standard errors for a range of estimates have been approximated using a statistical software package (STATA).[6] These standard errors are listed individually in Tables 8.1–8.3 of the WERS 2004 Technical Report (Chaplin *et al.*, 2005). To ascertain the precision of any particular estimate presented in this book the reader is advised, where possible, to identify its standard error from those tables, referring to the columns presenting the standard errors of estimates within the sub-sample of establishments with 10 or more employees. However, in order to provide a simple guide to the likely precision of estimates presented in the book, Tables A4–A6 indicate the likely standard errors for various percentages based on different numbers of observations. These are based on a calculation of the extent to which the various features of the WERS sample-design inflate standard errors in comparison with a simple random sample, averaged over the variables cited in the relevant tables of the WERS 2004 Technical Report (ibid.).

Table A4 presents approximate standard errors for estimates derived from the WERS 2004 Cross-Section Surveys of Managers and Employee Representatives, and is based on the sub-sample of establishments with 10 or more employees. In this sub-sample, the average degree of inflation in standard errors due to the sample design (the 'design factor') is 1.45. This average design factor can also be used as a multiplier in conjunction with the standard formulae for calculating the standard errors of estimates from simple random samples. Table A5 presents the equivalent information for estimates derived from the Survey of Employees, again in the sub-sample of establishments with 10 or more employees. Here, the average design factor is 1.55. Table A6 presents the same

*Table A4* Approximate standard errors for estimates derived from the WERS 2004 Cross-Section Surveys of Managers and Employee Representatives

| | Number of observations (unweighted) | | | | | | | | | |
|---|---|---|---|---|---|---|---|---|---|---|
| *Estimate (%)* | 100 | 250 | 500 | 750 | 1,000 | 1,250 | 1,500 | 1,750 | 2,000 | 2,250 |
| 10 | 4.4 | 2.8 | 1.9 | 1.6 | 1.4 | 1.2 | 1.1 | 1.0 | 1.0 | 0.9 |
| 20 | 5.8 | 3.7 | 2.6 | 2.1 | 1.8 | 1.6 | 1.5 | 1.4 | 1.3 | 1.2 |
| 30 | 6.6 | 4.2 | 3.0 | 2.4 | 2.1 | 1.9 | 1.7 | 1.6 | 1.5 | 1.4 |
| 40 | 7.1 | 4.5 | 3.2 | 2.6 | 2.2 | 2.0 | 1.8 | 1.7 | 1.6 | 1.5 |
| 50 | 7.3 | 4.6 | 3.2 | 2.6 | 2.3 | 2.1 | 1.9 | 1.7 | 1.6 | 1.5 |
| 60 | 7.1 | 4.5 | 3.2 | 2.6 | 2.2 | 2.0 | 1.8 | 1.7 | 1.6 | 1.5 |
| 70 | 6.6 | 4.2 | 3.0 | 2.4 | 2.1 | 1.9 | 1.7 | 1.6 | 1.5 | 1.4 |
| 80 | 5.8 | 3.7 | 2.6 | 2.1 | 1.8 | 1.6 | 1.5 | 1.4 | 1.3 | 1.2 |
| 90 | 4.4 | 2.8 | 1.9 | 1.6 | 1.4 | 1.2 | 1.1 | 1.0 | 1.0 | 0.9 |

Notes:
1. Based on the sub-sample of establishments with 10 or more employees.
2. Average (median) design factor for this sub-sample: 1.45.

*Table A5* Approximate standard errors for estimates derived from the WERS 2004 Cross-Section Survey of Employees

| | Number of observations (unweighted) | | | | | | | | | |
|---|---|---|---|---|---|---|---|---|---|---|
| *Estimate (%)* | 1,000 | 2,500 | 5,000 | 7,500 | 10,000 | 12,500 | 15,000 | 17,500 | 20,000 | 22,500 |
| 10 | 1.5 | 0.9 | 0.7 | 0.5 | 0.5 | 0.4 | 0.1 | 0.4 | 0.3 | 0.3 |
| 20 | 2.0 | 1.2 | 0.9 | 0.7 | 0.6 | 0.6 | 0.2 | 0.5 | 0.4 | 0.4 |
| 30 | 2.2 | 1.4 | 1.0 | 0.8 | 0.7 | 0.6 | 0.2 | 0.5 | 0.5 | 0.5 |
| 40 | 2.4 | 1.5 | 1.1 | 0.9 | 0.8 | 0.7 | 0.2 | 0.6 | 0.5 | 0.5 |
| 50 | 2.5 | 1.6 | 1.1 | 0.9 | 0.8 | 0.7 | 0.2 | 0.6 | 0.5 | 0.5 |
| 60 | 2.4 | 1.5 | 1.1 | 0.9 | 0.8 | 0.7 | 0.2 | 0.6 | 0.5 | 0.5 |
| 70 | 2.2 | 1.4 | 1.0 | 0.8 | 0.7 | 0.6 | 0.2 | 0.5 | 0.5 | 0.5 |
| 80 | 2.0 | 1.2 | 0.9 | 0.7 | 0.6 | 0.6 | 0.2 | 0.5 | 0.4 | 0.4 |
| 90 | 1.5 | 0.9 | 0.7 | 0.5 | 0.5 | 0.4 | 0.1 | 0.4 | 0.3 | 0.3 |

Notes:
1. Based on the sub-sample of employees in establishments with 10 or more employees.
2. Average (median) design factor for this sub-sample: 1.55.

*Table A6* Approximate standard errors for estimates derived from the WERS 1998–2004 Panel Survey

| Estimate (%) | Number of observations (unweighted) | | | | | | | | | |
|---|---|---|---|---|---|---|---|---|---|---|
| | *100* | *200* | *300* | *400* | *500* | *600* | *700* | *800* | *900* | *950* |
| 10 | 5.9 | 4.1 | 3.4 | 2.9 | 2.6 | 2.4 | 2.2 | 2.1 | 2.0 | 1.9 |
| 20 | 7.8 | 5.5 | 4.5 | 3.9 | 3.5 | 3.2 | 2.9 | 2.8 | 2.6 | 2.5 |
| 30 | 8.9 | 6.3 | 5.2 | 4.5 | 4.0 | 3.6 | 3.4 | 3.2 | 3.0 | 2.9 |
| 40 | 9.6 | 6.8 | 5.5 | 4.8 | 4.3 | 3.9 | 3.6 | 3.4 | 3.2 | 3.1 |
| 50 | 9.8 | 6.9 | 5.6 | 4.9 | 4.4 | 4.0 | 3.7 | 3.4 | 3.3 | 3.2 |
| 60 | 9.6 | 6.8 | 5.5 | 4.8 | 4.3 | 3.9 | 3.6 | 3.4 | 3.2 | 3.1 |
| 70 | 8.9 | 6.3 | 5.2 | 4.5 | 4.0 | 3.6 | 3.4 | 3.2 | 3.0 | 2.9 |
| 80 | 7.8 | 5.5 | 4.5 | 3.9 | 3.5 | 3.2 | 2.9 | 2.8 | 2.6 | 2.5 |
| 90 | 5.9 | 4.1 | 3.4 | 2.9 | 2.6 | 2.4 | 2.2 | 2.1 | 2.0 | 1.9 |

Notes:
1. Standard errors apply to estimates derived from the 1998 or 2004 interviews.
2. Average (median) design factor: 1.95.

information for estimates derived from the 1998 or 2004 interviews in the Panel Survey, where the average design factor is 1.95. It should be noted that, to calculate the standard error of an estimated *change* between the 1998 and 2004 observations in the Panel Survey, one additionally requires an estimate of the proportion of establishments that have not changed their behaviour on the item in question, since the two samples are not independent.

Once the likely standard error of an estimate has been obtained from the tables, the confidence interval around that estimate can also be gauged by multiplication. For instance, the 95 per cent confidence interval extends to two standard errors either side of the estimate. Ninety-five out of 100 unbiased survey estimates would lie within this interval, and one could therefore be 95 per cent certain that the population parameter also lay within this range.

# Further information

Additional resources accompanying this book, including data tables and full results from the multivariate analysis conducted in Chapter 10, are available from the Routledge companion website at: http://www.routledge.com/textbooks/ 0415378133.

A report accompanying the sourcebook of main findings, published by the WERS Sponsors in collaboration with the Small Business Service, examines employment relations in small and medium-sized enterprises (Forth *et al.*, 2006). Copies of this report are available via the DTI's publication order line on 0845 0150 010 (+44 845 0150 010) or email: publications@dti.gsi.gov.uk. The publication is also available to download from the DTI's Employment Relations (ER) Directorate website: http://www.dti.gov.uk/employment/research-evaluation/ wers-2004/index.html

The booklet of first findings from the 2004 WERS, published by the Sponsors in July 2005, is also available from the DTI's publication order line and available to download from the DTI's ER Directorate website.

Additional information about the design and development of WERS 2004 is currently available from the DTI website: http://www.dti.gov.uk/employment/ research-evaluation/wers-2004/index.html, alongside information about the 1998 survey and a bibliography of papers based on data from the WERS series. The full technical report based on the 2004 survey is also available to download from the same website.

# Accessing the data

The data collected in WERS 2004 are publicly available for research purposes and may be obtained, along with accompanying documentation, from the UK Data Archive at the University of Essex. The previous surveys in the WERS series are also available from the Archive. The data have been anonymized to protect the identity of individual respondents and participating establishments. To add further protections, region identifiers and a detailed industry classification are also being withheld from general release until April 2007 and, prior to that date, data from the Financial Performance Questionnaire will be available only via the Micro-Data Laboratory operated by the Business Data Linking section at the Office for National Statistics.

Secondary analysis of WERS 2004 is being supported by the establishment of an information and advice service at the National Institute of Economic and Social Research. This service is funded by the Economic and Social Research Council.

## The UK Data Archive

Telephone:    01206 872 143
E-mail:       help@esds.ac.uk
Website:      http://www.data-archive.ac.uk/

## Business Data Linking (ONS)

Telephone:    0845 601 3034
E-mail:       bdl@ons.gov.uk
Website:      http://www.statistics.gov.uk/about/bdl/

## WERS 2004 Information and Advice Service

Telephone:    020 7654 1954
E-mail:       wers2004@niesr.ac.uk
Website:      http://www.wers2004.info

# Notes

## 1 Introduction

1 Information about the ESRC's 'Future of Work' programme can be found at: http://www.leeds.ac.uk/esrcfutureofwork/. Information about the Leverhulme Trust's funded programme of work into the 'Future of Unions' can be found at: http://158.143.49.27/future_of_unions/.

2 Further information about the development of WERS 2004 can be found at: http://www.dti.gov.uk/employment/research-evaluation/wers-2004/index.html. The website includes the papers which arose from the consultation exercise, including the full paper setting out the Sponsors' decisions about how the fifth WERS would proceed.

3 Cases which did not conform to the standard definition of the workplace included 'aggregate returns', where the IDBR local unit referred to more than one establishment or a group of employees located at a number of different establishments (e.g. all teachers employed by a Local Education Authority) and 'partial units', where the IDBR local unit referred to a sub-section of an establishment (e.g. one department within a head office).

4 The survey population was all British workplaces with five or more employees, excluding those within the following Sections of the *Standard Industrial Classification (2003)*: A (Agriculture, hunting and forestry); B (Fishing); C (Mining and quarrying); P (Private households with employed persons); and Q (Extra-territorial organizations and bodies). The sample for the Cross-Section was drawn from the Inter-Departmental Business Register (IDBR) during September 2003. In addition to the industry exclusions, workplaces that took part in the 1998 WERS were also excluded to avoid duplication in sample selection between the Cross-Section and the Panel.

5 The weighting strategy differs from that used in 1998 when weights were applied simply to reflect the inverse of the probability of selection. This approach ignored the variations in the out of scope rates across strata and any non-response bias. For comparisons to be made between the 2004 and 1998 Cross-Section Surveys of Managers, new weights have been devised for the 1998 survey in line with the approach taken for the 2004 survey data.

6 A copy of the 2004 WERS Technical Report can be downloaded from the DTI's WERS page: http://www.dti.gov.uk/employment/research-evaluation/wers-2004/index.html.

7 The selection rule adopted for the survey of worker representatives in WERS 2004 was: (1) either the most senior representative of the largest recognized union or, if there were no recognized unions, the most senior representative of the largest non-recognized union; and (2) either the most senior non-union employee representative on the most wide-ranging consultative committee at the workplace or, in the absence of such a committee, the most senior stand-alone non-union employee representative.

8 The development of the Employee Representative Questionnaire and the Panel Survey involved a single pilot rather than the two-stage pilot adopted for the other elements.

9 For full details on how the response rates for each of the survey instruments were calculated refer to the WERS 2004 Technical Report (Chaplin *et al.*, 2005).

10 Some 2,046 interviews were achieved with managers in workplaces with at least 10 employees and 249 interviews were achieved in workplaces with between five and nine employees.

11 Questionnaires were distributed in 76 per cent of workplaces with 10 or more employees; the response rate in these workplaces was 60 per cent. The equivalent figures in 1998 were 81 per cent and 66 per cent respectively. The calculation of the reported response rate for the Survey of Employees is different to the approach adopted in 1998 and reported in the 1998 WERS Technical Report (Airey *et al.*, 1999). In 1998, the response rate was calculated as a proportion of the number of employee surveys *distributed* by employers, whereas in 2004 it is calculated as a proportion of those placed in workplaces from which at least one productive employee survey was returned.

12 Information about employment legislation in Great Britain can be found at http://www.dti.gov.uk/employment.

13 Organizations with 100 or more employees will come within the scope of the legislation in April 2007, and those with 50 or more employees in April 2008.

14 The Routledge companion website can be found at: http://www.routledge.com/textbooks/0415378133.

## 2 A profile of workplaces and employees

1 The exception to this rule would be a situation in which the sampled workplace was itself an employment agency that engaged the staff it supplied to clients on contracts of employment. This is not usually the case for employment agencies.

2 For the purposes of WERS 2004, 'continuing workplaces' are those which had at least 10 employees in both 1998 and 2004, and which had employed at least one member of staff at all times in the intervening period between the two surveys. Changes in name, activity, ownership or location did not institute a break in continuity, so long as these two conditions were met.

3 As an exception, the convention was retained from its predecessor – *Standard Industrial Classification (1992)* – whereby head offices and administrative offices are classified under the main activity of the wider organization which they serve. For example, the head office of a chain of hotels would be coded under 'Hotels and restaurants' in our tables, rather than under the dedicated *SIC (2003)* code 74.15 which is categorized under 'Other business services'. Ten per cent of workplaces in our sample were head offices.

4 Micro firms (those with 0–9 employees) are ignored as they are beyond the scope of this book.

5 An example might be an estate agent's office that also brokers mortgages. In such situations, the industrial classification introduced in Table 2.1 addresses this complexity by classifying workplaces on the basis of their main activity.

6 Figures indicate a trade deficit of £3.9 billion for the UK in 2005 (Office for National Statistics, 2005).

7 Articles describing the pattern of employment using data from the Labour Force Survey are frequently published in *Labour Market Trends*.

8 The Autumn 2004 LFS indicated that 48 per cent of employees were female in workplaces with 11 or more employees.

9 This sums to 93 rather than 94 per cent because of rounding errors.

10 These proportions correspond well to those obtained from the Autumn 2004 Labour Force Survey.

11 This compared to 9 per cent of all employees in workplaces with 11 or more employees according to the Autumn 2004 LFS.

12 The LFS indicated that 2 per cent of employees were in this age range in workplaces with 11 or more employees during the Autumn of 2004.

13 This compared to 23 per cent of employees in workplaces with 11 or more employees according to the LFS.

14 This compared to 42 per cent of employees in workplaces with 11 or more employees according to the Autumn 2004 LFS.

## 3  The management of employment relations

1 The terms 'employment relations management', 'people management', and 'personnel management' are used throughout the chapter as *generic* terms to denote the management of the employment relationship. The term 'human resource management' is used, in contrast, to denote a distinctive approach to employment management.

2 In 14 per cent of workplaces, the interview was conducted with a manager who was not based at the sampled address, typically at a head office.

3 Specialization as used here and throughout the chapter refers to *functional* specialization; it does not imply that there is a low degree of integration of the personnel function in business strategy. The integration of the personnel function in the business strategy is covered separately later in the chapter.

4 In this instance, the data from management respondents who were not based at the sampled establishment were included as the focus was on presence of a personnel function in the organization. Their responses, even if they referred to the head office rather than the sampled establishment, were therefore valid.

5 Sampled establishments that were head offices were excluded from the analysis because they are the highest level in an organization, and this would have resulted in an under-estimation of the extent to which the personnel function was based at a higher level.

6 The percentage of workplaces with only a workplace specialist increased slightly but the difference was not statistically significant.

7 Only respondents whose major job responsibility was employment relations or who were equally responsible for employment relations and other matters were asked about their experience in personnel. In addition, in 1998, only these respondents were asked about their qualifications in personnel. For consistency purposes, the figures provided on qua-lifications, job tenure and experience are restricted to these respondents and exclude the 20 per cent of specialists and the 52 per cent of generalists who were primarily concerned with other non-employment relations related matters.

8 The equivalent figures for *all* specialists and *all* generalists regardless of whether employment relations was their major job responsibility were 50 per cent and 17 per cent, respectively.

9 As per note 5.

10 As per note 5.

11 The proportion of male specialists should be treated with caution, as the unweighted base is between 20 and 49 observations.

12 This section excludes 10 per cent of managers who were not primarily responsible for employment relations matters.

13 The bodies listed were: Acas, DTI, Business Link/Small Business Service, other government departments, management consultants, external lawyers, external accountants, employers' associations, Citizens Advice Bureaux, and other professional bodies, such as the CIPD.

14 For the public sector the equivalent figures were 14 per cent in 2004 and 10 per cent in 1998.

15 The analysis reported refers to *all* managers. The findings for those managers who were more likely to have responsibility for these non-employment issues, i.e. proprietors or general managers who spent less than half of their time on employment relations issues, were found to be similar to those for all managers, and therefore the latter are reported.

16 Seventy per cent had qualifications, 27 per cent had been five or more years in their jobs, and 54 per cent had 10 or more years of personnel experience.

17 The other issues on the showcard were 'product or service development', 'improving quality of product or service', 'forecasts of staffing requirements', and 'market strategy/ developing new markets'.

18 The questions on competitive strategy are discussed in Chapter 2.

19 The items were: introduction of performance related pay; introduction or upgrading of computers; introduction or upgrading of other types of new technology; changes in working time arrangements; changes in the organization of work; changes in work techniques or procedures; introduction of initiatives to involve employees; and introduction of technologically new or significantly improved product or service.

20 The labour costs estimate comes from a question asking 'About what proportion of this establishment's sales revenue/operating costs is accounted for by wages, salaries and other labour costs like pensions and national insurance?' with four banded responses of 'less than 25 per cent', '25–49 per cent', '50–74 per cent', '75 per cent or more'.

## 4 Recruitment, training and work organization

1 See, for example, European Commission (1998); HM Treasury (2003); EEF and CIPD (2003); Department for Education and Skills (2005); and TUC (2005). These various publications include numerous references to research in this broad area. Recent survey evidence is also presented in Chapters 2 and 3 of White *et al.* (2004).

2 The number of response categories to this question was different in 1998 and 2004. In 1998, respondents could say that internal applicants were preferred or that internal and external applicants were treated equally. In 2004, respondents were also given the option of saying that external applicants were given preference. The comparison is based on the assumption that in those workplaces where external applicants might have been given preference in 1998, respondents chose the category 'treated equally'.

3 This corresponds with 23 per cent of employees in workplaces with 11 or more employees in the Autumn 2004 LFS.

4 In the Survey of Employees questionnaire, employees were specifically instructed to include overtime or extra hours. No specific instruction was given in the Employee Profile Questionnaire, and so it is likely that some managers based their reports solely on employees' contracted hours.

5 One half of all workplaces were open from Monday to Friday only, while 12 per cent were open six days per week and 38 per cent were open seven days per week.

6 Around one-fifth (18 per cent) of workplaces operated around the clock on those days that they were open, while 57 per cent operated in the core hours of 8 am–6.30 pm and 25 per cent operated outside of these hours.

7 This was similar to the Autumn 2004 LFS which showed that 93 per cent of employees had a permanent contract.

8 The period 1964–1998 represents the exception, during which training levies were operated by the Industrial Training Boards, and the Manpower Services Commission administered public training levies (Keep and Rainbird, 2003).

9 The definition of off-the-job training given in the 1998 and 2004 surveys also differed slightly. In 1998, employees were asked to include only 'training away from your normal place of work, but it could be on or off the premises'.

10 The difference in the proportion of workplaces linking appraisals to employees' pay was significant only at the 10 per cent level.

11 The method combines separate estimates for continuing workplaces, joiners and leavers using the population proportions presented in Figure 2.2, and uses comparisons between the cross-section and panel estimates for continuing workplaces in 2004 to gauge the likely impact of changes in question wording on other parts of the population. The approach is equivalent to that outlined by Millward *et al.* (2000: 118–120) in earlier analyses of WERS data.

12 The Cronbach Alpha for the single scale was 0.85.

13 Further evidence is provided by Kersley *et al.* (2005: 18–20, n. 38).

## 5  Representation, consultation and communication

1  The Information and Consultation of Employee Regulations 2004 came into force on 6 April 2005, giving employees in organizations with 150 or more employees the right to be informed and consulted on a regular basis about issues in their organization. Organizations with 100–149 employees will come within the scope of the regulations in April 2007, and organizations with 50–99 employees will follow in April 2008.

2  The data do not distinguish between members of trade unions and members of independent staff associations; the term 'union membership' is used hereafter for brevity. The figure cited here is slightly higher than the official estimate of union membership density in Great Britain, which stood at 29 per cent in Autumn 2004 (Grainger and Holt, 2005). This reflects the fact that density is particularly low among employees working in very small workplaces, who fall outside the scope of WERS.

3  Summing across workplaces, managers estimated that 28 per cent of all employees were members of trade unions.

4  Among workplaces with at least some union members, the proportion with members from two or more unions remained stable (53 per cent in 1998 and 55 per cent in 2004). The Certification Officer's Annual Reports record that 30 unions were involved in mergers between 1998 and 2004, but most occurred among small unions and so would not have had any substantial bearing on the overall pattern observed across all unionized workplaces.

5  A small proportion of managers who expressed neutrality about employees' membership of unions (4 per cent) said that they did, nevertheless, encourage or discourage membership among employees at their workplace. These are coded as actively encouraging or discouraging membership, rather than as neutral, in Table 5.2.

6  A more precise estimate is not provided as the figure is computed on a base of only 20 observations.

7  Among workplaces where recruitment had not been attempted, or was unsuccessful, density had risen in 30 per cent of cases, remained stable in 55 per cent and fallen in 15 per cent.

8  Estimates obtained from new analysis of the WERS 1990–1998 Panel Survey.

9  Direct questions on the incidence of new recognition agreements and derecognitions suggest that there is a degree of measurement error, with less than one half of apparent 'new recognitions' and 'derecognitions' being identified as such by managerial respondents in 2004. There is no way of examining this issue in the 1990–1998 Panel Survey.

10  This excludes union representatives that were concerned exclusively with health and safety.

11  In the remaining 3 per cent of workplaces, there were no on-site representatives, but managers did not know whether members had access to a representative at another site in the organization.

12  In workplaces where there was more than one on-site multi-issue committee, managers were asked to focus on the committee that dealt with the widest range of issues.

13  The majority of those non-union committee representatives not providing an answer were, in fact, not asked the question, because of a routing error.

14  The question that was asked of managers covered meetings in which senior managers met with employees either all together or group by group.

## 6  Employee representatives

1  Seniority was determined by position and responsibility, not by the number of years of experience, although the two may have been related. If the members of the largest recognized union were represented by a lay representative at another site in the organization, interviews were sought with this off-site representative. After weighting, 31 per cent of representatives of the largest recognized union were based off-site, compared with 13 per cent in 1998. Interviews with representatives of non-recognized unions and

with non-union representatives were conducted only with on-site lay representatives. Paid full-time officers of trade unions were not interviewed for the purposes of the survey.

2 Around one quarter (24 per cent) of non-union JCC representatives and 8 per cent of stand-alone non-union representatives held trade union membership, but it was determined as part of the interview that their union membership was unrelated to their representative role.

3 Among workplaces with 10 or more employees, there were 689 interviews with the representative of the largest recognized union, 35 interviews with the representative of the largest non-recognized union, 179 interviews with a non-union JCC representative and 61 interviews with a stand-alone non-union representative.

4 The reader is reminded of the selection criteria for the survey, which focused on those representatives with greatest responsibility or seniority at the workplace.

5 Any recent influx of representatives who might differ from the stereotype may be under-represented in the survey as it would be expected that they would take some time to enter senior positions.

6 Such provisions are contained within the Trade Union and Labour Relations Consolidation Act 1992 (for representatives of recognized trade unions), the Employment Act 2002 (for Union Learning Representatives) and the Information and Consultation of Employees Regulations 2004 (for representatives appointed to bodies within the scope of those regulations).

7 'Working practices' and 'absence or staff sickness' were not among the 12 items present on the showcard.

8 The incidence of ULRs as reported by managers is provided in Chapter 5. In workplaces with union representatives, 12 per cent of managers reported that at least some on-site union representatives were ULRs.

9 Union representatives were asked whether there were any other representatives of their union; JCC representatives were asked how many other representatives sat on the committee; and stand-alone non-union representatives were asked how many other non-union representatives were present at the workplace.

10 This figure includes the sampled representative and other representatives on their committee, whether union or non-union. Throughout this section median figures are reported rather than the mean, due to a small number of cases with high values present in the data relating to union representatives' constituency sizes.

11 This hypothesis could not be tested because of changes in the question wording between 1998 and 2004.

12 It was apparent in a number of cases that representatives found it difficult to choose between the two options (individual employees or groups of employees) and felt that the two were evenly balanced (although this was not given as an option).

13 The figure is computed on a base of 120 observations after excluding a further 55 cases for which data were not available due to an error in the question wording during the early part of fieldwork.

14 Managers were not asked the questions in instances where members of recognized unions were represented only by off-site representatives. Accordingly, the responses from off-site representatives of recognized unions are not utilized here and the results therefore relate only to the relationships between managers and on-site representatives.

## 7 The determination of pay and other terms and conditions

1 In addition to occupation-level pay determination information (FSOC), the derivation of collective bargaining coverage draws on two other data sources in the managerial questionnaire. First, it uses information on the most recent pay settlement for core employees at the workplace. In instances where there is a recognized trade union and this settlement involved negotiation with trade unions, but the FSOC data does not identify any collective bargaining, the coverage data are altered to afford bargaining coverage to core

employees. Coverage is also assumed to extend to other occupations in that workplace sharing the core employees' FSOC code. Second, the derivation used to derive coverage calls upon a banded estimate of coverage (FCOVER) obtained by asking managers to estimate the 'proportion of all employees here [who] have their pay set through nego-tiations with trade unions, either at this workplace or at a higher level'. Where there is a recognized union and FCOVER identifies covered workers, but the edited FSOC data do not, collective bargaining coverage is imputed using the mid-point of the banded esti-mate in FCOVER. All data items have been edited to account for instances in which managers in the public sector mistake collective bargaining for pay setting by an Inde-pendent Pay Review Body, and *vice versa*. Full details are available on the Routledge website at: http://www.routledge.com/textbooks/0415378133.

2  These data are not directly comparable to those contained in the Labour Force Survey: the WERS measure is based on employers' responses, rather than those of employees; the LFS includes employees in very small establishments; and the LFS covers a broader range of industries. Compared to the LFS estimates for the UK for Autumn 2004, the WERS estimates tend to be higher, although there are exceptions (Table 29, Grainger and Holt, 2005). However, the industry rankings are very similar.

3  To obtain a time-consistent measure of collective bargaining that is available in the 1998 and 2004 Cross-Section Surveys of Managers, these estimates are based on the occupa-tion-level data in FSOC and the detailed information on pay setting for core employees. The banded coverage variable (FCOVER) is not used since the 1998 question wording is not comparable to that used in the 2004 Cross-Section. The time-consistent estimate is a lower bound: in 2004, the FCOVER adjustment raises aggregate collective bargaining coverage from 35 per cent to 40 per cent.

4  The aggregate collective bargaining coverage figures in this paragraph and in Table 7.5 use the measure described in endnote 3. If the data are not edited using information on pay setting for core employees, aggregate bargaining coverage is lower (33 per cent in 1998 instead of 38 per cent, and 31 per cent in 2004 instead of 35 per cent). Using this unadjusted measure, the fall in aggregate bargaining coverage is not statistically significant.

5  The annual rate of change is calculated as $r=(((CB_{2004}/CB_{1998})^{1/6.5})-1)$ where $CB_{2004}$ is coverage in 2004, $CB_{1998}$ is coverage in 1998 and 6.5 is the number of years that have elapsed between the median interview dates for the 1998 and 2004 surveys.

6  The newly re-weighted estimate of aggregate collective bargaining coverage for the 25+ workplace population in 1998 is 41 per cent, a percentage point above the figure repor-ted by Millward *et al.* (2000: 197), implying that the rate of decline in the 1990s was actually a little slower than their estimate of 3.3 per cent per annum.

7  Whether variable payment methods do, in fact, elicit increased employee motivation and commitment seems to depend, in part, on employee perceptions that rewards are dis-tributed fairly (Makinson, 2000; Marsden, 2004; Kessler, 2000).

8  The Pearson correlation coefficients, all of which are statistically significant at a 99 per cent confidence level, were: performance-related payments and employee share schemes 0.19; performance-related payments and profit-related bonuses 0.25; employee share schemes and profit-related bonuses 0.28.

9  This distinction between incentive payments relying on subjective and objective assess-ments of performance was explained to survey respondents using a showcard.

10  It is likely that the 1998 question format elicits a lower incidence of performance-related pay schemes than the 2004 question. The 2004 question is similar to the question used in the 1990 survey. For a discussion of comparisons with the question asked in 1998 see Millward *et al.* (2000: 212–213).

11  Note, however, that the 2004 panel question relating to variable pay schemes includes the interviewer instruction 'these questions relate only to pay schemes currently in operation', an instruction not issued in 1998.

12  The 1998 showcard simply refers to the generic term 'employee share ownership schemes' as one of five variable pay schemes employers might use.

13 The 1998 survey also asked about the incidence of deferred profit-sharing schemes. Eight per cent of trading sector workplaces had them. These schemes have subsequently been outlawed, but the question was retained in the panel nevertheless. Among continuing panel workplaces in the trading sector, the incidence of deferred profit-sharing schemes fell from 7 per cent in 1998 to 3 per cent in 2004. Adding deferred schemes to other PRP schemes the percentage of panel workplaces in the trading sector with PRP schemes was 45 per cent in 1998 and 41 per cent in 2004.

14 The data are not comparable with similar 1998 items because, in the case of union involvement, WERS 2004 adds: 'If any of these issues are dealt with at a higher level in the organization or through an employers' association, please tell me how they are dealt with at that level.' This instruction was absent in 1998.

15 Each of the 12 items were recoded into (0,1) dummy variables scoring '1' if the managerial respondent said negotiations normally took place over that particular item. The principal components' eigenvalues were 5.4, 2.2 and 1.2 respectively, with the Cronbach Alphas for each factor being 0.90, 0.87 and 0.87 respectively.

16 Managers were asked, 'How many employees at this establishment aged 22 or over are currently paid ... ' with respondents invited to fill in boxes for each of the four categories presented in the table, split by males and females. It appears that many respondents ignored the request to confine figures to those aged 22 or more since the box totals conform more closely to the total number of employees at the workplace. The percentages cited in column 1 therefore use the total number of employees at the workplace as the denominator (ZALLEMPS). They also exclude 363 cases where the number of employees cited is more than 10 percentage points above or below ZALLEMPS.

17 Entitlements to fringe benefits for the largest non-managerial occupational group were based on managerial responses to the question: 'Looking at this card, are [core employees] entitled to any of these non-pay terms and conditions: employer pension scheme; company car or car allowance; private health insurance; more than four weeks of paid annual leave (excluding public holidays); sick pay in excess of statutory requirements'.

18 Control variables were: gender; age (nine dummies); academic qualifications (eight dummies); vocational qualifications (three dummies); disability; ethnicity; household status (four dummies); union membership (three dummies); and sector of ownership. The sample size varied between 14,516 and 21,351 for the whole economy models, depending on the variables introduced.

19 This figure is the sum of all redundancies divided by the sum of all employees 12 months previously, multiplied by 100. The figures are employee-weighted. The redundancy rate in the Autumn 2004 Labour Force Survey was 1.8. This is significantly higher than the WERS rate (the 95 per cent confidence interval around the mean of 1.3 being 1.0–1.6).

20 The questions for 1998 and 2004 are not identical. WERS 2004 asked for the number of full-time and part-time employees on the payroll 12 months ago, and then asked how many of these employees had stopped working because they were made redundant. WERS 1998 asked 'During the last twelve months how many permanent employees (full and part time) stopped working here because they were made redundant?' The latter is more restrictive in specifying 'permanent' employees, but less restrictive in that it might include employees who were not on the payroll 12 months previously, that is, those who arrived and left within the year.

21 Changes to the wording and format of redundancy questions mean it is not possible to compare information on redundancy consultations in 1998 and 2004. In 1998, managers were asked whether there had been any workforce reductions in the previous 12 months and, if so, why, with responses including 'compulsory redundancy'. In 2004, on the other hand, there is no reference to compulsion, and, before asking the redundancy consultation questions the manager is prompted to recall that he/she had identified redundancies in the Employee Profile Questionnaire completed prior to the survey interview.

22 Managers were also asked whether redundancy proposals had been withdrawn as a direct result of consultation. Unfortunately the number of cases answering this question was too small to analyse with 12 cases saying 'yes' and 13 saying 'no'.

23 In contrast to the analysis presented by Cully *et al.* (1999), this analysis augments the primary information on health and safety arrangements collected from Section I of the Cross-Section management questionnaire with additional (sometimes inconsistent) information collected in Section D of the questionnaire.

24 There can be occasions when one party to discussions believes the engagement constitutes negotiation, whereas the other party perceives it to be consultation. Case study research offers 'some evidence . . . that the [union and employer] parties [to negotiation] may have had an entirely different understanding of the process in which they were involved' (Moore *et al.*, 2004: 62).

## 8 Workplace conflict

1 Drinkwater and Ingram (2005), for example, consider the sharp increase in Employment Tribunal applications in the context of the downward trend in strike activity.

2 The standard error around the mean rate for 2004 was 0.42, whilst that around the mean rate for 1998 was 0.18. The difference between the two rates is therefore not statistically significant. Monger (2005) also records a similar number of stoppages in 1998 and 2004, but a greater number of working days lost in the more recent of the two years, suggesting that stoppages in 2004 were of longer duration, on average. WERS collects cursory information on strike duration, but such action is sufficiently rare to prohibit meaningful comparisons.

3 It is possible to analyse the number of occurrences of non-strike action in each workplace. However, there was great variation in the number of events occurring within those few workplaces where non-strike action had taken place, meaning that this rate was imprecisely estimated in the survey. For this reason, mean rates of non-strike action, and combined rates for strike and non-strike action, are not reported.

4 Workplaces with no union members (12 per cent of all workplaces) were excluded from the set of questions on threatened industrial action in the first three months of fieldwork because of a routing error in the questionnaire. The incidence of threatened action was 2 per cent among non-union workplaces that *were* asked the question after the routing was corrected; the figure of 4 per cent was calculated by assuming an equivalent incidence among workplaces that were originally excluded. The incidence of threatened action among workplaces where union members were present was 8 per cent.

5 It is possible that a ballot in support of industrial action may have been conducted prior to the 12-month recall period: lawful action may begin up to eight weeks after a ballot.

6 WERS does not identify instances where a dispute was avoided through use of the procedure at an early stage.

7 The question on disciplinary procedures referred to a formal procedure for dealing with 'discipline and dismissals, other than redundancies'. The term 'disciplinary procedure' is used as shorthand throughout the remainder of the chapter.

8 Further information about the sampling and contact procedures used in the survey can be found in the Technical appendix to this volume and in the WERS 2004 Technical Report (Chaplin *et al.*, 2005).

9 The difference remained of similar magnitude, and not significant, after also controlling for other factors that might feasibly be related to both the time taken to obtain an interview and the nature of dispute resolution procedures, namely: workplace size, organization size, industry, sector of ownership, union recognition and the presence of a personnel specialist.

10 Under the Employment Relations Act 1999, the statutory right to be accompanied applies to all workers, not just employees. The WERS questionnaires and accompanying papers use the term 'employee' throughout and for consistency this term was maintained (and is

reported here) in relation to questions on accompaniment. Similarly, whilst much of the good practice guidance and the law use the term 'hearing' when describing disciplinary and grievance arrangements, for simplicity, the WERS survey used the term 'meeting'.

11 The data on the right to be accompanied collected in 1998 are not directly comparable with 2004 and so an analysis of change is not possible. In WERS 2004, the right to accompaniment was explored only in workplaces in which formal meetings were reported to be part of the management of discipline and grievances. In WERS 1998, which preceded this legislation, accompaniment in grievance situations was explored among workplaces with a formal grievance procedure and, for disciplinary handling, all workplaces were asked about accompaniment. These changes, and the absence of questions on the use of formal meetings in WERS 1998, make comparison across the two surveys problematic.

12 The WERS Cross-Section Survey of Managers does not provide an overall picture of the proportion of workplaces subject to tribunal claims since it excludes workplaces with less than five employees, and the figures reported here are for workplaces with 10 or more employees. Analysis of the 2003 Survey of Employment Tribunal Applications indicates that 78 per cent of tribunal claims are brought in workplaces with 10 or more employees.

13 The standard error around the mean rate for 2004 was 0.18 (0.22 for 1998), suggesting that neither measure was very precise. Point-in-time estimates also provide an incomplete picture: the actual volume of Employment Tribunal claims has been rather volatile between 1998 and 2004. However, the rate observed in any one year does give a broad indication of the types of workplace in which the concentration of claims was highest. A single outlier was excluded from the computation in 2004 due to a suspected punching error.

14 Discontent may also be expressed through sabotage, pilfering or fiddles (Edwards, 1986), but WERS provides no data on these phenomena.

15 Eighteen per cent of managers in 2004 did not know the proportion of days lost due to sickness or absence at the establishment over the preceding 12 months (17 per cent in 1998). The standard error around the mean absenteeism rate for 2004 was 0.28 (0.54 for 1998).

16 The standard error around the mean rate of voluntary resignations was 0.42. It is not possible to provide an equivalent rate for 1998 because of differences in question wording.

## 9 Equality, diversity and work–life balance

1 The Sex Discrimination (Election Candidates) Act 2002 amends the Sex Discrimination Act 1975 and the Sex Discrimination (Northern Ireland) Order 1976.

2 The Race Relations Act Employment Code of Practice is available at: http://www.cre.gov.uk/gdpract/employ_cop_1.html. The Sex Discrimination Act Employment Code of Practice is available from: http://www.eoc.org.uk/default.aspx?page=1. The Disability Discrimination Act 1995 Employment Code of Practice is available to download from: http://www.drc-gb.org/documents/employment_occupation.pdf.

3 The average inter-item correlation was 0.82.

4 Note that the proportions do not sum to 100 as the question allowed for multiple responses.

5 For information about the Race Equality Duty, see http://www.cre.gov.uk/duty/index.html.

6 In 2004, managers were asked whether a points-rating system or some other method was used, while in 1980, 1984 and 1990 managers were asked about a number of different schemes used, including points-rating, factor comparisons, ranking, grading or any other.

7 Responses from the WERS 2004 Cross-Section Survey of Managers indicated that 68 per cent of workplaces with five or more employees, and 76 per cent of workplaces with 10 or more employees, provided two or more practices to at least some employees from a range of arrangements including: working reduced hours, job-sharing, flexitime, annual hours, term-time only working, compressed hours, or having some part-time workers.

This compares to 63 per cent and 70 per cent respectively according to analysis of the Second Work–Life Balance Survey (WLB2). This represents a statistically significant increase in the provision of flexible working practices in the region of 5 to 6 per cent broadly between 2003 and 2004. The Second Work–Life Balance Survey report indicated that two or more of these practices had been taken up by employees in the last 12 months in 44 per cent of workplaces with five or more employees. The WERS 2004 Cross-Section Survey of Managers did not ask whether there was any take-up in the past 12 months (with the exception of part-time work), so it is not possible to compare figures from the WLB2 and WERS 2004 surveys on this particular measure.

8 During Ordinary Maternity Leave most mothers will usually qualify to be paid Statutory Maternity Pay or Maternity Allowance.

9 Further information about maternity rights in Great Britain can be found on the DTI website: http://www.dti.gov.uk/employment/.

10 Details of the qualification criteria for paternity leave are available at: http://www.dti.gov.uk/employment/.

11 Neither the data from the 1998 management interview nor the 1998 Survey of Employees are fully comparable. This is particularly the case for parental leave. In 1998, managers were asked about the entitlement of *non-managerial* employees to a number of different family friendly working arrangements, including parental leave. A completely new question was devised for the 2004 survey to examine the availability of parental leave. Managers were asked, 'With the exception of maternity leave, paternity leave and time off for emergencies, how do mothers and fathers usually take their time off to look after their children?' with paid and unpaid parental leave as two possible response categories. In 1998, employees were asked about the availability of parental leave rather than paid parental leave as in 2004.

12 This compares to a mean average in the employees' main job of 19.8 hours a week for part-time employees and 42.8 hours for full-time employees in workplaces with 11 or more employees in the Autumn 2004 Labour Force Survey (LFS) (medians of 20.0 and 40.3, respectively). However, the LFS uses the respondent's own report of whether they work full-time or part-time, rather than allocating them to either category based on whether or not they work at least 30 hours a week, as in WERS. This difference in the definitions of part-time work probably explains the discrepancy in hours worked by full-time and part-time employees between the two surveys.

13 The Transport industry is defined as land, sea or air transport.

## 10 Workplace climate and performance

1 The 'poor' and 'very poor' categories were collapsed on both the management and employee indicators of climate, due to the small numbers in the 'very poor' category. The values assigned to these indicators ranged from one ('poor'/'very poor') to four ('very good').

2 Variables indicating these various events were coded 1 if the event had occurred in the 12 months prior to the survey, and 0 otherwise. The exception was a continuous variable indicating the percentage of working days lost through employee sickness or unauthorized absence.

3 The unweighted sample size was 2,045, with dummy variables identifying where data were missing for a particular workplace.

4 The reader should note that this does not represent an attempt to construct fully-specified models.

5 If a set of independant variables are jointly significant, it indicates that the inclusion of the full set within the regression model serves to explain a statistically-significant amount of additional variation in the dependant variable when compared with a model that does not include any of these variables. It does not necessarily indicate that each of the individual variables within the set are significantly associated with the dependant variable.

6 A number of cases had missing data on items required for this detailed typology. However, simpler typologies ignoring missing data on some items produced similar results.

7 Meetings with senior management were only counted as 'voice' where they occurred at least monthly and where at least 10 per cent of the time was available for employees to give their views. Problem-solving groups only counted as voice where they involved non-managerial employees.

8 These HIM zones were defined in the following way. 'Task practices' were present where one or more of the following were in place: at least 60 per cent of core employees work in semi-autonomous teams (depending on each other to do their job, jointly deciding how work is done, and given responsibility for specific products/services); at least 60 per cent of core employees formally trained to be able to do jobs other than their own; at least 60 per cent of core employees in problem-solving groups; management uses suggestion schemes to communicate or consult with employees; some core employees given time off from normal daily duties to undertake training on communication skills, team-working, or problem-solving methods in past 12 months. 'Recruitment, appraisal or development' occurred where at least one of the following were in place: internal applicants given preference over external applicants for vacancies; performance tests used in recruitment, except where known to be occasional; personality or attitude tests routinely used in filling vacancies for some non-managerial posts; regular formal performance appraisal for some non-managerial employees; formal off-the-job training given to at least 60 per cent of experienced core employees in the past 12 months. 'Communication' occurred where at least one of the following were in place: management regularly gave employees or their representatives information on internal investment plans, the financial position of the workplace, or staffing plans; there were monthly meetings between senior management and the whole workforce. 'Welfare practices' were present if any of the following were present: a job security guarantee covering non-managerial employees; managers and non-managerial employees had equal status across five terms and conditions; there was a three-step grievance procedure in place; there was a three-step disciplinary procedure in place. 'Financial incentives' were present where at least one of the following occurred: at least 60 per cent of non-managerial employees got profit-related payments in the last 12 months; at least 60 per cent of non-managerial employees were eligible for share ownership schemes; at least 60 per cent of non-managerial employees got payments-by-results or merit pay.

9 The region with the best managerial and employee perceptions of climate was Wales.

10 Adding a simpler four-way typology distinguishing representative voice, direct voice, the combination of the two and 'no voice' to the baseline model instead of the eight-way variable indicated that the combination of direct and representative voice was associated with poorer employee perceptions of climate than both the 'no voice' and direct voice-only regimes. (Similar models run on employer perceptions of climate revealed that direct voice only was associated with better employer perceptions of climate than the other three regimes.)

11 Specifically, having at least one practice from among the 'shift and night work' and 'hours flexibility' domains were negatively associated with managers' perceptions of climate. However, all of the count variables were not significant and, with the exception of the positive effect of annual hours contracts, nor were any of the practices in isolation.

12 For instance, a workplace's competitors may be defined more narrowly than standard industrial classifications, being determined in part by locality for example. Accounting measures, which are based on the market value of goods or services, may also conflate differences in productivity with differences in prices.

13 In fact, associations between financial performance and various measures of unionization suggested results were not particularly sensitive to alternative performance measures (Wilkinson, 2001; Bryson and Wilkinson, 2002).

14 If factors unobservable to the analyst which determine how the respondent rates productivity or performance happen to be correlated with observable features of the workplace that are

accounted for in the analysis, this can bias the estimated impact of those observable features on productivity, either upwardly or downwardly.

15  Technically, it is possible that such a distribution exists if respondents are comparing their workplace's performance against the mean performance in an industry with a very long tail of poor performers. In that case, mean performance would be dragged down below the median by the low performers such that most workplaces would be above the mean. However, the data to test this possibility were not available at the time of writing.

16  The estimation sample for the subjective measure of labour productivity was 1,317.

17  The implication is that the remaining respondent characteristics were generally not close to being statistically significant, such that it was not possible to determine with confidence that the set of respondent characteristics together explained a statistically-significant amount of additional variation in labour productivity.

18  Replacing the eight-way typology with a four-way one distinguishing between direct voice-only, representative voice-only, a combination of the two, and no voice, direct voice and representative voice combined were associated with higher productivity than 'no voice'.

19  The estimation sample for the subjective measure of financial performance was 1,347.

20  Separate bargaining by multiple unions was associated with significantly poorer perceptions of financial performance relative to non-union workplaces, though the effect was only statistically significant at a 90 per cent confidence level. The difference between joint bargaining and separate bargaining in multiple union environments was not statistically significant. Neither multiple unionism nor bargaining arrangements were significantly associated with managerial perceptions of labour productivity compared to the industry average, suggesting the association with poorer financial performance arose through the reallocation of profits towards employees, rather than through a direct productivity effect on performance.

21  Convergent validity would be demonstrated if the two measures exhibit a positive association with one another. Construct validity would be demonstrated if they are associated in similar ways with other relevant factors, such as workplace practices.

22  Private sector workplaces in Sections J and L of the *Standard Industrial Classification (2003)* were excluded from the WERS sample when computing these estimates, as these industries are not included in the Annual Business Inquiry aggregates.

23  The magnitude of the coefficients cannot be directly compared because the dependent variables have different metrics.

24  The lack of statistical significance of the capital–labour ratio in the model of value-added is noteworthy. It derives from a small coefficient which appears to be related to the predominance of small establishments in the weighted sample. These tended to have a low capital–labour ratio when compared with larger sites. When the analysis was restricted to establishments with 25 or more employees, the size and significance of the coefficient were in line with conventional expectations.

25  Such a test of consistency is also proposed by Gunderson (2002).

## 11  Conclusion

1  There are, however, limits to what can be achieved with WERS data. There may be a number of reasons as to why change has occurred and, even with a survey of this scale and complexity, it is impossible to control for all factors, thus making it difficult to tease out the impact of legislation from, say, changing labour market conditions.

2  For a more comprehensive assessment of the impact of the Government's work–life balance policies, empirical evidence on employee take-up of these arrangements is required. The WERS survey did not examine the use of these practices by employees. Other survey evidence suggests that employee take-up of several flexible working arrangements has increased between 2000 and 2003 (Stevens *et al.*, 2004). Evidence on the use of parental leave suggests that it was low in 2001 (Dickens *et al.*, 2005), as was the take-up of

emergency time off (although this might not involve a dependent), which stood at just under one half of all employees in 2003 (Stevens *et al.*, 2004).

3 Another indicator of the impact of the legislation in this area is employees' awareness of their individual rights and the arrangements which are available to them. The survey did not examine employees' awareness of their rights, but employees often did not know which flexible working and leave arrangements were available to them. There is potential for future analysis which investigates the types of respondents who 'did not know' which arrangements would be available to them, or did not answer the questions on the availability of arrangements.

4 The law is being phased in with respect to smaller organizations from April 2007.

5 There was no question on job evaluation schemes in WERS 1998.

## Technical appendix

1 The exceptions being local units that covered more than one establishment (referred to in this Appendix as aggregate units) and local units that covered only part of an establishment (referred to as partial units).

2 The issued sample was used as the basis for these exclusions in preference to the achieved sample, in order to avoid introducing selection biases caused by non-random patterns of non-response to the 1998 WERS Cross-Section Survey within each cell of the sampling matrix.

3 This was a departure from earlier surveys in the series, in which interviewers were responsible for all approaches to sampled establishments.

4 Eighteen of these cases were subsequently dropped prior to analysis because of concerns about the consistency of the definition of the establishment in 1998 and 2004.

5 Post-stratification by employment size was applied in WIRS 1990. It was done on that occasion to account for a deficiency of small workplaces in the achieved sample that was caused by the absence of recent updates to the sampling frame.

6 Most statistical software packages do not allow for all of the departures from simple random sampling to be taken into account when estimating true standard errors, and Stata is no exception. However, the estimated standard errors reported here take account of the most important departures, namely: the stratification of the population prior to sampling; the use of unequal sampling fractions; and the clustering of employee observations.

# Bibliography

Advisory, Conciliation and Arbitration Service (2003) *Job Evaluation: An Introduction*, London: Acas.
——(2004) *Annual Report and Resource Accounts 2003/04*, London: Acas.
——(2005) *Acas Telephone Helpline: Findings from the 2005 Customer Survey*, London: Acas.
Agree, E., Bissett, B. and Rendall, M.S. (2003) 'Simultaneous care for parents and care for children among mid-life British women and men', *Population Trends*, 112: 29–35.
Airey, C., Hales, J., Hamilton, R., Korovessis, C., McKernan, A. and Purdon, S. (1999) *The Workplace Employee Relations Survey (WERS) 1997–1998: Technical Report (Main and Panel Surveys)*, London: Social Community Planning Research.
Alpin, C., Shackleton, J.R. and Walsh, S. (1998) 'Over- and under-education in the UK graduate labour market', *Studies in Higher Education*, 23, 1: 17–34.
Appelbaum, E., Bailey, T., Berg, P. and Kalleberg, A.L. (2000) *Manufacturing Advantage: Why High-Performance Work Systems Pay Off*, Ithaca, NY: ILR Press.
Applebaum, E. and Batt, R. (1994) *The New American Workplace: Transforming Work Systems in the United States*, Ithaca, NY: ILR Press.
Armstrong, M. (2000) 'The name has changed but has the game remained the same?', *Employee Relations*, 22, 6: 576–593.
Arrowsmith, J. and Sisson, K. (1999) 'Pay and working time: towards organisation-based arrangements?', *British Journal of Industrial Relations*, 37, 1: 51–75.
Bach, S. (2000) 'From performance appraisal to performance management', in S. Bach and K. Sisson (eds) *Personnel Management*, Oxford: Blackwell.
Bach, S. and Sisson, K. (2000) 'Personnel management in perspective', in S. Bach and K. Sisson (eds) *Personnel Management*, Oxford: Blackwell.
Bach, S. and Winchester, D. (2003) 'Industrial relations in the public sector', in P. Edwards (ed.) *Industrial Relations: Theory and Practice*, 2nd edn, Oxford: Blackwell.
Bacon, N. (2003) 'Human resource management and industrial relations', in P. Ackers and A. Wilkinson (eds) *Understanding Work and Employment*, Oxford: Oxford University Press.
Bacon, N. and Storey, J. (2000) 'New employee relations strategies in Britain: towards individualism or partnership?', *British Journal of Industrial Relations*, 38, 3: 407–427.
Baldwin, M.L. and Schumacher, E.J. (2002) 'A note on job mobility among workers with disabilities', *Industrial Relations*, 41, 3: 430–441.
Barmby, T. and Stephan, G. (2000) 'Worker absenteeism: why firm size may matter', *The Manchester School*, 68, 5: 568–577.
Batstone, E., Boraston, I. and Frenkel, S. (1977) *Shop Stewards in Action*, Oxford: Basil Blackwell.
Bevan, S., Dench, S., Tamkin P. and Cummings, J. (1999) *Family Friendly Employment: The Business Case*, Research Report No.16, London: Department for Education and Employment.

Bewley, H. and Fernie, S. (2003) 'What do unions do for women?', in H. Gospel and S. Wood (eds) *Representing Workers: Union Recognition and Membership in Britain*, vol. 1, London: Routledge.

Blackaby, D.H., Leslie, D.G., Murphy, P.D. and O'Leary, N.C. (2002) 'White/ethnic minority earnings and employment differentials in Britain: evidence from the LFS', *Oxford Economic Papers*, 54, 2: 270–297.

Blackburn, R.M., Brooks, B. and Jarman, J. (2001) 'Occupational stratification: the vertical dimension of occupational segregation', *Work, Employment and Society*, 15, 3: 511–538.

Blanchflower, D. and Bryson, A. (2003) 'Changes over time in union relative wage effects in the UK and the US revisited', in J.T. Addison and C. Schnabel (eds) *International Handbook of Trade Unions*, Cheltenham: Edward Elgar.

Blanden, J., Machin, S. and Van Reenan, J. (2005) 'New survey evidence on recent changes in UK union recognition', Discussion Paper No. 685, London: Centre for Economic Performance, London School of Economics.

Blinkhorn, S. and Johnson, C. (1990) 'The insignificance of personality testing', *Nature*, 348: 671–672.

Bonner, C. and Gollan, P. (2004) 'A bridge over troubled water: a decade of representation at South West Water', *Employee Relations*, 27, 3: 238–258.

Booth, A., Francesconi, M. and Frank, J. (2000) 'Temporary jobs: stepping stones or dead ends?', *The Economic Journal*, 112: F189–F213.

Boxall, P. and Purcell, J. (2003a) 'Managing individual performance and development', in P. Boxall and J. Purcell, *Strategy and Human Resource Management*, Basingstoke: Palgrave Macmillan.

——(2003b) *Strategy and Human Resource Management*, Basingstoke: Palgrave Macmillan.

Brannen, J. and Moss, P. (1991) *Managing Mothers: Dual Earner Households After Maternity Leave*, London: Unwin Hyman.

Brynjolfsson, E. and Hitt, L. (2000) 'Beyond computation: information technology, organizational transformation and business performance', *Journal of Economic Perspectives*, 14, 4: 24–48.

Bryson, A. (2004) 'Unions and workplace closure in Britain, 1990–1998', *British Journal of Industrial Relations*, 42, 2: 283–302.

——(2005) 'Union effects on employee relations in Britain', *Human Relations*, 58, 9: 1111–1139.

Bryson, A., Cappellari, L. and Lucifora, C. (2004) 'Does union membership really reduce job satisfaction?', *British Journal of Industrial Relations*, 42, 3: 439–459.

Bryson, A., Forth, J. and Kirby, S. (2005) 'High-involvement management practices, trade union representation and workplace performance in Britain', *Scottish Journal of Political Economy*, 52, 3: 451–491.

Bryson, A. and Gomez, R. (2005) 'Why have employees stopped joining unions? The rise in never-membership in Britain', *British Journal of Industrial Relations*, 43, 1: 67–92.

Bryson, A. and Wilkinson, D. (2002) *Collective Bargaining and Workplace Performance: An Investigation Using the Workplace Employee Relations Survey 1998*, Employment Relations Research Series, No. 12, London: Department of Trade and Industry.

Budd, J. (2004) *Employment with a Human Face: Balancing Efficiency, Equity and Voice*, Ithaca, NY: Cornell University Press.

Budd, J.W. and Mumford, K. (2004) 'Trade unions and family-friendly policies in Britain', *Industrial and Labor Relations Review*, 57, 2: 204–222.

Buyens, D. and De Vos, A. (2001) 'Perceptions of the value of the HR function', *Human Resource Management Journal*, 11, 3: 70–89.

Buzzard, R. and Shaw, W. (1952) 'An analysis of absence under a scheme of paid sick leave', *British Journal of Industrial Medicine*, 9: 282–295 (cited in T. Barmby, M. Ercolani and J. Treble (2002) 'Sickness absence: an international comparison', *The Economic Journal*, 112: 315–331).

Cabinet Office (2000) *Winning the Generation Game: Improving Opportunities for People Aged 50–65 in Work and Community Activity*, London: Cabinet Office.

Caldwell, R. (2001) 'Champions, adapters, consultants and synergists: the new change agents in HRM', *Human Resource Management Journal*, 11, 3: 39.

Capelli, P. and Neumark, D. (2001) 'Do "high-performance" work practices improve establishment-level outcomes?', *Industrial and Labor Relations Review*, 54, 4: 737–775.

Chaplin, J., Mangla, J., Purdon, S. and Airey, C. (2005) *The Workplace Employment Relations Survey 2004 (WERS 2004) Technical Report (Cross-Section and Panel Surveys)*, London: National Centre for Social Research.

Chevalier, A. (2003) 'Measuring over-education', *Economica*, 70: 509–531.

Clegg, H. (1975) 'Pluralism in industrial relations', *British Journal of Industrial Relations*, 13, 2: 309–316.

Colvin, A. (2003a) 'Institutional pressures, human resource strategies, and the rise of non-union dispute resolution procedures', *Industrial and Labor Relations Review*, 56, 3: 375–392.

——(2003b) 'The dual transformation of workplace dispute resolution', *Industrial Relations*, 42, 4: 712–735.

Coyne, I. and Bartram, D. (2000) 'Personnel managers' perceptions of dishonesty in the workplace', *Human Resource Management Journal*, 10, 3: 38–45.

Crompton, R., Brockmann, M. and Lyonette, C. (2005) 'Attitudes, women's employment and the domestic division of labour: a cross-national analysis in two waves', *Work, Employment and Society*, 19, 2: 213–233.

Crompton, R., Dennett, J. and Wigfield, A. (2003) *Organisations, Careers and Caring*, Bristol: Policy Press.

Cully, M. (1998) *A Survey in Transition: The Design of the 1998 Workplace Employee Relations Survey*, London: Department of Trade and Industry.

Cully, M., Woodland, S., Reilly, A. and Dix, G. (1999) *Britain at Work, as Depicted by the 1998 Workplace Employee Relations Survey*, London: Routledge.

Currie, G. and Procter, S. (2001) 'Exploring the relationship between HR and middle managers', *Human Resource Management Journal*, 11, 3: 53–69.

Dastmalchian, A., Blyton, P. and Adamson, R. (1989) 'Industrial relations climate: testing a construct', *Journal of Occupational Psychology*, 62: 21–32.

——(1991) *The Climate of Workplace Relations*, London: Routledge.

Deery, S., Erwin, P. and Iverson, R. (1999) 'Industrial relations climate, attendance behaviour and the role of trade unions', *British Journal of Industrial Relations*, 37, 4: 533–558.

Department for Education and Skills (2005) *Skills: Getting on in Business, Getting on at Work*, London: Department for Education and Skills.

Department for Work and Pensions (2001a) *Evaluation of the Code of Practice on Age Discrimination in Employment*, Sheffield: Department for Work and Pensions.

——(2001b) *Ageism: Attitudes and Experiences of Young People*, Research Report No. 301, Sheffield: Department for Work and Pensions.

Dex, S. and Scheibl, F. (1999) 'Business performance and family-friendly policies', *Journal of General Management*, 24, 4: 22–37.

Dex, S. and Smith, C. (2002) *The Nature and Pattern of Family-Friendly Employment Policies in Britain*, London: Policy Press.

Dickens, L. (1999) 'Beyond the business case: a three-pronged approach to equality action', *Human Resource Management Journal*, 9, 1: 9–19.

Dickens, L. and Hall, M. (2003) 'Labour law and industrial relations: a new settlement?' in P. Edwards (ed.) *Industrial Relations: Theory and Practice*, 2nd edn, Oxford: Blackwell.

Dickens, L., Hall, M. and Wood, S., (2005) *Review of Research into the Impact of Employment Relations Legislation*, Employment Relations Research Series, No. 45, London: Department of Trade and Industry.

Dietz, G. (2004) 'Partnership and the development of trust in British workplaces', *Human Resource Management Journal*, 14, 1: 5–24.

Dietz, G., Cullen, J. and Coad, A. (2005) 'Can there be non-union forms of workplace partnership?', *Employee Relations*, 27, 3: 289–306.

Dix, G. and Oxenbridge, S. (2003) *Information and Consultation at Work: From Challenges to Good Practice*, Acas Research Paper 03/03, London: Advisory Conciliation and Arbitration Service.

Dixon, S. (2003) 'Implications of population ageing for the labour market', *Labour Market Trends*, 111, 2: 67–76.

Drinkwater, S. and Ingram, P. (2005) 'Have industrial relations in the UK really improved?', *Labour*, 19, 3: 373–398.

DTI/Acas/ESRC/PSI (2003) *Design Issues for a Fifth Workplace Employment Relations Survey.* Online. Available http://www.dti.gov.uk/employment/research-evaluation/wers-2004/index.html (accessed 29 November 2005).

Dundon, T., Wilkinson, A., Marchington, M. and Ackers, P. (2005) 'The management of voice in non-union organisations: managers' perspectives', *Employee Relations* 27, 3: 307–319.

Earnshaw, J., Goodman, J., Harrison, R. and Marchington, M. (1998) *Industrial Tribunals, Workplace Disciplinary Procedures and Employment Practice*, Employment Relations Research Series, No. 2, London: Department of Trade and Industry.

Edwards, P. (1986) *Conflict at Work: A Materialist Analysis of Workplace Relations*, Oxford: Blackwell.

——(1995) 'The employment relationship', in P. Edwards (ed.) *Industrial Relations: Theory and Practice*, 1st edn, Oxford: Blackwell.

——(2000) 'Discipline: towards trust and self-discipline?', in S. Bach and K. Sisson (eds) *Personnel Management: A Comprehensive Guide to Theory and Practice*, 3rd edn, Oxford: Blackwell.

——(2003) 'The employment relationship and the field of industrial relations', in P. Edwards (ed.) *Industrial Relations: Theory and Practice*, Oxford: Blackwell.

EEF and CIPD (2003) *Maximising Employee Potential and Business Performance: The Role of High Performance Working*, London: Engineering Employers Federation.

Employment Tribunals Service (2005) *The Employment Tribunals Service: Annual Report and Accounts 2004–05*, HC180, London: The Stationery Office.

European Commission (1998) *Modernising the Organisation of Work: A Positive Approach to Change*, COM (98) 592, Luxembourg: Office for Official Publications of the European Communities.

Farnham, D. and Horton, S. (1992) 'Human resources management in the new public sector: leading or following private employer practice?', *Public Policy and Administration*, 7, 3: 42–55.

Ferner, A. (2003) 'Foreign multinationals and IR innovation in Britain', in P. Edwards (ed.) *Industrial Relations: Theory and Practice*, 2nd edn, Oxford: Blackwell.

Fernie, S. and Metcalf, D. (1995) 'Participation, contingent pay, representation and workplace performance: evidence from Great Britain', *British Journal of Industrial Relations*, 33, 3: 379–415.

——(2005) *Trade Unions: Resurgence or Demise?*, London: Routledge.

Fernie, S., Metcalf, D. and Woodland, S. (1994) 'Does HRM boost employee-management relations?', Centre for Economic Performance Working Paper No. 548, London: Centre for Economic Performance, London School of Economics.

Ford, G., Watkins, B., Bosley, S., Hawthorn, R., McGowan, B. and Grattan, P. (2003) *Challenging Age: Information, Advice and Guidance for Older Age Groups*, London: Department for Education and Skills.

Forth, J. (2000) *Compositional Versus Behavioural Change: Combined Analysis of WERS98 Panel Survey, Closures and New Workplaces*, NIESR mimeo, London: National Institute for Economic and Social Research.

——(2002) *Initial Review of WERS98: Final Report to the Sponsors of WERS98*. Online. Available http://www.dti.gov.uk/employment/research-evaluation/wers-2004/index.html.

Forth, J., Bewley, H. and Bryson, A. (2006) *Employment Relations in SMEs: Findings from the 2004 Workplaces Employment Relations Survey*, London: Department of Trade and Industry.

Forth, J. and Millward, N. (2000) 'The determinants of pay levels and fringe benefit provision in Britain', NIESR Discussion Paper 171, London: National Institute for Economic and Social Research.

——(2002a) *The Growth of Direct Communication*, London: Chartered Institute of Personnel and Development.

——(2002b) 'Union effects on pay levels in Britain', *Labour Economics*, 9, 4: 547–561.

——(2004) 'High involvement management and pay in Britain', *Industrial Relations*, 43, 1: 98–119.

Fox, A. (1974) *Beyond Contract: Work Power and Trust Relations*, London: Faber and Faber.

Freeman, R. (1980) 'The exit-voice tradeoff in the labour market: unionism, job tenure, quits and separations', *Quarterly Journal of Economics*, 94, 4: 643–674.

——(1984) 'Longitudinal analysis of the effects of trade unions', *Journal of Labor Economics*, 2, 1: 1–26.

Freeman, R. and Medoff, J. (1984) *What Do Unions Do?*, New York: Basic Books.

Gall, G. (1993) 'What happened to single union deals? A research note', *Industrial Relations Journal*, 24, 1: 71–75.

——(1996) 'All year round: the growth of annual hours in Britain', *Personnel Review*, 25, 3: 35–52.

——(2004) 'Trade union recognition in Britain, 1995–2002: turning a corner?', *Industrial Relations Journal*, 35, 3: 249–270.

Gallie, D., White, M., Cheng, Y. and Tomlinson, M. (1998) *Restructuring the Employment Relationship*, Oxford: Clarendon Press.

Geary, J. (2003) 'New forms of work organisation: still limited, still controlled, but still welcome?', in P. Edwards (ed.) *Industrial Relations: Theory and Practice*, 2nd edn, Oxford: Blackwell.

Godard, J. (2001a) 'Beyond the high-performance paradigm? An analysis of variation in Canadian managerial perceptions of reform programme effectiveness', *British Journal of Industrial Relations*, 39, 1: 25–52.

——(2001b) 'New dawn or bad moon rising? Large scale government administered workplace surveys and the future of Canadian IR research', *Relations Industrielles / Industrial Relations*, 56, 1.

——(2004) 'A critical assessment of the high-performance paradigm', *British Journal of Industrial Relations*, 42, 2: 25–52.

Godard, J. and Delaney, J.T. (2000) 'Reflections on the "high performance" paradigm's implications for industrial relations as a field', *Industrial and Labor Relations Review*, 53, 3: 482–502.

——(2002) 'On the paradigm guiding industrial relations theory and research: reply to Thomas A. Kochan', *Industrial and Labor Relations Review*, 55, 3: 552–554.

Gollan, P. (2000) 'Nonunion forms of employee representation in the United Kingdom and Australia', in B. Kaufman and D. Taras (eds) *Nonunion Employee Representation: History, Contemporary Practice and Policy*, Armonk, NY: M.E.Sharpe.

Gooch, L. and Ledwith, S. (1996) 'Women in personnel management: re-visioning of a handmaiden's role?', in S. Ledwith and F. Colgan (eds) *Women in Organizations: Challenging Gender Politics*, London: Macmillan.

Gospel, H. (2003) *Quality of Working Life: A Review on Changes in Work Organization, Conditions of Employment and Work–Life Arrangements*, Conditions of Work and Employment Series, No. 1, Geneva: International Labour Organization.

Goss, D. and Adam-Smith, D. (2001) 'Pragmatism and compliance: employer responses to the working time regulations', *Industrial Relations Journal*, 32, 3: 195–208.

Grainger, H. and Holt, H. (2005) *Trade Union Membership 2004*, London: Department of Trade and Industry.

Green, F. (2001) 'Its been a hard day's night: the concentration and intensification of work in late twentieth-century Britain', *British Journal of Industrial Relations*, 39, 1: 53–80.

——(2004) 'Why has work effort become more intense?', *Industrial Relations*, 43: 709–741.

Green, F., McIntosh, S., and Vignoles, A. (2002) 'The utilisation of education and skills: evidence from Britain', *The Manchester School*, 70, 6: 792–811.

Guest, D. (1999) 'Human resource management: the workers' verdict', *Human Resource Management Journal*, 9, 3: 5.

——(2001) 'Industrial relations and human resource management', in J. Storey (ed.) *Human Resource Management: A Critical Text*, London: Thomson Learning.

Guest, D. and Conway, N. (1999) 'Peering into the black hole: the downside of the new employment relations in the UK', *British Journal of Industrial Relations*, 37, 3: 367–389.

Guest, D., Michie, J., Conway, N. and Sheehan, M. (1999) 'Partnership and performance: an analysis using the 1998 Workplace Employee Relations Survey', paper presented at BJIR/WERS98 Conference, Cumberland Lodge.

Guest, D. and Peccei, R. (1994) 'The nature and causes of effective human resource management', *British Journal of Industrial Relations*, 32, 2: 219–242.

——(2001) 'Partnership at work: mutuality and the balance of advantage', *British Journal of Industrial Relations* 39, 2: 207–236.

Gunderson, M. (2002) 'Rethinking productivity from a workplace perspective', Canadian Policy Research Networks Discussion Paper No. W17, Ottawa: Canadian Policy Research Networks.

Hall, M. and Edwards, P. (1999) 'Reforming the statutory redundancy consultation procedure', *Industrial Law Journal*, 28, 4: 299–319.

Hall, M. and Terry, M. (2004) 'The emerging system of statutory worker representation', in G. Healy, E. Heery, P. Taylor and W. Brown (eds) *The Future of Worker Representation*, Basingstoke: Palgrave Macmillan.

Handy, L. (1968) 'Absenteeism and attendance in the British coal mining industry: an examination of post-war trends', *British Journal of Industrial Relations*, 6, 1: 27–50.

Harris, R., Reid, R. and MacAdam, R. (2004) 'Consultation and communication in family-owned businesses in Great Britain', *International Journal of Human Resource Management*, 15, 8: 1424–1434.

Haskel, J. 'Unions and productivity again: new evidence from matched WERS and Business Census data', paper presented at the WPEG Conference, Cardiff, 2005.

Hayward, B., Peters, M., Rousseau, N. and Seeds, K. (2004) *Findings from the Survey of Employment Tribunal Applications 2003*, Employment Relations Research Series, No. 33, London: Department of Trade and Industry.

Healy, G., Bradley, H. and Mukherjee, N. (2004) 'Inspiring activists: the experience of minority ethnic women in trade unions', in G. Healy, E. Heery, P. Taylor and W. Brown (eds) *The Future of Worker Representation*, Basingstoke: Palgrave Macmillan.

Heery, E., Conley, H., Delbridge, R., Simms, M. and Stewart, P. (2004a) 'Trade union responses to non-standard work', in G. Healy, E. Heery, P. Taylor and W. Brown (eds) *The Future of Worker Representation*, Basingstoke: Palgrave Macmillan.

Heery, E., Healy, G. and Taylor, P. (2004b) 'Representation at work: themes and issues', in G. Healy, E. Heery, P. Taylor and W. Brown (eds) *The Future of Worker Representation*, Basingstoke: Palgrave Macmillan.

Heywood, J. and Jirjahn, U. (2004) 'Teams, teamwork and absence', *Scandinavian Journal of Economics*, 106, 4: 765–782.

Hindess, G. (2003) 'Population review of England and Wales, 2001', *Population Trends*, 112: 7–14.

HM Treasury (2003) *EMU and Labour Market Flexibility*, London: The Stationery Office.

Holzer, H. (1988) 'Search method use of unemployed youth', *Journal of Labor Economics*, 6, 2: 1–20.

Hoque, K. (2003) 'All in all it's just another plaque on the wall: the incidence and impact of the Investors in People Standard', *Journal of Management Studies*, 40, 2: 543–572.

Hoque, K. and Noon, M. (2001) 'Counting angels: a comparison of personnel and HR specialists', *Human Resource Management Journal*, 11, 3: 5–23.

Hyman, J. and Mason, B. (1995) *Managing Employee Involvement and Participation*, London: Sage.

Hyman, R. (1996) 'Is there a case for statutory works councils in Britain?', in A. McColgan (ed.) *The Future of Labour Law*, London: Pinter.

Ichniowski, C., Kochan, T., Levine, D., Olson, C. and Strauss, G. (1996) 'What works at work: overview and assessment', *Industrial Relations*, 35, 3: 299–333.

IRS (1997) 'The state of selection: an IRS survey', *Employee Development Bulletin*, 85, January: 8–13.

——(1999) 'New ways to perform appraisal', *Employment Trends*, 676, March: 7–16.

James, P. and Walters, D. (1997) 'Non-union rights of involvement: the case of health and safety at work', *Industrial Law Journal*, 26, 1: 35–50.

Jewson, N. and Mason, D. (1986) 'The theory and practice of equal opportunities policies: liberal and radical approaches', *Sociological Review*, 34, 2: 307–334.

Keep, E. and Mayhew, K. (1999) 'The assessment: knowledge, skills and competitiveness', *Oxford Review of Economic Policy*, 15, 1: 1–15.

Keep, E. and Rainbird, H. (2003) 'Training', in P. Edwards (ed.) *Industrial Relations: Theory and Practice*, 2nd edn, Oxford: Blackwell.

Kelly, J. (1996) 'Works councils: union advance or marginalization?', in A. McColgan (ed.) *The Future of Labour Law*, London: Pinter.

Kelly, J. and Gennard, J. (2000) 'Getting to the top: career paths of personnel directors', *Human Resource Management Journal*, 10, 3: 22.

Kersley, B., Alpin, C., Forth, J., Bryson, A., Bewley, H., Dix, G. and Oxenbridge, S. (2005) *Inside the Workplace: First Findings from the 2004 Workplace Employment Relations Survey*. London: Department of Trade and Industry. Online. Available http://www.dti.gov.uk/employment/research-evaluation/wers-2004/index.html.

Kessler, I. (2000) 'Remuneration systems', in S. Bach and K. Sisson (eds) *Personnel Management*, Oxford: Blackwell.

Kingsmill, D. (2001) *Report into Women's Employment and Pay*, London: Women and Equality Unit.

Kochan, T.A. (2000) 'On the paradigm guiding industrial relations theory and research: comment on John Godard and John T. Delaney's "Reflections on the 'high performance' paradigm's implications for industrial relations as a field"', *Industrial and Labor Relations Review*, 53, 4: 704–711.

Kodz, J., Davis, S., Lain, D., Strebler, M., Rick, J., Bates, P., Cummings, J., Meager, N., Anxo, D., Gineste, S., Trinczek, R. and Pamer, S. (2003) *Working Long Hours: A Review of the Evidence*, vol. 1: *Main Report*, Employment Relations Research Series, No. 16, London: Department of Trade and Industry.

Labour Research (2004) 'Be organised, be consulted', *Labour Research*, November.

Lane, N. (1998) 'Barriers to women's progression into nurse management in the National Health Service', *Women in Management Review*, 13, 5: 184–191.

Leighton, P. (2002) 'Problems continue for zero-hours workers', *Industrial Law Journal*, 31, 1: 71–78.

Lewin, D. and Peterson, R. (1999) 'Behavioural outcomes of grievance activity', *Industrial Relations*, 38: 4: 554–576.

Lewis, S. (1997) '"Family friendly" employment policies: a route to changing organizational culture or playing about at the margins?', *Gender, Work and Organization*, 4, 1: 13–23.

Liff, S. (2003) 'The Industrial Relations of a diverse workforce', in P. Edwards (ed.) *Industrial Relations: Theory and Practice*, Oxford: Blackwell.

Liff, S. and Ward, K. (2001) 'Distorted views through the glass ceiling: the construction of women's understandings of promotion and senior management positions', *Gender, Work and Organization*, 8, 1: 19–36.

Lindsay, C. and Doyle, P. (2003) 'Experimental consistent time series of historical Labour Force Survey data', *Labour Market Trends*, 111, 9: 467–475.

Lloyd, C. (2001) 'What do employee councils do? The impact of non-union forms of representation on trade union organisation', *Industrial Relations Journal* 32, 4: 313–327.

Long, P. (1986) *Performance Appraisal Revisited*, London: Institute of Personnel Management.

Lupton, B. and Shaw, S. (2001) 'Are public sector personnel managers the profession's poor relations?' *Human Resource Management Journal*, 11, 3: 23.

Machin, S. (2001) 'The changing nature of labour demand in the new economy and skill-biased technology change', *Oxford Bulletin of Economics and Statistics*, 63 (Special Issue): 753–776.

Machin, S. and Stewart, M. (1996) 'Trade unions and financial performance', *Oxford Economic Papers*, 48, 2: 213–241.

Makinson, J. (2000) *Incentives for Change: Rewarding Performance in National Government Networks*, Public Services Productivity Panel, London: HM Treasury.

Marks, A., Findlay, P., Hine, J., McKinlay, A. and Thompson, P. (1998) 'The politics of partnership? Innovation in employment relations in the Scottish spirits industry', *British Journal of Industrial Relations*, 36, 2: 209–226.

Marsden, D. (1999) *A Theory of Employment Systems: Micro-Foundations of Diversity*, Oxford: Oxford University Press.

——(2004) 'Unions and procedural justice: an alternative to the "common rule"', in A. Verma and T.A. Kochan (eds) *Unions in the 21st Century: An International Perspective*, London: Palgrave Macmillan.

Martinez Lucio, M. and Stuart, M. (2004) 'Swimming against the tide: social partnership, mutual gains and the revival of "tired" HRM', *International Journal of Human Resource Management*, 15, 2: 410–424.

Metcalf, D. (2005) 'Trade unions: resurgence or perdition? An economic analysis', in S. Fernie and D. Metcalf (eds) *Trade Unions: Resurgence or Demise?*, London: Routledge.

Millward, N., Bryson, A. and Forth, J. (2000) *All Change at Work? British Employment Relations 1980–98, as Portrayed by the Workplace Industrial Relations Survey Series*, London: Routledge.

Millward, N., Forth, J. and Bryson, A. (1999) 'Changes in employment relations, 1980–1998', in M. Cully, S. Woodland, A. Reilly and G. Dix (eds) *Britain at Work: As Depicted by the 1998 Workplace Employee Relations Survey*, London: Routledge.

Millward, N., Stevens, M., Smart, D. and Hawes, W. (1992) *Workplace Industrial Relations in Transition: The ED/ESRC/PSI/ACAS Surveys*, Aldershot: Dartmouth.

Monger, J. (2005) 'Labour disputes in 2004', *Labour Market Trends*, 113, 6: 239–253.

Moore, J., Tilson, B. and Whitting, G. (1994) *An International Overview of Employment Policies and Practices Towards Older Workers*, Research Series 29, Sheffield: Department of Employment.

Moore, S., McKay, S. and Bewley, H. (2004) *The Content of New Voluntary Trade Union Recognition Agreements 1998–2002*, vol. 1: *An Analysis of New Agreements and Case Studies*, Employment Relations Research Series, No. 26, London: Department of Trade and Industry.

——(2005) *The Content of New Voluntary Trade Union Recognition Agreements 1998–2002*, vol. 2: *Findings from the Survey of Employers*, Employment Relations Research Series, No. 43. London: Department of Trade and Industry.

Mullarkey, S., Wall, T., Warr, P., Clegg, C. and Stride, C. (1999) *Measures of Job Satisfaction, Mental Health and Job-Related Well-Being: A Bench-Marking Manual*, Sheffield: Institute of Work Psychology.

Munro, A. and Rainbird, H. (2004) 'The workplace learning agenda – new opportunities for trade unions?', in G. Healy, E. Heery, P. Taylor and W. Brown (eds) *The Future of Worker Representation*, Basingstoke: Palgrave Macmillan.

Office for National Statistics (2003) 'Labour market spotlight', *Labour Market Trends*, 112, 12: 598–599.

——(2004) 'Work and family: 1 in 2 mums of under 5s are in the labour force', Office for National Statistics. Online. Available http://www.statistics.gov.uk/CCI/nugget.asp?ID=436&Pos=2&ColRank=1&Rank=176 (accessed 23 August 2005).

——(2005) *UK Trade (First Release)*, September 2005, London: Office for National Statistics.

O'Higgins, N. (2001) *Youth Unemployment and Employment Policy: A Global Perspective*, Geneva: International Labour Organization.

Oswick, C. and Grant, D. (1996) 'Personnel management in the public sector: power, roles and relationships', *Personnel Review*, 25, 2: 4–18.

Palmore, E. (1990) *Ageism: Negative or Positive?*, New York: Springer.

Pelizzari, M. (2004) 'Do friends and relatives really help in getting a good job?', Discussion Paper 623, London: Centre for Economic Performance, London School of Economics.

Pencavel, J. (2004) 'The surprising retreat of union Britain', in R. Blundell, D. Card and R. Freeman (eds) *Seeking a Premier League Economy*, Chicago: University of Chicago Press for NBER.

Perotin, V. and Robinson, A. (2000) 'Employee participation and equal opportunities practices: productivity effect and potential complementarities', *British Journal of Industrial Relations*, 38, 4: 557–583.

Pfeffer, J. (1995) 'Producing sustainable competitive advantage through effective management of people', *Academy Journal of Management Executive*, 9, 1: 55–69.

Poole, M., Mansfield, R., Gould-Williams, J. and Mendes, P. (2005) 'British managers' attitudes and behaviour in industrial relations: a twenty year study', *British Journal of Industrial Relations*, 43, 1: 117–134.

Purcell, J. (2001a) 'Personnel and human resource managers: power, prestige and potential', *Human Resource Management Journal*, 11, 3: 3–4.

——(2001b) 'The meaning of strategy in human resource management', in J. Storey (ed.) *Human Resource Management: A Critical Text*, London: Thomson Learning.

Purcell, J. and Kinnie, N. (2006) 'HRM and business performance', in P. Boxall, J. Purcell and P. Wright (eds) *Handbook of Human Resource Management*, Oxford: Oxford University Press.

Purdon, S. (2002) *Sampling Issues for a Fifth WERS*, London: National Centre for Social Research. Online. Available http://www.dti.gov.uk/employment/research-evaluation/wers-2004/index.html.

Ram, M. and Edwards, P. (2003) 'Praising Caesar not burying him: what we know about employment relations in small firms', *Work, Employment and Society*, 17, 4: 719–730.

Ramsay, H., Scholarios, D. and Harley, B. (2000) 'Employees and high performance work systems: testing inside the black box', *British Journal of Industrial Relations*, 38, 4: 501–531.

Saks, A.M. and Waldman, D.A. (1998) 'The relationship between age and job performance evaluations for entry-level professionals', *Journal of Organizational Behaviour*, 19, 4: 409–419.

Sapsford, D. and Turnbull, P. (1994) 'Strikes and industrial conflict in Britain's docks: balloons or icebergs', *Oxford Bulletin of Economics and Statistics*, 56, 3: 249–265.

Scase, R. (2003) 'Employment relations in small firms', in P. Edwards (ed.) *Industrial Relations: Theory and Practice*, 2nd edn, Oxford: Blackwell.

Simon, J.C. and Warner, T. (1992) 'Matchmaker, matchmaker: the effect of old boy networks on jobmatch quality, earnings and tenure', *Journal of Labor Economics*, 10, 3: 306–330.

Sisson, K. (2001) 'Human resource management and the personnel function: a case of partial impact?', in J. Storey (ed.) *Human Resource Management: A Critical Text*, London: Thomson Learning.

Sisson, K. and Marginson, P. (2003) 'Management: systems, structures and strategy', in P. Edwards (ed.) *Industrial Relations: Theory and Practice*, 2nd edn, Oxford: Blackwell.

Sisson, K. and Storey, J. (2000a) 'Improving competencies and capabilities I: training and development', in K. Sisson and J. Storey *The Realities of Human Resource Management*, Buckingham: Open University Press.

——(2000b) *The Realities of Human Resource Management*, Buckingham: Open University Press.

Spilsbury, D. (2003) *Learning and Training at Work 2002*, Department for Education and Skills Research Report RR399, London: Department for Education and Skills.

Stevens, J., Brown, J. and Lee, C. (2004) *The Second Work–Life Balance Study: Results from the Employee Survey*, Employment Relations Research Series, No. 27, London: Department of Trade and Industry.

Storey, J. (1992) *Developments in the Management of Human Resources*, Oxford: Blackwell.

——(2001) 'Human resource management today: an assessment', in J. Storey (ed.) *Human Resource Management: A Critical Text*, London: Thomson Learning.

Suff, P. (2002) *Consultation with Practitioners and Think-Tanks about a Fifth Workplace Employment Relations Survey (WERS5)*, IRS Research. Online. Available http://www.dti.gov.uk/employment/research-evaluation/wers-2004/index.html.

Taylor, P. and Urwin, P. (2001) 'Age and participation in vocational education and training', *Work, Employment and Society*, 15, 4: 763–779.

Terry, M. (1999) 'Systems of collective employee representation in non-union firms in the UK', *Industrial Relations Journal*, 30, 1: 16–30.

——(2003) 'Employee representation: stewards and the new legal framework', in P. Edwards (ed.) *Industrial Relations: Theory and Practice*, 2nd edn, Oxford: Blackwell.

——(2004) '"Partnership": a serious strategy for UK trade unions?', in A. Verma and T.A. Kochan (eds) *Unions in the 21st Century: An International Perspective*, London: Palgrave Macmillan.

Terry, M. and Smith, J. (2003) *Evaluation of the Partnership at Work Fund*, Employment Relations Research Series, No. 17, London: Department of Trade and Industry.

TUC (2005) *Learning is the Business: How Workplace Learning Boosts Company Performance*, London: TUC.

Ulrich, D. (1997) *Human Resource Champions: The Next Agenda for Adding Value to HR Practices*, Cambridge, MA: Harvard Business School Press.

Undy, R. (1999) 'Annual review article: New Labour's "industrial relations settlement": the Third Way?', *British Journal of Industrial Relations*, 37: 315–336.

Urwin, P. and Shackleton, J.R. (1999) 'Search methods and transitions into employment and inactivity', *International Journal of Manpower*, 20, 3/4: 189–230.

Waddington, J. (2003) 'Trade union organization', in P. Edwards (ed.) *Industrial Relations: Theory and Practice*, 2nd edn, Oxford: Blackwell.

Wall, T.D., Michie, J., Patterson, M., Wood, S.J., Sheenhan, M., Clegg, C.W. and West, M. (2004) 'On the validity of subjective measures of company performance', *Personnel Psychology*, 57: 95–118.

Walling, A. (2005) 'Families and work', *Labour Market Trends*, 113, 7: 275–283.

Webb, J. and Liff, S. (1988) 'Play the white man – the social construction of fairness and competition in equal opportunity policies', *Sociological Review*, 36, 3: 532–551.

White, M., Hill, S., Mills, C. and Smeaton, D. (2004) *Managing to Change? British Workplaces and the Future of Work*, Basingstoke: Palgrave Macmillan.

Whitfield, K. (2002) *Academic Consultation Exercise about a Fifth Workplace Employment Relations Survey. Report to the Economic and Social Research Council.* Online. Available http://www.dti.gov.uk/employment/research-evaluation/wers-2004/index.html.

Wilkinson, D. (2001) *Collective Bargaining and Workplace Financial Performance in Britain*, mimeo, London: Policy Studies Institute.

Wills, J. (2004) 'Trade unionism and partnership in practice: evidence from the Barclays-Unifi agreement', *Industrial Relations Journal* 35, 4: 329–343.

Winchester, D. and Bach, S. (1995) 'The state: the public sector', in P. Edwards (ed.) *Industrial Relations*, Oxford: Blackwell.

Wood, S. (1999) 'Human resource management and performance', *International Journal of Management Reviews*, 1, 4: 367–413.

Wood, S. and de Menezes, L. (1998) 'High commitment management in the UK: evidence from the Workplace Industrial Relations Survey, and Employers' Manpower and Skills Practices Survey', *Human Relations*, 51, 4: 485–515.

Woodland, S., Simmonds, N., Thornby, M., Fitzgerald, R. and McGee, A. (2003) *The Second Work–Life Balance Study: Results from the Employers' Survey – Main Report*, Employment Relations Research Series, No. 22. London: Department of Trade and Industry.

# Index